Taste All-New Recipes from the World's #1 Cooking Magazine!

WHEN a cookbook's recipes come straight from the most popular cooking magazine in the world, you know they're the very best. And that's exactly what you get inside this exciting, brand-new *Taste of Home Annual Recipes 2010.*

The 17th edition in our best-selling series, this can't-miss collection gives you a full year's worth of scrumptious favorites published in *Taste of Home* magazine. Plus, you get over 100 bonus recipes never before seen in *Taste of Home.* That's a total of 506 recipes—all in one convenient cookbook!

Packed with gorgeous color photos and helpful cooking hints from our Test Kitchen pros, each chapter is designed with you in mind. For those extra busy weeknights, rely on "Meals in Minutes" to get dinner on the table fast. Or, for special occasions, turn to "Holiday & Seasonal Celebrations" to make your event the most memorable ever.

We've also featured slimmed-down fare in "Cooking Lighter"...crowd-size foods in "Potluck Pleasers"... "Meals on a Budget" to help you watch your wallet ...festive party ideas in "Getting in the Theme of Things"...plus 12 other chock-full chapters.

You'll even enjoy the winners from *Taste of Home's* 2009 national recipe contests:

• **Party-Perfect Appetizers.** For small bites that have big flavor, this contest delivered a buffet of impressive hors d'oeuvres. The Grand Prize went to Brie Cherry Pastry Cups (p. 21), while Sesame Chicken Dip (p. 17) finished second.

• **Standout Quick Breads.** These lickety-split loaves give you the comfort of home-baked bread without the wait. The entries included first-place Peppery Cheese Bread (p. 86) and runner-up Savory Dill & Caraway Scones (p. 91).

• **Breakfast and Brunch.** Wake up your family with scrumptious Ham & Cheese Breakfast Strudels (p. 163), the Grand Prize winner, and second-place Oatmeal Brulee with Ginger Cream (p. 164). There's no better way to start the day!

• **You Say Tomato.** What to do with all of that garden produce? Enjoy these fresh-picked favorites. South-of-the-Border Caprese Salad (p. 27) took the top prize, while Summertime Spaghetti Sauce (p. 60) was the worthy runner-up.

• **5-Ingredient.** The short list of winners for this contest included a number of exceptional recipes. Among them were first-rate "Secret's in the Sauce" BBQ Ribs (p. 68) and the judges' number-two choice, Grilled Shrimp with Apricot Sauce (p. 56).

• **30-Minute Entrees.** Dinner's done in a flash when you rely on fast-but-fabulous main courses such as Flatbread Tacos with Ranch Sour Cream (p. 71)—the top winner—and second-place Glazed Shrimp & Asparagus (p. 78).

With all of those prize-winning delights and hundreds of other family-favorite main dishes, sides, soups, breads, desserts and more, you'll always have exactly the recipes you need right at your fingertips. So make *Taste of Home Annual Recipes 2010* part of your kitchen library of cookbooks...and enjoy the unbeatable "taste of home" today!

BEST OF THE BRUNCH. Oven-baked Ham & Cheese Breakfast Strudels (pictured above) won the Grand Prize in *Taste of Home* magazine's "Breakfast and Brunch" recipe contest. That outstanding dish is just one of the delights you'll find in this cookbook's "Holiday and Seasonal Celebrations" chapter (p. 156).

taste of home 2010
ANNUAL RECIPES

Editor in Chief Catherine Cassidy
Vice President, Executive Editor/Books
Heidi Reuter Lloyd
Creative Director Ardyth Cope
Food Director Diane Werner RD
Senior Editor/Books Mark Hagen
Editor Michelle Bretl
Art Director Gretchen Trautman
Content Production Supervisor Julie Wagner
Layout Designer Kathy Crawford
Proofreader Linne Bruskewitz
Recipe Asset Systems Coleen Martin, Sue A. Jurack
Editorial Assistant Barb Czysz

Chief Marketing Officer Lisa Karpinski
Vice President/Book Marketing Dan Fink
Creative Director/Creative Marketing James Palmen

taste of home

Editor Ann Kaiser
Managing Editor Barbara Schuetz
Senior Art Director Sandra L. Ploy
Food Editor Patricia Schmeling
Associate Editor Cheri Mantz
Recipe Editors Mary King, Christine Rukavena
Copy Editor Susan Uphill
Editorial Assistants Jane Stasik, Joanne Wied
Executive Assistant Marie Brannon
Senior Web Editor Sarah Marx Feldner
Web Community Manager Erik Bergstrom

Test Kitchen Manager Karen Scales
Associate Food Editors Alicia Bozewicz RD,
Tina Johnson, Marie Parker, Annie Rundle,
Jenni Warren
Test Kitchen Associates Rita Krajcir, Kristy Martin,
Sue Megonigle, Laura Scharnott, Megan Taylor
Photographers Rob Hagen, Dan Roberts,
Jim Wieland, Lori Foy
Set Stylists Jenny Bradley Vent, Stephanie Marchese,
Melissa Haberman, Dee Dee Jacq
Food Stylist Manager Sarah Thompson
Food Stylist Kaitlyn Besasie
Assistant Food Stylists Alynna Malson,
Shannon Roum, Leah Rekau
Photo Studio Coordinator Kathy Swaney

The Reader's Digest Association, Inc.
President and Chief Executive Officer Mary G. Berner
President, Food & Entertaining Suzanne M. Grimes
President, Consumer Marketing Dawn M. Zier
SVP, Chief Marketing Officer Amy J. Radin

Taste of Home Books
©2010 Reiman Media Group, Inc.
5400 S. 60th St., Greendale WI 53129

International Standard Book Number (10):
0-89821-529-3
International Standard Book Number (13):
978-0-89821-529-8
International Standard Serial Number: 1094-3463

All rights reserved. Printed in U.S.A.

"Timeless Recipes from Trusted Home Cooks" is a
registered trademark of Reiman Media Group.

PICTURED AT RIGHT: Clockwise from upper left:
Lime Tartlets (p. 123), Double-Cheese Macaroni
(p. 138), Coffee-Flavored Beef Roast (p. 68), Sweet
Potato Pie & Maple Praline Sauce (p. 108) and
Philly Cheesesteak Pizza (p. 82).

2010 taste of home ANNUAL RECIPES

PICTURED ON FRONT COVER. Clockwise from upper left: Peach Melba Cheesecake (p. 124), Potato Vegetable Medley (p. 190) and Lemon Basil Chicken (p. 288).

PICTURED ON BACK COVER. Cranberry-Kissed Pork Chops (p. 59).

Front cover photo by Rob Hagen. Food styled by Diane Armstrong. Set styled by Stephanie Marchese.

For other *Taste of Home* books and products, visit *www.ShopTasteofHome.com*.

Appetizers & Beverages

Holiday get-togethers, Super Bowl parties, after-school snacktime...no matter what the occasion, this chapter has you covered with fun finger foods, extra-special hors d'oeuvres, cool thirst-quenchers, munchies and more!

A BITE BEFORE DINNER. Clockwise from upper left: Watermelon Sherbet Smoothies (p. 19), Marinated Cheese (p. 13), Mediterranean Tomato Bites (p. 10), Thai Steak Skewers (p. 7) and Sour Cream Cheese Puffs (p. 8).

Meanwhile, in a large resealable plastic bag, combine the flour, salt, paprika, cayenne, garlic powder and remaining celery seed. Add wings, a few at a time, and shake to coat.

In an electric skillet or deep-fat fryer, heat oil to 375°. Fry the wings, a few at a time, for 6-8 minutes or until no longer pink, turning once. Drain on paper towels. Place in a large bowl; add the sauce and toss to coat. **Yield:** about 4 dozen.

Microwave Potato Chips

PREP: 10 min. **COOK:** 10 min./batch

Can you make golden, crispy homemade potato chips in the microwave? The answer is, absolutely! OurTest Kitchen cooks show you how with the simple recipe here.

> 3 **medium red potatoes**
> 1/4 **cup olive oil**
> 1 **teaspoon salt**
> **Curry powder**

Layer three paper towels on a microwave-safe plate; set aside.

Scrub potatoes and cut into 1/16-in.-thick slices. Brush slices on both sides with olive oil and lightly sprinkle with salt and curry. Arrange on the prepared plate (do not overlap).

Microwave on high for 3 minutes; turn and microwave 2-3 minutes longer or until the chips are dry and brittle. Repeat with remaining potatoes, oil and seasonings. Let chips cool for at least 1 minute before serving. Store in an airtight container. **Yield:** 5 servings.

Editor's Note: This recipe was tested in a 1,100-watt microwave.

Waldorf Celery Sticks

PREP/TOTAL TIME: 15 min.

I added blue cheese to the traditional Waldorf salad filling to create these creamy, crunchy snacks. I like how the sharpness of the cheese complements the sweetness of the apples. For variety, use feta cheese instead. —Stacie Hull, Seneca, South Carolina

☑ **This recipe includes Nutrition Facts.**

> 1/2 **cup finely chopped apple**
> 1/4 **cup finely chopped walnuts**
> 3 **tablespoons mayonnaise**
> 2 **tablespoons crumbled blue cheese**
> 12 **celery ribs**

In a small bowl, combine the apple, walnuts, mayonnaise and blue cheese. Spoon filling into celery ribs, a scant 3 tablespoons in each. Chill until serving. **Yield:** 1 dozen.

Nutrition Facts: 1 stuffed celery rib equals 55 calories, 5 g fat (1 g saturated fat), 2 mg cholesterol, 70 mg sodium, 2 g carbohydrate, 1 g fiber, 1 g protein.

Spicy Hot Wings

(Pictured above)

PREP: 20 min. **COOK:** 10 min./batch

After searching in vain for a good wings recipe, I came up with my own. They get snatched up almost as fast as I can fry them!
—Brent Burns, Long Grove, Illinois

> 5 **pounds chicken wings**
> 1/2 **cup butter, cubed**
> 1/2 **cup Louisiana-style hot sauce**
> 1/4 **cup balsamic vinegar**
> 1/4 **cup soy sauce**
> 3 **tablespoons brown sugar**
> 3 **tablespoons honey**
> 2 **tablespoons plus 1 teaspoon celery seed, divided**
> 2 **tablespoons lemon juice**
> 2/3 **cup all-purpose flour**
> 1 **teaspoon *each* salt, paprika and cayenne pepper**
> 1/2 **teaspoon garlic powder**
> **Oil for deep-fat frying**

Cut wings into three sections; discard wing tip sections. In a large saucepan, bring the butter, hot sauce, vinegar, soy sauce, brown sugar, honey, 2 tablespoons celery seed and lemon juice to a boil. Reduce the heat; simmer, uncovered, until reduced by half.

Thai Steak Skewers

(Pictured below and on page 4)

PREP: 20 min. + marinating **GRILL:** 10 min.

The combo of peanut butter and coconut milk in these slightly spicy kabobs is delicious! Include a side of rice for a meal instead of an appetizer. —Amy Frye, Goodyear, Arizona

- 1/4 **cup packed brown sugar**
- 2 **tablespoons lime juice**
- 2 **tablespoons soy sauce**
- 1 **tablespoon curry powder**
- 1 **teaspoon lemon juice**
- 1 **can (14 ounces) coconut milk,** *divided*
- 1-1/2 **teaspoons crushed red pepper flakes,** *divided*
- 2 **pounds boneless beef sirloin steak, cut into 1/4-inch slices**
- 2 **medium limes, halved and thinly sliced, optional**
- 1/4 **cup creamy peanut butter**
- 1 **tablespoon chopped salted peanuts**

In a large resealable plastic bag, combine the first five ingredients. Add 1/4 cup coconut milk and 1 teaspoon pepper flakes. Add the steak; seal bag and turn to coat. Refrigerate 2-4 hours.

Drain and discard the marinade. Thread the beef onto 16 metal or soaked wooden skewers, alternately threading beef with lime slices if desired. Grill, covered, over medium-hot heat for 6-8 minutes or until desired doneness, turning occasionally.

In a small saucepan, combine peanut butter with the remaining coconut milk and pepper flakes. Heat through.

Transfer to a small bowl; sprinkle with peanuts. Serve with skewers. **Yield:** 16 skewers.

Roasted Garlic & Tomato Spread

(Pictured above)

PREP: 45 min. + cooling

With bold flavors and a velvety consistency, this spread is a real crowd-pleaser. Serve it warm or chilled with pita chips, crackers or breads. —Tara McDonald, Kansas City, Missouri

- 2 **whole garlic bulbs**
- 3 **teaspoons olive oil,** *divided*
- 3 **plum tomatoes, quartered**
- 1 **carton (8 ounces) spreadable chive and onion cream cheese**
- 1/4 **teaspoon Italian seasoning**
- 1/4 **teaspoon salt**

Assorted crackers *or* **snack breads**

Remove papery outer skin from garlic (do not peel or separate cloves). Cut tops off of garlic bulbs; brush each with 1/2 teaspoon oil. Wrap each bulb in heavy-duty foil. Place garlic and tomatoes in a foil-lined 9-in. square baking pan. Brush tomatoes with remaining oil.

Bake at 425° for 30-35 minutes or until the garlic is softened. Cool for 10-15 minutes; squeeze garlic into a small bowl. Drain any liquid from tomatoes; chop and add to garlic. Stir in cream cheese, seasoning and salt. Serve with crackers or snack breads. **Yield:** 1-1/2 cups.

ROASTING RUNDOWN. When garlic is roasted, it turns golden and buttery. Its flavor mellows and becomes slightly sweet and nutty.

Roasted garlic is terrific in a variety of dishes (such as the appetizer above) or spread on bread and grilled meats. You can roast garlic and refrigerate it in an airtight container for up to 1 week.

Mexican Salsa Pizza

PREP/TOTAL TIME: 25 min.

This appetizer pizza always gets rave reviews. If you'd prefer to kick up the heat, just use a spicy salsa and pepper Jack cheese.
—Carla McMahon, Hermiston, Oregon

☑ This recipe includes Nutrition Facts and Diabetic Exchanges.

>   1 prebaked Italian bread shell crust (14 ounces)
>   1 cup (4 ounces) shredded Monterey Jack cheese, *divided*
> 3/4 cup salsa
>   2 tablespoons minced fresh cilantro

Place the Italian bread shell crust on an ungreased baking sheet or pizza pan. In a small bowl, combine 1/2 cup Monterey Jack cheese, salsa and cilantro. Spread over the crust to within 1/2 in. of edges. Sprinkle with remaining cheese.

   Bake at 350° for 20-25 minutes or until the cheese is melted. Cut into wedges. **Yield:** 2 dozen.

   Nutrition Facts: 1 wedge equals 64 calories, 2 g fat (1 g saturated fat), 4 mg cholesterol, 143 mg sodium, 8 g carbohydrate, trace fiber, 3 g protein. **Diabetic Exchanges:** 1/2 starch, 1/2 fat.

Sour Cream Cheese Puffs

(Pictured below and on page 4.)

PREP: 30 min. **BAKE:** 15 min.

I've made these pretty little puffs countless times for all sorts of occasions—from a football party to a wedding rehearsal dinner.
—Annie Darling, Minneapolis, Minnesota

>   1 package (8 ounces) cream cheese, softened
>   1 cup sour cream
> 1/3 cup finely chopped sweet red pepper
> 1/4 cup finely chopped onion
>   2 teaspoons lemon juice
> 3/4 teaspoon dill weed
> 1/4 teaspoon pepper
>   2 tubes (12 ounces *each*) refrigerated buttermilk biscuits
> 1/4 cup minced fresh cilantro

In a small bowl, beat the cream cheese, sour cream, red pepper, onion, lemon juice, dill and pepper until blended.

   Cut each biscuit in half horizontally; press into greased miniature muffin cups. Place a rounded tablespoonful of cream cheese mixture in each cup.

   Bake at 375° for 14-16 minutes or until golden brown. Sprinkle with cilantro. Serve warm. **Yield:** 40 appetizers.

Salsa Chorizo Pizzas

PREP: 30 min. **GRILL:** 5 min.

Grilled pizza is a snap when you start with frozen bread dough. Created by our Test Kitchen cooks, this version with a Mexican twist features a fresh homemade salsa and chorizo, a highly seasoned, coarsely ground pork sausage.

SALSA:
>   3 cups chopped seeded tomatoes
>   1 medium onion, chopped
>   2 jalapeno peppers, seeded and chopped
>   1 poblano pepper, seeded and chopped
> 1/3 cup minced fresh cilantro
> 1/4 cup lime juice
>   1 tablespoon olive oil
>   1 garlic clove, minced
>   1 teaspoon chili powder
>   1 teaspoon ground cumin
> 1/2 teaspoon salt

PIZZAS:
>   1 loaf (1 pound) frozen bread dough, thawed
>   3 tablespoons olive oil
>   2 cups (8 ounces) shredded Mexican cheese blend
> 1/2 pound chorizo, cooked and crumbled

In a large bowl, combine the salsa ingredients; set aside. Divide bread dough into fourths. On a lightly floured surface, roll each portion into an 8-in. circle. Lightly brush both sides of dough with oil; place on grill. Cover and grill over medium heat for 1-2 minutes or until the bottom is lightly browned.

   Remove from the grill. Top the grilled side of each pizza with 1/2 cup cheese, 1/4 cup chorizo and 1/2 cup salsa. Return to the grill. Cover and cook for 4-5 minutes or until the bottom is browned and cheese is melted. Refrigerate remaining salsa. **Yield:** 4 servings.

and salsa if desired. **Yield:** 16 servings.

Editor's Note: When cutting hot peppers, disposable gloves are recommended. Avoid touching your face.

Apple-Nut Blue Cheese Tartlets

(Pictured below)

PREP: 25 min. **BAKE:** 10 min.

These simple bites look and taste gourmet. The phyllo shells and filling can be made in advance—just fill the cups and warm them in the oven before serving. —*Trisha Kruse, Eagle, Idaho*

✓ This recipe includes Nutrition Facts and Diabetic Exchanges.

  1 large apple, peeled and finely chopped
  1 medium onion, finely chopped
  2 teaspoons butter
  1 cup (4 ounces) crumbled blue cheese
  4 tablespoons finely chopped walnuts, toasted, *divided*
1/2 teaspoon salt
  1 package (1.9 ounces) frozen miniature phyllo tart shells

In a small nonstick skillet, saute apple and onion in butter until tender. Remove from the heat; stir in the blue cheese, 3 tablespoons walnuts and salt. Spoon a rounded tablespoonful into each tart shell.

Place on an ungreased baking sheet. Bake at 350° for 5 minutes. Sprinkle with the remaining walnuts; bake 2-3 minutes longer or until lightly browned. **Yield:** 15 appetizers.

Nutrition Facts: 1 appetizer equals 76 calories, 5 g fat (2 g saturated fat), 7 mg cholesterol, 200 mg sodium, 5 g carbohydrate, trace fiber, 3 g protein. **Diabetic Exchanges:** 1 fat, 1/2 starch.

Taco Meatball Ring

(Pictured above)

PREP: 20 min. **COOK:** 30 min.

While this attractive meatball-filled ring looks complicated, it's really very easy to assemble. My family loves tacos, and we find that the crescent dough is a nice change from the usual tortilla shells or chips. —*Brenda Johnson, Davison, Michigan*

  2 cups (8 ounces) shredded cheddar cheese, *divided*
  2 tablespoons water
  2 to 4 tablespoons taco seasoning
1/2 pound ground beef
  2 tubes (8 ounces *each*) refrigerated crescent rolls
1/2 medium head iceberg lettuce, shredded
  1 medium tomato, chopped
  4 green onions, sliced
1/2 cup sliced ripe olives
  2 jalapeno peppers, sliced
Sour cream and salsa, optional

In a large bowl, combine 1 cup cheddar cheese, water and taco seasoning. Crumble beef over mixture and mix well. Shape into 16 balls.

Place meatballs on a greased rack in a shallow baking pan. Bake, uncovered, at 400° for 12 minutes or until the meat is no longer pink. Drain the meatballs on paper towels. Reduce heat to 375°.

Arrange crescent rolls on a greased 15-in. pizza pan, forming a ring with pointed ends facing the outer edge of the pan and wide ends overlapping.

Place a meatball on each roll; fold point over meatball and tuck under the wide end of roll (meatball will be visible). Repeat. Bake for 15-20 minutes or until rolls are golden brown.

Transfer the ring to a serving platter. Fill the center of the ring with lettuce, tomato, green onions, ripe olives, jalapenos, remaining cheddar cheese, and sour cream

Mediterranean Tomato Bites

(Pictured above and on page 4)

PREP: 20 min. **BAKE:** 15 min.

My friend, Mary, served these cute little appetizers at a summer get-together, and I've since adapted the recipe to suit my taste. Make them when tomatoes and herbs are at their freshest!
—*Susan Wilson, Milwaukee, Wisconsin*

 1 package (17.3 ounces) frozen puff pastry, thawed
 1-1/2 cups (6 ounces) shredded Gouda cheese
 6 plum tomatoes, cut into 1/4-inch slices
 1/4 cup pitted ripe olives, coarsely chopped
 1 cup (4 ounces) crumbled feta cheese
Minced fresh basil and oregano

Unfold the puff pastry; cut each sheet into 16 squares. Transfer the squares to greased baking sheets. Sprinkle with Gouda cheese; top with the tomatoes, olives and feta cheese.

Bake at 400° for 14-18 minutes or until golden brown; sprinkle with herbs. Serve appetizers warm or at room temperature. **Yield:** 32 appetizers.

Gouda Bites

PREP/TOTAL TIME: 25 min.

I season refrigerated crescent dough with garlic powder before baking it into golden, cheese-filled cups. It's hard to believe these delectable appetizers come from just three simple ingredients.
—*Phylis Behringer, Defiance, Ohio*

✓ **This recipe includes Nutrition Facts and Diabetic Exchanges.**

 1 tube (8 ounces) refrigerated reduced-fat crescent rolls

 1/2 teaspoon garlic powder
 5 ounces Gouda cheese, cut into 24 pieces

Unroll crescent roll dough into one long rectangle; seal seams and perforations. Sprinkle with garlic powder. Cut into 24 pieces; lightly press onto the bottom and up the sides of ungreased miniature muffin cups.

Bake at 375° for 3 minutes. Place a piece of Gouda cheese in each cup. Bake 8-10 minutes longer or until golden brown and the cheese is melted. Serve warm. **Yield:** 2 dozen.

Nutrition Facts: 2 bites equals 110 calories, 6 g fat (3 g saturated fat), 13 mg cholesterol, 252 mg sodium, 8 g carbohydrate, trace fiber, 4 g protein. **Diabetic Exchanges:** 1-1/2 fat, 1/2 starch.

Sparkling Kiwi Lemonade

PREP: 20 min. + freezing

Keep some of the kiwi ice cubes from this recipe in the freezer so they're ready whenever you crave a glass of the tangy lemonade.
—*Emily Seidel, Ainsworth, Nebraska*

 8 medium kiwifruit, peeled, *divided*
 3/4 cup sugar
 3/4 cup lemon juice
 1 liter carbonated water

Slice two kiwi into small pieces. Place in ice cube trays and fill with water. Freeze.

Cut the remaining kiwi into fourths; place in a food processor. Cover and process until smooth. Strain; discard pulp. In a 2-qt. pitcher, stir the sugar and lemon juice until sugar is dissolved. Stir in the kiwi puree. Refrigerate until chilled. Just before serving, stir in the carbonated water. Serve lemonade over kiwi ice cubes. **Yield:** 6 servings.

Scotch Eggs

PREP: 10 min. **BAKE:** 30 min.

Wrapped in sausage and coated with crispy cornflakes, these hard-cooked eggs make different but delicious snacks. They're fantastic hot out of the oven but can be enjoyed cold, too.
—*Dorothy Smith, El Dorado, Arkansas*

 1 pound bulk pork sausage
Salt and pepper to taste
 6 hard-cooked eggs
 1 egg, lightly beaten
 3/4 cup crushed cornflakes

Divide sausage into six portions; flatten and sprinkle with salt and pepper. Shape each portion around a peeled hard-cooked egg. Roll in beaten egg, then in cornflake crumbs. Place on a rack in a baking pan.

Bake, uncovered, at 400° for 30 minutes or until the meat is no longer pink, turning every 10 minutes. **Yield:** 6 servings.

Olive & Roasted Pepper Bruschetta

(Pictured at right)

PREP/TOTAL TIME: 15 min.

I've tried many versions of bruschetta, and I think this recipe featuring bits of chicken has the perfect blend of ingredients. It's also super-easy, and you can make the topping ahead of time.
—*Jennifer Mathis, Hilton Head, South Carolina*

☑ This recipe includes Nutrition Facts and Diabetic Exchanges.

- 1/2 cup grated Romano cheese
- 1/2 cup chopped pitted green olives
- 1/2 cup chopped roasted sweet red peppers
- 2 teaspoons olive oil
- 1/2 teaspoon dried basil
- 16 slices French bread baguette

In a small bowl, combine the first five ingredients. Top each bread slice with 1 tablespoon olive mixture. **Yield:** 16 appetizers.

Nutrition Facts: 1 appetizer equals 62 calories, 3 g fat (1 g saturated fat), 4 mg cholesterol, 251 mg sodium, 7 g carbohydrate, trace fiber, 3 g protein. **Diabetic Exchanges:** 1/2 starch, 1/2 fat.

So Very Berry Brie

(Pictured below)

PREP: 15 min. + standing **BAKE:** 10 min.

I needed a quick dish for a party and had some berries on hand. Combining them with warm Brie cheese made for an impressive starter.   —*Kristin Larson-Jantzi, Newton, Kansas*

- 1/2 cup sugar
- 2 tablespoons water

- 1/2 cup fresh *or* frozen raspberries, thawed
- 1/2 cup fresh *or* frozen blueberries, thawed
- 1/2 cup fresh *or* frozen blackberries, thawed
- 1 tablespoon cornstarch
- 2 tablespoons cold water
- 1 round (8 ounces) Brie cheese, halved horizontally

Baked pita chips *and/or* bagel

In a small saucepan, heat the sugar and water until the sugar is dissolved. Add berries. Bring to a boil. Reduce the heat; simmer, uncovered, for 3 minutes. Combine cornstarch and cold water until smooth; gradually stir into the pan. Bring to a boil. Cook and stir for 2 minutes or until thickened. Remove from the heat; let stand for 10 minutes.

Place the bottom half of the cheese in an ungreased ovenproof serving dish; pour 1/2 cup berry mixture over cheese. Top with remaining cheese and berry mixture. Bake, uncovered, at 400° for 8-10 minutes or until cheese is softened. Serve with chips. **Yield:** 8 servings.

BERRY BASICS. Plan to use fresh berries for So Very Berry Brie (above left)? Buy berries that are brightly colored and plump. At home, remove any berries that are soft, shriveled or moldy. Place berries in a single layer on a paper towel-lined plate, cover them loosely and refrigerate. Don't wash berries until you're ready to use them.

From Casual to Fancy

ON THOSE LAID-BACK occasions when friends drop by, ever-popular fare such as nachos, guacamole, cheese trays and hearty sandwiches always go over big. Why not enjoy the same crowd-pleasing flavors at your more elegant events as well?

These recipes take those favorite foods and dress them up for parties that call for something a little more special. Guests can savor the great tastes they love, and you'll be proud to serve these impressive appetizers!

Mini Muffuletta

(Pictured below)

PREP: 25 min. + chilling

Everyone likes these little Italian sandwich wedges. The recipe is fantastic for get-togethers and can be prepared the day before.
—Gareth Craner, Minden, Nevada

- 1 jar (10 ounces) pimiento-stuffed olives, drained and chopped
- 2 cans (4-1/4 ounces *each*) chopped ripe olives
- 2 tablespoons balsamic vinegar
- 1 tablespoon red wine vinegar
- 1 tablespoon olive oil
- 3 garlic cloves, minced
- 1 teaspoon dried basil
- 1 teaspoon dried oregano
- 6 French rolls, split
- 1/2 pound thinly sliced hard salami
- 1/4 pound sliced provolone cheese
- 1/2 pound thinly sliced cotto salami
- 1/4 pound sliced part-skim mozzarella cheese

In a large bowl, combine first eight ingredients; set aside. Hollow out tops and bottoms of rolls, leaving 3/4-in. shells (discard removed bread or save for another use).

Spread olive mixture over tops and bottoms of rolls. On roll bottoms, layer hard salami, provolone cheese, cotto salami and mozzarella cheese. Replace tops. Wrap tightly in plastic wrap. Refrigerate overnight. Cut each into wedges; secure with toothpicks. **Yield:** 3 dozen.

Corn Cakes with Shrimp & Guacamole

PREP: 30 min. **COOK:** 5 min./batch

Busy party hosts appreciate the convenience of these scrumptious appetizers. Make them a few hours ahead and keep them in an airtight container. —Carla Develder, Mishawaka, Indiana

☑ **This recipe includes Nutrition Facts.**

- 1/2 cup fresh *or* frozen corn
- 1-1/4 cups water, *divided*
- 1 cup complete buttermilk pancake mix
- 2 tablespoons grated Parmesan cheese
- 1/8 teaspoon hot pepper sauce
- 2 tablespoons finely chopped sweet red pepper
- 1 green onion, chopped
- 1 tablespoon minced fresh cilantro
- 1 medium ripe avocado, peeled and pitted
- 2 tablespoons finely chopped onion
- 1 tablespoon chopped seeded jalapeno pepper
- 1 tablespoon lime juice
- 1/8 teaspoon salt
- 24 cooked small shrimp, peeled and deveined
Small strips green onion *and/or* fresh cilantro leaves

In a small saucepan, bring the corn and 1/2 cup water to a boil. Reduce heat; cover and simmer for 4-6 minutes or until tender. Drain.

In a large bowl, combine the pancake mix and cheese. Add pepper sauce and remaining water; stir just until moistened. Fold in the corn, red pepper, green onion and minced cilantro.

Pour batter by tablespoonfuls onto a hot griddle coated with cooking spray; turn when bubbles form on top. Cook until the second side is golden brown. Set aside.

In a small bowl, mash avocado with onion, jalapeno, lime juice and salt. Top each pancake with a teaspoonful of guacamole and a shrimp. Garnish with green onion and/or cilantro. Serve immediately. **Yield:** 2 dozen.

Nutrition Facts: 1 appetizer equals 44 calories, 2 g fat (trace saturated fat), 15 mg cholesterol, 118 mg sodium, 6 g carbohydrate, 1 g fiber, 2 g protein.

Nacho Party Slices

(Pictured above)

PREP: 25 min. **BAKE:** 70 min. + chilling

A cheesecake doesn't always have to be a sweet dessert—as this savory version proves! Its nacho flavor and zesty crust never fail to get raves. —Melinda Messer, Benson, North Carolina

- 1-3/4 cups crushed nacho tortilla chips
- 1/3 cup butter, melted
- 3 packages (8 ounces *each*) cream cheese, softened
- 1/2 cup mayonnaise
- 1 envelope taco seasoning
- 2 tablespoons all-purpose flour
- 4 eggs, lightly beaten
- 1-1/2 cups finely chopped cooked chicken breasts
- 1-1/2 cups (6 ounces) shredded Mexican cheese blend
- 1/3 cup finely chopped green onions
- 1 cup (8 ounces) sour cream

Whole kernel corn, cubed avocado, chopped tomato and sliced ripe olives

Salsa, optional

Assorted crackers *or* additional nacho tortilla chips, optional

Combine crushed tortilla chips and butter; press onto the bottom of a greased 9-in. springform pan.

In a large bowl, beat the cream cheese, mayonnaise, taco seasoning and flour until smooth. Add eggs; beat on low speed just until combined. Stir in the chicken, cheese blend and onions. Pour over crust. Place pan on a baking sheet.

Bake at 325° for 60-70 minutes or until center is almost set. Gently spread the sour cream over the top; bake 10 minutes longer or until set.

Cool on a wire rack for 10 minutes. Carefully run a knife around edge of pan to loosen; cool 1 hour longer. Refrigerate for 8 hours.

Just before serving, remove sides of pan. Garnish with corn, avocado, tomato and olives. Serve with salsa and crackers if desired. **Yield:** 24 servings.

Marinated Cheese

(Pictured below and on page 4)

PREP: 30 min. + marinating

This tongue-tingling cheese always appears at our neighborhood parties and is the first appetizer to disappear at the buffet table. Attractive and delicious, it's also easy to prepare—making it a great alternative to the usual tray of cheese slices and crackers. —Laurie Casper, Coraopolis, Pennsylvania

- 2 blocks (8 ounces *each*) white cheddar cheese
- 2 packages (8 ounces *each*) cream cheese, softened
- 3/4 cup chopped roasted sweet red peppers
- 1/2 cup olive oil
- 1/4 cup white wine vinegar
- 1/4 cup balsamic vinegar
- 3 tablespoons chopped green onions
- 3 tablespoons minced fresh parsley
- 2 tablespoons minced fresh basil
- 1 tablespoon sugar
- 3 garlic cloves, minced
- 1/2 teaspoon salt
- 1/2 teaspoon pepper

Toasted sliced French bread *or* assorted crackers

Slice each block of cheddar cheese into twenty 1/4-in. slices. Cut each block of cream cheese into 18 slices; sandwich between cheddar slices, using a knife to spread evenly. Create four 6-in.-long blocks of cheese; place in a 13-in. x 9-in. dish.

Combine the roasted peppers, oil, vinegars, onions, herbs, sugar, garlic, salt and pepper; pour over cheese. Cover and refrigerate overnight, turning once. Drain excess marinade. Serve cheese with bread or crackers. **Yield:** about 2 pounds.

cook, stirring occasionally, for 3-4 minutes or until thickened. Spoon about 1 teaspoonful of filling into each tart shell; place tarts on a baking sheet. Sprinkle with bacon and cheese.

Bake at 350° for 5-7 minutes or until heated through. Serve warm. **Yield:** 2-1/2 dozen.

Nutrition Facts: 1 tart equals 53 calories, 2 g fat (1 g saturated fat), 6 mg cholesterol, 90 mg sodium, 5 g carbohydrate, trace fiber, 2 g protein.

Parmesan Knots

(Pictured below)

PREP/TOTAL TIME: 15 min.

These buttery bites can be made in advance, then reheated when needed. And when I'm busy with other party preparations, that's just perfect! —Jane Paschke, Duluth, Minnesota

- 1 **tube (12 ounces) refrigerated buttermilk biscuits**
- 1/4 **cup canola oil**
- 3 **tablespoons grated Parmesan cheese**
- 1 **teaspoon garlic powder**
- 1 **teaspoon dried oregano**
- 1 **teaspoon dried parsley flakes**

Cut each biscuit into thirds. Roll each piece into a 3-in. rope and tie into a knot; tuck the ends under. Place 2 in. apart on a greased baking sheet. Bake at 400° for 8-10 minutes or until golden brown.

In a large bowl, combine remaining ingredients; add warm knots and gently toss to coat. **Yield:** 2-1/2 dozen.

Chicken, Pear & Gorgonzola Tarts

(Pictured above)

PREP: 30 min. **COOK:** 5 min.

I've been experimenting with candied bacon and tried fitting it into some of my favorite recipes. I loved what it did for these rich, delicious tarts. —Richard Boulanger, Williston, Vermont

☑ This recipe includes Nutrition Facts.

- 8 **bacon strips**
- 1-1/2 **teaspoons brown sugar**
- 1/4 **teaspoon ground cinnamon**
- 3/4 **cup finely chopped cooked chicken breast**
- 1/3 **cup pear nectar**
- 1/4 **cup finely chopped dried pears**
- 3 **tablespoons apricot preserves**
- 2 **teaspoons butter**
- 1/4 **teaspoon salt**
- 1/4 **teaspoon pepper**
- 2 **packages (1.9 ounces *each*) frozen miniature phyllo tart shells**
- 1/3 **cup crumbled Gorgonzola cheese**

Place bacon in a 15-in. x 10-in. x 1-in. baking pan; broil 4 in. from the heat for 4-6 minutes on each side or until crisp. Combine brown sugar and cinnamon; sprinkle over bacon. Broil 1 minute longer or until the bacon is glazed and bubbly. Drain on paper towels. Cool slightly and crumble.

In a small skillet, combine the chicken, pear nectar, pears, preserves, butter, salt and pepper. Bring to a boil;

Greek Pinwheels

(Pictured above)

PREP/TOTAL TIME: 30 min.

These little golden spirals look and taste so good, my guests were surprised to learn that the recipe is actually simple to make. You could even serve these as a side with salad, soup or stew.
—*Veronica Worlund, Pasco, Washington*

- 1 sheet frozen puff pastry, thawed
- 1 tablespoon beaten egg
- 3/4 teaspoon water
- 1/2 cup cream cheese, softened
- 1/3 cup marinated quartered artichoke hearts, drained and finely chopped
- 1/4 cup crumbled feta cheese
- 1 tablespoon finely chopped drained oil-packed sun-dried tomatoes
- 3 Greek olives, finely chopped
- 1 teaspoon Greek seasoning

Unfold puff pastry. Whisk egg and water; brush over pastry. Combine the remaining ingredients; spread over pastry to within 1/2 in. of edges. Roll up jelly-roll style. Cut into twenty 1/2-in. slices.

Place 2 in. apart on greased baking sheets. Bake at 425° for 9-11 minutes or until puffed and golden brown. Serve warm. **Yield:** 20 appetizers.

Spiced Honey Pretzels

PREP/TOTAL TIME: 15 min.

If you like the combination of sweet and spicy, you're sure to love these zesty pretzels with a twist. The coating is so yummy, you won't need a fattening dip to enjoy munching them.
—*Mary Lou Moon, Beaverton, Oregon*

✓ **This recipe includes Nutrition Facts and Diabetic Exchanges.**

- 4 cups thin pretzel sticks
- 3 tablespoons honey
- 2 teaspoons butter, melted
- 1 teaspoon onion powder
- 1 teaspoon chili powder

Line a 15-in. x 10-in. x 1-in. baking pan with foil; coat the foil with cooking spray. Place the pretzel sticks in a large bowl.

In a small bowl, combine the honey, butter, onion powder and chili powder. Pour over pretzels; toss to coat evenly. Spread into prepared pan.

Bake at 350° for 8 minutes, stirring once. Cool on a wire rack, stirring gently several times to separate.
Yield: 8 servings.

Nutrition Facts: One serving (1/2 cup) equals 98 calories, 1 g fat (1 g saturated fat), 3 mg cholesterol, 487 mg sodium, 20 g carbohydrate, 1 g fiber, 2 g protein.
Diabetic Exchange: 1-1/2 starch.

Fontina Asparagus Tart

(Pictured below)

PREP: 15 min.   **BAKE:** 20 min.

This lemony cheese and vegetable tart made with convenient frozen puff pastry can be assembled in a mere 15 minutes, but it looks so impressive that guests will think you slaved in the kitchen all day. They'll also be vying for every last tasty slice!
— *Heidi Meek, Grand Rapids, Michigan*

- 1 pound fresh asparagus, trimmed
- 1 sheet frozen puff pastry, thawed
- 1/2 pound fontina cheese, shredded, *divided*
- 2 tablespoons lemon juice
- 1 tablespoon olive oil
- 1 teaspoon grated lemon peel
- 1/4 teaspoon salt
- 1/4 teaspoon pepper

In a large skillet, bring 1 in. of water to a boil; add asparagus. Cover and cook for 3-5 minutes or just until crisp-tender; drain.

On a lightly floured surface, roll out pastry into a 12-in. x 16-in. rectangle; transfer to a parchment paper-lined baking sheet. Bake at 400° for 10 minutes or until golden brown.

Sprinkle 1-1/2 cups fontina cheese over the pastry. Arrange the asparagus on top; sprinkle with remaining cheese. Combine the lemon juice, oil, lemon peel, salt and pepper; sprinkle over the top.

Bake 10-15 minutes longer or until the asparagus is tender and the cheese is melted. Slice and serve warm. **Yield:** 1 tart (about 24 appetizers).

Stuffed Baby Red Potatoes

(Pictured above)

PREP: 45 min.   **COOK:** 15 min.

For a fun and popular party food, try these. The ingredients are basic, but the cute little spuds always get lots of attention on the appetizer table.   — *Carole Bess White, Portland, Oregon*

☑ This recipe includes Nutrition Facts and Diabetic Exchanges.

- 24 small red potatoes (about 2-1/2 pounds)
- 1/4 cup butter, cubed
- 1/2 cup shredded Parmesan cheese, *divided*
- 1/2 cup crumbled cooked bacon, *divided*
- 2/3 cup sour cream
- 1 egg, beaten
- 1/2 teaspoon salt
- 1/8 teaspoon pepper
- 1/8 teaspoon paprika

Scrub potatoes; place in a large saucepan and cover with water. Bring to a boil. Reduce heat; cover and cook for 15-20 minutes or until tender. Drain.

When cool enough to handle, cut a thin slice off the top of each potato. Scoop out the pulp, leaving a thin shell. (Cut thin slices from the potato bottoms to level if necessary.)

In a large bowl, mash the potato tops and pulp with butter. Set aside 2 tablespoons each of the Parmesan cheese and bacon for the garnish; add the remaining cheese and bacon to the potatoes. Stir in the sour cream, egg, salt and pepper. Spoon the mixture into the potato shells. Top with remaining cheese and bacon; sprinkle with paprika.

Place in an ungreased 15-in. x 10-in. x 1-in. baking pan. Bake at 375° for 12-18 minutes or until a thermometer reads 160°. **Yield:** 2 dozen.

Nutrition Facts: 1 stuffed potato equals 82 calories, 4 g fat (3 g saturated fat), 21 mg cholesterol, 135 mg sodium, 8 g carbohydrate, 1 g fiber, 3 g protein.
Diabetic Exchanges: 1 fat, 1/2 starch.

Presto Black Bean & Corn Salsa

PREP/TOTAL TIME: 25 min.

I like to tinker in the kitchen with a variety of foods, including salsa. This chunky version makes a big batch, but it will be gone before you know it! —Jan Daniels, Rochester, Minnesota

✓ This recipe includes Nutrition Facts.

   1 **can (15 ounces) black beans, rinsed and drained**
   2 **cups fresh *or* frozen corn, thawed**
   5 **plum tomatoes, chopped**
   1 **large sweet red pepper, chopped**
   1 **small green pepper, chopped**
   1 **can (4 ounces) chopped green chilies**
1/4 **cup chopped red onion**
1/4 **cup minced fresh cilantro**
   2 **tablespoons lime juice**
   2 **garlic cloves, minced**
   1 **teaspoon sugar**
   1 **teaspoon salt**
1/2 **teaspoon ground cumin**
   1 **jar (16 ounces) salsa**
Tortilla chips

In a large bowl, combine the beans, corn, tomatoes, peppers, chilies, onion, cilantro, lime juice, garlic, sugar, salt and cumin. Stir in salsa until blended. Serve with chips. **Yield:** 28 servings (1/4 cup each).

Nutrition Facts: 1/4 cup (calculated without chips) equals 35 calories, trace fat (trace saturated fat), 0 cholesterol, 195 mg sodium, 7 g carbohydrate, 1 g fiber, 1 g protein.

German-Style Pickled Eggs

PREP: 20 min. + chilling

I make these eggs and refrigerate them in a glass gallon jar for my husband to sell at his tavern, and the customers can't get enough of them. I found the recipe in an old cookbook years ago. —Marjorie Hennig, Green Valley, Arizona

   2 **cups cider vinegar**
   1 **cup sugar**
1/2 **cup water**
   2 **tablespoons prepared mustard**
   1 **tablespoon salt**
   1 **tablespoon celery seed**
   1 **tablespoon mustard seed**
   6 **whole cloves**
   2 **medium onions, thinly sliced**
 12 **hard-cooked eggs, peeled**

In a large saucepan, combine the first eight ingredients. Bring to a boil. Reduce the heat; cover and simmer for 10 minutes. Cool completely. Place the onions and eggs in a large jar; add enough vinegar mixture to completely cover. Cover and refrigerate for at least 8 hours or overnight. Use a clean spoon each time you remove eggs for serving. May be refrigerated for up to 1 week. **Yield:** 12 servings.

Sesame Chicken Dip

(Pictured below)

PREP: 35 min. + chilling

We always have a "holiday feast" at work, and everyone brings a dish to pass. One of my co-workers made this crunchy dip, and it went over so well that I've since adopted it as my own! —Dawn Schutte, Sheboygan, Wisconsin

   2 **tablespoons soy sauce**
   4 **teaspoons sesame oil**
   2 **garlic cloves, minced**
   4 **cups shredded cooked chicken breast**
   3 **package (8 ounces *each*) reduced-fat cream cheese**
   8 **green onions, thinly sliced**
1/2 **cup chopped salted peanuts**
   2 **cups chopped fresh baby spinach**
   1 **jar (10 ounces) sweet-and-sour sauce**
Sesame rice crackers

In a large resealable plastic bag, combine the soy sauce, sesame oil and garlic; add the chicken. Seal the bag and turn to coat; refrigerate for at least 1 hour.

Spread cream cheese onto a large serving platter; top with chicken mixture. Sprinkle with onions, peanuts and spinach. Drizzle with sweet-and-sour sauce. Cover and refrigerate for at least 2 hours. Serve with crackers. **Yield:** 36 servings (1/4 cup each).

Mexican Salsa

(Pictured above)

PREP: 40 min.

In the summertime, I like to make this zesty salsa using fresh tomatoes and peppers from my garden. There's no better way to savor the season. —*Roger Stenman, Batavia, Illinois*

☑ **This recipe includes Nutrition Facts.**

- **3 jalapeno peppers**
- **1 medium onion, quartered**
- **1 garlic clove, halved**
- **2 cans (one 28 ounces, one 14-1/2 ounces) whole peeled tomatoes, drained**
- **4 fresh cilantro sprigs**
- **1/2 teaspoon salt**
- **Tortilla chips**

Heat a small ungreased cast-iron skillet over high heat. With a small sharp knife, pierce jalapenos; add to the hot skillet. Cook for 15-20 minutes or until peppers are blistered and blackened, turning occasionally.

Immediately place jalapenos in a small bowl; cover and let stand for 20 minutes. Peel off and discard the charred skins. Remove stems and seeds.

Place onion and garlic in a food processor; cover and pulse four times. Add the tomatoes, cilantro, salt and jalapenos. Cover and process until desired consistency. Chill until serving. Serve with chips. **Yield:** 3-1/2 cups.

Editor's Note: When cutting hot peppers, disposable gloves are recommended. Avoid touching your face.

Nutrition Facts: 1/4 cup (calculated without chips) equals 23 calories, trace fat (trace saturated fat), 0 cholesterol, 241 mg sodium, 5 g carbohydrate, 1 g fiber, 1 g protein.

Southwest Egg Rolls & Cool Avocado Dip

(Pictured below)

PREP: 35 min. **COOK:** 5 min./batch

A friend of mine prepared these egg rolls for my birthday treat several years ago…and what a treat it was! They're the best I've ever eaten. I love the Southwestern twist on a traditional Asian specialty. —*Becky Aylor, Sisters, Oregon*

- **2-1/2 cups shredded cooked chicken**
- **1-1/2 cups (6 ounces) shredded Mexican cheese blend**
- **2/3 cup frozen corn, thawed**
- **2/3 cup canned black beans, rinsed and drained**
- **5 green onions, chopped**
- **1/4 cup minced fresh cilantro**
- **1 teaspoon salt**
- **1 teaspoon ground cumin**
- **1 teaspoon grated lime peel**
- **1/4 teaspoon cayenne pepper**
- **1 package (16 ounces) egg roll wrappers**
- **Oil for deep-fat frying**
- **DIP:**
- **1 cup ranch salad dressing**
- **1 medium ripe avocado, peeled and mashed**
- **1 tablespoon minced fresh cilantro**
- **1 teaspoon grated lime peel**

In a large bowl, combine the first 10 ingredients. Place 1/4 cup of the chicken mixture in the center of one egg roll wrapper. (Keep the remaining wrappers covered with a damp paper towel until ready to use.) Fold the bottom corner over the filling. Fold the sides toward the center over the filling. Moisten the remaining

corner with water; roll up tightly to seal. Repeat.

In an electric skillet or deep-fat fryer, heat oil to 375°. Fry egg rolls, a few at a time, for 2 minutes on each side or until golden brown. Drain on paper towels.

Meanwhile, combine the dip ingredients. Serve with egg rolls. **Yield:** 20 egg rolls (1-1/2 cups sauce).

Fried Clams

PREP/TOTAL TIME: 30 min.

My state of Maine has some of the best seafood anywhere, and my favorite event is the Yarmouth Clam Festival. It's perfect for people who crave clams, clams and more clams! This recipe is a fantastic way to bring a taste of it into your own home.
—*Lee Ann Lowe, Gray, Maine*

  1-1/2 cups yellow cornmeal, *divided*
     1/2 cup cake flour, *divided*
     2/3 cup water
      12 fresh cherrystone clams, shucked
Oil for deep-fat frying
     1/2 teaspoon salt
Tartar sauce *or* **seafood cocktail sauce, optional**

In a shallow bowl, combine 3/4 cup cornmeal and 1/4 cup flour with the water, forming a batter. In another bowl, combine the remaining cornmeal and flour.

Dip the clams in batter; shake off excess. Coat with cornmeal mixture.

In an electric skillet or deep-fat fryer, heat oil to 375°. Fry clams, a few at a time, for 4-5 minutes or until golden brown. Drain on paper towels; sprinkle with salt. Serve immediately with sauce if desired. **Yield:** 1 dozen.

Tomato-Jalapeno Granita

PREP: 15 min. + freezing

Everyone says "wow" after a spoonful of this icy refresher. Even my grandchildren enjoy the zippy blend of tomato, pepper, mint and lime. —*Paula Marchesi, Lenhartsville, Pennsylvania*

✓ This recipe includes Nutrition Facts and Diabetic Exchanges.

    2 cups tomato juice
  1/3 cup sugar
    4 mint sprigs
    1 jalapeno pepper, sliced
    2 tablespoons lime juice
Fresh mint leaves, optional

In a small saucepan, bring the tomato juice, sugar, mint sprigs and jalapeno to a boil. Cook and stir until sugar is dissolved. Remove from the heat; cover and let stand for 15 minutes.

Strain and discard solids. Stir in lime juice. Transfer to a 1-quart dish; cool to room temperature. Freeze for 1 hour; stir with a fork. Freeze 2-3 hours longer or until completely frozen, stirring every 30 minutes. Scrape the granita with a fork just before serving; spoon into

dessert dishes. Garnish with additional mint if desired. **Yield:** 6 servings.

Editor's Note: When cutting hot peppers, disposable gloves are recommended. Avoid touching your face.

Nutrition Facts: 1 serving equals 59 calories, trace fat (trace saturated fat), 0 cholesterol, 218 mg sodium, 15 g carbohydrate, trace fiber, 1 g protein. **Diabetic Exchange:** 1 starch.

Watermelon Sherbet Smoothies

(Pictured above and on page 4)

PREP/TOTAL TIME: 10 min.

These quick-to-fix smoothies have become a mainstay for my sons when the weather warms up. Nothing beats the heat like these chilly drinks! —*Jamie Cockerel, Kalamazoo, Michigan*

✓ This recipe includes Nutrition Facts and Diabetic Exchanges.

    3 cups cubed seedless watermelon
    1 cup crushed ice
    1 cup watermelon, raspberry *or* **lime sherbet**
    4 teaspoons lime juice
    2 teaspoons miniature semisweet chocolate chips

In a blender, combine the watermelon, ice, sherbet and lime juice; cover and process for 30 seconds or until smooth. Stir if necessary. Pour into chilled glasses; sprinkle with chocolate chips. Serve immediately. **Yield:** 4 servings.

Nutrition Facts: 3/4 cup equals 93 calories, 1 g fat (1 g saturated fat), 0 cholesterol, 21 mg sodium, 23 g carbohydrate, 2 g fiber, 1 g protein. **Diabetic Exchanges:** 1 starch, 1/2 fruit.

Crab Cakes
With Red Chili Mayo
(Pictured below)

PREP: 35 min. + chilling **COOK:** 10 min./batch

This is one of the most popular appetizers I've made and is so attractive for a party. The spicy mayo is just the right accent for the crab cakes. —Tiffany Anderson–Taylor, Gulfport, Florida

- **1-1/3 cups mayonnaise**
- **2 tablespoons Thai chili sauce**
- **2 teaspoons lemon juice,** *divided*
- **1/4 cup** *each* **finely chopped celery, red onion and sweet red pepper**
- **1 jalapeno pepper, seeded and finely chopped**
- **4 tablespoons olive oil,** *divided*
- **1/2 cup soft bread crumbs**
- **1 egg, beaten**
- **1 pound fresh crabmeat**
- **1/4 cup all-purpose flour**

In a small bowl, combine the mayonnaise, chili sauce and 1-1/4 teaspoons lemon juice. Set aside.

In a small skillet, saute the celery, onion, red pepper and jalapeno in 1 tablespoon oil until tender. Transfer to a large bowl; stir in the bread crumbs, egg, 1/2 cup reserved mayonnaise mixture and remaining lemon juice. Fold in the crab. Cover and refrigerate for at least 2 hours. Cover and refrigerate remaining mayonnaise mixture for sauce.

Place flour in a shallow bowl. Drop crab mixture by 2 tablespoonfuls into flour. Gently coat and shape into a 1/2-in.-thick patty. Repeat with remaining mixture. In a large skillet over medium-high heat, cook patties in the remaining oil in batches for 3-4 minutes on each side or until golden brown. Serve crab cakes with the reserved sauce. **Yield:** 2 dozen (1 cup sauce).

Editor's Note: When cutting hot peppers, disposable gloves are recommended. Avoid touching your face.

Frozen Lemon-Berry
Margaritas

PREP/TOTAL TIME: 15 min.

Whether you're having friends over for a barbecue or are just trying to cool off on a hot summer's day, this thirst–quencher is terrific. Everyone loves the blend of sweet and tart ingredients. —Julie Hieggelke, Grayslake, Illinois

- **6 lime wedges**
- **3 tablespoons coarse sugar**
- **2/3 cup lemonade concentrate**
- **1 cup frozen unsweetened raspberries**
- **2 cups ice cubes**
- **1 package (16 ounces) frozen sweetened sliced strawberries, partially thawed**
- **1/2 cup frozen blueberries**
- **1 tablespoon sugar**
- **1/2 cup tequila, optional**

Using lime wedges, moisten the rims of six margarita or cocktail glasses. Set aside limes for garnish. Sprinkle coarse sugar on a plate; hold each glass upside down and dip rim into sugar. Set aside. Discard remaining sugar on plate.

In a blender, combine the lemonade concentrate and raspberries; cover and process until blended. Press the mixture through a fine meshed sieve; discard the seeds. Return the raspberry mixture to blender; add the ice, strawberries, blueberries, sugar and tequila if desired. Cover and process until smooth.

Pour into prepared glasses. Garnish with the reserved limes. **Yield:** 6 servings.

Spiced Nuts

PREP: 10 min. **COOK:** 10 min. + cooling

These seasoned mixed nuts are great not only to set out for guests, but also to give as a hostess gift or to pack in a tin as a Christmas present. I often add another teaspoon of cardamom, a flavor we really enjoy. —Judi Oudekerk, Buffalo, Minnesota

- **1/4 cup butter, cubed**
- **1/2 cup plus 3 tablespoons sugar,** *divided*
- **2 teaspoons ground cardamom**
- **1 cup salted cashews**
- **1 cup salted peanuts**
- **1 cup pecan halves**

In a large heavy skillet, melt butter. Add 1/2 cup sugar; cook and stir over high heat until sugar is dissolved. Meanwhile, place cardamom and remaining sugar in a large bowl; set aside.

Reduce heat to medium; add the cashews, peanuts and pecans to butter mixture. Cook and stir until nuts are toasted, about 3 minutes. Add hot nuts to reserved cardamom mixture; toss to coat. Spread on foil to cool. **Yield:** 3-1/2 cups.

1 tablespoon canned chopped green chilies
1/2 teaspoon chipotle pepper in adobo sauce
1/8 teaspoon garlic salt
4 teaspoons salsa
1-1/2 teaspoons thinly sliced green onion
1 pitted ripe olive, quartered

Cut the eggs in half lengthwise. Remove the yolks; set whites aside. In a small bowl, mash yolks. Stir in the mayonnaise, chilies, chipotle pepper and garlic salt. Stuff or pipe into egg whites.

Top with salsa, onion and an olive piece. Refrigerate until serving. **Yield:** 2 servings.

Cordon Bleu Appetizers

(Pictured below)

PREP/TOTAL TIME: 30 min.

Looking for a cheesy snack with mass appeal? I've found that adults and kids alike will snatch up these baked ham–and–Swiss bread slices. —Susan Mello, Jackson Heights, New York

4 ounces cream cheese, softened
1 teaspoon Dijon mustard
1 cup (4 ounces) shredded Swiss cheese
3/4 cup diced fully cooked ham
1/2 cup minced chives, *divided*
18 slices French bread (1/2 inch thick)

In a small bowl, beat cream cheese and mustard until smooth. Stir in the Swiss cheese, ham and 1/4 cup chives. Spread 1 tablespoon mixture over each bread slice; place on an ungreased baking sheet.

Bake appetizers at 350° for 12-15 minutes or until lightly browned. Sprinkle with remaining chives. **Yield:** 1-1/2 dozen.

Brie Cherry Pastry Cups

(Pictured above)

PREP/TOTAL TIME: 30 min.

With the cherry preserves and airy pastry, these yummy little appetizers almost taste like a dessert. But they always go over big as before–dinner snacks. —Marilyn Mcsween, Mentor, Ohio

☑ This recipe includes Nutrition Facts and Diabetic Exchanges.

1 sheet frozen puff pastry, thawed
1/2 cup cherry preserves
4 ounces Brie *or* Camembert cheese, cut into 1/2-inch cubes
1/4 cup chopped pecans *or* walnuts
2 tablespoons minced chives

Unfold puff pastry; cut into 36 squares. Gently press squares onto the bottoms of 36 miniature muffin cups coated with cooking spray.

Bake at 375° for 10 minutes. Using the end of a wooden spoon handle, make a 1/2-in.-deep indentation in the center of each. Bake 6-8 minutes longer or until golden brown. With the spoon handle, press squares down again.

Spoon a rounded 1/2 teaspoonful of preserves into each cup. Top with the cheese; sprinkle with nuts and chives. Bake for 3-5 minutes or until cheese is melted. **Yield:** 3 dozen.

Nutrition Facts: 1 appetizer equals 61 calories, 3 g fat (1 g saturated fat), 3 mg cholesterol, 42 mg sodium, 7 g carbohydrate, 1 g fiber, 1 g protein. **Diabetic Exchanges:** 1/2 starch, 1/2 fat.

Santa Fe Deviled Eggs

PREP/TOTAL TIME: 15 min.

For a change of pace from the usual deviled egg recipe, try this one. It gives eggs a kick with chilies, chipotle pepper and salsa. —Patricia Harmon, Baden, Pennsylvania

2 hard-cooked eggs
1 tablespoon mayonnaise

Salads & Dressings

From crowd-pleasers for picnics to speedy weeknight sides and take-along lunches, these mouth-watering medleys will toss great taste into your menus.

BEST DRESSED. Clockwise from top left: Grilled Steak Bruschetta Salad (p. 29), Rainbow Pasta Salad (p. 30), South-of-the-Border Caprese Salad (p. 27), Caroline's Basil Boats (p. 28) and Parmesan, Walnut & Arugula Baskets (p. 28).

Fabulous Fruit Salad

(Pictured above)

PREP: 45 min. + chilling

This pretty salad is a must-have for our family gatherings and is packed with 11 kinds of fruit. The lemonade-pudding coating goes well with every one! —Rhonda Eads, Jasper, Indiana

- 1 **medium honeydew, peeled, seeded and cubed**
- 1 **medium cantaloupe, peeled, seeded and cubed**
- 2 **cups cubed seedless watermelon**
- 2 **medium peaches, peeled and sliced**
- 2 **medium nectarines, sliced**
- 1 **cup seedless red grapes**
- 1 **cup halved fresh strawberries**
- 1 **can (11 ounces) mandarin oranges, drained**
- 2 **medium kiwifruit, peeled, halved and sliced**
- 2 **medium firm bananas, sliced**
- 1 **large Granny Smith apple, cubed**
- 1 **can (12 ounces) frozen lemonade concentrate, thawed**
- 1 **package (3.4 ounces) instant vanilla pudding mix**

In a large bowl, combine the first nine ingredients. Cover and refrigerate for at least 1 hour.

Just before serving, stir in the bananas and apple. Combine the lemonade concentrate and pudding mix; pour over the fruit and toss to coat. **Yield:** 20 servings (3/4 cup each).

Pear Harvest Salad

PREP/TOTAL TIME: 25 min.

We came up with this delightful dish as a way to use up leftover Thanksgiving turkey...but it looks and tastes good enough to serve company. —Nancy Prewitt, Beaverton, Oregon

- 2 **packages (5 ounces *each*) spring mix salad greens**
- 4 **cups cubed cooked turkey breast**
- 2 **medium pears, sliced**
- 1 **medium ripe avocado, peeled and cubed**
- 1/2 **cup pomegranate seeds**
- 1/2 **small red onion, thinly sliced**

DRESSING:
- 6 **tablespoons cider vinegar**
- 1/4 **cup olive oil**
- 3 **tablespoons honey**
- 1 **teaspoon Dijon mustard**
- 1/2 **teaspoons salt**
- 1/4 **teaspoons pepper**

TOPPINGS:
- 1/2 **cup crumbled blue cheese**
- 1/2 **cup honey-roasted sliced almonds**

Divide spring mix among six plates. Top with turkey, pears, avocado, pomegranate seeds and onion.

Whisk the dressing ingredients; drizzle over salads. Sprinkle with cheese and almonds. Serve immediately. **Yield:** 6 servings.

Spicy Crunchy Veggies

PREP: 15 min. + chilling

This simple salad offers a lot of crunch and plenty of spice. If you like, top it off with ranch-flavored almonds instead of toasting them yourself. —Grady Jones, Midland, Texas

☑ This recipe includes Nutrition Facts and Diabetic Exchanges.

- 2 **cups fresh broccoli florets**
- 1/3 **cup finely chopped red onion**
- 1/4 **cup fresh cauliflowerets**
- 1/4 **cup julienned carrot**
- 2 **tablespoons chopped sweet red pepper**
- 1 **small jalapeno pepper, seeded and chopped**
- 2 **ounces reduced-fat Monterey Jack cheese, cut into small cubes**
- 2 **tablespoons fat-free plain yogurt**
- 2 **tablespoons reduced-fat mayonnaise**
- 1/2 **teaspoon salt-free spicy seasoning blend**
- 1/8 **teaspoon salt**
- 1 **tablespoon slivered almonds, toasted**

In a large bowl, combine the first six ingredients. Stir in cheese. In a small bowl, combine yogurt, mayonnaise, seasoning blend and salt. Stir into the vegetable mixture. Cover and refrigerate for at least 1 hour. Just

before serving, sprinkle with almonds. **Yield:** 4 servings.
Nutrition Facts: 3/4 cup equals 87 calories, 5 g fat (2 g saturated fat), 12 mg cholesterol, 281 mg sodium, 7 g carbohydrate, 2 g fiber, 6 g protein. **Diabetic Exchanges:** 1 vegetable, 1 fat.

French Dressing With Tomatoes

(Pictured below)

PREP/TOTAL TIME: 10 min.

Every time I prepare this recipe, it takes me back to the country. I can picture myself in the garden among the fresh tomatoes.
—*Dana Barnes, Beaufort, South Carolina*

 1 **can (10-3/4 ounces) condensed tomato soup, undiluted**
 1 **cup vegetable oil**
 1/2 **cup sugar**
 1/2 **cup cider vinegar**
 1 **tablespoon Worcestershire sauce**
 1 **tablespoon prepared mustard**
 2 **to 3 teaspoons pepper**
 1 **teaspoon salt**
 1/4 **teaspoon garlic powder**
Tomato wedges
Lettuce leaves

In a blender, combine the first nine ingredients; cover and process until blended. Place tomato wedges in a bowl; add enough dressing to cover. Let stand at room temperature for 1 hour. Pour remaining dressing into a jar; cover and refrigerate for another use.

To serve, use a slotted spoon to place tomato wedges on lettuce leaves; drizzle with dressing left in bowl. **Yield:** 3 cups.

Pina Colada Molded Salad

(Pictured above)

PREP/TOTAL TIME: 25 min.

This gelatin mold gets a tropical twist from coconut, pineapple and macadamia nuts. It's a wonderful treat on special occasions or anytime. —*Carol Gillespie, Chambersburg, Pennsylvania*

 1 **can (20 ounces) unsweetened crushed pineapple**
 2 **envelopes unflavored gelatin**
 1/2 **cup cold water**
 1 **cup cream of coconut**
 1 **cup (8 ounces) sour cream**
 3/4 **cup lemon-lime soda**
 3/4 **cup flaked coconut**
 1/2 **cup chopped macadamia nuts**
Pineapple chunks and freshly shredded coconut, optional

Drain pineapple, reserving juice; set pineapple aside. In a large saucepan, sprinkle gelatin over cold water; let stand for 1 minute. Cook and stir over low heat until the gelatin is completely dissolved, about 2 minutes.

Remove from the heat; stir in the cream of coconut, sour cream, soda and reserved pineapple juice. Transfer to a large bowl. Cover and refrigerate for 30 minutes or until thickened, stirring occasionally.

Fold in the flaked coconut, macadamia nuts and reserved pineapple. Pour into a 6-cup ring mold coated with cooking spray. Cover and refrigerate for 3 hours or until firm.

To serve, unmold salad onto a platter. Fill the center with pineapple chunks and shredded coconut if desired. **Yield:** 8 servings.

Editor's Note: This recipe was tested with Coco Lopez cream of coconut.

Asparagus & Pear Salad

(Pictured below)

PREP/TOTAL TIME: 15 min.

I always look forward to the fresh asparagus my husband grows in his garden, and this salad is the perfect opportunity to use it.
—Nancy Zimmerman, Cape May Court House, New Jersey

☑ This recipe includes Nutrition Facts and Diabetic Exchanges.

> 1 pound fresh asparagus, trimmed
> 1 large pear, sliced
> 2 teaspoons lemon juice
> 2 green onions, thinly sliced
> 1/4 cup chopped walnuts, toasted
> 2 tablespoons prepared honey Dijon salad dressing
> 8 romaine lettuce leaves

In a large skillet, bring 1/2 in. of water to a boil. Add the asparagus; cover and boil for 3-5 minutes or until crisp-tender. Drain and immediately place asparagus in ice water. Drain and pat dry; cut into 1/2-in. pieces and set aside.

   In a large bowl, combine pear and lemon juice. Add the onions, walnuts and reserved asparagus; drizzle with dressing and toss to coat. Arrange lettuce on four salad plates; top with asparagus mixture. Serve immediately. **Yield:** 4 servings.

   Nutrition Facts: 1 cup with 2 lettuce leaves equals 128 calories, 7 g fat (1 g saturated fat), 0 cholesterol, 60 mg sodium, 15 g carbohydrate, 3 g fiber, 4 g protein. **Diabetic Exchanges:** 1 vegetable, 1 fat, 1/2 fruit.

Chunky Cranberry Salad

PREP: 10 min. **COOK:** 15 min.

This is a recipe I discovered while taking a cooking class. The fruity, nutty gelatin salad makes a lively alternative to jellied cranberry sauce.   —Joyce Butterfield, Nancy, Kentucky

> 4 cups fresh *or* frozen cranberries
> 3-1/2 cups unsweetened pineapple juice
> 2 envelopes unflavored gelatin
> 1/2 cup cold water
> 2 cups sugar
> 1 can (20 ounces) unsweetened pineapple tidbits, drained
> 1 cup chopped pecans
> 1 cup green grapes, chopped
> 1/2 cup finely chopped celery
> 2 teaspoons grated orange peel

In a large saucepan, combine the cranberries and pineapple juice. Cook over medium heat until berries pop, about 15 minutes.

   Meanwhile, in a small bowl, sprinkle gelatin over cold water; let stand for 5 minutes. In a large bowl, combine the berry mixture, sugar and softened gelatin. Chill until partially set.

   Fold in the pineapple, pecans, grapes, celery and orange peel. Pour into individual serving dishes. Chill until firm. **Yield:** 12 servings.

Greek Salad with Greek Artisan's Olives

PREP/TOTAL TIME: 20 min.

From Jungle Jim's International Market in Fairfield, Ohio, this green salad is packed with Greek flavor. The simple homemade dressing is just the right finishing touch.

☑ This recipe includes Nutrition Facts.

> 2 packages (5 ounces *each*) spring mix salad greens
> 3 plum tomatoes, chopped
> 1 small red onion, halved and thinly sliced
> 1 cup Greek olives
> 2/3 cup chopped peeled cucumber
> 1/2 cup olive oil
> 1/4 cup lemon juice
> 1 tablespoon minced fresh oregano
> 1 garlic clove, minced
> 1/4 teaspoon salt
> 1/8 teaspoon pepper
> 1 cup (4 ounces) crumbled feta cheese

In a salad bowl, combine the first five ingredients. Combine the oil, lemon juice, oregano, garlic, salt and pepper; drizzle over salad and toss to coat. Sprinkle

with cheese. **Yield:** 21 servings (3/4 cup each).
   Nutrition Facts: 3/4 cup equals 84 calories, 8 g fat
(2 g saturated fat), 3 mg cholesterol, 190 mg sodium,
2 g carbohydrate, 1 g fiber, 1 g protein.

South-of-the-Border Caprese Salad

(Pictured above and on page 23)

PREP/TOTAL TIME: 30 min.

*Plump heirloom tomatoes are the stars of this garden-fresh
medley, topped with a sweet-tart dressing and crumbled cheese.
It's a treat!*   —Kathleen Merkley, Layton, Utah

CILANTRO VINAIGRETTE:
   1/3 cup white wine vinegar
   1/2 cup fresh cilantro leaves
      3 tablespoons sugar
      1 jalapeno pepper, seeded and chopped
      1 garlic clove, peeled and quartered
   3/4 teaspoon salt
   2/3 cup olive oil
SALAD:
      4 cups torn mixed salad greens
      3 large heirloom *or* other tomatoes, sliced
   1/2 cup crumbled queso fresco *or* diced part-skim
         mozzarella cheese
   1/4 teaspoon salt
   1/8 teaspoon pepper
1-1/2 teaspoons fresh cilantro leaves

In a blender, combine the first six ingredients. While
processing, gradually add oil in a steady stream.
   Arrange greens on a serving platter; top with
tomatoes. Sprinkle with cheese, salt and pepper.
   Just before serving, drizzle salad with 1/2 cup
dressing; garnish with cilantro leaves. Refrigerate
leftover dressing. **Yield:** 2 dozen.
   Editor's Note: When cutting hot peppers, disposable
gloves are recommended. Avoid touching your face.

Thai Beef Salad

(Pictured below)

PREP/TOTAL TIME: 30 min

*A local restaurant served this unique salad, and we loved it so
much that we created our own version. Try it the next time you
have leftover beef.*   —Alma Winberry, Great Falls, Montana

      8 ounces uncooked spaghetti
THAI SALAD DRESSING:
   1/2 cup rice vinegar
   1/3 cup peanut *or* canola oil
      2 tablespoons lime *or* lemon juice
      1 tablespoon sugar
1-1/2 teaspoons minced fresh gingerroot
1-1/2 teaspoons hot pepper sauce
1-1/2 teaspoons soy sauce
      1 teaspoon salt
      1 garlic clove, minced
   1/2 teaspoon crushed red pepper flakes
SALAD:
      1 package (5 ounces) spring mix salad greens
      1 small sweet red pepper, thinly sliced
      4 green onions, chopped
      1 pound deli roast beef, cut into strips
      2 tablespoons chopped salted peanuts, optional

Cook spaghetti according to package directions.
Meanwhile, in a small bowl, whisk dressing ingredients.
   Drain spaghetti and rinse in cold water; toss with 1/2
cup dressing. Place in a large serving dish.
   In a large bowl, combine salad greens, red pepper and
onions. Drizzle with remaining dressing; toss to coat.
Arrange lettuce mixture over spaghetti. Top with roast
beef; sprinkle with peanuts if desired. **Yield:** 6 servings.

Parmesan, Walnut & Arugula Baskets

(Pictured below and on page 22)

PREP/TOTAL TIME: 30 min.

Really want to impress at your next luncheon or dinner party? Serve up this green salad in crispy, edible Parmesan baskets and just watch the reaction! They'll be the talk of the meal.
—*Anna Maria Wharton, Staten Island, New York*

- 1 cup plus 2 tablespoons shredded Parmesan cheese
- 2 tablespoons finely chopped walnuts

SALAD:

- 4 cups fresh arugula *or* spring mix salad greens
- 1/2 cup green grapes, halved
- 2 tablespoons chopped walnuts
- 2 tablespoons olive oil
- 1 tablespoon raspberry vinegar
- 1/4 teaspoon salt
- 1/8 teaspoon pepper

Heat a small nonstick skillet over medium-high heat. Sprinkle 3 tablespoons cheese and 1 teaspoon walnuts over the bottom of the skillet. Cook for 1-2 minutes or until edges are golden brown and cheese is bubbly. Remove from the heat and let stand for 30 seconds.

Using a spatula, carefully remove the cheese mixture and immediately drape over an inverted glass with a 2-in. diameter bottom to form a basket shape; cool completely. Repeat with remaining cheese and walnuts, forming six baskets.

For salad, in a large bowl, combine the arugula, grapes and walnuts. Whisk the oil, vinegar, salt and pepper; pour over arugula mixture and toss to coat. Place 1/2 cup salad in each basket. Serve immediately. **Yield:** 6 servings.

Caroline's Basil Boats

(Pictured above and on page 22)

PREP/TOTAL TIME: 15 min.

When I saw the basil and tomatoes in my grandparents' garden, I thought of creating these boats. They're fun to make and eat.
—*Caroline Elswick, Myrtle Beach, South Carolina*

✓ This recipe includes Nutrition Facts and Diabetic Exchanges.

- 8 large fresh basil leaves
- 1/2 cup finely chopped tomato
- 1/2 cup finely chopped carrot
- 3 tablespoons shredded part-skim mozzarella cheese
- 4 teaspoons shredded Parmesan cheese
- 3 tablespoons Italian salad dressing

Place basil leaves on a serving plate. Combine the tomato, carrot and mozzarella cheese; spoon into basil leaves. Sprinkle with Parmesan cheese; drizzle with dressing. **Yield:** 8 servings.

Nutrition Facts: 1 filled basil leaf equals 36 calories, 3 g fat (1 g saturated fat), 2 mg cholesterol, 127 mg sodium, 2 g carbohydrate, trace fiber, 1 g protein. **Diabetic Exchange:** 1/2 fat.

Harvest Turkey Bread Salad

PREP: 25 min. **BAKE:** 50 min.

One year when we were trying to use up our Thanksgiving dinner leftovers, this delicious panzanella was the result. It's now a family favorite. —Mary Beth Harris-Murphree, Tyler, Texas

- **8 cups cubed day-old Italian bread**
- **1/4 cup whole-berry cranberry sauce *or* chutney of your choice**
- **6 tablespoons olive oil, *divided***
- **6 tablespoons balsamic vinegar, *divided***
- **2 teaspoons salt, *divided***
- **1 large sweet potato, peeled and cubed**
- **1 large sweet onion, peeled and cut into wedges**
- **2 tablespoons minced fresh thyme**
- **1/2 teaspoon coarsely ground pepper**
- **5 cups cubed cooked turkey breast**
- **1/4 cup minced fresh parsley**
- **1/3 cup dried cranberries**
- **1/3 cup chopped pecans *or* hazelnuts, toasted**

Place bread cubes in an ungreased 15-in. x 10-in. x 1-in. baking pan. Bake at 250° for 12-15 minutes or until lightly browned. Set aside. Increase heat to 400°.

In a large bowl, combine the cranberry sauce, 2 tablespoons oil, 2 tablespoons vinegar and 1 teaspoon salt. Add sweet potato and onion; toss to coat. Place in a foil-lined 15-in. x 10-in. x 1-in. baking pan. Bake for 30-40 minutes or until tender, stirring once.

In a small bowl, combine thyme and pepper with the remaining oil, vinegar and salt. In a large bowl, combine the bread cubes, roasted vegetables, turkey and parsley. Drizzle with dressing and toss to coat. Sprinkle with cranberries and pecans. **Yield:** 8 servings.

Sweet Pepper Pesto Pasta

PREP: 20 min. **BAKE:** 15 min.

What's a summer gathering or potluck without at least one pasta salad? This Italian-style medley with peppers and pesto can be served hot or cold and is still good for several days after it's made. —Karen Hentges, Bakersfield, California

- **4-1/2 cups uncooked bow tie pasta**
- **1 large sweet red pepper, chopped**
- **1 large sweet yellow pepper, chopped**
- **2 teaspoons olive oil**
- **1/2 teaspoon garlic powder**
- **1 cup prepared pesto**
- **1 can (2-1/4 ounces) sliced ripe olives, drained**
- **1/3 cup grated Parmesan cheese**

Cook the pasta according to the package directions. Meanwhile, in a bowl, combine the peppers, oil and garlic powder; toss to coat. Arrange in a single layer in a greased 15-in. x 10-in. x 1-in. baking pan. Bake at 350° for 15-18 minutes or until peppers are tender.

Drain pasta and rinse in cold water. In a large salad bowl, toss the pasta, pesto, olives and pepper mixture. Refrigerate until serving. Sprinkle with Parmesan cheese. **Yield:** 8 servings.

Grilled Steak Bruschetta Salad

(Pictured above and on page 22)

PREP/TOTAL TIME: 30 min.

You'll want to fire up the grill just to make this impressive entree. The steaks cook quickly, and the salad prep takes almost no time at all. —Devon Delaney, Princeton, New Jersey

- **1-1/2 pounds beef tenderloin steaks (1 inch thick)**
- **1/2 teaspoon salt**
- **1/4 teaspoon pepper**
- **6 slices Italian bread (1/2 inch thick)**
- **3 cups fresh arugula *or* baby spinach**
- **3/4 cup prepared bruschetta topping *or* vegetable salad of your choice**
- **Crumbled blue cheese, optional**
- **3/4 cup blue cheese salad dressing**

Sprinkle steaks with salt and pepper. Grill, covered, over medium heat for 6-8 minutes on each side or until meat reaches desired doneness (for medium-rare, a meat thermometer should read 145°; medium, 160°; well-done, 170°). Let stand for 5 minutes.

Grill bread, covered, for 1-2 minutes on each side or until toasted; place on salad plates.

Thinly slice steak; arrange over toast. Top with arugula and bruschetta topping; sprinkle with cheese if desired. Drizzle with dressing. **Yield:** 6 servings.

Asian Veggie Gelatin

(Pictured below)

PREP/TOTAL TIME: 15 min.

The combination of ingredients in this gelatin mold—soy sauce, bean sprouts, water chestnuts and other veggies—may seem odd, but everyone who samples this sweet–savory salad loves the taste. Even people who hesitate to try it are pleasantly surprised.
—*Janice Scott, Spokane Valley, Washington*

☑ This recipe includes Nutrition Facts and Diabetic Exchanges.

    1 **package (.3 ounce) sugar-free orange gelatin**
  3/4 **cup boiling water**
    1 **cup cold water**
4-1/2 **teaspoons reduced-sodium soy sauce**
    1 **tablespoon lemon juice**
  1/2 **cup canned bean sprouts**
  1/2 **cup sliced celery**
  1/2 **cup shredded carrots**
  1/4 **cup sliced water chestnuts, halved**
    1 **tablespoon chopped green onion**

In a large bowl, dissolve gelatin in boiling water. Stir in the cold water, soy sauce and lemon juice. Add the bean sprouts, celery, carrots, water chestnuts and onion; mix well.

    Spoon into four 6-oz. bowls coated with cooking spray. Refrigerate for 1 hour or until set. Invert onto salad plates. **Yield:** 4 servings.

    Nutrition Facts: 1 serving equals 30 calories, trace fat (trace saturated fat), 0 cholesterol, 307 mg sodium, 5 g carbohydrate, 1 g fiber, 2 g protein. **Diabetic Exchange:** Free food.

Rainbow Pasta Salad

(Pictured above and on page 23)

PREP: 40 min. **COOK:** 20 min.

This colorful, meatless salad is hearty enough to be a light meal in itself. Because the full flavors of the herbs and vegetables need a little time to blend, it's a great choice when you need to make something ahead. —*Sue Ellen Clark, Warsaw, New York*

  2 **packages (12 ounces *each*) tricolor spiral pasta**
  2 **packages (16 ounces *each*) frozen California-blend vegetables, thawed**
  2 **pints grape tomatoes**
  1 **large zucchini, halved and thinly sliced**
  1 **large yellow summer squash, quartered and thinly sliced**
  1 **large red onion, finely chopped**
  1 **block (8 ounces) cheddar cheese, cubed**
  1 **block (8 ounces) Monterey Jack cheese, cubed**
  2 **packages (4 ounces *each*) crumbled tomato and basil feta cheese**
  1 **bottle (16 ounces) Italian salad dressing**
  3 **tablespoons minced fresh parsley**
  1 **tablespoon minced fresh basil**
  1 **teaspoon Italian seasoning**
  1 **teaspoon seasoned salt**
1/2 **teaspoon pepper**
  1 **can (3.8 ounces) sliced ripe olives, drained**
Grated Romano cheese, optional

Cook pasta according to package directions. Rinse with cold water; drain well. In two large bowls, combine the California vegetables, tomatoes, zucchini, yellow squash, onion, cheeses and pasta.

    In a small bowl, combine the salad dressing, parsley, basil, Italian seasoning, seasoned salt and pepper. Pour over pasta mixture; toss to coat. Stir in olives. Cover and refrigerate for 8 hours or overnight.

    Toss before serving. Serve with grated Romano cheese if desired. **Yield:** 36 servings.

Next-Generation German Potato Salad

PREP: 15 min. **COOK:** 15 min.

For family reunions and other big gatherings, this quick-cooking German-style potato salad is a keeper. Balsamic vinegar and bacon give it a twist. —*Mary Shivers, Ada, Oklahoma*

- **4 pounds small red potatoes, quartered**
- **10 bacon strips, chopped**
- **1 large onion, chopped**
- **3 tablespoons chopped celery**
- **2 tablespoons chopped green pepper**
- **1 tablespoon all-purpose flour**
- **1 tablespoon sugar**
- **1 teaspoon salt**
- **1/2 teaspoon pepper**
- **1 cup water**
- **1/3 cup white balsamic vinegar**

Place the potatoes in a Dutch oven and cover with water. Bring to a boil. Reduce heat; cover and simmer for 15-20 minutes or until tender.

Meanwhile, in a large skillet, cook bacon over medium heat until crisp. Using a slotted spoon, remove to paper towels. In the drippings, saute the onion, celery and green pepper until tender. Stir in the flour, sugar, salt and pepper until blended.

Combine the water and balsamic vinegar; stir into the vegetable mixture. Bring to a boil; cook and stir for 2 minutes or until thickened.

Drain potatoes and place in a large serving bowl. Pour dressing over potatoes. Add bacon and toss to coat. Serve salad warm or at room temperature. Refrigerate leftovers. **Yield:** 14 servings.

Tortellini-Shrimp Caesar Salad

PREP/TOTAL TIME: 25 min.

This fun main-dish salad from our Test Kitchen staff dresses up ordinary Caesar salad with two surprise ingredients—cheese tortellini and breaded popcorn shrimp. The result is a fantastic and filling combo you're sure to enjoy.

- **2 cups frozen breaded popcorn shrimp**
- **1 package (9 ounces) refrigerated cheese tortellini**
- **8 cups torn romaine**
- **1 medium tomato, chopped**
- **1/2 cup creamy Caesar salad dressing**

Prepare shrimp and tortellini according to package directions. In a large salad bowl, combine the romaine and tomato; drizzle with dressing and toss to coat. Drain the tortellini; toss with salad. Top with shrimp. **Yield:** 4 servings.

Spring Greens with Beets & Goat Cheese

(Pictured below)

PREP/TOTAL TIME: 20 min.

I make variations of this recipe depending on what I happen to have in my kitchen at the time, but this version is my absolute favorite. The medley of salad greens, sliced beets, goat cheese, glazed pecans and a homemade dressing is hard to beat. —*Kristin Kossak, Bozeman, Montana*

- **2/3 cup pecan halves**
- **3 tablespoons balsamic vinegar, *divided***
- **1 tablespoon water**
- **1 tablespoon sugar**
- **1/4 cup olive oil**
- **2 tablespoons maple syrup**
- **1 teaspoon whole grain mustard**
- **1/8 teaspoon salt**
- **1 package (5 ounces) spring mix salad greens**
- **1 can (14-1/2 ounces) sliced beets, drained**
- **1 cup crumbled goat cheese**

In a large heavy skillet, cook the pecans, 1 tablespoon vinegar and water over medium heat until nuts are toasted, about 4 minutes. Sprinkle with sugar. Cook and stir for 2-4 minutes or until sugar is melted. Spread on foil to cool.

For dressing, in a small bowl, combine the oil, maple syrup, mustard, salt and remaining vinegar. Refrigerate until serving.

In a large bowl, combine salad greens and prepared dressing; toss to coat. Divide among eight salad plates. Top with beets, goat cheese and glazed pecans. **Yield:** 8 servings.

Soups & Sandwiches

This always-popular combo gets jazzed up thanks to the exciting new recipes for stew, burgers, chowder, panini and more in this chapter.

CASUAL AND COMFORTING. Clockwise from top left: Very Veggie Soup (p. 34), Vegetarian Polka Dot Stew (p. 37), Crab Toast (p. 38), Cheddar French Dip Sandwiches (p. 40) and North Pacific Chowder (p. 38).

Chicken Taco Burgers

PREP/TOTAL TIME: 20 min.

Taco seasoning gives this moist chicken burger a Southwestern flair everyone loves. It's a great alternative to the usual ground beef patty. —Maria Regakis, Somerville, Massachusetts

>   1 egg, beaten
>   1/4 cup chopped onion
>   2 tablespoons taco seasoning
>   1 garlic clove, minced
>   1/4 teaspoon pepper
>   1 pound ground chicken
>   4 whole wheat hamburger buns, split
>   and toasted

In a large bowl, combine the first five ingredients. Crumble chicken over mixture and mix well. Shape into four patties. Grill the burgers, covered, over medium heat for 4-6 minutes on each side or until a meat thermometer reads 165° and juices run clear. Serve on buns with desired toppings. **Yield:** 4 servings.

Very Veggie Soup

(Pictured above and on page 32)

PREP: 20 min. **COOK:** 35 min.

I came up with this recipe in an effort to make my family's diet healthier. With so many vegetables, this flavorful soup is packed with nutrition. —Jaime Sargent, Farmington, New York

>   1 medium zucchini, chopped
>   1-1/3 cups chopped fresh mushrooms
>   1 small onion, chopped
>   4 garlic cloves, minced
>   1 teaspoon canola oil
>   1 carton (32 ounces) reduced-sodium chicken
>   broth
>   2 cans (14-1/2 ounces *each*) diced tomatoes with
>   basil, oregano and garlic, undrained
>   1 package (16 ounces) frozen chopped broccoli,
>   thawed
>   2 medium carrots, shredded
>   1 cup meatless spaghetti sauce
>   1 teaspoon Italian seasoning
>   1 teaspoon adobo seasoning
>   1 package (10 ounces) frozen chopped spinach,
>   thawed and squeezed dry
>   Parmesan curls

In a Dutch oven, saute the zucchini, mushrooms, onion and garlic in oil until tender. Add the broth, tomatoes, broccoli, carrots, spaghetti sauce and seasonings.

Bring to a boil. Reduce the heat; cover and simmer 10-15 minutes or until the vegetables are tender. Stir in the spinach; heat through. Garnish each serving with cheese. **Yield:** 6 servings (2 qts.).

Speedy Jambalaya

(Pictured below)

PREP/TOTAL TIME: 30 min.

With spicy sausage and colorful sweet peppers, this classic Cajun dish looks as appetizing as it tastes. It's impossible to turn down a second helping! —Nicole Filizetti, Grand Marais, Michigan

>   1-1/3 cups uncooked long grain rice
>   1 large onion, halved and sliced
>   1 medium green pepper, sliced
>   1 medium sweet red pepper, sliced
>   2 teaspoons olive oil
>   3 garlic cloves, minced
>   1 can (28 ounces) diced tomatoes, undrained
>   3 bay leaves
>   1 teaspoon salt

1 teaspoon paprika

1/2 teaspoon dried thyme

1/2 teaspoon pepper

1/4 teaspoon hot pepper sauce

2 cans (15-1/2 ounces *each*) black-eyed peas, rinsed and drained

3/4 pound fully cooked andouille *or* Italian sausage links, sliced

1/4 cup minced fresh parsley

Cook rice according to package directions. Meanwhile, in a large skillet, saute onion and peppers in oil for 4 minutes. Add garlic; cook 1 minute longer. Stir in the tomatoes, bay leaves, salt, paprika, thyme, pepper and pepper sauce. Bring to a boil.

Reduce heat; simmer, uncovered, for 5 minutes. Stir in peas and sausage; heat through. Discard bay leaves. Serve with rice. Sprinkle each serving with parsley. **Yield:** 8 servings.

Buffalo Beef Burgers

PREP/TOTAL TIME: 30 min.

This tangy, amped-up burger puts a new twist on ever-popular buffalo wings. The zippy mayo topping gives these sandwiches their kick. —Michael Cohen, Los Angeles, California

2 tablespoons butter, softened

2 tablespoons brown sugar

3/4 cup mayonnaise

1/4 cup Louisiana-style hot sauce

2 pounds ground beef

1 teaspoon salt

1/2 teaspoon coarsely ground pepper

6 kaiser rolls, split

1 celery rib, finely chopped

6 tablespoons crumbled blue cheese

In a small bowl, beat butter and brown sugar until light and fluffy. Add mayonnaise and hot sauce; beat until smooth. Set aside.

Crumble beef into a large bowl; sprinkle with salt and pepper and mix well. Shape into six patties.

Grill the burgers, covered, over medium heat for 5-7 minutes on each side or until a meat thermometer reads 160° and juices run clear. Place on rolls. Top each with 2 tablespoons buffalo mayonnaise and 1 tablespoon each of celery and cheese. **Yield:** 6 servings.

BEST BURGERS. To keep grilled burgers from drying out, be careful not to overhandle the meat before cooking. Also, avoid flattening the burgers with your spatula as they cook. You'll press out the juices that make burgers moist.

Turkey Focaccia Club

(Pictured above)

PREP/TOTAL TIME: 20 min.

Homemade cranberry-pecan mayo makes this hearty sandwich pure heaven. It's delicious the day after Thanksgiving or any day of the year. —Judy Wilson, Sun City West, Arizona

CRANBERRY PECAN MAYONNAISE:

1/2 cup mayonnaise

1/2 cup whole-berry cranberry sauce

2 tablespoons Dijon mustard

2 tablespoons chopped pecans, toasted

1 tablespoon honey

SANDWICH:

1 loaf (8 ounces) focaccia bread

3 lettuce leaves

1/2 pound thinly sliced cooked turkey

1/4 pound sliced Gouda cheese

8 slices tomato

6 bacon strips, cooked

In a small bowl, combine the mayonnaise, cranberry sauce, mustard, pecans and honey.

Cut bread in half horizontally; spread with cranberry pecan mayonnaise. Layer with lettuce, turkey, cheese, tomato and bacon; replace bread top. Cut into wedges. **Yield:** 4 servings.

Best Bet Burgers

PREP/TOTAL TIME: 25 min.

A well-seasoned classic, this fool-proof burger makes mouths water as soon as it hits the grill! You can't go wrong choosing this recipe for your cookout.   —Lucy Meyring, Walden, Colorado

- **2 eggs, beaten**
- **1 tablespoon prepared mustard**
- **1 tablespoon chili sauce**
- **2 teaspoons Worcestershire sauce**
- **1 small onion, finely chopped**
- **1 teaspoon seasoned salt**
- **1 garlic clove, minced**
- **2 pounds ground beef**
- **6 hamburger buns, split**

In a large bowl, combine the first seven ingredients. Crumble beef over mixture and mix well. Shape into six patties.

Grill, covered, over medium heat 5-7 minutes on each side or until a meat thermometer reads 160° and juices run clear. Serve on buns with your favorite toppings. **Yield:** 6 servings.

Bistro Breakfast Panini

(Pictured below)

PREP/TOTAL TIME: 25 min.

I tried an omelet that contained Brie cheese, bacon and apples and thought it would be tasty as a breakfast panini—so I created this recipe.   —Kathy Harding, Richmond, Missouri

- **6 bacon strips**
- **1 teaspoon butter**
- **4 eggs, beaten**
- **4 slices sourdough bread (3/4 inch thick)**
- **1/8 teaspoon salt**
- **1/8 teaspoon pepper**
- **3 ounces Brie *or* Camembert cheese, thinly sliced**
- **8 thin slices apple**
- **1/2 cup fresh baby spinach**
- **2 tablespoons butter, softened**

In a large skillet, cook bacon over medium heat until crisp. Remove to paper towels to drain.

Meanwhile, heat butter in a large skillet over medium heat. Add eggs; cook and stir until set.

Place the eggs on two slices of bread; sprinkle with salt and pepper. Layer with the cheese, apple, bacon, spinach and remaining bread. Butter the outsides of sandwiches. Cook on a panini maker or indoor grill for 3-4 minutes or until bread is browned and cheese is melted. **Yield:** 2 servings.

Apple Cider Beef Stew

(Pictured above)

PREP: 20 min. **COOK:** 6-1/4 hours

This slow cooker version of beef stew uses convenience products to cut down on preparation time. Apple cider and cinnamon are the special touches that add unbeatable home-style flavor.
*   —Margaret Wilson, Hemet, California*

✓ This recipe includes Nutrition Facts and Diabetic Exchanges.

- **4 cups frozen vegetables for stew (about 24 ounces), thawed**
- **1 can (8 ounces) sliced water chestnuts, drained**
- **1 jar (4-1/2 ounces) sliced mushrooms, drained**
- **1 tablespoon dried minced onion**
- **2 envelopes brown gravy mix**
- **2 tablespoons onion soup mix**
- **2 teaspoons steak seasoning**
- **1/8 teaspoon ground cinnamon**
- **2 pounds beef stew meat, cut into 1-inch cubes**
- **1 can (14-1/2 ounces) beef broth**
- **1-1/4 cups apple cider *or* unsweetened apple juice**
- **1 can (8 ounces) tomato sauce**
- **1 bay leaf**

3 tablespoons cornstarch
1/3 cup cold water

Place the vegetables, water chestnuts, mushrooms and onion in a 5-qt. slow cooker. In a large resealable plastic bag, combine the gravy mix, soup mix, steak seasoning and cinnamon; add beef, a few pieces at a time, and shake to coat. Add to slow cooker.

Combine the broth, cider and tomato sauce; pour over beef. Add bay leaf. Cover and cook on low for 6-7 hours or until meat is tender.

Combine cornstarch and water until smooth; stir into stew. Cover and cook on high for 15 minutes or until thickened. Discard bay leaf. **Yield:** 12 servings.

Nutrition Facts: 1 cup (prepared with lean beef stew meat, reduced-sodium beef broth, unsweetened apple juice and no-salt-added tomato sauce) equals 197 calories, 6 g fat (2 g saturated fat), 48 mg cholesterol, 748 mg sodium, 18 g carbohydrate, 1 g fiber, 17 g protein. **Diabetic Exchanges:** 2 lean meat, 2 vegetable, 1/2 fruit.

Herbed Tuna Sandwiches

PREP/TOTAL TIME: 20 min.

With a delightful combination of herbs and cheese, this tuna sandwich stands out. Plus, fat-free and reduced-fat ingredients make it lighter. —Marie Connor, Virginia Beach, Virginia

☑ This recipe includes Nutrition Facts and Diabetic Exchanges.

2 cans (6 ounces *each*) light water-packed tuna, drained and flaked
2 hard-cooked eggs, chopped
1/3 cup fat-free mayonnaise
1/4 cup minced chives
2 teaspoons minced fresh parsley
1/2 teaspoon dried basil
1/4 teaspoon onion powder
8 slices whole wheat bread, toasted
1/2 cup shredded reduced-fat cheddar cheese

In a small bowl, combine the first seven ingredients. Place four slices of toast on an ungreased baking sheet; top with tuna mixture and sprinkle with cheese.

Broil 3-4 in. from heat for 1-2 minutes or until cheese is melted. Top with remaining toast. **Yield:** 4 servings.

Nutrition Facts: 1 sandwich equals 332 calories, 9 g fat (4 g saturated fat), 144 mg cholesterol, 864 mg sodium, 30 g carbohydrate, 4 g fiber, 34 g protein. **Diabetic Exchanges:** 4 very lean meat, 2 starch, 1 fat.

Vegetarian Polka Dot Stew

(Pictured at right and on page 33)

PREP/TOTAL TIME: 30 min.

Here's a speedy version of traditional minestrone soup. The fun polka-dot shapes of the couscous, carrots and beans give this stew its name. —Teagan O'Toole, Boston, Massachusetts

☑ This recipe includes Nutrition Facts.

2 cups water
1 cup Israeli couscous
2 medium carrots, sliced
1 plum tomato, chopped
1/4 cup chopped onion
1 garlic clove, minced
2 cans (19 ounces *each*) ready-to-serve tomato soup
1 can (15 ounces) black beans, rinsed and drained
1 package (10 ounces) frozen chopped spinach, thawed and squeezed dry
1 tablespoon minced fresh basil *or* 1 teaspoon dried basil
1/2 teaspoon salt
1/2 teaspoon dried oregano
1/2 teaspoon dried marjoram
1/4 teaspoon pepper
Shredded Parmesan cheese

In a large saucepan, bring water to a boil. Stir in the couscous, carrots, tomato, onion and garlic. Bring to a boil. Reduce heat; simmer, uncovered, for 10-15 minutes or until tender and the water is absorbed. Stir in the remaining ingredients; heat through. Sprinkle with cheese. **Yield:** 5 servings.

Editor's Note: You may substitute 1 cup quick-cooking barley for the couscous if desired.

Nutrition Facts: 1-1/2 cups (calculated without cheese) equals 309 calories, 2 g fat (trace saturated fat), 0 cholesterol, 879 mg sodium, 60 g carbohydrate, 10 g fiber, 14 g protein.

North Pacific Chowder

(Pictured above and on page 32)

PREP: 15 min.　**COOK:** 35 min.

Tender vegetables and tarragon add great flavor to this savory fish soup. A side of your favorite bread makes a complete meal.
—*Pam Woolgar, Qualicum Beach, British Columbia*

- 8　bacon strips
- 1　small onion, chopped
- 1　celery rib, chopped
- 1　carton (32 ounces) chicken broth
- 4　medium red potatoes, cubed
- 2　tablespoons all-purpose flour
- 1　pint half-and-half cream
- 1　pound halibut fillets, cubed
- 1　tablespoon minced fresh tarragon
  or 1 teaspoon dried tarragon
- 1/2　teaspoon salt
- 1/4　teaspoon pepper

Tarragon sprigs, optional

In a large saucepan over medium heat, cook bacon until crisp. Drain, reserving 1 teaspoon drippings. Crumble bacon and set aside. Saute onion and celery in the drippings. Add broth and potatoes. Bring to a boil. Reduce heat; cover and cook for 15-20 minutes or until potatoes are tender.

Combine flour and cream until smooth; gradually stir into soup. Bring to a boil; cook and stir for 2 minutes. Stir in halibut, tarragon, salt, pepper and reserved bacon. Reduce heat; simmer, uncovered, for 5-10 minutes or until fish flakes easily with a fork. Garnish with tarragon sprigs if desired. **Yield:** 9 servings (2-1/4 qts.).

Crab Toast

(Pictured below and on page 33)

PREP: 20 min.　**BAKE:** 20 min.

When you're in the mood for casual dining, try this oven-baked, open-face sandwich that's crunchy, creamy and delightfully rich. You could also serve it as appetizer by cutting thinner slices.
—*Teri Rasey-Bolf, Cadillac, Michigan*

- 1　loaf (16 ounces) French bread
- 1/4　cup butter, cubed
- 4　plum tomatoes, peeled and finely chopped, *divided*
- 1　jalapeno pepper, seeded and chopped
- 2　garlic cloves, minced
- 2　teaspoons minced fresh cilantro
- 2　packages (8 ounces *each*) imitation crabmeat
- 3/4　cup ricotta cheese
- 1/2　cup sour cream
- 2　cups (8 ounces) shredded Italian cheese blend, *divided*

Cut bread in half horizontally; hollow out top and bottom, leaving 1-in. shells. Crumble removed bread; set aside.

In a large skillet, melt butter over medium heat; add half of the tomatoes. Add the jalapeno, garlic and cilantro; cook and stir for 4 minutes. Remove from the heat.

In a large bowl, combine the crab, ricotta and sour cream. Stir in the tomato mixture, reserved bread crumbs and 1 cup cheese blend. Spoon into bread shells. Place on an ungreased baking sheet. Bake at 375° for 15 minutes. Top with remaining cheese blend and tomatoes. Bake 5-7 minutes longer or until cheese is melted. **Yield:** 6 servings.

Editor's Note: When cutting hot peppers, disposable gloves are recommended. Avoid touching your face.

Asian Burgers

PREP/TOTAL TIME: 30 min.

With their distinctive East-meets-West taste, these Asian-style burgers have been a family favorite for more than 20 years. We enjoy them whether they're cooked in a skillet or on the grill.
—*Charlotte Giltner, Mesa, Arizona*

- 2 tablespoons soy sauce
- 1 tablespoon sesame oil
- 1 can (8 ounces) sliced water chestnuts, drained and chopped
- 1 cup fresh bean sprouts
- 1/2 cup finely chopped fresh mushrooms
- 1 celery rib, finely chopped
- 4 green onions, finely chopped
- 1 teaspoon pepper
- 1/2 teaspoon salt
- 2 pounds ground beef
- 4 teaspoons canola oil
- 1/2 cup mayonnaise
- 1 tablespoon prepared wasabi
- 8 sesame seed hamburger buns, split
- 3 cups shredded Chinese *or* napa cabbage

In a large bowl, combine the first nine ingredients. Crumble beef over mixture and mix well. Shape into eight patties.

In two large skillets, cook burgers in oil over medium heat for 5-6 minutes on each side or until a meat thermometer reads 160°.

Meanwhile, combine the mayonnaise and wasabi; spread over buns. Serve burgers on buns with cabbage. **Yield:** 8 servings.

Grilled Pork Burgers

PREP/TOTAL TIME: 25 min.

Try something a little different at your next cookout with these patties made of ground pork. They're jazzed up with Parmesan and plenty of seasonings. —*Dawnita Phillips, Drexel, Missouri*

- 1 egg, lightly beaten
- 3/4 cup soft bread crumbs
- 3/4 cup grated Parmesan cheese
- 1 tablespoon dried parsley flakes
- 2 teaspoons dried basil
- 1/2 teaspoon salt
- 1/2 teaspoon garlic powder
- 1/4 teaspoon pepper
- 2 pounds ground pork
- 6 hamburger buns, split

Lettuce leaves, sliced tomato and sweet onion, optional

In a large bowl, combine first eight ingredients. Crumble pork over mixture and mix well. Shape into six patties.

Grill burgers, covered, over medium heat for 4-6 minutes on each side or until a meat thermometer reads 160° and juices run clear.

Serve on buns with lettuce, tomato and onion if desired. **Yield:** 6 servings.

Chicken Alphabet Soup

(Pictured above)

PREP/TOTAL TIME: 25 min.

I'm a teenager and love making this fun chicken soup for my family. It makes me so happy when they tell me how much they like it! —*Sarah Mackey, New Smyrna Beach, Florida*

- 3 medium carrots, chopped
- 2 celery ribs, chopped
- 3/4 cup chopped sweet onion
- 1 tablespoon olive oil
- 2 quarts chicken broth
- 3 cups cubed cooked chicken breast
- 1/4 teaspoon dried thyme
- 1-1/2 cups uncooked alphabet pasta
- 3 tablespoons minced fresh parsley

In a Dutch oven, saute the carrots, celery and onion in oil until tender. Stir in the broth, chicken and thyme. Bring to a boil. Stir in pasta. Reduce heat; simmer, uncovered, for 10 minutes or until tender. Stir in parsley. **Yield:** 10 servings (2-1/2 qt.).

Yellow Tomato Soup with Goat Cheese Croutons

(Pictured below)

PREP: 45 min. **COOK:** 30 min.

Get your next dinner party off to an impressive start with this creamy, roasted tomato soup topped with crispy bread. In the summer, I grill the tomatoes instead of baking them.
— *Patterson Watkins, Philadelphia, Pennsylvania*

- **3 pounds yellow tomatoes, halved (about 9 medium)**
- **2 tablespoons olive oil, *divided***
- **4 garlic cloves, minced, *divided***
- **1 teaspoon salt**
- **1 teaspoon pepper**
- **1 teaspoon minced fresh rosemary**
- **1 teaspoon minced fresh thyme**
- **1 large onion, chopped**
- **1 cup vegetable broth**
- **1/2 cup milk**
- **1/2 cup heavy whipping cream**

CROUTONS:
- **12 slices French bread baguette (1/2 inch thick)**
- **1 tablespoon olive oil**
- **2 tablespoons prepared pesto**
- **1/2 cup crumbled goat cheese**
- **1 teaspoon pepper**

Place tomatoes, cut side down, in a greased 15-in. x 10-in. x 1-in. baking pan; brush with 1 tablespoon oil. Sprinkle with 2 teaspoons garlic and the salt, pepper, rosemary and thyme.

Bake at 400° for 25-30 minutes or until tomatoes are tender and skins are charred. Cool slightly. Discard tomato skins. In a blender, process the tomatoes until blended.

In a large saucepan, saute onion in remaining oil until tender. Add remaining garlic; saute 1 minute longer. Add broth and milk; bring to a boil. Carefully stir in tomato puree. Simmer, uncovered, for 15 minutes to allow flavors to blend. Stir in cream; heat through (do not boil).

Meanwhile, for croutons, place bread on a baking sheet and brush with oil. Bake for 5-6 minutes or until golden brown. Spread with pesto and sprinkle with goat cheese and pepper. Bake 2 minutes longer. Ladle soup into bowls and top with croutons. **Yield:** 6 servings.

Cheddar French Dip Sandwiches

(Pictured above and on page 32)

PREP/TOTAL TIME: 20 min.

With leftover roast beef or deli beef, it takes almost no time at all to fix these satisfying hot sandwiches. They're perfect for those hectic days. — *Holly Szwej, Bridgeport, New York*

- **1/4 cup butter, cubed**
- **2 garlic cloves, minced**
- **4 ciabatta rolls, split**
- **1 cup (4 ounces) shredded cheddar cheese**
- **1 pound thinly sliced roast beef**
- **1 can (14-1/2 ounces) beef broth**

In a small skillet, melt butter. Add the garlic; saute for 1 minute. Place rolls on a baking sheet; brush cut sides with garlic butter. Sprinkle with cheese. Broil 3-4 in. from the heat for 2-3 minutes or until cheese is melted.

In a large saucepan, combine beef and broth; heat through. Using tongs or a slotted spoon, place beef on rolls. Serve sandwiches with remaining broth for dipping. **Yield:** 4 servings.

Greek Chickpea & Walnut Burgers

PREP: 30 min. + chilling **GRILL:** 10 min.

Even meat eaters love this easy vegetarian burger featuring feta cheese, nuts and veggies. The flavor's so good, you'll enjoy it with or without the bun. —Jessie Apfel, Berkeley, California

- 2 eggs
- 1/2 cup dry bread crumbs
- 1/2 cup chopped walnuts
- 1 medium carrot, shredded
- 1/3 cup crumbled reduced-fat feta cheese
- 1/4 cup coarsely chopped onion
- 1/4 cup Greek olives
- 4 sprigs fresh parsley, stems removed
- 1 tablespoon lemon juice
- 2 garlic cloves, minced
- 1/4 teaspoon *each* salt and pepper
- 1 can (15 ounces) chickpeas *or* garbanzo beans, rinsed and drained
- 5 whole wheat hamburger buns

In a food processor, combine the first 11 ingredients; cover and pulse four times. Add chickpeas; pulse until chopped. Refrigerate for at least 45 minutes.

Shape chickpea mixture by 2/3 cupfuls into patties. Coat the grill rack with cooking spray before starting the grill. Grill burgers, covered, over medium heat for 3-5 minutes on each side or until a thermometer reads 160°. Serve on buns with your favorite toppings. **Yield:** 5 servings.

Holiday Tortellini Soup

PREP: 15 min. **COOK:** 35 min.

From Michelle Goggins of the Taste of Home Cooking School, this special Italian–style soup packed with cheese tortellini is hearty and delicious. It also freezes well if you want to make it ahead or to save leftovers for another day.

- 2 tablespoons olive oil
- 2 ounces pancetta *or* bacon, finely diced
- 1 medium onion, finely chopped
- 3 garlic cloves, minced
- 1 can (49-1/2 ounces) chicken broth
- 2 teaspoons Italian seasoning
- 1 package (9 ounces) cheese tortellini
- 1 can (28 ounces) crushed tomatoes in puree
- 8 ounces fresh spinach, rinsed, stemmed and chopped

Salt and pepper to taste
- 1 cup freshly shredded Parmesan cheese

Heat the olive oil in a Dutch oven over medium heat. Add the pancetta. Cook until crisp. Add the onion; cook 3-4 minutes or until soft. Add the garlic; cook 1 more

minute. Add broth and Italian seasoning; bring to a boil and simmer for 5 minutes.

Meanwhile, cook tortellini according to package directions; drain. Add cooked tortellini to soup mixture. Stir in tomatoes and simmer 5 minutes. Add spinach and cook just until wilted. Season with salt and pepper. Garnish with cheese. **Yield:** 8 servings (2-1/2 qts.).

Chilled Melon Soup

(Pictured below)

PREP: 25 min. + chilling

Want to put some zip in a summer luncheon? Try this pretty soup that gets a kick from cayenne pepper. It's sure to have guests talking! —Mary Lou Timpson, Colorado City, Arizona

☑ This recipe includes Nutrition Facts and Diabetic Exchanges.

- 3/4 cup orange juice
- 1 cup (8 ounces) plain yogurt
- 1 medium cantaloupe, peeled, seeded and cubed
- 1 tablespoon honey
- 1/4 teaspoon salt
- 1/4 teaspoon ground nutmeg
- 1/8 teaspoon cayenne pepper
- 6 mint sprigs

Place the orange juice, yogurt and cantaloupe in a blender; cover and process until pureed. Add the honey, salt, nutmeg and cayenne; cover and process until smooth. Refrigerate for at least 1 hour before serving. Garnish with mint sprigs. **Yield:** 6 servings.

Nutrition Facts: 2/3 cup equals 82 calories, 2 g fat (1 g saturated fat), 5 mg cholesterol, 126 mg sodium, 16 g carbohydrate, 1 g fiber, 2 g protein. **Diabetic Exchange:** 1 fruit.

Side Dishes & Condiments

A memorable menu just isn't complete without those on-the-side sensations that perfectly complement the main course. Look here for rave-winning recipes.

IDEAL ACCOMPANIMENTS. Clockwise from top left: Roasted Veggie Platter (p. 48), Garden Tomato Relish (p. 48), Scarborough Fair Stuffing (p. 46), Speedy Spanish Rice (p. 52) and Chipotle Sweet Potatoes (p. 45).

Veggie Noodle Side Dish

(Pictured above)

PREP/TOTAL TIME: 20 min.

I love to cook with fresh vegetables, especially when they're from my garden. Pair this colorful side dish with grilled chicken for an easy, filling meal. —*Wendy Myers, Thompson Falls, Montana*

✓ This recipe includes Nutrition Facts and Diabetic Exchanges.

- 1 small sweet red pepper, julienned
- 3/4 cup cut fresh green beans
- 3/4 cup thinly sliced fresh carrots
- 1/4 cup chopped red onion
- 1 tablespoon canola oil
- 1 package (3 ounces) ramen noodles
- 1 yellow summer squash, sliced
- 1 medium zucchini, sliced
- 1/4 cup chicken broth
- 1 tablespoon soy sauce
- 1 teaspoon fajita seasoning mix

In a large skillet or wok, stir-fry the pepper, green beans, carrots and onion in oil for 4 minutes. Meanwhile, cook noodles according to package directions (discard the seasoning packet or save for another use).

Add the remaining ingredients to the vegetable mixture; cook and stir until vegetables are crisp-tender. Drain noodles; add to vegetables and stir until blended. **Yield:** 4 servings.

Nutrition Facts: 1 cup equals 173 calories, 7 g fat (2 g saturated fat), trace cholesterol, 471 mg sodium, 23 g carbohydrate, 3 g fiber, 5 g protein. **Diabetic Exchanges:** 2 vegetable, 1 starch, 1 fat.

Tzatziki Topping

PREP/TOTAL TIME: 15 min.

The name of this recipe may be unfamiliar, but the fresh taste of the thick, chunky Greek-style cucumber sauce complements any kind of burger patty. —*Jessie Apfel, Berkeley, California*

- 1 cup finely chopped cucumber
- 1/2 cup reduced-fat plain yogurt
- 1/4 cup fat-free sour cream
- 1 tablespoon minced fresh mint *or* 1 teaspoon dried mint
- 1 tablespoon lemon juice
- 1 garlic clove, minced
- 1/4 teaspoon salt
- 5 lettuce leaves
- 5 slices tomato

For tzatziki sauce, combine the first seven ingredients; refrigerate until serving. Serve sauce on your favorite burger with lettuce and tomato. **Yield:** 5 servings.

Refrigerator Dill Pickles

(Pictured below)

PREP: 40 min. + chilling

These fresh, crispy, no-fuss pickles have a wonderful dill flavor and irresistible crunch. No one will believe they're homemade! —*Jake Haen, Ocala, Florida*

- 6 to 8 pounds pickling cucumbers
- 40 fresh dill sprigs
- 2 large onions, thinly sliced

5 garlic cloves, sliced
1 quart water
1 quart white vinegar
3/4 cup sugar
1/2 cup canning salt

Cut each cucumber lengthwise into four spears. In a large bowl, combine cucumbers, dill, onions and garlic; set aside. In a Dutch oven, combine the remaining ingredients. Bring to a boil; cook and stir just until salt is dissolved. Pour over cucumber mixture; cool.

Cover tightly and refrigerate for at least 24 hours. Store in the refrigerator for up to 2 months. **Yield:** 100 pickle spears.

Cheese & Parsnip Mashed Potatoes

PREP: 20 min. **BAKE:** 40 min.

Even young children will eat parsnips when you serve this side dish. Everyone who tries it likes the rich, slightly smoky taste.
—Jim Rude, Janesville, Wisconsin

2 medium Yukon Gold potatoes
4 small red potatoes
3 medium parsnips, peeled and cut into 1-inch pieces
2 bacon strips, cut into 1-inch pieces
2 tablespoons butter, melted
1/4 teaspoon salt
1/4 teaspoon seasoned salt
1/4 teaspoon coarsely ground pepper
1/2 cup shredded Havarti cheese
1/2 cup shredded Parmesan cheese
1/2 cup heavy whipping cream, warmed
1 tablespoon minced chives
2 tablespoons crumbled blue cheese

Scrub potatoes and cut into 1-in. pieces; place in a large bowl. Add the parsnips, bacon, butter, salt, seasoned salt and pepper; toss to coat. Transfer to a greased 15-in. x 10-in. x 1-in. baking pan. Bake at 425° for 40-45 minutes or until parsnips are tender, stirring once.

In a large bowl, mash the potato mixture with Havarti cheese, Parmesan cheese, cream and chives. Stir in blue cheese. **Yield:** 6 servings.

PARSNIP POINTERS. Look for small to medium parsnips that are firm and have smooth skin. Don't buy parsnips that are shriveled, limp, cracked or spotted.

Store parsnips in a plastic bag for up to 2 weeks. Peel and trim the ends just before using.

Chipotle Sweet Potatoes

(Pictured above and on page 42)

PREP: 15 min. **BAKE:** 25 min.

Tired of the same old sweet potato recipe? Try this spicy-sweet creation. It's a great way to add this nutritious veggie to your diet any time of year. —Kim Jones, Mount Juliet, Tennessee

☑ This recipe includes Nutrition Facts and Diabetic Exchanges.

3 large sweet potatoes (about 2-1/2 pounds), peeled and cut into 1/2-inch cubes
1 cup balsamic vinaigrette, *divided*
1/4 teaspoon salt
1/4 teaspoon pepper
1/3 cup minced fresh cilantro
3 tablespoons honey
2 chipotle peppers in adobo sauce, minced

Place sweet potatoes in two greased 15-in. x 10-in. x 1-in. baking pans. Drizzle with 1/2 cup vinaigrette and sprinkle with salt and pepper; toss to coat. Bake at 400° for 25-30 minutes or until tender, stirring once. Cool slightly; transfer to a large bowl.

In a small bowl, whisk the remaining vinaigrette with the cilantro, honey and chipotle peppers. Pour over potatoes and gently stir to coat. **Yield:** 8 servings.

Nutrition Facts: 3/4 cup equals 168 calories, 5 g fat (1 g saturated fat), 0 cholesterol, 357 mg sodium, 30 g carbohydrate, 3 g fiber, 1 g protein. **Diabetic Exchanges:** 2 starch, 1 fat.

Scarborough Fair Stuffing

(Pictured below and on page 43)

PREP: 30 min. **BAKE:** 25 min.

A variety of types and textures of breads is the key to making this scrumptious herb stuffing. Serve it as a side dish anytime, or see the Editor's Note at the end of the recipe to use it to stuff your Thanksgiving turkey. For a delicious variation, add cooked sausage or pine nuts. —April Greenwood, Lakewood, Colorado

- 10 **cups torn assorted breads, such as French, whole wheat, rye, pumpernickel and plain bagels**
- 1/4 **cup minced fresh parsley**
- 1/4 **cup minced fresh sage**
- 2 **tablespoons minced fresh rosemary**
- 2 **tablespoons minced fresh thyme**
- 1/2 **teaspoon salt**
- 1/4 **teaspoon pepper**
- 2 **eggs, beaten**
- 1 **can (14-1/2 ounces) reduced-sodium chicken broth**
- 1/2 **cup butter, melted**

In a large bowl, combine the breads, herbs, salt and pepper. Combine the eggs, broth and butter; add to bread mixture and stir until moistened.

Transfer stuffing to a greased 13-in. x 9-in. baking dish. Bake, uncovered, at 350° for 25-30 minutes or until a thermometer reads 160°. **Yield:** 9 servings.

Editor's Note: This recipe may also be doubled to stuff a 14-lb. turkey (use 1/2 cup egg substitute in place of the 2 eggs). Bake until a meat thermometer reads 180° for the turkey and 165° for the stuffing.

Oodles of Noodles

(Pictured above)

PREP: 50 min. + standing **COOK:** 15 min.

My mother made the most delicious noodles from scratch using our own farm-fresh eggs, flour and salt. I remember her rolling out the dough paper-thin on our big dining room table.
—Karen Ann Bland, Gove, Kansas

☑ **This recipe includes Nutrition Facts.**

- 3-1/4 to 3-1/2 **cups all-purpose flour**
- 3/4 **teaspoon salt**
- 6 **eggs, beaten**

In a small bowl, combine 3-1/4 cups flour and salt. Make a well in the center. Pour eggs into well. Stir together, forming a dough. Turn dough onto a floured surface; knead for 3-4 minutes or until smooth, adding the remaining flour if necessary.

Divide the dough into nine portions; cover and let rest for 15 minutes. Roll each portion of dough into a 12-in. x 5-in. rectangle. Roll up jelly-roll style, starting with a short side; cut into 1/4-in.-thick strips. Unroll noodles and allow to dry on kitchen towels for 1 hour before cooking.

To cook, fill a Dutch oven three-fourths full with water. Bring to a boil. Add the noodles; cook for 9-12 minutes or until tender. Drain. **Yield:** 9 servings.

Nutrition Facts: 3/4 cup equals 212 calories, 4 g fat (1 g saturated fat), 141 mg cholesterol, 244 mg sodium, 35 g carbohydrate, 1 g fiber, 9 g protein.

Plum Sauce

(Pictured at right)

PREP/TOTAL TIME: 15 min.

This sauce makes any Asian dish simply mouth-watering. And the bonus is, you won't need a lot of extra time to prepare the recipe. —Doris Chamberlain, South Weymouth, Massachusetts

- **1/2 cup plum preserves**
- **1/4 cup finely chopped onion**
- **1/4 cup apricot preserves**
- **2 tablespoons brown sugar**
- **2 tablespoons apple cider *or* juice**
- **2 tablespoons soy sauce**
- **2 tablespoons ketchup**
- **1 garlic clove, minced**

In a small saucepan, combine all ingredients. Cook, stirring occasionally, over low heat to allow flavors to blend. **Yield:** 1 cup.

Blazing Mustard

(Pictured at right)

PREP/TOTAL TIME: 5 min.

Here's a great condiment for your Asian cooking, but don't stop there! Save some to slather on hot dogs, hamburgers, submarine sandwiches...anything that can get jazzed up with mustard.
—Harry Goeschko, Waukesha, Wisconsin

- **1/2 cup ground mustard**
- **1-1/2 teaspoons sugar**
- **1/2 teaspoon salt**
- **3 tablespoons water**
- **2 tablespoons white vinegar**

In a small bowl, combine the mustard, sugar and salt. Stir in water and vinegar until smooth. Chill until serving. **Yield:** 1/2 cup.

Sweet & Sour Sauce

(Pictured at right)

PREP/TOTAL TIME: 5 min.

You won't want to buy bottled sweet-and-sour sauce from the store after sampling this tongue-tingling recipe. It goes together in mere moments and requires only a handful of ingredients.
—Flo Weiss, Seaside, Oregon

- **1/2 cup orange marmalade**
- **2 tablespoons vinegar**
- **1 tablespoon diced pimientos**
- **1/8 teaspoon paprika**

Dash salt

Combine all ingredients in a small bowl; cover and refrigerate until serving. **Yield:** 2/3 cup.

Roasted Veggie Platter

(Pictured above and on page 42)

PREP/TOTAL TIME: 30 min.

These colorful, well-seasoned vegetables baked in the oven are so good. For an extra-special presentation, thread them on skewers before roasting. —*Margaret Allen, Abingdon, Virginia*

☑ **This recipe includes Nutrition Facts and Diabetic Exchanges.**

- 1 **medium sweet red pepper, cut into 1-1/2-inch pieces**
- 1 **medium red onion, cut into wedges**
- 1 **medium yellow summer squash, cut into 1/2-inch slices**
- 1/2 **pound whole fresh mushrooms**
- 1/4 **pound fresh green beans, trimmed**
- 1/4 **cup prepared Italian salad dressing**
- 1/4 **teaspoon *each* dried basil, thyme and rosemary, crushed**

Place the vegetables in a greased 15-in. x 10-in. x 1-in. baking pan. Drizzle with salad dressing and sprinkle with herbs; toss to coat.

Bake, uncovered, at 425° for 15-20 minutes or until vegetables are tender, stirring occasionally. **Yield:** 6 servings.

Nutrition Facts: 1/2 cup equals 69 calories, 4 g fat (trace saturated fat), 0 cholesterol, 173 mg sodium, 7 g carbohydrate, 2 g fiber, 2 g protein. **Diabetic Exchanges:** 1 vegetable, 1 fat.

Garden Tomato Relish

(Pictured below and on page 43)

PREP: 2-1/2 hours **PROCESS:** 20 min.

What a great way to use your garden harvest—and have a tasty topping on hand for hot dogs, hamburgers and more. The relish is also a wonderful homemade gift to share with a neighbor.
—*Kelly Martel, Tillsonburg, Ontario*

☑ **This recipe includes Nutrition Facts.**

- 10 **pounds tomatoes**
- 3 **large sweet onions, finely chopped**
- 2 **medium sweet red peppers, finely chopped**
- 2 **medium green peppers, finely chopped**
- 2 **teaspoons mustard seed**
- 1 **teaspoon celery seed**
- 4-1/2 **cups white vinegar**
- 2-1/2 **cups packed brown sugar**
- 3 **tablespoons canning salt**
- 2 **teaspoons ground ginger**
- 2 **teaspoons ground cinnamon**
- 1 **teaspoon ground allspice**
- 1 **teaspoon ground cloves**
- 1 **teaspoon ground nutmeg**

In a large saucepan, bring 8 cups water to a boil. Add tomatoes, a few at a time; boil for 30 seconds. Drain and immediately place tomatoes in ice water. Drain and pat dry; peel and finely chop. Place in a stockpot. Add onions and peppers.

Place mustard and celery seed on a double thickness of cheesecloth; bring up corners of cloth and tie with string to form a bag. Add spice bag and remaining ingredients to pot. Bring to a boil. Reduce heat; cover and simmer for 60-70 minutes or until slightly thickened. Discard spice bag.

Carefully ladle relish into hot 1-pint jars, leaving 1/2-in. headspace. Remove air bubbles; wipe rims and adjust

lids. Process for 20 minutes in a boiling-water canner. **Yield:** 10 pints.

Editor's Note: Processing time listed is for altitudes of 1,000 feet or less. For altitudes up to 3,000 feet, add 5 minutes; 6,000 feet, 10 minutes; 8,000 feet, 15 minutes; 10,000 feet, 20 minutes.

Nutrition Facts: 2 tablespoons equals 20 calories, trace fat (trace saturated fat), 0 cholesterol, 136 mg sodium, 5 g carbohydrate, trace fiber, trace protein.

Caramel-Drizzled Spoons

(Pictured above, at left)

PREP: 20 min. + standing

Our Test Kitchen home economists are so sweet on coffee drinks, they created these pretty stirrers with white chocolate and a dressy caramel drizzle—perfect for coffee, tea or even hot cocoa.

- **4 squares (1 ounce *each*) white baking chocolate, *divided***
- **12 metal *or* plastic spoons**
- **8 caramels**
- **2 teaspoons heavy whipping cream**

In a microwave-safe bowl, melt two squares of white baking chocolate; stir until smooth. Dip six spoons into melted chocolate; tap the spoon handles on the edge of the bowl to remove the excess chocolate. Place the dipped spoons on waxed paper; let stand until set. Repeat with remaining chocolate and spoons.

In a microwave-safe bowl, melt caramels and cream; stir until smooth. Drizzle over spoons. Let stand until set. **Yield:** 1 dozen.

Chocolate-Dipped Spoons

(Pictured above, at right)

PREP: 20 min. + standing

Coffee goes down in the most delightful way when stirred with these sugar–coated spoons from our Test Kitchen. They add a refreshing hint of raspberry to your favorite warm drinks.

- **1/2 cup raspberry chocolate chips**
- **2 teaspoons shortening, *divided***
- **12 metal *or* plastic spoons**
- **2 squares (1 ounce *each*) semisweet chocolate**
- **4 teaspoons coarse sugar**

In a microwave-safe bowl, melt the raspberry chocolate chips and 1 teaspoon shortening; stir until smooth. Dip each spoon into the melted chocolate; tap the spoon handles on the edge of the bowl to remove the excess chocolate. Place the dipped spoons on waxed paper; let stand until set.

In a microwave-safe bowl, melt semisweet chocolate and remaining shortening; stir until smooth. Dip coated spoons into chocolate mixture; tap spoon handles on edge of bowl to remove excess chocolate. Place on waxed paper; sprinkle with coarse sugar. Let stand until set. **Yield:** 1 dozen.

Butter—Made Better!

WHY STICK to plain butter when you can dress it up deliciously to suit your menus? The recipes here give you easy ways to do just that.

From an orange-ginger spread for accenting asparagus to a spicy Cajun version for corn on the cob, these flavorful butters are sure to get you pats on the back!

Asparagus with Orange-Ginger Butter

(Pictured below)

PREP/TOTAL TIME: 20 min.

The combination of orange, ginger and balsamic vinegar is the perfect complement to the fresh asparagus spears in this winning side dish. —Lisa Feld, Grafton, Wisconsin

- 1-1/2 **pounds fresh asparagus, trimmed**
- 1/2 **cup butter, softened**
- 1/2 **cup orange marmalade**
- 1 **tablespoon minced candied** *or* **crystallized ginger**
- 1 **tablespoon balsamic vinegar**
- 2 **tablespoons grated orange peel**

In a large skillet, bring 1/2 in. of water to a boil. Add the asparagus; cover and boil for 3-5 minutes or until crisp-tender. Drain; transfer to a serving platter and keep warm.

In a small bowl, beat the butter, marmalade, ginger, vinegar and orange peel until blended. Spoon over asparagus. **Yield:** 6 servings.

Cinnamon Espresso Butter

(Pictured at left in photo at right)

PREP/TOTAL TIME: 5 min.

I've enjoyed this sweet spiced butter on everything from bagels to biscotti. If you like, use a teaspoon of espresso powder for the instant coffee granules. —Diane Hixon, Niceville, Florida

✓ This recipe includes Nutrition Facts and Diabetic Exchanges.

- 2 **teaspoons instant coffee granules**
- 2 **teaspoons water**
- 1/2 **teaspoon vanilla extract**
- 1/2 **cup butter, softened**
- 1 **tablespoon confectioners' sugar**
- 1 **teaspoon ground cinnamon**

In a small bowl, combine the coffee granules, water and vanilla. In a small bowl, cream the butter, confectioners' sugar and cinnamon until light and fluffy. Add coffee mixture; beat until smooth. Store in the refrigerator for up to 1 month. **Yield:** 1/2 cup.

Nutrition Facts: 1 teaspoon equals 35 calories, 4 g fat (2 g saturated fat), 10 mg cholesterol, 27 mg sodium, trace carbohydrate, trace fiber, trace protein. **Diabetic Exchange:** 1 fat.

ENTERTAINING IDEAS. Impress your guests with butter in fun and festive shapes:
- To create butter cutouts, cut a chilled stick of butter into 1/4-inch slices. Cut out shapes with small cookie cutters. Simple shapes with little detail work best.
- To make balls of butter, dip a melon baller in hot water and cut balls from a chilled 1-pound block of butter.
- Butter cutouts and balls can be made early in the day and refrigerated in an airtight container. Just before serving, arrange the cutouts or balls on a small lettuce-lined serving plate or on individual bread and butter plates.

Cajun Butter

(Pictured above, at top)

PREP/TOTAL TIME: 10 min.

Melt this zippy spread over grilled corn on the cob, and your guests will be grinning from ear to ear! The home economists in our Test Kitchen jazzed up ordinary butter with chili powder, cayenne pepper, garlic powder and more to create a memorable condiment you'll want to serve again and again.

  1/2 **cup butter, softened**
    1 **teaspoon brown sugar**
    1 **teaspoon chili powder**
  1/2 **teaspoon dried thyme**
  1/2 **teaspoon cayenne pepper**
  1/4 **teaspoon garlic powder**
  1/4 **teaspoon pepper**
Hot cooked corn on the cob

In a small bowl, combine the first seven ingredients. Serve butter with corn on the cob. Refrigerate leftovers.
Yield: 1/2 cup.

Basil Butter

(Pictured above, at right)

PREP/TOTAL TIME: 20 min.

I whip up this tasty butter during the growing season and freeze it for later use. This allows my family and me to enjoy the flavor of fresh basil all year long. I use it to enhance vegetables, fish and chicken—and no one seems to miss the salt that I deliberately leave out.
                                  —Emily Chaney, Penobscot, Maine

1-1/2 **cups loosely packed fresh basil leaves**
  1/2 **pound butter, softened**
    1 **teaspoon lemon juice**
    1 **teaspoon seasoned pepper**
  1/2 **teaspoon garlic salt**

In a food processor, chop the basil. Add the butter, lemon juice, seasoned pepper and garlic salt; blend until smooth. Drop by half-tablespoons onto a baking sheet; freeze. Remove from the baking sheet and store in freezer bags. Use to flavor chicken, fish or vegetables.
Yield: 4 dozen butter balls.

heat. Fry tomato sandwiches in batches for 3-4 minutes on each side or until golden brown. Drain on paper towels. Serve immediately. **Yield:** 8 servings.

Buffalo Burger Topping

PREP/TOTAL TIME: 10 min.

Fans of blue cheese are sure to appreciate this zippy topping, a takeoff on popular buffalo wings. It's terrific on a big, juicy burger. —Michael Cohen, Los Angeles, California

   2 tablespoons butter, softened
   2 tablespoons brown sugar
 3/4 cup mayonnaise
 1/4 cup Louisiana-style hot sauce
   1 celery rib, finely chopped
   6 tablespoons crumbled blue cheese

In a small bowl, beat butter and brown sugar until light and fluffy. Add mayonnaise and hot sauce; beat until smooth. Chill until serving. Spoon onto your favorite burger; top with celery and cheese. **Yield:** 6 servings.

Speedy Spanish Rice

(Pictured below and on page 42)

PREP/TOTAL TIME: 25 min.

Mexican food is really popular in our family. In fact, one of my nephews loves this dish so much that he requests it as his birthday dinner! —Angie Rorick, Fort Wayne, Indiana

✓ **This recipe includes Nutrition Facts and Diabetic Exchanges.**

 1-1/2 cups uncooked instant brown rice
   1 medium onion, chopped
   1 small green pepper, chopped
   1 garlic clove, minced
   1 tablespoon butter
 1-1/2 cups water
   1 tablespoon minced fresh cilantro

Country-Style Tomatoes

(Pictured above)

PREP: 25 min. **COOK:** 10 min./batch

This is an excellent vegetable course when your garden is bursting with tomatoes, and it always gets lots of attention on a buffet table. For a special treat, I'll use beefsteak tomatoes. —Cathy Dwyer, Freedom, New Hampshire

   4 large tomatoes
   1 package (8 ounces) cream cheese, softened
 1/4 cup minced fresh parsley
 1-1/2 teaspoons minced fresh basil *or* 1/2 teaspoon dried basil
   1 garlic clove, minced
 1/4 teaspoon salt
 1/4 cup all-purpose flour
   1 cup panko (Japanese) bread crumbs
   1 egg
   1 tablespoon milk
   3 tablespoons butter
   3 tablespoons olive oil

Cut each tomato into four thick slices; place on paper towels to drain. Meanwhile, in a small bowl, beat the cream cheese, parsley, basil, garlic and salt until blended. Spread cream cheese mixture over eight tomato slices; top with remaining tomato slices.

  Place flour and bread crumbs in separate shallow bowls. In another bowl, whisk egg and milk. Coat the top and bottom of each sandwich with flour, dip into egg mixture, then coat with crumbs.

  In a large skillet, heat butter and oil over medium-hot

2 teaspoons ground cumin
1-1/2 teaspoons chicken bouillon granules
1/4 teaspoon pepper
1 cup picante sauce

In a large nonstick skillet, saute the rice, onion, green pepper and garlic in butter until rice is lightly browned and vegetables are crisp-tender. Stir in the water, cilantro, cumin, bouillon and pepper; bring to a boil. Reduce heat; cover and simmer for 5 minutes.

Remove from the heat; let stand for 5 minutes. Fluff with a fork. Stir in picante sauce. **Yield:** 4 servings.

Nutrition Facts: 3/4 cup equals 201 calories, 4 g fat (2 g saturated fat), 8 mg cholesterol, 615 mg sodium, 35 g carbohydrate, 3 g fiber, 4 g protein. **Diabetic Exchanges:** 2 starch, 1 vegetable, 1 fat.

Southwest Burger Topping

PREP/TOTAL TIME: 5 min.

Here's an easy way to give plain burgers a little pizzazz. The tasty topping combination is great on ground beef, chicken or turkey patties. —*Maria Regakis, Somerville, Massachusetts*

4 slices pepper Jack cheese
1 medium ripe avocado, peeled and sliced
1 jalapeno pepper, seeded and chopped
1/2 cup salsa

Top your favorite burger with cheese; cook for 1-2 minutes or until cheese is melted. Top with avocado, jalapeno and salsa. **Yield:** 4 servings.

Editor's Note: When cutting hot peppers, disposable gloves are recommended. Avoid touching your face.

Classic Turkey Gravy

(Pictured at right)

PREP/TOTAL TIME: 15 min.

This flavorful gravy comes out smooth and creamy every time. For an even richer taste, add cooked neck meat and giblets after stirring in the broth. —*Virginia Watson, Kirksville, Missouri*

GOOD GRAVY. When making gravy, keep in mind these tips and tricks from our Test Kitchen:
• If your finished gravy is lumpy, pour it into a blender and pulse for no more than 15 seconds. Reheat before serving.
• Always taste your gravy before adding salt and pepper. If the meat was highly seasoned, you may not need them.
• Gravy thickens upon standing, so resist the urge to add more thickener while cooking.

✓ This recipe includes Nutrition Facts.

Drippings from 1 roasted turkey
1 to 1-1/2 cups turkey *or* chicken broth
1/4 cup all-purpose flour
Salt and white pepper to taste

Pour turkey drippings into a 2-cup measuring cup. Skim fat, reserving 2 tablespoons; set aside. Add enough broth to the drippings to measure 2 cups.

In a small saucepan, combine flour and reserved fat until smooth. Gradually stir in the drippings mixture. Bring to a boil; cook and stir for 2 minutes or until thickened. Season with salt and white pepper to taste. **Yield:** 2 cups.

Nutrition Facts: 1/4 cup equals 45 calories, 3 g fat (1 g saturated fat), 4 mg cholesterol, 127 mg sodium, 3 g carbohydrate, trace fiber, 1 g protein.

Main Dishes

Elegant Chicken Saltimbocca for a dinner party...brunch-perfect Spiral Omelet
Supreme on Saturday morning...hearty Beef Stroganoff for a busy weeknight...
no matter what type of entree you need, you'll find it in this extra-big chapter!

CENTER OF ATTENTION. Clockwise from top left: Philly Cheesesteak Pizza (p. 82), Coffee-Flavored Beef Roast
(p. 68), Cranberry-Kissed Pork Chops (p. 59), Turkey with Curried Cream Sauce (p. 79) and Broccoli Rabe & Garlic
Pasta (p. 65).

drippings. Cover loosely with foil if turkey browns too quickly. Cover and let stand for 20 minutes before carving turkey. Discard vegetables; use drippings to make gravy. **Yield:** 14 servings.

Cabernet Marinara Pasta

PREP: 20 min. **COOK:** 20 min.

Red wine and fresh herbs accent the sweet sauce that highlights this fancy but fuss-free pasta dish. It makes an excellent meatless entree but can also be served on the side with meat or poultry.
—*Sarah Vasques, Milford, New Hampshire*

> 1 **cup chopped sweet onion**
> 2 **tablespoons olive oil**
> 3 **garlic cloves, crushed**
> 1/2 **cup Cabernet Sauvignon *or* other dry red wine**
> 1 **can (28 ounces) crushed tomatoes**
> 3 **plum tomatoes, chopped**
> 1 **tablespoon sugar**
> 1 **fresh basil sprig**
> 1 **fresh thyme sprig**
> 2 **cups uncooked penne pasta**
> **Parmesan and Romano cheeses**

In a large saucepan, cook the onion in oil over medium heat until tender. Add the garlic; cook 1 minute longer. Stir in wine and bring to a boil. Reduce heat; cook for 6-8 minutes or until liquid is reduced by half.

Add crushed tomatoes, plum tomatoes, sugar, basil and thyme; bring to a boil. Reduce the heat; cover and simmer for 15 minutes. Meanwhile, cook the pasta according to package directions.

Discard basil and thyme. Drain pasta; toss with sauce. Top with cheeses. **Yield:** 4 servings.

Grilled Shrimp With Apricot Sauce

PREP/TOTAL TIME: 30 min.

Served on skewers, this is a mouth-watering main attraction for a summertime dinner. Succulent, bacon-wrapped shrimp get a tongue-tingling boost from the chunky, sweet hot sauce.
—*Carole Resnick, Cleveland, Ohio*

> 1/2 **cup apricot preserves**
> 2 **tablespoons apricot nectar**
> 1/4 **teaspoon ground chipotle powder**
> 12 **uncooked large shrimp, peeled and deveined**
> 6 **slices Canadian bacon, halved**

In a small bowl, combine the preserves, apricot nectar and chipotle powder. Chill until serving.

Thread shrimp and bacon onto four metal or soaked wooden skewers. Grill, covered, over medium heat for 6-8 minutes or until the shrimp turn pink, turning once. Serve with sauce. **Yield:** 4 skewers (2/3 cup sauce).

Herb-Roasted Turkey

(Pictured above)

PREP: 20 min. **BAKE:** 3-1/4 hours + standing

Our Test Kitchen home economists gave this impressive turkey an extra-special touch...sage enhances its moist flavor and shows up beautifully beneath the golden-brown skin. The turkey does not need a roasting rack when roasted over root vegetables.

> 1/2 **cup olive oil, *divided***
> 4 **garlic cloves, minced**
> 1 **teaspoon salt**
> 1/4 **teaspoon pepper**
> 1 **turkey (14 to 16 pounds)**
> 8 **fresh sage leaves plus 4 fresh sage sprigs, *divided***
> 6 **fresh thyme sprigs, *divided***
> 4 **medium onions**
> 5 **celery ribs**
> 5 **medium carrots**
> 3 **medium parsnips**

In a small bowl, combine 1/4 cup oil, garlic, salt and pepper. With your fingers, carefully loosen skin from turkey breast; rub mixture under the skin. Place sage leaves and two thyme sprigs under the skin. Secure skin to underside of breast with toothpicks.

Cut the onions into wedges and the celery, carrots and parsnips into 2-in. lengths. Place about a fifth of the onions, celery and carrots in turkey cavity; add sprigs and remaining thyme. Place remaining vegetables in a roasting pan. Place the turkey, breast side up, over the vegetables. Brush with remaining oil.

Bake at 325° for 3-1/4 to 3-3/4 hours or until a meat thermometer reads 180°, basting occasionally with pan

Gingered Beef Stir-Fry

(Pictured below)

PREP: 20 min. + marinating **COOK:** 20 min.

A friend who owns a bed-and-breakfast in Maryland shared this exceptional dish with me. It's a deliciously different way to use fresh asparagus. —Sonja Blow, Nixa, Missouri

- 3 tablespoons reduced-sodium soy sauce, *divided*
- 1 tablespoon sherry
- 1/4 teaspoon minced fresh gingerroot *or* dash ground ginger
- 1/2 pound beef flank steak, cut into thin strips
- 1 teaspoon cornstarch
- 1/2 cup beef broth
- 1-1/2 teaspoons hoisin sauce
- 1/8 teaspoon sugar
- 2 tablespoons canola oil, *divided*
- 2 pounds fresh asparagus, trimmed and cut into 1-inch pieces
- 1 garlic clove, minced
- 3 cups hot cooked rice

In a large resealable plastic bag, combine 2 tablespoons soy sauce, sherry and ginger; add the beef. Seal bag and turn to coat; refrigerate for 30 minutes.

In a small bowl, combine the cornstarch, broth, hoisin sauce, sugar and remaining soy sauce until smooth; set aside.

In a large skillet or wok, stir-fry beef in 1 tablespoon oil until no longer pink. Remove and set aside. Stir-fry asparagus in remaining oil until crisp-tender. Add garlic; cook 1 minute longer.

Stir cornstarch mixture and add to the pan. Bring to a boil; cook and stir for 2 minutes or until thickened. Return beef to the pan; heat through. Serve with rice.
Yield: 4 servings.

Curried Chicken with Apples

(Pictured above)

PREP: 20 min. **COOK:** 30 min.

I got this recipe from an Indian neighbor of mine, who passed along her favorite recipes to me and even showed me how to prepare them. —Janice Fakhoury, Raleigh, North Carolina

- 1 pound boneless skinless chicken breasts, cut into 1-inch cubes
- 1 large sweet onion, halved and sliced
- 3 garlic cloves, minced
- 2 tablespoons canola oil
- 2 medium tart apples, peeled and sliced
- 1/2 cup water
- 1 teaspoon salt
- 1 teaspoon ground coriander
- 1 teaspoon minced fresh gingerroot
- 1/2 teaspoon ground turmeric
- 1/4 teaspoon cayenne pepper
- 1 can (14-1/2 ounces) diced tomatoes, drained
- 1 jalapeno pepper, seeded and chopped
- 2 tablespoons minced fresh cilantro

Hot cooked rice

In a large skillet or wok, stir-fry the chicken, onion and garlic in oil until onion is tender. Stir in the apples, water and seasonings. Bring to a boil. Reduce heat; simmer, uncovered, for 12-15 minutes or until chicken is no longer pink, stirring occasionally. Stir in the tomatoes, jalapeno and cilantro; heat through. Serve with rice. **Yield:** 4 servings.

Sole with Shrimp Sauce

(Pictured below)

PREP: 25 min.   **BAKE:** 15 min.

I discovered this saucy seafood recipe years ago when I was first married. I cut down the butter and flour, but I think it's just as good as the original.   —Laura McDowell, Lake Villa, Illinois

☑ This recipe includes Nutrition Facts and Diabetic Exchanges.

- 1-1/2 **pounds sole fillets**
- 1/4 **teaspoon *each* salt, paprika and coarsely ground pepper**
- 3/4 **pound sliced fresh mushrooms**

SAUCE:
- 1-1/2 **teaspoons grated onion**
- 4-1/2 **teaspoons butter**
- 4 **teaspoons all-purpose flour**
- 1/4 **teaspoon *each* salt, paprika and coarsely ground pepper**
- 3/4 **cup fat-free milk**
- 1/4 **cup reduced-sodium chicken broth**
- 3/4 **pound cooked medium shrimp, peeled and deveined**
- 4 **tablespoons grated Parmesan cheese, *divided***
- 1 **teaspoon minced fresh parsley**
- 1/4 **teaspoon dried basil**
- 1/8 **teaspoon cayenne pepper**

Place the fish fillets in a 15-in. x 10-in. x 1-in. baking pan coated with cooking spray; sprinkle with seasonings. In a large nonstick skillet coated with cooking spray, cook mushrooms over medium heat until tender. Spoon over fish. Bake at 350° for 10-15 minutes or until fish flakes easily with a fork.

Meanwhile, in the same skillet, cook onion in butter over medium heat until tender. Stir in the flour, salt, paprika and pepper until blended. Gradually stir in milk and broth. Bring to a boil; cook and stir for 1-2 minutes or until thickened. Stir in the shrimp, 3 tablespoons cheese, parsley and basil; heat through. Spoon sauce over fish; sprinkle with cayenne and remaining cheese. **Yield:** 4 servings.

Nutrition Facts: 1 serving equals 338 calories, 9 g fat (4 g saturated fat), 224 mg cholesterol, 741 mg sodium, 9 g carbohydrate, 1 g fiber, 52 g protein. **Diabetic Exchanges:** 7 very lean meat, 1 vegetable, 1 fat.

Banana Pancake Snowman

PREP: 15 min.   **COOK:** 5 min./batch

Both children and adults will love these yummy pancakes shaped like snowmen. Let little ones help decorate their characters with pretzels for arms and chocolate chips, raisins or cranberries for faces and buttons.   —Phyllis Schmalz, Kansas City, Kansas

☑ This recipe includes Nutrition Facts and Diabetic Exchanges.

- 1 **cup complete buttermilk pancake mix**
- 3/4 **cup water**
- 1/3 **cup mashed ripe banana**
- 14 **pretzel sticks**
- 1/2 **cup semisweet chocolate chips, raisins *and/or* dried cranberries**
- 1 **teaspoon confectioners' sugar**

In a small bowl, stir the pancake mix, water and banana just until moistened.

Using a 1/4-cup measuring cup, drop batter in three graduated sizes to resemble a snowman onto a greased hot griddle. Turn when bubbles form on top. Cook until the second side is golden brown.

Arrange snowmen on plates. For arms, push pretzels into bodies of snowmen. Add eyes, noses and buttons as desired. Sprinkle with confectioners' sugar. **Yield:** 7 servings.

Nutrition Facts: 1 pancake snowman equals 143 calories, 4 g fat (2 g saturated fat), 0 cholesterol, 296 mg sodium, 27 g carbohydrate, 2 g fiber, 2 g protein. **Diabetic Exchanges:** 1-1/2 starch, 1 fat.

Creole Black Beans 'n' Sausage

PREP: 25 min.   **COOK:** 6 hours

This slow cooker entree is easy to add to my table any day of the week. I simply brown the meat, cut up veggies and measure spices the night before, then assemble it and start it cooking the next morning. When I get home, I make the rice...and dinner is served!   —Cheryl Landers, LaTour, Missouri

- 2 **pounds smoked sausage, cut into 1-inch slices**
- 3 **cans (15 ounces *each*) black beans, rinsed and drained**
- 1-1/2 **cups *each* chopped onion, celery and green pepper**
- 1 **cup water**

Remove chops and keep warm. Add cranberries and vinegar to skillet, stirring to loosen browned bits from pan. Bring to a boil; cook until liquid is reduced to about 1/2 cup. Serve with chops. **Yield:** 6 servings.

Nutrition Facts: 1 pork chop with about 1 tablespoon sauce equals 229 calories, 8 g fat (3 g saturated fat), 68 mg cholesterol, 119 mg sodium, 10 g carbohydrate, 1 g fiber, 27 g protein. **Diabetic Exchanges:** 4 lean meat, 1 starch.

Taos Steak

(Pictured below)

PREP/TOTAL TIME: 25 min.

My husband had a steak at a Taos, New Mexico restaurant that inspired me to create this one. It has distinctive flavor that really stands out. —*Lorna Byrd, Colorado Springs, Colorado*

   1-1/2 teaspoons paprika
      1 teaspoon fennel seeds
    1/2 teaspoon whole peppercorns
    1/4 teaspoon white pepper
    1/8 teaspoon cayenne pepper
      1 beef top sirloin steak (1 inch thick and 1-1/2 pounds)
      6 slices Havarti cheese
    1/3 cup green chili salsa

In a spice grinder or with a mortar and pestle, combine the first five ingredients; grind until mixture becomes a fine powder. Rub over both sides of steak.

Grill, covered, over medium heat for 8-11 minutes on each side or until meat reaches desired doneness (for medium-rare, a meat thermometer should read 145°; medium, 160°; well-done, 170°).

Top with cheese; cover and grill for 1-2 minutes or until cheese is melted. Let stand for 5 minutes before slicing. Top with salsa. **Yield:** 6 servings.

---

      1 can (8 ounces) tomato sauce
      4 garlic cloves, minced
      2 teaspoons dried thyme
      1 teaspoon chicken bouillon granules
      1 teaspoon white pepper
    1/4 teaspoon cayenne pepper
      2 bay leaves
Hot cooked rice

In a large skillet, brown the sausage over medium heat; drain. Transfer to a 5-qt. slow cooker.

In a large bowl, combine beans, onion, celery, green pepper, water, tomato sauce, garlic, thyme, chicken bouillon, white pepper, cayenne and bay leaves; pour over sausage. Cover and cook on low for 6 hours or until vegetables are tender. Discard bay leaves. Serve with rice. **Yield:** 10 servings.

Cranberry-Kissed Pork Chops

(Pictured above and on page 54)

PREP/TOTAL TIME: 25 min.

I enjoy coming up with new recipes for my health-conscious family. I serve these succulent, tangy chops over cooked noodles or white rice. —*Betty Nichols, Eugene, Oregon*

✓ This recipe includes Nutrition Facts and Diabetic Exchanges.

      6 boneless pork loin chops (5 ounces *each*)
    1/4 teaspoon coarsely ground pepper
    1/3 cup jellied cranberry sauce
  4-1/2 teaspoons stone-ground mustard
      3 tablespoons dried cranberries
      2 tablespoons raspberry vinegar

Sprinkle the pork chops with pepper. In a large skillet coated with cooking spray, brown chops on both sides over medium-high heat. Combine cranberry sauce and mustard; spoon over chops. Reduce heat; cover and cook for 6-8 minutes or until a meat thermometer reads 160°.

Lamb Kabobs with Bulgur Pilaf

(Pictured above)

PREP: 15 min. + marinating **COOK:** 35 min.

For a grilled main course that's different and special, consider this. The tender chunks of lamb are marinated for terrific flavor.
—Ruth Hartunion Alumbaugh, Willimantic, Connecticut

- 30 garlic cloves, crushed (1-1/2 to 2 bulbs)
- 1/2 cup balsamic vinegar
- 3/4 cup chopped fresh mint *or* 1/4 cup dried mint
- 1/4 cup olive oil
- 2 pounds lean boneless lamb, cut into 1-1/2-inch cubes

PILAF:
- 1/2 cup butter, cubed
- 1 large onion, chopped
- 1 cup uncooked mini spiral pasta
- 2 cups bulgur
- 3 cups beef broth

In a large resealable plastic bag, combine the garlic, vinegar, mint and oil; add the lamb. Seal bag and turn to coat; refrigerate for several hours or overnight.

For the pilaf, in a large skillet, melt the butter. Add onion and pasta; saute until pasta is lightly browned. Add the bulgur and stir to coat. Stir in the beef broth. Bring to a boil. Reduce the heat; cover and simmer for 25-30 minutes or until tender. Remove from the heat; let stand for 5 minutes. Fluff with a fork.

Drain the lamb and discard marinade. Thread onto six metal or soaked wooden skewers.

Grill the kabobs, covered, over medium heat for 8-10 minutes or until the meat reaches desired doneness, turning frequently. Serve with pilaf. **Yield:** 6 servings.

Editor's Note: This recipe was tested with Barilla brand mini fusilli pasta.

Summertime Spaghetti Sauce

(Pictured below)

PREP: 30 min. **COOK:** 30 min.

My husband and I look forward to this fresh-tasting sauce when the tomatoes from our garden are at their peak ripeness. It's a real summertime treat. —Kay Kaepp, Coldwater, Michigan

☑ This recipe includes Nutrition Facts and Diabetic Exchanges.

- 3 Italian sausage links (4 ounces *each*)
- 1 tablespoon olive oil
- 3 medium onions, chopped
- 1 small green pepper, chopped
- 3 cups chopped seeded peeled tomatoes (about 8 medium)
- 1 jalapeno pepper, seeded and chopped
- 1 tablespoon brown sugar
- 1 tablespoon Italian seasoning
- 1-1/4 teaspoons salt
- 1/4 teaspoon pepper

Hot cooked spaghetti
Parmesan cheese

Remove casings from sausage; cut sausage into 1-in. pieces. In a large skillet, brown sausage over medium heat. Drain and set aside. Heat oil in the same skillet; add onions and green pepper. Cook and stir until tender.

Add the tomatoes, jalapeno, brown sugar, Italian seasoning, salt and pepper. Return sausage to the pan. Cook, stirring occasionally, for 12-15 minutes or until meat is no longer pink and sauce is thickened.

Serve the sauce with spaghetti; top with Parmesan cheese. **Yield:** 5 cups.

Editor's Note: When cutting hot peppers, disposable gloves are recommended. Avoid touching your face.

Nutrition Facts: 3/4 cup sauce (calculated without spaghetti and cheese) equals 173 calories, 10 g fat (3 g saturated fat), 23 mg cholesterol, 767 mg sodium, 14 g carbohydrate, 3 g fiber, 8 g protein. **Diabetic Exchanges:** 2 vegetable, 2 fat, 1 lean meat.

Benedict Eggs in Pastry

PREP: 30 min. **BAKE:** 20 min.

Here's a new twist on an old favorite. Inside these puffy golden bundles is an omelet-like filling of eggs, ham, cheese and lemony hollandaise sauce. —Catherine Slussler, Tomball, Texas

- **2 egg yolks**
- **2 tablespoons lemon juice**
- **1 teaspoon Dijon mustard**
- **1/2 cup butter, melted**
- **Dash cayenne pepper**
- **2 cups cubed fully cooked ham**
- **2 green onions, chopped**
- **1 tablespoon butter**
- **7 eggs, *divided***
- **2 tablespoons milk**
- **1 package (17.3 ounces) frozen puff pastry, thawed**
- **1 cup (4 ounces) shredded cheddar cheese**
- **1 tablespoon water**
- **Minced fresh tarragon, optional**

In a double boiler over simmering water or a small heavy saucepan, constantly whisk the egg yolks, lemon juice and mustard until mixture begins to thicken and reaches 160°. Reduce heat to low. Slowly drizzle in warm melted butter, whisking constantly. Whisk in cayenne.

Transfer to a small bowl if necessary. Place the bowl in a larger bowl of warm water. Keep warm, stirring occasionally, until ready to use.

In a large skillet over medium heat, cook and stir ham and onions in butter until onions are tender. In a large bowl, whisk six eggs and milk. Add egg mixture to the pan; cook and stir until set. Remove from the heat; stir in 1/3 cup reserved hollandaise sauce. Set aside.

On a lightly floured surface, unfold puff pastry. Roll each sheet into a 12-in. x 9-1/2-in. rectangle; cut each in half widthwise. Place 1 cup egg mixture on half of each rectangle; sprinkle with cheese.

Beat the water and remaining egg; brush over pastry edges. Bring an opposite corner of pastry over the egg mixture; pinch seams to seal. With a small sharp knife, cut several slits in the top.

Transfer to a greased baking sheet; brush with the remaining egg mixture. Bake at 400° for 18-22 minutes or until golden brown. Serve with remaining hollandaise sauce. Sprinkle with tarragon if desired. **Yield:** 4 servings.

BISCUIT TIP. Biscuits baked on top of casseroles, potpies and stews such as Quick Chicken and Dumplings (recipe above right) can easily become doughy on the bottom. To help avoid this, arrange the biscuits so they are not touching each other, allowing for better heat circulation.

Quick Chicken and Dumplings

(Pictured above)

PREP/TOTAL TIME: 30 min.

Using precooked chicken and ready-made biscuits, this hearty dish is home-style comfort food made simple. It's the perfect way to quickly warm up your family on chilly autumn nights. —Lakeya Astwood, Schenectady, New York

- **6 individually frozen biscuits**
- **1/4 cup chopped onion**
- **1/4 cup chopped green pepper**
- **1 tablespoon olive oil**
- **4 cups shredded cooked rotisserie chicken**
- **2 cans (14-1/2 ounces *each*) reduced-sodium chicken broth**
- **1 can (4 ounces) mushroom stems and pieces, drained**
- **1 teaspoon chicken bouillon granules**
- **1 teaspoon minced fresh parsley**
- **1/2 teaspoon dried sage leaves**
- **1/4 teaspoon dried rosemary, crushed**
- **1/4 teaspoon pepper**

Cut each biscuit into fourths; set aside. In a large saucepan, saute the onion and green pepper in oil until tender. Stir in the shredded chicken, chicken broth, mushrooms, chicken bouillon granules, parsley, sage, rosemary and pepper.

Bring to a boil. Reduce the heat; add the biscuit pieces for the dumplings. Cover and simmer for 10 minutes or until a toothpick inserted near the center of a dumpling comes out clean (do not lift the cover while simmering). **Yield:** 6 servings.

Beef Stroganoff

(Pictured below)

PREP/TOTAL TIME: 30 min.

Creamy and comforting, this hearty Stroganoff is perfect for cool autumn or winter days. But it's so good, your family is sure to crave it year-round. —Patty Rody, Puyallup, Washington

>   5 tablespoons all-purpose flour, *divided*
>   1/2 teaspoon salt
>   1 pound boneless beef sirloin steak, cut into thin strips
>   4 tablespoons butter, *divided*
>   1 cup sliced fresh mushrooms
>   1/2 cup chopped sweet onion
>   1 garlic clove, minced
>   1 tablespoon tomato paste
> 1-1/4 cups beef broth
>   1 cup (8 ounces) sour cream
>   2 tablespoons sherry *or* beef broth
> **Hot cooked egg noodles *or* brown rice**

In a large resealable plastic bag, combine 2 tablespoons flour and salt. Add the beef, a few pieces at a time, and shake to coat.

In a large skillet over medium-high heat, brown the coated beef in 2 tablespoons butter. Add the fresh mushrooms and sweet onion; cook and stir until the vegetables are tender. Add the garlic; cook 1 minute longer. Remove and keep warm.

In the same skillet, melt the remaining butter. Stir in the tomato paste and remaining flour until smooth. Gradually add beef broth; bring to a boil. Cook and stir for 2 minutes or until thickened.

Carefully return beef mixture to the pan. Add sour cream and sherry; heat through (do not boil). Serve with noodles or rice.

Editor's Note: This recipe was not tested using organic ingredients, but all ingredients listed are available in organic versions. **Yield:** 5 servings.

His Favorite Ravioli

(Pictured above)

PREP/TOTAL TIME: 30 min.

Want terrific pasta—pronto? This recipe transforms refrigerated ravioli into a gourmet dinner in no time. The rich flavors and interesting textures give this dish its distinctive character.
—Christa Rispoli, Newfoundland, New Jersey

>   2 packages (8.8 ounces *each*) refrigerated pumpkin ravioli *or* ravioli of your choice
> 1-2/3 cups sliced baby portobello mushrooms
>   1 small onion, finely chopped
>   4 thin slices prosciutto *or* deli ham, chopped
>   1 teaspoon olive oil
>   1/2 teaspoon minced fresh sage
>   2 cups half-and-half cream
>   1/2 cup frozen peas, thawed
>   2 tablespoons grated Parmigiano-Reggiano cheese
>   1/4 teaspoon salt
>   1/4 teaspoon pepper

Cook the ravioli according to the package directions. Meanwhile, in a large skillet, saute the mushrooms, onion and prosciutto in oil until vegetables are tender. Add sage; cook 1 minute longer. Stir in half-and-half cream. Bring to a boil over medium heat. Reduce the heat; simmer, uncovered, for 8-10 minutes or until slightly thickened.

Stir in the peas, cheese, salt and pepper; heat through. Drain ravioli; toss with sauce. **Yield:** 4 servings.

Braided Pork Tenderloins

PREP: 30 min. + marinating **GRILL:** 10 min.

I cook for my family three or four times a week and always like to experiment or do something special. These marinated and grilled tenderloins are braided and jazzed up with jerk seasoning, as well as a burst of mango. —*Jim Rude, Janesville, Wisconsin*

- 2 pork tenderloins (1 pound *each*)
- 1/2 cup mango nectar
- 1/4 cup plus 1 tablespoon spiced rum *or* additional mango nectar, *divided*
- 2 tablespoons olive oil
- 2 tablespoons Caribbean jerk seasoning, *divided*
- 2 garlic cloves, minced
- 1 cup chopped peeled mango
- 1 tablespoon heavy whipping cream

Cut the pork tenderloins in half lengthwise; cut each half into three strips to within 1 in. of one end. In a large resealable plastic bag, combine mango nectar, 1/4 cup rum, oil, 1 tablespoon jerk seasoning and garlic; add the pork. Seal the bag and turn to coat; refrigerate for up to 4 hours.

Drain and discard the marinade. Place the tenderloin halves on a clean cutting board and braid; secure the loose ends with toothpicks. Sprinkle with the remaining jerk seasoning.

Grill the tenderloin braids, covered, over medium heat for 8-10 minutes or until a meat thermometer reads 160°, turning once. Discard the toothpicks. Let stand for 5 minutes before slicing.

Meanwhile, place chopped mango, heavy whipping cream and remaining rum in a food processor. Cover and process until smooth. Transfer to a small saucepan; heat through. Serve sauce with pork. **Yield:** 8 servings (3/4 cup sauce).

Glazed Pork Chops

PREP: 10 min. + marinating **GRILL:** 10 min.

I've served these tasty chops for birthdays, Easter dinner…and no particular reason at all. The recipe is easy to double or even triple to feed a crowd. —*Sondra Warson, Madrid, Iowa*

- 2/3 cup apricot preserves
- 1/2 cup Italian salad dressing
- 2 tablespoons Dijon mustard
- 4 boneless pork loin chops (1 inch thick and 6 ounces *each*)

In a small bowl, combine the apricot preserves, Italian salad dressing and mustard. Pour 3/4 cup marinade into a large resealable bag; add the pork. Seal bag and turn to coat; refrigerate for 8 hours or overnight. Cover and refrigerate remaining marinade for basting.

Coat the grill rack with cooking spray before starting the grill. Drain the pork chops and discard marinade. Grill the pork chops, covered, over medium heat for

4-5 minutes on each side or until a meat thermometer reads 160°, basting frequently with reserved marinade. **Yield:** 4 servings.

Bruschetta Pizza

(Pictured below)

PREP: 25 min. **BAKE:** 10 min.

To eat this loaded Italian–style pie, you might need a knife and fork! It's a a real treat for family pizza night. Sometimes I use a homemade whole wheat crust instead of a purchased bread shell crust. —*Debra Keil, Owasso, Oklahoma*

- 1/2 pound reduced-fat bulk pork sausage
- 1 prebaked Italian bread shell crust (14 ounces)
- 1 package (6 ounces) sliced turkey pepperoni
- 2 cups (8 ounces) shredded part-skim mozzarella cheese
- 1-1/2 cups chopped plum tomatoes
- 1/2 cup fresh basil leaves, thinly sliced
- 1 tablespoon olive oil
- 2 garlic cloves, minced
- 1/2 teaspoon minced fresh thyme *or* 1/8 teaspoon dried thyme
- 1/2 teaspoon balsamic vinegar
- 1/4 teaspoon salt
- 1/8 teaspoon pepper

Additional fresh basil leaves, optional

In a small skillet, cook the sausage over medium heat until no longer pink; drain. Place crust on an ungreased baking sheet. Top with pepperoni, sausage and cheese. Bake at 450° for 10-12 minutes or until cheese is melted.

In a small bowl, combine the tomatoes, sliced basil, oil, garlic, thyme, balsamic vinegar, salt and pepper. Spoon over the pizza. Garnish with additional basil if desired. **Yield:** 8 slices.

Black Bean Cakes With Mole Salsa

(Pictured above)

PREP/TOTAL TIME: 30 min.

A fresh-tasting homemade salsa adds extra flair to these nicely spiced bean cakes. Serve them on a bun for a great veggie burger!
—Roxanne Chan, Albany, California

☑ This recipe includes Nutrition Facts and Diabetic Exchanges.

    1 can (15 ounces) black beans, rinsed and drained
    1 egg, beaten
    1 cup shredded zucchini
1/2 cup dry bread crumbs
1/4 cup shredded Mexican cheese blend
    2 tablespoons chili powder
1/4 teaspoon salt
1/4 teaspoon baking powder
1/4 teaspoon ground cumin
    2 tablespoons olive oil
SALSA:
    2 medium tomatoes, chopped
    1 small green pepper, chopped
    3 tablespoons grated chocolate
    1 green onion, thinly sliced
    2 tablespoons minced fresh cilantro
    1 tablespoon lime juice
    1 to 2 teaspoons minced chipotle pepper in
        adobo sauce
    1 teaspoon honey

In a small bowl, mash the beans. Add the egg, zucchini, bread crumbs, cheese, chili powder, salt, baking powder and cumin; mix well. Shape into six patties; brush both sides with oil. Place on a baking sheet.

Broil 3-4 in. from the heat for 3-4 minutes on each side or until a thermometer reads 160°.

Meanwhile, in a small bowl, combine salsa ingredients.

Serve the salsa with black bean cakes. **Yield:** 6 servings (1-1/4 cups salsa).

Nutrition Facts: 1 cake with about 3 tablespoons salsa equals 206 calories, 10 g fat (3 g saturated fat), 39 mg cholesterol, 397 mg sodium, 23 g carbohydrate, 6 g fiber, 8 g protein. **Diabetic Exchanges:** 2 fat, 1 starch, 1 very lean meat.

Eggs Bravo

PREP: 15 min. **COOK:** 20 min.

I stir leftover ham and hard-cooked eggs into a creamy cheese sauce, then drape it over toasted English muffins. The simple stovetop dish is wonderful for breakfast, brunch or a light lunch.
—Erika Anderson, Wausau, Wisconsin

1/3 cup all-purpose flour
1/8 to 1/4 teaspoon salt
Dash pepper
1-3/4 cups milk
    4 ounces process cheese (Velveeta), cubed
1-1/2 cups cubed fully cooked ham
    4 hard-cooked eggs, chopped
1/2 cup mayonnaise
1/4 cup sliced green onions
1/4 cup chopped pimientos
    6 to 8 English muffins, split and toasted

In a saucepan, combine the flour, salt, pepper and milk until smooth. Bring to a boil; cook and stir for 2 minutes or until thickened. Add the cheese; cook and stir until melted. Stir in the ham, eggs, mayonnaise, onions and pimientos; heat through. Serve over English muffins. **Yield:** 6-8 servings.

German Oktoberfest Pizza

PREP/TOTAL TIME: 20 min.

There's a little bit of Deutschland in every slice of this quick but creative pizza. If you're a fan of sausage and sauerkraut, you'll love this!
—Angela Spengler, Clovis, New Mexico

    1 tube (13.8 ounces) refrigerated pizza crust
    1 pound smoked kielbasa *or* Polish sausage, cut
        into 1/4-inch slices
    2 teaspoons butter
    2 cups leftover *or* refrigerated mashed potatoes
    1 cup sauerkraut, rinsed and well drained
    1 cup (4 ounces) shredded cheddar cheese
    1 teaspoon caraway seeds

Unroll dough into a greased 15-in. x 10-in. x 1-in. baking pan; flatten dough and build up edges slightly. Bake at 425° for 8-10 minutes or until lightly golden brown.

Meanwhile, in a large skillet, saute kielbasa in butter until browned. Spread potatoes over crust. Top with sauerkraut, kielbasa, cheese and caraway seeds. Bake for 10-15 minutes or until golden brown. **Yield:** 6 pieces.

Chicken Saltimbocca

(Pictured below)

PREP: 25 min. **COOK:** 20 min.

This saucy main course is one of my favorites. The traditional recipe calls for veal, but I created this version that uses chicken instead. —Kristin Kossak, Bozeman, Montana

- 2 **medium onions, chopped**
- 2 **tablespoons butter**
- 2 **cups uncooked long grain rice**
- 4 **cups chicken broth**
- 8 **boneless skinless chicken breast halves (4 ounces** *each***)**
- 4 **thin slices prosciutto** *or* **deli ham, halved**
- 8 **fresh sage leaves**
- 1/2 **teaspoon salt**
- 1/4 **teaspoon pepper**
- 2 **tablespoons olive oil**
- 1/2 **cup white wine**
- 1/4 **cup sour cream**
- 1/2 **teaspoon sugar**
- 1 **teaspoon minced fresh sage**

In a large saucepan, saute onions in butter until tender. Add rice and stir to coat. Stir in broth and bring to a boil. Reduce the heat; cover and simmer for 15-20 minutes or until tender. Fluff with a fork.

Meanwhile, cut a slit lengthwise through the thickest part of each chicken breast; fill with prosciutto and two sage leaves. Sprinkle with salt and pepper.

In a large skillet over medium heat, brown the chicken in oil for 1-2 minutes on each side. Reduce heat to low; cover and cook for 8-10 minutes or until juices run clear. Remove and keep warm.

Add the wine to the pan. Bring to a boil. Reduce heat; simmer, uncovered, for 2-3 minutes or until slightly reduced. Stir in the sour cream, sugar and minced sage; heat through (do not boil). Serve with chicken and rice. **Yield:** 8 servings.

Broccoli Rabe & Garlic Pasta

(Pictured above and on page 54)

PREP/TOTAL TIME: 30 min.

Broccoli rabe, or rapini, pairs so well with the garlic in this dish. It's a terrific way to get your greens and enjoy pasta at the same time. —Mary Ann Lee, Clifton Park, New York

- 12 **ounces uncooked linguine**
- 1 **pound broccoli rabe**
- 3 **garlic cloves, minced**
- 2 **tablespoons olive oil**
- 1/4 **teaspoon salt**
- 1/4 **teaspoon pepper**
- 1/4 **teaspoon crushed red pepper flakes**
- 1 **cup chicken broth,** *divided*
- 1/4 **cup minced fresh parsley**
- 1/4 **cup shredded Parmesan cheese**

Cook the linguine according to the package directions. Meanwhile, trim 1/4 in. off the bottoms of broccoli rabe stems; discard coarse outer leaves. Rinse broccoli rabe in cold water and cut into 2-in. pieces; set aside.

In a large skillet, saute the garlic in oil for 1 minute. Add the broccoli rabe, salt, pepper, red pepper flakes and 1/2 cup broth. Bring to a boil.

Reduce heat; cover and cook for 3-5 minutes or until broccoli rabe is tender. Drain linguine; add to the pan. Stir in parsley and enough remaining broth to moisten the linguine. Sprinkle with cheese. **Yield:** 4 servings.

Penne & Sausage Casseroles

(Pictured below)

PREP: 50 min. **BAKE:** 30 min.

This recipe makes two satisfying, meal-in-one casseroles. I'm the regular cook in our family, and this is a dinner I can always rely on. —John Venturino, Concord, California

- 1-1/2 pounds uncooked penne pasta
- 1 pound bulk Italian sausage
- 1 pound sliced fresh mushrooms
- 1 large onion, chopped
- 3 tablespoons olive oil
- 6 garlic cloves, minced
- 1 tablespoon dried oregano
- 1-1/2 cups dry red wine *or beef broth*, *divided*
- 2 cans (14-1/2 ounces *each*) stewed tomatoes, cut up
- 1 can (15 ounces) tomato sauce
- 1 cup beef broth
- 4 cups (16 ounces) shredded part-skim mozzarella cheese
- 4 cups (16 ounces) shredded fontina cheese

Minced fresh parsley, optional

Cook the pasta according to the package directions. Meanwhile, in a Dutch oven, cook sausage over medium heat until no longer pink; drain and set aside.

In the same Dutch oven, saute mushrooms and onion in oil until tender. Add garlic and oregano; cook 1 minute longer. Stir in 1 cup wine. Bring to a boil; cook until liquid is reduced by half. Stir in tomatoes, tomato sauce, broth, sausage and remaining wine. Bring to a boil. Reduce the heat; cover and simmer for 15 minutes.

Drain the pasta. Spread 1/2 cup sauce in each of two greased 13-in. x 9-in. baking dishes. Divide half of the pasta between the dishes; top each with 2-1/2 cups sauce and 1 cup each of the cheeses. Repeat layers.

Cover and bake at 350° for 25 minutes. Uncover; bake 5-10 minutes longer or until bubbly and the cheese is melted. Sprinkle with minced parsley if desired. **Yield:** 2 casseroles (8 servings each).

Garlic Lemon Shrimp

PREP/TOTAL TIME: 20 min.

You'll be amazed that you can fix this elegant entree so quickly. Serve it with crusty bread to soak up all of the delicious, garlicky sauce. —Athena Russell, Florence, South Carolina

- 1 pound uncooked large shrimp, peeled and deveined
- 2 tablespoons olive oil
- 3 garlic cloves, sliced
- 1 tablespoon lemon juice
- 1 teaspoon ground cumin
- 1/4 teaspoon salt
- 2 tablespoons minced fresh parsley

Hot cooked pasta *or* rice

In a large skillet, saute shrimp in oil for 3 minutes. Add the garlic, lemon juice, cumin and salt; cook and stir until shrimp turn pink. Stir in parsley. Serve with pasta or rice. **Yield:** 4 servings.

Thai Shrimp

PREP/TOTAL TIME: 30 min.

There's fantastic Thai flavor in this restaurant-quality shrimp stir-fry. Once you try it, you'll want to skip going out for dinner and enjoy the comforts of home instead with this superb dish. —Genise Krause, Sturgeon Bay, Wisconsin

- 1 tablespoon cornstarch
- 1 cup vegetable broth
- 1/4 cup soy sauce
- 3 tablespoons rice vinegar
- 1 to 2 tablespoons Thai chili sauce
- 1 tablespoon minced fresh gingerroot
- 1 teaspoon minced garlic
- 1 pound uncooked medium shrimp, peeled and deveined
- 2 teaspoons sesame oil
- 1 can (14 ounces) water-packed artichoke hearts, rinsed, drained and chopped
- 3 tablespoons chopped green onions
- 1 head bok choy, trimmed

Hot cooked rice, optional

In a small bowl, combine cornstarch and broth until smooth; stir in the soy sauce, vinegar, chili sauce, ginger and garlic. Set aside.

In a large skillet or wok, stir-fry shrimp in oil until shrimp turn pink. Remove and keep warm.

Stir the soy sauce mixture and add to the pan. Bring to a boil. Cook and stir for 2 minutes or until thickened. Stir in the artichokes and green onions; top with the bok choy. Reduce the heat; cover and cook for 5 minutes or until the bok choy is wilted. Return the shrimp to the pan; heat through. Serve with rice if desired. **Yield:** 4 servings.

form; fold into batter. Bake in a preheated waffle iron according to the manufacturer's directions until golden brown. Serve with syrup. **Yield:** 10 waffles.

Orange-Cashew Chicken and Rice

(Pictured below)

PREP/TOTAL TIME: 30 min.

I like to experiment with different ingredients when I prepare this popular dish. Try celery instead of bok choy...or toasted almonds instead of cashews. The recipe is so versatile, every combination turns out great! —Aysha Schurman, Ammon, Idaho

- 1 cup instant brown rice
- 1 can (11 ounces) mandarin oranges
- 1/4 cup chopped cashews
- 1/4 cup chicken broth
- 2 tablespoons soy sauce
- 2 tablespoons teriyaki sauce
- 3/4 pound boneless skinless chicken breasts, cut into 1/2-inch pieces
- 1 tablespoon canola oil
- 1/2 cup chopped bok choy
- 1/4 cup minced chives

Cook the rice according to the package directions. Meanwhile, drain mandarin oranges, reserving 1/2 cup oranges and 2 tablespoons juice (save the remainder for another use).

In a small bowl, combine the cashews, broth, soy sauce, teriyaki sauce and reserved juice; set aside. In a large wok or skillet, stir-fry chicken in oil until no longer pink. Add cashew mixture; cook 1 minute longer. Add the bok choy, chives and reserved oranges; cook and stir for 2 minutes.

Fluff the rice with a fork; serve with chicken mixture. **Yield:** 3 servings.

Sweet Potato Waffles

(Pictured above)

PREP: 20 min. **COOK:** 5 min./batch

With cardamom and chopped pecans, these special waffles really stand out. They're perfect for using up leftover sweet potatoes from last night's dinner. —Mickey Turner, Grants Pass, Oregon

- 1-1/2 cups all-purpose flour
- 1 tablespoon sugar
- 1-1/2 teaspoons baking powder
- 1 teaspoon ground cardamom
- 1/2 teaspoon salt
- 3 eggs, *separated*
- 1 cup (8 ounces) sour cream
- 1 cup cold mashed sweet potatoes
- 1/2 cup milk
- 1/4 cup butter, melted
- 3/4 cup chopped pecans
- Maple syrup, optional

In a large bowl, combine the flour, sugar, baking powder, cardamom and salt. In another bowl, whisk the egg yolks, sour cream, sweet potatoes, milk and butter; stir into dry ingredients just until moistened. Fold in pecans.

In a small bowl, beat the egg whites until stiff peaks

FRESH TASTE. The shelf life for baking powder is about 6 months. Want to make Sweet Potato Waffles (above) but aren't sure if your baking powder is still fresh? You can quickly find out using a simple test:

Place 1 teaspoon baking powder in a cup and add 1/3 cup hot tap water to the cup. If active bubbling occurs, the baking powder is fine to use. If not, it should be replaced.

"Secret's in the Sauce" BBQ Ribs

(Pictured above)

PREP: 10 min. **COOK:** 6 hours

You'll be amazed that just five ingredients are needed for this sweet, rich sauce. It makes the slow-cooked ribs so tender, the meat falls off the bones. And the aroma during cooking is out of this world! —*Tanya Reid, Winston-Salem, North Carolina*

> 2 racks pork baby back ribs (about 4-1/2 pounds)
> 1-1/2 teaspoons pepper
> 2-1/2 cups barbecue sauce
> 3/4 cup cherry preserves
> 1 tablespoon Dijon mustard
> 1 garlic clove, minced

Cut ribs into serving-size pieces; sprinkle with pepper. Place in a 5- or 6-qt. slow cooker. Combine the remaining ingredients; pour over ribs.

Cover and cook on low for 6-8 hours or until meat is tender. Serve with sauce. **Yield:** 5 servings.

Moist & Tender Turkey Breast

PREP: 10 min. **COOK:** 4 hours

This tasty turkey breast recipe is the easiest I've ever prepared and always turns out perfect. What more could a cook ask for?
—*Heidi Vawdrey, Riverton, Utah*

> 1 bone-in turkey breast (6 to 7 pounds)
> 4 fresh rosemary sprigs
> 4 garlic cloves, peeled
> 1 tablespoon brown sugar

> 1/2 teaspoon coarsely ground pepper
> 1/4 teaspoon salt

Place turkey in a 6-qt. slow cooker. Place rosemary and garlic around turkey. Combine the brown sugar, pepper and salt; sprinkle over turkey.

Cover and cook on low for 4 to 6 hours or until turkey is tender. **Yield:** 12 servings.

Coffee-Flavored Beef Roast

(Pictured below and on page 54)

PREP: 35 min. **COOK:** 6 hours

Coffee and chili powder give this beef roast so much flavor. With red potatoes, carrots, mushrooms and gravy, you get a complete dinner in one. —*Jean Collier, Hanford, California*

> 6 medium red potatoes, cut into wedges
> 6 medium carrots, cut into 1-inch lengths
> 2 beef sirloin tip roasts (2 to 3 pounds *each*)
> 1 teaspoon salt, *divided*
> 1/2 teaspoon pepper, *divided*
> 2 teaspoons canola oil
> 1 medium onion, halved and sliced
> 2 cups whole fresh mushrooms, quartered
> 2 garlic cloves, minced
> 1-1/2 cups brewed coffee
> 1 teaspoon chili powder
> 3 tablespoons cornstarch
> 1/4 cup cold water

Place the potatoes and carrots in a 6-qt. slow cooker. Sprinkle the beef with half of the salt and pepper. In a large skillet, brown the beef in oil on all sides. Transfer to slow cooker.

In the same skillet, saute the onion in the drippings for 2 minutes. Add the mushrooms and garlic; cook 2 minutes longer. Stir in the coffee, chili powder and

remaining salt and pepper. Pour over meat. Cover and cook on low for 6-8 hours or until meat is tender.

Remove the meat and vegetables to a serving platter; keep warm. Skim fat from the cooking juices; transfer to a small saucepan. Bring the liquid to a boil. Combine cornstarch and water until smooth; gradually stir into the pan. Bring to a boil; cook and stir for 2 minutes or until thickened. Serve with meat and vegetables. **Yield:** 8 servings (2 cups gravy).

Bear's Breakfast Burritos

PREP: 45 min. **COOK:** 15 min.

My husband, Larry, makes these for our church's taco booth on the Fourth of July. Everyone likes the Southwestern taste of these breakfast burritos. Plus, you can assemble them up to 1 month in advance and freeze them. —Sandy Kelley, Grangeville, Idaho

- 2 packages (22-1/2 ounces *each*) frozen hash brown patties
- 15 eggs
- 2 tablespoons chili powder
- 2 tablespoons garlic salt
- 1 tablespoon ground cumin
- 1/2 pound uncooked chorizo *or* bulk spicy pork sausage
- 6 jalapeno peppers, seeded and minced
- 1 large green pepper, chopped
- 1 large sweet red pepper, chopped
- 1 large onion, chopped
- 1 bunch green onions, chopped
- 3 cups salsa
- 1 package (28 ounces) flour tortillas (12 inches), warmed
- 4 cups (16 ounces) shredded Monterey Jack cheese

Sour cream, optional

Cook hash browns according to package directions; crumble and keep warm. Meanwhile, in a large bowl, whisk eggs, chili powder, garlic and cumin. Set aside.

Crumble chorizo into a large skillet; add jalapenos, peppers and onions. Cook and stir over medium heat until meat is fully cooked; drain. Add reserved egg mixture; cook and stir over medium heat until eggs are set. Stir in salsa.

Spoon 1/2 cup hash browns and 1/2 cup egg mixture off center on each tortilla; sprinkle with 1/3 cup cheese. Fold sides and ends over filling and roll up. Wrap each burrito in waxed paper and foil. Serve warm with sour cream if desired. Cool the remaining burritos to room temperature; freeze for up to 1 month.

To use frozen burritos: Remove the foil and waxed paper. Place burritos 2 in. apart on an ungreased baking sheet. Bake, uncovered, at 350° for 50-55 minutes or until heated through. **Yield:** 12 servings.

Editor's Note: When cutting hot peppers, disposable gloves are recommended. Avoid touching your face.

Spiral Omelet Supreme

(Pictured above)

PREP: 20 min. **BAKE:** 20 min.

Feel free to replace the vegetables in this fun recipe with 2 cups of any combination of your favorite omelet fillings. A serrated knife works well for slicing it. —Debbie Morris, Hamilton, Ohio

- 4 ounces cream cheese, softened
- 3/4 cup milk
- 1/4 cup plus 2 tablespoons grated Parmesan cheese, *divided*
- 2 tablespoons all-purpose flour
- 12 eggs
- 1 large green pepper, chopped
- 1 cup sliced fresh mushrooms
- 1 small onion, chopped
- 2 teaspoons canola oil
- 1-1/2 cups (6 ounces) shredded part-skim mozzarella cheese
- 1 plum tomato, seeded and chopped
- 1-1/4 teaspoons Italian seasoning, *divided*

Line the bottom and sides of a greased 15-in. x 10-in. x 1-in. baking pan with parchment paper; grease paper and set aside.

In a small bowl, beat the cream cheese and milk until smooth. Beat in 1/4 cup Parmesan cheese and flour until blended. In a large bowl, beat eggs; add the cream cheese mixture and mix well. Pour into prepared pan.

Bake at 375° for 20-25 minutes or until set. Meanwhile, in a large skillet, saute pepper, mushrooms and onion in oil until crisp-tender. Keep warm.

Turn omelet onto a work surface; peel off parchment paper. Sprinkle with the vegetable mixture, mozzarella cheese, tomato and 1 teaspoon Italian seasoning. Roll up jelly-roll style, starting with a short side. Place on a serving platter. Sprinkle with the remaining Parmesan cheese and Italian seasoning. **Yield:** 8 servings.

Cider Mushroom Brisket

PREP: 10 min. **COOK:** 6 hours

Apple juice and gingersnaps bring an autumn feel to this tender brisket. It's quick to get in the slow cooker, and the aroma is simply irresistible. —*Colleen Weston, Denver, Colorado*

- 1 fresh beef brisket (6 pounds)
- 2 jars (12 ounces *each*) mushroom gravy
- 1 cup apple cider *or* juice
- 1 envelope onion mushroom soup mix
- 6 gingersnap cookies, crushed

Cut brisket into thirds; place in a 5- or 6-qt. slow cooker. In a large bowl, combine the gravy, cider, soup mix and cookie crumbs; pour over beef. Cover and cook on low for 6-8 hours or until meat is tender.

Thinly slice the meat across the grain. Skim fat from cooking juices; thicken if desired. **Yield:** 12 servings.

Editor's Note: This is a fresh beef brisket, not corned beef.

Grilled Salmon With Garlic Mayo

(Pictured below)

PREP/TOTAL TIME: 15 min.

I've shared this recipe with people from Maine to California, and everyone loves it. Lemon juice and yogurt give the mayo a nice tang. —*Donna Noel, Gray, Maine*

- 3 tablespoons plus 1 teaspoon olive oil, *divided*
- 1/2 teaspoon dried rosemary, crushed
- 4 salmon fillets (6 ounces *each*)
- 8 garlic cloves, peeled
- 1 tablespoon lemon juice

- 3/4 cup mayonnaise
- 2 tablespoons plain yogurt
- 1 tablespoon Dijon mustard

Coat grill rack with cooking spray before starting the grill. Combine 3 tablespoons oil and rosemary; brush over salmon. Place salmon skin side down on grill rack.

Grill, covered, over medium heat for 10-12 minutes or until fish flakes easily with a fork.

Meanwhile, in a small microwave-safe bowl, combine garlic and remaining oil. Microwave, uncovered, on high for 20-30 seconds or until softened; place in a blender. Add the remaining ingredients. Cover and process until blended. Serve with salmon. **Yield:** 4 servings.

Raspberry Cheese Blintz Bake

PREP: 25 min. **BAKE:** 40 min. + standing

For a special breakfast, try this twist on traditional blintzes. It puffs during baking and falls a bit while standing, but it looks beautiful on the table. —*Kristi Twohig, Waterloo, Wisconsin*

- 1/2 cup orange juice
- 6 eggs
- 2 egg whites
- 1-1/2 cups (12 ounces) sour cream
- 1 cup all-purpose flour
- 1/2 cup sugar
- 1/4 cup butter, softened
- 2 teaspoons baking powder
- 1 teaspoon grated orange peel
- 1 teaspoon vanilla extract

Dash salt

FILLING:

- 2 egg yolks
- 1 teaspoon vanilla extract
- 2 cups (16 ounces) 4% cottage cheese
- 1 package (8 ounces) cream cheese, softened
- 1/4 cup sugar

TOPPING:

- 1 package (12 ounces) frozen unsweetened raspberries, thawed
- 2 tablespoons cornstarch
- 3/4 cup orange juice

Mandarin oranges, optional

Combine the first 11 ingredients in a blender. Cover and process until smooth. Set aside 2 cups batter; pour remaining batter into a greased 13-in. x 9-in. baking dish.

For the filling, combine the egg yolks, vanilla, cottage cheese, cream cheese and sugar in a blender. Cover and process until smooth. Spoon filling over the batter; cut through with a knife to swirl. Top with reserved batter. Bake, uncovered, at 350° for 40-45 minutes or until the center is just set (the mixture will jiggle). Let stand for 10 minutes before cutting.

For the topping, press raspberries through a strainer;

biscuit for 30-60 seconds on each side or until golden brown; keep warm.

To serve, spread each flatbread with 2 tablespoons ranch sour cream; top each with 2/3 cup meat mixture. Sprinkle with toppings if desired. **Yield:** 8 servings.

Porcini-Crusted Pork with Polenta

(Pictured below)

PREP: 20 min. **BAKE:** 20 min.

Porcini mushrooms surround these mouth-watering chops with delectable flavor. Rosemary and Parmesan make the polenta a sophisticated accompaniment to this restaurant-quality entree.
—*Casandra Rittenhouse, North Hollywood, California*

- 1 **package (1 ounce) dried porcini mushrooms**
- 1/4 **teaspoon salt**
- 1/4 **teaspoon pepper**
- 4 **bone-in pork loin chops (7 ounces** *each*)
- 2 **teaspoons olive oil**
- 1 **tube (1 pound) polenta**
- 1/2 **cup grated Parmesan cheese**
- 1/4 **teaspoon dried rosemary, crushed**

Process mushrooms in a food processor until coarsely chopped. Transfer to a shallow bowl; stir in salt and pepper. Press one side of each pork chop into the mushroom mixture.

In a large ovenproof skillet coated with cooking spray, heat oil over medium-high heat. Place the chops, mushroom side down, in skillet; cook for 2 minutes. Turn over; cook 2 minutes longer. Bake, uncovered, at 375° for 20-25 minutes or until a meat thermometer reads 160°.

Prepare polenta according to package directions for soft polenta. Stir in Parmesan cheese and rosemary. Serve with pork chops. **Yield:** 4 servings.

discard seeds and pulp. In a small saucepan, combine the cornstarch and orange juice until smooth; stir in the berry puree. Bring to a boil. Cook and stir for 2 minutes or until thickened. Serve with blintz bake. Top with mandarin oranges if desired. **Yield:** 12 servings.

Flatbread Tacos with Ranch Sour Cream

(Pictured above)

PREP/TOTAL TIME: 30 min.

Made with convenient refrigerated biscuits, these flatbread tacos are perfect for serving buffet style. Just set out shredded cheddar cheese, lettuce, ripe olives or other favorite toppings, then let your guests assemble their own. You'll see lots of happy faces!
—*Jennifer Eggebraaten, Delton, Michigan*

- 1 **cup (8 ounces) sour cream**
- 2 **teaspoons ranch salad dressing mix**
- 1 **teaspoon lemon juice**
- 1-1/2 **pounds ground beef**
- 1 **can (15 ounces) pinto beans, rinsed and drained**
- 1 **can (14-1/2 ounces) diced tomatoes, undrained**
- 1 **envelope taco seasoning**
- 1 **tablespoon hot pepper sauce**
- 1 **tube (16.3 ounces) large refrigerated buttermilk biscuits**
- **Optional toppings: sliced ripe olives and shredded lettuce and cheddar cheese**

In a small bowl, combine the sour cream, dressing mix and lemon juice; chill until serving.

In a large skillet, cook ground beef over medium heat until no longer pink; drain. Add the beans, tomatoes, taco seasoning and pepper sauce; heat through.

Meanwhile, roll out each biscuit into a 6-in. circle. In a small nonstick skillet over medium heat, cook each

Dilled Salmon Omelets With Creme Fraiche

(Pictured above)

PREP: 15 min. **COOK:** 5 min./batch

This simple but elegant recipe from the Nutmeg Country Inn in Wilmington, Vermont gives ordinary omelets an extra-special treatment with salmon, Swiss cheese, fresh dill and a dollop of creme fraiche. Try hash browns or breakfast potatoes on the side for a breakfast you won't soon forget!

- 12 eggs
- 2 tablespoons milk
- Salt and pepper to taste
- 2 tablespoons butter
- 1 pound salmon fillets, cooked and flaked
- 3 cups (12 ounces) shredded Swiss cheese
- 2 tablespoons snipped fresh dill
- 3/4 cup creme fraiche *or* sour cream
- 6 fresh dill sprigs

In a large bowl, whisk the eggs, milk, salt and pepper until blended.

For each omelet, in an 8-in. ovenproof skillet, melt 1 teaspoon butter over medium heat. Pour 1/2 cup egg mixture into the pan. Sprinkle with 1/3 cup salmon, 1/2 cup cheese and 1 teaspoon snipped dill. As eggs set, lift edges, letting uncooked portion flow underneath. Cook until eggs are nearly set.

Broil 6 in. from the heat for 1-2 minutes or until eggs are completely set. Fold omelet in half; transfer to a plate. Top with 2 tablespoons creme fraiche and a dill sprig. Serve immediately. Repeat for remaining omelets. **Yield:** 6 servings.

Ginger Pork Stir-Fry

PREP/TOTAL TIME: 25 min.

My recipe box is full of delicious pork recipes, but this stir-fry really stands out. My family just loves the citrus glaze that coats the pork and veggies. —Jackie Hannahs, Fountain, Michigan

☑ This recipe includes Nutrition Facts and Diabetic Exchanges.

- 1 tablespoon cornstarch
- 1 cup orange juice
- 2 tablespoons soy sauce
- 2 garlic cloves, minced
- 1/4 teaspoon ground ginger
- 1 pork tenderloin (1 pound), cut into thin strips
- 1 tablespoon canola oil
- 1 small onion, chopped
- 1/4 pound fresh snow peas
- 1/4 cup chopped sweet red pepper
- Hot cooked rice

In a small bowl, combine the cornstarch, orange juice, soy sauce, garlic and ginger until smooth; set aside.

In a large skillet or wok, stir-fry the pork in oil for 5 minutes or until lightly browned; drain. Add the onion, peas and red pepper; cook and stir for 3-5 minutes or until crisp-tender.

Stir the orange juice mixture; add to the skillet. Bring to a boil; cook and stir for 2 minutes or until thickened. Serve with rice. **Yield:** 4 servings.

Nutrition Facts: 3/4 cup serving (prepared with reduced-sodium soy sauce; calculated without rice) equals 230 calories, 7 g fat (2 g saturated fat), 74 mg cholesterol, 361 mg sodium, 14 g carbohydrate, 1 g fiber, 26 g protein. **Diabetic Exchanges:** 3 lean meat, 1 vegetable, 1/2 fruit.

Easy Stuffed Shells

PREP: 20 min. **BAKE:** 40 min.

I threw these together one day when we had unexpected guests. The four-ingredient pasta was a hit—and is now a mainstay in our house! —Dolores Betchner, Cudahy, Wisconsin

- 1 package (12 ounces) jumbo pasta shells
- 1 jar (26 ounces) spaghetti sauce
- 36 frozen cooked Italian meatballs (1/2 ounce *each*), thawed
- 2 cups (8 ounces) shredded part-skim mozzarella cheese

Cook the pasta according to package directions; drain and rinse in cold water. Place 1/2 cup sauce in a greased 13-in. x 9-in. baking dish. Place a meatball in each shell; transfer to prepared dish. Top with remaining sauce and sprinkle with cheese.

Cover and bake at 350° for 35 minutes. Uncover; bake 5-10 minutes longer or until bubbly and the cheese is melted. **Yield:** 12 servings.

Seafood Medley

(Pictured below)

PREP: 25 min. **COOK:** 10 min.

This creamy main course is the traditional Christmas Eve dinner for our family...but you'll find it's wonderful any time of year.
—*Marilyn Bishop, Redbridge, Ontario*

- 5 cups water
- 2 tablespoons lemon juice
- 1/2 teaspoon salt
- 2 pounds fresh *or* frozen orange roughy fillets, thawed
- 1 pound uncooked medium shrimp, peeled and deveined
- 1/2 pound bay scallops
- 2 tablespoons butter
- 3 tablespoons all-purpose flour
- 1 teaspoon chicken bouillon granules
- 1 teaspoon Dijon mustard

Dash pepper
- 1 cup heavy whipping cream
- 1 cup (4 ounces) shredded Gruyere *or* Swiss cheese

Hot cooked pasta

In a Dutch oven, bring the water, lemon juice and salt to a boil. Reduce heat; carefully add orange roughy fillets and cook, uncovered, for 4 minutes. Add the shrimp; cook for 3 minutes. Add the scallops; cook 3-4 minutes longer or until the fish flakes easily with a fork, the shrimp turn pink and the scallops are firm and opaque. Strain, reserving 1-1/2 cups cooking liquid.

In a large saucepan, melt the butter. Stir in the flour, bouillon, mustard and pepper until smooth. Gradually add cream and reserved liquid. Bring to a boil; cook and stir for 1-2 minutes or until thickened. Stir in the cheese and seafood mixture; heat through. Serve with pasta. **Yield:** 6 servings.

Skillet Shepherd's Pie

(Pictured above)

PREP/TOTAL TIME: 20 min.

Leftover mashed potatoes are put to perfect use in this stovetop version of a classic main dish. I like the tasty twist it gets from the taco seasoning. —*Sharon Tipton, Orlando, Florida*

- 1-1/2 pounds ground beef
- 1 medium onion, chopped
- 2 garlic cloves, minced
- 1/2 cup water
- 1 envelope taco seasoning
- 2 cups (8 ounces) shredded cheddar cheese, *divided*
- 3 cups leftover *or* refrigerated mashed potatoes, warmed

In a large ovenproof skillet, cook the beef, onion and garlic over medium heat until meat is no longer pink. Stir in water and taco seasoning; heat through. Stir in 1 cup cheese.

Combine potatoes and remaining cheese; spread over beef. Broil 4-6 in. from the heat for 5-6 minutes or until golden brown. **Yield:** 4 servings.

Asian Orange Beef

(Pictured below)

PREP: 20 min. **COOK:** 20 min.

Here is the fastest stir–fry I've ever found! Fresh ginger is a must for this recipe and really sparks it up. We also love the splash of orange flavor. —Nancy Bellomo, St. Charles, Missouri

☑ This recipe includes Nutrition Facts and Diabetic Exchanges.

- **3 large navel oranges**
- **1 bunch green onions**
- **3 tablespoons sugar**
- **2 tablespoons cornstarch**
- **3 tablespoons reduced-sodium soy sauce**
- **3 garlic cloves, minced**
- **1 tablespoon minced fresh gingerroot**
- **1-1/2 pounds boneless beef sirloin steak, cut into 1/2-inch cubes**
- **1 tablespoon canola oil**
- **3 cups hot cooked rice**

Finely grate the peel from two oranges; set aside. Cut thin strips of orange peel from the remaining orange for the garnish; set aside. Squeeze juice from all oranges. Cut the green onions to separate the white and green parts. Thinly slice the white parts; cut the green parts into 1-in. lengths for garnish.

For the sauce, in a small bowl, combine the sugar and cornstarch; stir in orange juice until smooth. Stir in the soy sauce, garlic, ginger, grated orange peel and white parts of onions; set aside.

In a large nonstick skillet or wok coated with cooking spray, stir-fry the beef in oil until no longer pink. Stir the sauce and add to the pan. Bring to a boil; cook and stir for 2 minutes or until thickened. Serve with rice. Garnish with the orange peel strips and remaining onions. **Yield:** 6 servings.

Nutrition Facts: 2/3 cup beef mixture with 1/2 cup

rice equals 351 calories, 8 g fat (2 g saturated fat), 64 mg cholesterol, 352 mg sodium, 44 g carbohydrate, 3 g fiber, 25 g protein. **Diabetic Exchanges:** 3 lean meat, 2 starch, 1 fruit.

Spicy Chorizo & Shrimp Rice

(Pictured above)

PREP/TOTAL TIME: 30 min.

Looking for an easy, one–skillet meal for dinner tonight? This filling dish has a Southwestern taste your family is sure to enjoy. —Cheryl Perry, Hertford, North Carolina

- **1/2 pound uncooked chorizo *or* bulk spicy pork sausage**
- **4 tomatillos, husks removed, chopped**
- **1 cup uncooked long grain rice**
- **1/4 cup chopped onion**
- **1/4 cup chopped celery leaves**
- **1/4 cup chopped carrot**
- **1/2 teaspoon garlic powder**
- **1/4 teaspoon pepper**
- **2 cups chicken broth**
- **1/2 pound uncooked medium shrimp, peeled and deveined**
- **1/4 cup crumbled queso fresco *or* diced part-skim mozzarella cheese**
- **2 teaspoons minced fresh cilantro**

Crumble chorizo into a large skillet; add tomatillos. Cook over medium heat for 6-8 minutes or until meat is fully cooked. Add the rice, onion, celery leaves, carrot, garlic powder and pepper; cook and stir for 2 minutes.

Add the chicken broth; bring to a boil. Reduce heat; cover and simmer for 10 minutes. Stir in shrimp; cover and cook 5 minutes longer or until shrimp turn pink and rice is tender. Sprinkle with cheese and cilantro. **Yield:** 4 servings.

Lemon Shrimp Stir-Fry

PREP: 25 min. **COOK:** 10 min.

I got this healthier-for-you recipe from a friend about 10 years ago. With a tangy sauce, it makes you feel like you're indulging.
—Caroline Elliott, Grants Pass, Oregon

☑ This recipe includes Nutrition Facts and Diabetic Exchanges.

- 1 tablespoon cornstarch
- 1/2 teaspoon sugar
- 1/2 teaspoon chicken bouillon granules
- 1/4 teaspoon grated lemon peel
- Dash pepper
- 1/2 cup water
- 4-1/2 teaspoons lemon juice
- 1/2 pound uncooked medium shrimp, peeled and deveined
- 1 tablespoon canola oil
- 3/4 cup sliced celery
- 1/2 medium green pepper, cut into strips
- 1/2 medium sweet red pepper, cut into strips
- 1 cup sliced fresh mushrooms
- 3/4 cup fresh sugar snap peas
- 1 green onion, sliced
- 1 cup hot cooked long grain rice

In a small bowl, combine the first five ingredients. Stir in water and lemon juice until blended; set aside.

In a large skillet or wok, stir-fry the shrimp in oil for 1-2 minutes or until no longer pink. Remove with a slotted spoon and keep warm. In the same pan, stir-fry celery and peppers for 2 minutes. Add the mushrooms, peas and onion; stir-fry 3-4 minutes longer or until the vegetables are crisp-tender.

Stir cornstarch mixture and add to the pan. Bring to a boil; cook and stir for 2 minutes or until thickened. Add shrimp; heat through. Serve with rice. **Yield:** 2 servings.

Nutrition Facts: 1-1/2 cups shrimp mixture with 1/2 cup rice equals 326 calories, 9 g fat (1 g saturated fat), 168 mg cholesterol, 449 mg sodium, 39 g carbohydrate, 4 g fiber, 24 g protein. **Diabetic Exchanges:** 3 very lean meat, 2 starch, 2 vegetable.

Creamy Pasta with Bacon

PREP/TOTAL TIME: 20 min.

My son loves bacon, so he dug right into this saucy linguine. Add leftover chicken if you want a heartier main dish...or serve it as-is for a substantial side. *—Kim Uhrich, Cabot, Arkansas*

- 1 package (9 ounces) refrigerated linguine
- 1 medium onion, chopped
- 1 tablespoon canola oil
- 2 garlic cloves, minced
- 2 tablespoons all-purpose flour
- 1-1/2 cups heavy whipping cream
- 3 eggs, beaten
- 8 cooked bacon strips, chopped
- 1/2 cup grated Parmesan cheese

Cook the linguine according to the package directions. Meanwhile, in a large skillet, saute the onion in oil until tender. Add garlic; cook 1 minute longer.

In a small bowl, whisk flour and cream until smooth; stir into the pan. Bring to a boil, stirring constantly. Reduce the heat; cook and stir for 1 minute or until thickened. Remove from the heat. Stir a small amount of the hot mixture into the eggs; return all to the pan, stirring constantly. Bring to a gentle boil; cook and stir 2 minutes longer.

Drain linguine; add to the pan. Stir in the bacon and cheese; heat through. **Yield:** 6 servings.

Chicken Enchilada Bake

(Pictured below)

PREP: 20 min. **BAKE:** 50 min. + standing

Kids and adults alike eat up this cheesy, south-of-the-border chicken bake...and ask for it again and again. It's true comfort food! *—Melanie Burns, Pueblo West, Colorado*

- 4-1/2 cups cubed cooked rotisserie chicken
- 1 can (28 ounces) green enchilada sauce
- 1-1/4 cups (10 ounces) sour cream
- 9 corn tortillas (6 inches), cut into 1-1/2-inch pieces
- 4 cups (16 ounces) shredded Monterey Jack cheese

In a greased 13-in. x 9-in. baking dish, layer half of the chicken, enchilada sauce, sour cream, tortillas and cheese. Repeat layers.

Cover and bake at 375° for 40 minutes. Uncover; bake 10 minutes longer or until bubbly. Let casserole stand for 15 minutes before serving. **Yield:** 10 servings.

Best-Loved Contest Winners

WHEN *Taste of Home* magazine kicked off its America's Best Loved Recipe Contest, cooks from all over sent in recipes—more than 10,000 in all! George Schroeder of Port Murray, New Jersey won the top prize with Gorgonzola Penne with Chicken. You'll find his outstanding recipe—as well as the runners-up—right here.

Italian Meatball Tortes

(Pictured below)

PREP: 1-1/4 hours + rising **BAKE:** 30 min.

This from-scratch entree is great for a special occasion. I love making it for my five grown children and their families when they visit.   —Sandy Blessing, Ocean Shores, Washington

      1 **package (1/4 ounce) active dry yeast**
   1/4 **cup warm water (110° to 115°)**
   3/4 **cup warm milk (110° to 115°)**
   1/4 **cup sugar**
   1/4 **cup shortening**
      1 **egg**
      1 **teaspoon salt**
3-1/2 to 3-3/4 **cups all-purpose flour**
MEATBALLS:
      1 **can (5 ounces) evaporated milk**
      2 **eggs, beaten**
      1 **cup quick-cooking oats**
      1 **cup crushed saltines**
   1/2 **cup chopped onion**
   1/2 **cup chopped celery**
      2 **teaspoons salt**
      2 **teaspoons chili powder**
   1/2 **teaspoon garlic powder**
   1/2 **teaspoon pepper**
      3 **pounds ground beef**

FILLING:
      1 **can (15 ounces) crushed tomatoes**
   1/2 **cup chopped onion**
   1/3 **cup grated Parmesan cheese**
      1 **teaspoon minced fresh parsley**
1-1/2 **teaspoons dried basil**
1-1/2 **teaspoons dried oregano**
      1 **teaspoon salt**
1-1/2 **cups (6 ounces) shredded part-skim mozzarella cheese**

In a large bowl, dissolve yeast in warm water. Add the milk, sugar, shortening, egg, salt and 2 cups flour. Beat until smooth. Stir in enough remaining flour to form a soft dough.

Turn onto a floured surface; knead until smooth and elastic, about 6-8 minutes. Place in a greased bowl, turning once to grease the top. Cover and let rise in a warm place until doubled, 1 to 1-1/2 hours.

In a large bowl, combine the milk, eggs, oats, saltines, onion, celery and seasonings. Crumble the beef over the mixture and mix well. Shape into 1-1/2-in. balls. In a large skillet over medium heat, cook the meatballs in batches until no longer pink.

Meanwhile, place the tomatoes and onion in a small saucepan. Bring to a boil. Reduce the heat; simmer, uncovered, for 10 minutes or until slightly thickened. Stir in the Parmesan cheese, herbs and salt.

Punch the dough down. Divide into three portions. Roll two portions into 11-in. circles; line the bottoms and press partially up the sides of two greased 9-in. springform pans. Roll third portion into a 12-in. x 10-in. rectangle; cut into twelve 10-in. x 1-in. strips.

Place meatballs in prepared crusts; top with tomato mixture and mozzarella. Make a lattice crust with dough strips; trim and seal edges. Cover; let rise for 30 minutes. Bake at 350° for 30-35 minutes or until golden brown. Cut into wedges. **Yield:** 2 tortes (6 servings each).

Mango Chicken with Plum Sauce

PREP: 25 min. **COOK:** 15 min.

I'm a retired nurse and enjoy all kinds of food, but particularly dishes that are low in calories, fat and carbs. This one fills the bill—deliciously!   —Christine Vaught, Salem, Oregon

      1 **tablespoon sugar**
      1 **tablespoon cornstarch**
   1/2 **teaspoon salt**
   1/2 **cup chicken broth**
   1/4 **cup teriyaki sauce**
   1/2 **pound fresh snow peas, trimmed**

2 large carrots, sliced diagonally
2 medium zucchini, sliced
1/2 cup chopped red onion
1/2 medium sweet red pepper, sliced
1 can (4 ounces) sliced water chestnuts, drained
2 tablespoons canola oil
1 pound finely chopped cooked chicken breast (about 3 cups)
2 medium mangoes, peeled and mashed
1/2 cup plum sauce
2 cups hot cooked brown rice
1/4 cup slivered almonds, toasted

In a small saucepan, combine the sugar, cornstarch and salt; stir in broth and teriyaki sauce until smooth. Cook and stir until thickened. Set aside.

In a large skillet or wok, stir-fry snow peas, carrots, zucchini, onion, pepper and water chestnuts in oil until crisp-tender. Add chicken, mangoes and broth mixture; heat through. Stir in the plum sauce. Serve with rice. Sprinkle with almonds. **Yield:** 6 servings.

Asian-Style Baby Back Ribs

PREP: 1-1/4 hours **GRILL:** 10 min.

My husband and I are empty nesters with two grown children and four grandkids. If you're cooking for two, these glazed ribs are a treat. —*Esther Danielson, San Marcos, California*

1-1/2 pounds pork baby back ribs
4-1/2 teaspoons molasses
1 tablespoon garlic salt
1 teaspoon onion powder
1 teaspoon Worcestershire sauce
GLAZE:
1/2 cup reduced-sodium soy sauce
3 tablespoons thawed pineapple juice concentrate
2 tablespoons rice vinegar
2 tablespoons hoisin sauce
2 tablespoons ketchup
1 teaspoon lemon juice
1 teaspoon whole grain mustard
1 teaspoon Worcestershire sauce
1 teaspoon minced fresh gingerroot
1/2 teaspoon minced garlic
Chopped green onion

Pat ribs dry. Combine the molasses, garlic salt, onion powder and Worcestershire sauce; brush over meat. Place ribs on a rack in a small shallow roasting pan. Cover and bake at 300° for 1 hour or until tender.

In a small saucepan, combine soy sauce, juice concentrate, vinegar, hoisin sauce, ketchup, lemon juice, mustard, Worcestershire, ginger and garlic. Bring to a boil. Reduce heat; simmer, uncovered, for 10 minutes or until slightly thickened, stirring occasionally.

Coat grill rack with cooking spray before starting grill. Brush ribs with some of glaze; grill over medium heat for 8-12 minutes or until browned, turning frequently and brushing with additional glaze. Serve remaining glaze on the side. Garnish with onion. **Yield:** 2 servings.

Penne Gorgonzola with Chicken

(Pictured above)

PREP/TOTAL TIME: 30 min.

I've been cooking since I was 16, but this is the first recipe contest I've ever entered. My wife cooks, too, and this pasta dish is one of our favorites. —*George Schroeder, Port Murray, New Jersey*

1 package (16 ounces) penne pasta
1 pound boneless skinless chicken breasts, cut into 1/2-inch pieces
1 tablespoon olive oil
1 large garlic clove, minced
1/4 cup white wine
1 cup heavy whipping cream
1/4 cup chicken broth
2 cups (8 ounces) crumbled Gorgonzola cheese
6 to 8 fresh sage leaves, thinly sliced
Salt and pepper to taste
Grated Parmigiano-Reggiano cheese and minced fresh parsley

Cook penne pasta according to the package directions. Meanwhile, in a large skillet over medium heat, brown the chicken in oil on all sides. Add garlic; cook 1 minute longer. Add the wine, stirring to loosen browned bits from pan.

Add cream and broth; cook until sauce is slightly thickened and chicken is no longer pink. Stir in the Gorgonzola cheese, sage, salt and pepper; cook just until cheese is melted.

Drain the penne pasta; toss with the sauce. Sprinkle with the Parmigiano-Reggiano cheese and parsley. **Yield:** 8 servings.

Mushroom-Blue Cheese Tenderloin

(Pictured above)

PREP: 10 min. + marinating **BAKE:** 45 min. + standing

This restaurant-style entree is so impressive and special-looking. I often double the mushroom-cheese sauce because it disappears quickly. —Eric Schoen, Lincoln, Nebraska

- 1-1/2 **cups soy sauce**
- 3/4 **cup Worcestershire sauce**
- 1 **beef tenderloin (3-1/2 to 4 pounds)**
- 4 **garlic cloves, minced**
- 1 **tablespoon coarsely ground pepper**
- 1 **can (10-1/2 ounces) condensed beef broth, undiluted**

SAUCE:
- 1/2 **cup butter, cubed**
- 1/2 **pound sliced fresh mushrooms**
- 2 **garlic cloves, minced**
- 1 **cup (4 ounces) crumbled blue cheese**
- 1 **tablespoon Worcestershire sauce**
- 1/4 **teaspoon caraway seeds**
- 4 **green onions, chopped**

In a large resealable plastic bag, combine soy sauce and Worcestershire sauce. Add the beef; seal bag and turn to coat. Refrigerate for 2 hours, turning occasionally.

Drain and discard marinade. Rub the beef with garlic and pepper; place in a shallow roasting pan. Add broth to the pan. Bake, uncovered, at 425° for 45-55 minutes or until meat reaches desired doneness (for medium-rare, a meat thermometer should read 145°; medium, 160°; well-done, 170°). Let stand for 10 minutes before slicing.

Meanwhile, in a small saucepan, melt the butter. Add the mushrooms and garlic; saute until tender. Add the

cheese, Worcestershire sauce and caraway seeds; cook and stir over low heat until the cheese is melted. Stir in the onions; heat through. Serve sauce with beef. **Yield:** 10 servings (1-1/2 cups sauce).

Chops with Corn Salsa

PREP: 15 min. + chilling **COOK:** 15 min.

I'll fix these south-of-the-border pork chops on just about any occasion. The recipe is not only popular with family and friends, but it's also fuss-free. —Diane Halferty, Corpus Christi, Texas

- 4-1/2 **teaspoons chili powder**
- 6 **boneless pork loin chops (3/4 inch thick *each*)**
- 2 **teaspoons canola oil**
- 1 **can (14-1/2 ounces) diced tomatoes with garlic and onion, undrained**
- 1 **can (11 ounces) Mexicorn, drained**
- 1 **can (2-1/4 ounces) sliced ripe olives, drained**
- 2 **tablespoons minced fresh cilantro**

Rub chili powder over both sides of pork chops. Cover and refrigerate for 20 minutes.

In a large skillet over medium-high heat, brown chops in oil; drain. Add the tomatoes, corn and olives. Reduce heat; cover and simmer for 12-16 minutes or until meat is tender and juices run clear. Remove chops and keep warm. Stir cilantro into corn mixture; serve with chops. **Yield:** 6 servings.

Glazed Shrimp & Asparagus

(Pictured below)

PREP/TOTAL TIME: 30 min.

With spicy Asian flavor, this 30-minute shrimp and asparagus combo is excellent for special dinners as well as busy weeknights. —Joan Duckworth, Lee's Summit, Missouri

- 8 **ounces uncooked whole wheat angel hair pasta**
- 1 **tablespoon cornstarch**
- 3/4 **cup water**

1 tablespoon soy sauce
1 tablespoon honey
1 pound uncooked large shrimp, peeled and deveined
3 teaspoons peanut *or* canola oil, *divided*
1 teaspoon sesame oil
1 pound fresh asparagus, trimmed and cut into 2- to 3-inch lengths
1 tablespoon minced fresh gingerroot
2 garlic cloves, minced
1/4 teaspoon crushed red pepper flakes
1 tablespoon sesame seeds

Cook pasta according to package directions. In a small bowl, combine the cornstarch, water, soy sauce and honey until smooth; set aside.

In a large skillet or wok, stir-fry shrimp in 1 teaspoon peanut oil and the sesame oil until shrimp turn pink. Remove and keep warm.

Stir-fry the asparagus in the remaining peanut oil for 2 minutes. Add ginger, garlic, pepper flakes and sesame seeds; stir-fry 2 minutes longer or until the asparagus is crisp-tender.

Stir cornstarch mixture and add to the pan. Bring to a boil; cook and stir for 2 minutes or until thickened. Add shrimp; heat through. Drain pasta; serve with shrimp mixture. **Yield:** 4 servings.

Cashew Beef Stir-Fry

PREP/TOTAL TIME: 30 min.

Cashews bring an added crunch to this mix of beef and colorful vegetables served over rice. Expect requests for second helpings!
—*Rhonda Ragen, Naples, Florida*

2 tablespoons cornstarch
2 cups cold water
4 tablespoons soy sauce, *divided*
1 bunch broccoli, chopped
3 medium carrots, julienned
2 tablespoons canola oil, *divided*
1 pound boneless beef sirloin steak, cut into thin strips
3 garlic cloves, minced
1/2 teaspoon pepper
2 medium green peppers, cut into strips
2 medium sweet red peppers, cut into strips
2 medium onions, halved and sliced
1 yellow summer squash, sliced
1-1/2 cups salted cashews
Hot cooked rice

In a small bowl, combine the cornstarch, water and 2 tablespoons soy sauce until smooth; set aside. In a very large skillet or a wok, stir-fry broccoli and carrots in 1 tablespoon oil until vegetables begin to soften. Add the beef, garlic, pepper and remaining soy sauce; stir-fry

until meat is no longer pink. Remove and keep warm.

In same pan, stir-fry green and red peppers, onions and squash in remaining oil until crisp-tender. Return beef to pan. Stir cornstarch mixture; add to pan. Bring to a boil; cook and stir for 2 minutes or until thickened. Stir in cashews. Serve with rice. **Yield:** 7 servings.

Turkey with Curried Cream Sauce

(Pictured below and on page 54)

PREP/TOTAL TIME: 30 min.

When we have extra turkey, we use it for this saucy dinner. But we call it a "turkey encore"—it's too good to be called leftovers.
—*Lori Lockrey, Scarborough, Ontario*

2 tablespoons butter
2 tablespoons all-purpose flour
1/2 teaspoon curry powder
1 cup chicken broth
1/4 cup milk
1 small yellow summer squash, sliced
1 small zucchini, sliced
1/2 small onion, thinly sliced
2 teaspoons canola oil
2 cups cubed cooked turkey breast
1/2 teaspoon grated lemon peel
Hot cooked rice
3 tablespoons chopped cashews

In a small saucepan, melt butter; stir in flour and curry until smooth. Gradually add broth and milk. Bring to a boil; cook and stir for 1-2 minutes or until thickened. Remove from the heat; set aside.

In a large skillet, saute the squash, zucchini and onion in oil until tender. Add turkey, lemon peel and reserved sauce; heat through. Serve with rice. Sprinkle each serving with cashews. **Yield:** 3 servings.

Orange Flank Steak

(Pictured below)

PREP: 10 min. + marinating **BROIL:** 10 min.

I've sampled many different steak recipes, but this is my all-time favorite. The homemade marinade is a breeze to create using everyday ingredients I usually have on hand. Best of all, it makes this inexpensive cut of meat taste like a tender, juicy treat.
—*Gloria Bisck, Deerwood, Minnesota*

- 1/4 **cup orange juice**
- 1/4 **cup canola oil**
- 2 **tablespoons ketchup**
- 4-1/2 **teaspoons soy sauce**
- 2 **garlic cloves, minced**
- 1 **teaspoon grated orange peel**
- 1/8 **teaspoon hot pepper sauce**
- 1 **beef flank steak (1 pound)**
- 1 **medium orange, sliced**

In a large resealable plastic bag, combine the first seven ingredients. Add the beef; seal bag and turn to coat. Refrigerate for 8 hours or overnight.

Broil steak 4-6 in. from the heat or grill, covered, over medium-hot heat for 4-6 minutes on each side or until meat reaches desired doneness (for medium-rare, a meat thermometer should read 145°; medium, 160°; well-done, 170°). Let stand for 10 minutes.

Meanwhile, broil or grill orange slices for 2 minutes. To serve, thinly slice steak across the grain. Garnish with orange slices. **Yield:** 4 servings.

Seafood Kabobs

PREP: 25 min. + marinating **BROIL:** 10 min.

These are delicious, easy—and fast! The recipe calls for halibut, shrimp and scallops, but feel free to use any firm, fresh fish or shellfish you like. —*Michelle Armistead, Marlboro, New Jersey*

- 1/4 **cup lemon juice**
- 1/4 **cup olive oil**
- 3 **teaspoons snipped fresh dill,** *divided*
- 1/2 **teaspoon salt**
- 1/2 **teaspoon white pepper**
- 1-1/2 **pounds halibut steaks, cut into 1-1/2-inch pieces**
- 18 **uncooked large shrimp, peeled and deveined**
- 18 **sea scallops**
- 1 *each* **large green, sweet red and yellow peppers, cut into 1-inch pieces**

In a small bowl, combine lemon juice, oil, 1 teaspoon dill, salt and pepper. Place halibut, shrimp and scallops in a large resealable plastic bag; place peppers in another large resealable plastic bag. Divide marinade between both bags. Seal bags and turn to coat; refrigerate for 15-20 minutes. Drain and discard marinade.

On six metal or soaked wooden skewers, alternately thread halibut, shrimp, scallops and peppers. Sprinkle with remaining dill. Broil 6 in. from heat or grill, covered, over medium heat for 4-5 minutes on each side or until halibut flakes easily with a fork, shrimp turn pink and scallops are firm and opaque. **Yield:** 6 servings.

Chicken Mushroom Stir-Fry

PREP: 20 min. + marinating **COOK:** 10 min.

When I had co-workers sample this colorful stir-fry, the dish ended up empty in no time. After that, I knew it was a winner.
—*Christina Thompson, Howell, Michigan*

- 1 **tablespoon soy sauce**
- 1 **egg white**
- 1 **teaspoon sesame oil**
- 1/2 **teaspoon brown sugar**
- 1 **teaspoon cornstarch**
- 1/8 **teaspoon white pepper**
- 1 **pound boneless skinless chicken breasts, cut into 1/2-inch cubes**
- 2 **tablespoons cornstarch**
- 1/2 **cup chicken broth**
- 1/4 **cup oyster sauce**
- 2 **tablespoons cold water**
- 4 **tablespoons vegetable oil,** *divided*
- 1-1/2 **teaspoons minced fresh gingerroot**
- 2 **garlic cloves, minced**
- 2 **green onions, sliced**
- 4 **medium carrots, cubed**
- 1 **pound fresh mushrooms, quartered**
- 1/4 **pound fresh snow pea pods, trimmed and cut in half**

In a bowl, combine the first six ingredients; toss with chicken. Refrigerate for 30 minutes. In a small bowl, combine the cornstarch, broth, oyster sauce and water until smooth. Set aside.

In a wok or large skillet, heat 2 tablespoons oil over medium-high. Add the ginger, garlic and onions; stir-fry 1 minute. Add the chicken and continue to stir-fry until the chicken is no longer pink. Remove the chicken and vegetables from pan. Add remaining oil; stir-fry carrots 3 minutes or until crisp-tender. Add mushrooms and pea pods; stir-fry 1 minute. Return chicken and vegetables to pan. Stir broth mixture and pour into skillet, cook and stir until the sauce is thickened. Serve immediately. **Yield:** 6 servings.

Chicken with Rosemary Butter Sauce

(Pictured above)

PREP/TOTAL TIME: 25 min.

This simply elegant entree requires a minimum of effort but is sure to win you kudos from your family or guests. They'll love the butter sauce! —Connie McDowell, Greenwood, Delaware

- **4 boneless skinless chicken breast halves (4 ounces *each*)**
- **4 tablespoons butter, *divided***
- **1/2 cup white wine *or* chicken broth**
- **1/2 cup heavy whipping cream**
- **1 tablespoon minced fresh rosemary**

In a large skillet over medium heat, cook the chicken in 1 tablespoon butter for 4-5 minutes on each side or until juices run clear. Remove and keep warm.

Add wine to pan; cook over medium-low heat, stirring to loosen browned bits from pan. Add cream and bring to a boil. Reduce heat; cook and stir until slightly thickened. Stir in rosemary and remaining butter until blended. Serve sauce with chicken. **Yield:** 4 servings.

Barbecued Ribs

PREP: 2-1/4 hours **GRILL:** 10 min.

You'll need just a handful of ingredients to jazz up these grilled ribs. They always turn out juicy and have lip-smacking flavor. —Catherine Santich, Alamo, California

- **1 teaspoon salt**
- **1 teaspoon Italian seasoning**
- **1/2 teaspoon pepper**
- **1 rack pork spareribs (3 to 4 pounds)**
- **1 bottle (12 ounces) beer**
- **2/3 cup barbecue sauce**

Rub the salt, Italian seasoning and pepper over the ribs and place in a shallow roasting pan; add beer. Cover and bake at 325° for 2 hours.

Coat the grill rack with cooking spray before starting the grill. Drain ribs. Spoon some of the sauce over ribs. Grill, covered, over medium heat for 8-10 minutes or until browned, turning occasionally and brushing with sauce. **Yield:** 3 servings.

Hamburger Stir-Fry

(Pictured above)

PREP/TOTAL TIME: 25 min.

Here's a quick teriyaki stir–fry that features ground beef instead of the usual beef strips. It's different enough to be a treat for the taste buds. —*Kathi and John Horst, Westfield, New York*

☑ This recipe includes Nutrition Facts and Diabetic Exchanges.

- 1 tablespoon sugar
- 1 tablespoon cornstarch
- 1 tablespoon ground mustard
- 1/3 cup water
- 1/3 cup reduced-sodium teriyaki sauce
- 1 pound lean ground beef
- 1 package (16 ounces) frozen asparagus stir-fry vegetable blend
- 1 medium onion, halved and thinly sliced
- 2 teaspoons canola oil
- 2 cups hot cooked rice
- 2 teaspoons sesame seeds

In a small bowl, combine the sugar, cornstarch and mustard. Stir in water and teriyaki sauce until smooth; set aside.

In a large skillet or wok, stir-fry beef until no longer pink; drain and set aside. In the same pan, stir-fry the vegetable blend and onion in oil until crisp-tender.

Stir cornstarch mixture and add to the pan. Bring to a boil; cook and stir for 1-2 minutes or until thickened. Add beef; heat through. Serve with rice. Sprinkle with sesame seeds. **Yield:** 4 servings.

Nutrition Facts: 1 cup stir-fry with 1/2 cup rice equals 399 calories, 12 g fat (4 g saturated fat), 56 mg cholesterol, 516 mg sodium, 42 g carbohydrate, 3 g fiber, 28 g protein. **Diabetic Exchanges:** 3 lean meat, 2 starch, 2 vegetable, 1/2 fat.

Philly Cheesesteak Pizza

(Pictured below and on page 54)

PREP: 30 min. **BAKE:** 10 min.

Using leftover beef and a prebaked bread shell saves time when you're in the mood for great homemade pizza. And this is truly a great one! —*Laura McDowell, Lake Villa, Illinois*

- 1 small green pepper, julienned
- 1 small sweet red pepper, julienned
- 1-3/4 cups sliced fresh mushrooms
- 1 small onion, halved and sliced
- 1-1/2 teaspoons canola oil
- 4 garlic cloves, minced
- 1 prebaked Italian bread shell crust (14 ounces)
- 1/2 cup pizza sauce
- 2 ounces cream cheese, cubed
- 2 cups (8 ounces) shredded provolone cheese, *divided*
- 1 cup shredded *or* julienned cooked roast beef
- 1/3 cup pickled pepper rings
- 1/4 cup grated Parmesan cheese
- 1/2 teaspoon dried oregano

In a large skillet, saute peppers, mushrooms and onion in oil until tender. Add garlic; cook 1 minute longer.

Place the bread shell crust on an ungreased 12-in. pizza pan. Spread the pizza sauce over the crust and dot with cream cheese. Sprinkle with 1 cup provolone cheese. Top with pepper mixture, beef, pepper rings and

remaining provolone cheese. Sprinkle with Parmesan cheese and oregano.

Bake at 450° for 10-12 minutes or until the cheese is melted. **Yield:** 6 slices.

Creamy Prosciutto Pasta

PREP/TOTAL TIME: 10 min.

I'm always looking for dinners I can put together quickly. Here, I relied on grocery store convenience products to re-create a favorite pasta dish from an Italian restaurant. Add bread and a salad for a complete meal. —Christine Ward, Austin, Texas

- 1 package (9 ounces) refrigerated fettuccine *or* refrigerated linguine
- 1/2 pound sliced fresh mushrooms
- 1 small onion, chopped
- 1 tablespoon butter
- 1 package (10 ounces) fresh baby spinach
- 1 jar (17 ounces) Alfredo sauce
- 1/3 pound thinly sliced prosciutto, chopped

Cook the pasta according to the package directions. Meanwhile, in a large saucepan, saute the mushrooms and onion in the butter until tender. Add the spinach. Bring to a boil. Reduce the heat; cook just until the spinach is wilted.

Stir in the Alfredo sauce and prosciutto; cook for 1-2 minutes or until heated through. Drain pasta; add to sauce and toss to coat. **Yield:** 4 servings.

Cilantro Chicken

PREP/TOTAL TIME: 30 min.

If you like cilantro, you'll definitely like this! It enhances plain chicken breasts with fresh herb flavor, as well as caramelized onions, lemon juice and cumin. I serve this entree with rice. —Mary Pipkin, Melba, Idaho

- 1 pound boneless skinless chicken breasts, cut into 1-inch cubes
- 1/2 teaspoon salt
- 1/2 teaspoon ground cumin
- 1/4 teaspoon pepper
- 4 tablespoons butter, *divided*
- 2 large onions, sliced
- 1/2 cup lemon juice
- 1/4 cup minced fresh cilantro

Hot cooked rice

Sprinkle chicken with salt, cumin and pepper. In a large skillet over medium heat, cook and stir the chicken in 2 tablespoons butter until no longer pink. Remove and keep warm.

In the same skillet, saute onions in remaining butter until tender and golden brown. Return chicken to the pan. Stir in the lemon juice and cilantro; bring to a boil. Serve with rice. **Yield:** 4 servings.

Ravioli with Shrimp Tomato Sauce

(Pictured above)

PREP/TOTAL TIME: 30 min.

After sampling a similar dish when my husband and I went out to dinner for our 25th anniversary, I came up with this recipe I can make at home. —Nettie Smith, Loveland, Colorado

- 1/2 cup chopped onion
- 2 tablespoons butter
- 2 tablespoons all-purpose flour
- 1 can (14-1/2 ounces) Italian stewed tomatoes
- 1 tablespoon brown sugar
- 1 bay leaf
- 1 whole clove
- 1/2 teaspoon dried basil
- 1/2 teaspoon salt
- 1/8 to 1/4 teaspoon pepper
- 2 packages (9 ounces *each*) fresh *or* frozen cheese ravioli
- 1-1/2 cups heavy whipping cream
- 1/2 pound cooked medium shrimp, peeled and deveined
- 1 tablespoon grated Parmesan cheese
- 1 tablespoon minced chives

In a large skillet, saute the onion in butter until tender. Stir in flour until blended. Bring to a boil; cook and stir until thickened.

Place tomatoes in a blender, cover and process until pureed; add to onion mixture. Stir in the brown sugar, bay leaf, clove, basil, salt and pepper. Bring to a boil. Reduce heat; cover and simmer for 10 minutes.

Meanwhile, cook the ravioli according to the package directions. Remove and discard the bay leaf and clove from the sauce. Reduce heat; gradually stir in cream. Add shrimp; heat through. Drain ravioli; top with sauce, Parmesan cheese and chives. **Yield:** 5 servings.

Breads, Rolls & Muffins

What a treat—freshly baked cinnamon buns, spiced loaves and other golden goodies warm from the oven. They're as close as the tempting recipes here!

FRESH FAVORITES. Clockwise from top left: Peanut Butter Banana Bread (p. 90), Rhubarb Coffee Cake with Caramel Sauce (p. 87), Hot Cross Buns (p. 92), Corn Bread with a Kick (p. 87) and Orange Nut Bread & Cream Cheese Spread (p. 91).

Peppery Cheese Bread

(Pictured above)

PREP: 15 min. **BAKE:** 45 min. + cooling

This is my daughter Kendra's favorite savory quick bread, and a loaf never lasts long at our house. When you bite into a warm, moist slice, it's just heavenly! —Sharon Boren, Salem, Oregon

- 2-1/2 **cups all-purpose flour**
-     1 **tablespoon sugar**
- 1-1/2 **teaspoons coarsely ground pepper**
-     1 **teaspoon baking powder**
-   3/4 **teaspoon salt**
-   1/2 **teaspoon baking soda**
-     2 **eggs**
-     1 **cup (8 ounces) reduced-fat plain yogurt**
-   1/2 **cup canola oil**
-   1/4 **cup milk**
-     1 **tablespoon spicy brown mustard**
-     1 **cup (4 ounces) shredded cheddar cheese**
-     2 **green onions, thinly sliced**

In a large bowl, combine the first six ingredients. In a small bowl, whisk the eggs, yogurt, oil, milk and mustard. Stir into dry ingredients just until moistened. Fold in cheese and onions.

Transfer to a greased 9-in. x 5-in. loaf pan. Bake at 350° for 45-55 minutes or until a toothpick inserted near the center comes out clean. Cool for 10 minutes before removing from pan to a wire rack. **Yield:** 1 loaf (16 slices).

Chive & Lemon Biscuits

PREP/TOTAL TIME: 30 min.

An unexpected pairing of flavors makes these biscuits delightfully different. They're wonderful fresh from the oven and spread with a little butter. —Jim Gales, Glendale, Wisconsin

- 2 **cups all-purpose flour**
- 3 **teaspoons baking powder**
- 1 **teaspoon sugar**
- 1 **teaspoon salt**
- 1/2 **cup cold butter**
- 3/4 **cup half-and-half cream**
- 1/2 **cup minced chives**
- 1-1/2 **teaspoons grated lemon peel**
- 1 **egg**
- 1 **tablespoon water**

In a large bowl, combine the flour, baking powder, sugar and salt. Cut in butter until mixture resembles coarse crumbs. Stir in cream just until moistened. Stir in chives and lemon peel. Turn onto a lightly floured surface; knead 8-10 times.

Pat or roll out to 3/4-in. thickness; cut with a floured 2-1/2-in. biscuit cutter. Place 2 in. apart on a greased baking sheet. In a small bowl, whisk egg and water; brush over biscuits. Bake at 400° for 15-20 minutes or until golden brown. Serve warm. **Yield:** 9 biscuits.

Chocolate Chai Mini Loaves

PREP: 25 min. **BAKE:** 35 min. + cooling

This popular bread is irresistible. A friend of mine "complains" when I give her a loaf because she just can't help but eat the whole thing! —Lisa Christensen, Poplar Grove, Illinois

- 2 **squares (1 ounce *each*) semisweet chocolate, chopped**
- 1/2 **cup water**
- 1/2 **cup butter, softened**
- 1 **cup packed brown sugar**
- 2 **eggs**
- 1 **teaspoon vanilla extract**
- 1-1/2 **cups all-purpose flour**
- 3 **tablespoons chai tea latte mix**
- 1 **teaspoon baking soda**
- 1/2 **teaspoon salt**
- 1/2 **cup sour cream**

FROSTING:
- 1 **cup confectioners' sugar**
- 1 **tablespoon butter, softened**
- 1 **tablespoon chai tea latte mix**
- 1/2 **teaspoon vanilla extract**
- 4 **to 5 teaspoons milk**

In a microwave, melt chocolate with the water; stir until smooth. Cool slightly. In a large bowl, cream butter and brown sugar until light and fluffy. Add eggs, one at a time, beating well after each addition. Beat in vanilla, then chocolate mixture.

Combine the flour, latte mix, baking soda and salt; add to creamed mixture alternately with sour cream.

Transfer to three greased 5-3/4-in. x 3-in. x 2-in. loaf pans. Bake at 350° for 35-40 minutes or until a toothpick inserted near the center comes out clean. Cool for 10 minutes before removing from pans to a wire rack to cool completely.

For frosting, combine the confectioners' sugar, butter, latte mix, vanilla and enough milk to achieve desired consistency. **Yield:** 3 mini loaves (6 slices each).

Rhubarb Coffee Cake With Caramel Sauce

(Pictured below and on page 85)

PREP: 20 min. **BAKE:** 35 min. + cooling

When I was growing up, I couldn't wait for the rhubarb to ripen so Mom could bake this luscious coffee cake. Now, the recipe is part of my own collection. —Angie Fehr, Ottosen, Iowa

- **1/2 cup shortening**
- **1-1/2 cups sugar**
- **1 egg**
- **2 cups all-purpose flour**
- **1 teaspoon baking soda**
- **1 cup buttermilk**
- **1-1/2 cups finely chopped fresh *or* frozen rhubarb**

TOPPING:
- **1/2 cup packed brown sugar**
- **1/4 cup all-purpose flour**
- **1 teaspoon ground cinnamon**
- **3 tablespoons cold butter**

SAUCE:
- **1/2 cup butter, cubed**
- **1 cup packed brown sugar**
- **1/2 cup heavy whipping cream**

In a large bowl, cream shortening and sugar until light and fluffy. Add egg; beat well. Combine flour and baking soda; add to creamed mixture alternately with buttermilk. Fold in rhubarb. Transfer to a greased 13-in. x 9-in. baking pan.

For topping, in a small bowl, combine the brown sugar, flour and cinnamon; cut in butter until crumbly. Sprinkle over batter.

Bake at 350° for 35-40 minutes or until a toothpick inserted near the center comes out clean. Cool for 10 minutes before serving.

For sauce, in a small saucepan, melt butter. Stir in brown sugar and cream; bring to a boil. Reduce heat; simmer for 3-4 minutes or until slightly thickened. Serve with warm coffee cake. **Yield:** 18 servings (1-2/3 cups sauce).

Corn Bread with a Kick

(Pictured above and on page 84)

PREP: 20 min. **BAKE:** 20 min.

To me, nothing says Southern cooking like crisp corn bread made in a cast–iron skillet. I use a very old skillet that belonged to my great–aunt. —Geordyth Sullivan, Cutler Bay, Florida

- **2/3 cup all-purpose flour**
- **2/3 cup cornmeal**
- **1 tablespoon sugar**
- **1/2 teaspoon baking powder**
- **1/2 teaspoon salt**
- **1/4 teaspoon baking soda**
- **1 egg**
- **1 cup buttermilk**
- **3 tablespoons butter**
- **3 chipotle peppers in adobo sauce, drained and chopped**
- **6 bacon strips, cooked and crumbled**

In a large bowl, combine the first six ingredients. In another bowl, whisk egg and buttermilk.

Place butter in an 8-in. ovenproof skillet; heat skillet in a 425° oven for 3-5 minutes or until butter is melted. Meanwhile, stir egg mixture into dry ingredients just until moistened. Fold in peppers and bacon.

Carefully swirl the butter in the skillet to coat the sides and bottom of pan; add batter. Bake at 425° for 18-22 minutes or until golden brown. Cut into wedges; serve warm. **Yield:** 8 servings.

Tomato & Brie Focaccia

(Pictured below)

PREP: 20 min. + rising **BAKE:** 25 min.

Combine tender yeast bread with creamy, melted Brie cheese and tomatoes, and you've got an appetizer that guests will line up for. This focaccia can also make an ideal side for salad or soup.
—*Laurie Figone, Petaluma, California*

2-1/2 to 3 cups all-purpose flour
  2 packages (1/4 ounce *each*) quick-rise yeast
  1 teaspoon sugar
  1 teaspoon salt
  1 cup water
1/4 cup plus 1 tablespoon olive oil, *divided*
  1 can (14-1/2 ounces) diced tomatoes, drained
  2 garlic cloves, minced
  1 teaspoon Italian seasoning
  6 ounces Brie cheese, cut into 1/2-inch cubes

In a large bowl, combine 2 cups flour, yeast, sugar and salt. In a small saucepan, heat the water and 1/4 cup oil to 120°-130°. Add to the dry ingredients; beat just until moistened. Stir in enough remaining flour to form a soft dough.

Turn the dough onto a floured surface; knead until smooth and elastic, about 6-8 minutes. Place in a greased bowl, turning once to grease the top. Cover and let rise for 20 minutes.

Punch dough down. Press into a greased 13-in. x 9-in. baking pan. Cover and let rest for 10 minutes.

In a small bowl, combine the tomatoes, garlic, Italian seasoning and remaining oil. Spread over dough; top with cheese. Bake at 375° for 25-30 minutes or until golden brown and cheese is melted. Place pan on a wire rack. **Yield:** 12 servings.

Lambertville Station Coconut Bread

PREP: 10 min. + rising **BAKE:** 40 min. + cooling

Hearty bread made with toasted coconut is a long-time specialty at Lambertville Station in Lambertville, New Jersey. Enjoy this sweet treat the next time you crave distinctive bakery.

✓ This recipe includes Nutrition Facts and Diabetic Exchanges.

  3 cups all-purpose flour
  1 cup sugar
  3 teaspoons baking powder
3/4 teaspoon salt
  1 egg
1-1/2 cups milk
3/4 teaspoon vanilla extract
1/4 teaspoon almond extract
  1 cup flaked coconut, toasted

In a large bowl, combine the flour, sugar, baking powder and salt. Combine the egg, milk and extracts. Stir into dry ingredients just until moistened. Fold in coconut.

Transfer to a greased 9-in. x 5-in. loaf pan. Bake at 350° for 40-50 minutes or until a toothpick comes out clean. Cool for 10 minutes before removing from pan to a wire rack. **Yield:** 1 loaf (16 slices).

Nutrition Facts: 1 slice equals 182 calories, 3 g fat (2 g saturated fat), 16 mg cholesterol, 215 mg sodium, 34 g carbohydrate, 1 g fiber, 4 g protein. **Diabetic Exchanges:** 2 starch, 1/2 fat.

Perfect Pizza Crust

PREP: 20 min. + rising **BAKE:** 10 min.

I've spent years trying different recipes and techniques to achieve the perfect pizza crust, and I think this is it! My family actually prefers it to the pizza parlor's. —*Lesli Dustin, Nibley, Utah*

  1 tablespoon active dry yeast
1-1/2 cups warm water (110° to 115°)
  2 tablespoons sugar
1/2 teaspoon salt
  2 cups bread flour
1-1/2 cups whole wheat flour
Cornmeal
Pizza toppings of your choice

In a large bowl, dissolve yeast in warm water. Add the sugar, salt, 1 cup bread flour and the whole wheat flour. Beat until smooth. Stir in enough remaining bread flour to form a soft dough (dough will be sticky).

Turn onto a floured surface; knead until smooth and elastic, about 6-8 minutes. Place in a greased bowl, turning once to grease the top. Cover and let rise in a warm place until doubled, about 1 hour.

Punch dough down; roll into a 15-in. circle. Grease a 14-in. pizza pan and sprinkle with cornmeal. Transfer

cheese) equals 124 calories, 3 g fat (trace saturated fat), 1 mg cholesterol, 145 mg sodium, 23 g carbohydrate, 2 g fiber, 3 g protein. **Diabetic Exchange:** 1-1/2 starch.

Sweet Potato Bread & Pineapple Butter

(Pictured below)

PREP: 20 min. **BAKE:** 50 min. + cooling

You won't want to skip the special butter when making this unique bread. The combination of tangy pineapple and spicy sweetness is delicious. —*Diane Goss, Chester, Virginia*

- 1-3/4 **cups all-purpose flour**
- 1-1/2 **cups sugar**
- 1-1/2 **teaspoons ground cinnamon**
  - 1 **teaspoon ground nutmeg**
- 1/2 **teaspoon baking soda**
- 1/2 **teaspoon baking powder**
- 1/2 **teaspoon salt**
  - 2 **eggs**
  - 1 **cup mashed sweet potatoes**
- 1/2 **cup canola oil**
- 1/3 **cup water**

BUTTER:
- 1/2 **cup butter, softened**
  - 1 **can (8 ounces) crushed pineapple, well drained**

In a large bowl, combine the first seven ingredients. In a small bowl, combine the eggs, potatoes, oil and water. Stir into dry ingredients just until moistened.

Transfer to a greased 9-in. x 5-in. loaf pan. Bake at 350° for 50-60 minutes or until a toothpick inserted near the center comes out clean. Cool for 10 minutes before removing from pan to a wire rack.

In a small bowl, combine butter and pineapple. Serve with bread. **Yield:** 1 loaf (16 slices) and 1 cup butter.

dough to prepared pan; build up edges slightly.

Add toppings of your choice. Bake at 425° for 10-15 minutes or until crust is golden brown and toppings are lightly browned and heated through. **Yield:** 8 servings.

Authentic Boston Brown Bread

(Pictured above)

PREP: 20 min. **COOK:** 50 min. + standing

The old-fashioned flavor of this rustic quick bread is out of this world. Spread a warm slice with cream cheese for a real treat. —*Sharon Delaney-Chronis, South Milwaukee, Wisconsin*

☑ This recipe includes Nutrition Facts and Diabetic Exchanges.

- 1/2 **cup cornmeal**
- 1/2 **cup whole wheat flour**
- 1/2 **cup rye flour**
- 1/2 **teaspoon baking powder**
- 1/2 **teaspoon baking soda**
- 1/4 **teaspoon salt**
  - 1 **cup buttermilk**
- 1/3 **cup molasses**
  - 2 **tablespoons brown sugar**
  - 1 **tablespoon canola oil**
  - 3 **tablespoons chopped walnuts, toasted**
  - 3 **tablespoons raisins**

Cream cheese, softened, optional

In a small bowl, combine the first six ingredients. In another bowl, combine the buttermilk, molasses, brown sugar and oil; stir into dry ingredients just until moistened. Fold in walnuts and raisins. Transfer to a greased 8-in. x 4-in. loaf pan; cover with foil.

Place pan on a rack in a deep kettle; add 1 in. of hot water to kettle. Bring to a gentle boil; cover and steam for 45-50 minutes or until a toothpick inserted near the center comes out clean, adding more water to the kettle as needed.

Remove pan from the kettle; let stand for 10 minutes before removing bread from pan to a wire rack. Serve with cream cheese if desired. **Yield:** 1 loaf (12 slices).

Nutrition Facts: 1 slice (calculated without cream

soda and cinnamon; stir into the creamed mixture just until moistened.

Divide half of the batter between two greased 8-in. x 4-in. loaf pans; sprinkle with half of the topping. Top with chocolate chips. Repeat layers of batter and topping.

Bake at 350° for 45-55 minutes or until a toothpick inserted near the center comes out clean. Cool for 10 minutes before removing from pans to wire racks. **Yield:** 2 loaves (12 slices each).

Peanut Butter Banana Bread

(Pictured above and on page 84)

PREP: 25 min. **BAKE:** 45 min. + cooling

Family members literally come running to the kitchen when they smell this bread baking. With a chocolate layer and crumbly topping, it's scrumptious. —Sherry Lee, Columbus, Ohio

TOPPING:
    1/2 **cup all-purpose flour**
    1/2 **cup packed brown sugar**
    1/4 **cup creamy peanut butter**
    1/2 **teaspoon ground cinnamon**
BATTER:
    1/2 **cup butter, softened**
      1 **package (8 ounces) cream cheese, softened**
  1-1/4 **cups sugar**
      2 **eggs**
      1 **cup mashed ripe bananas**
      1 **teaspoon vanilla extract**
  2-1/4 **cups all-purpose flour**
  1-1/2 **teaspoons baking powder**
    1/2 **teaspoon baking soda**
      1 **teaspoon ground cinnamon**
  1-1/2 **cups semisweet chocolate chips**

In a small bowl, stir the flour, brown sugar, peanut butter and cinnamon until crumbly; set aside.

In a large bowl, cream the butter, cream cheese and sugar until light and fluffy. Add eggs, one at a time, beating well after each addition. Beat in the bananas and vanilla. Combine the flour, baking powder, baking

Blue Cheese & Shallot Bread

PREP: 20 min. **BAKE:** 50 min. + cooling

You'll definitely want to cut yourself a thick slice of this savory, cheesy loaf. The robust taste will have everyone asking for the recipe—and seconds! —Rita Rowland, Auburn, Kentucky

    1/2 **cup chopped shallots**
      3 **tablespoons butter**
      2 **cups all-purpose flour**
      1 **tablespoon sugar**
  2-1/2 **teaspoons baking powder**
      1 **teaspoon salt**
      1 **teaspoon ground mustard**
    1/4 **cup cold butter**
      1 **egg**
      1 **cup milk**
    3/4 **cup crumbled blue cheese**
      2 **tablespoons grated Parmesan cheese**

In a small skillet, saute shallots in butter until tender; set aside.

In a large bowl, combine the flour, sugar, baking powder, salt and mustard. Cut in butter until mixture resembles coarse crumbs. In a small bowl, whisk egg and milk. Stir into crumb mixture just until moistened. Fold in cheeses and reserved shallot mixture.

Transfer to a greased 8-in. x 4-in. loaf pan. Bake at 325° for 50-60 minutes or until a toothpick inserted near the center comes out clean. Cool for 10 minutes before removing from pan to wire rack. **Yield:** 1 loaf (12 slices).

Spice Bread with Maple Butter

PREP: 25 min. **BAKE:** 40 min. + cooling

This hearty quick bread gets into the oven in a jiffy. I whip up the yummy maple-flavored butter for the perfect finishing touch. —Katherine Nelson, Centerville, Utah

    1/4 **cup butter, softened**
    3/4 **cup sugar**
      2 **eggs**
    1/2 **teaspoon vanilla extract**
      1 **cup all-purpose flour**
    1/2 **cup whole wheat flour**
      2 **teaspoons baking powder**

1/2 teaspoon ground cinnamon
1/4 teaspoon ground nutmeg
1/4 teaspoon ground allspice
1/4 teaspoon salt
1/3 cup milk
1/2 cup chopped walnuts
BUTTER:
1/2 cup butter, softened
2 tablespoons maple syrup
1/2 teaspoon ground cinnamon

In a large bowl, cream butter and sugar until light and fluffy. Add eggs, one at a time, beating well after each addition. Beat in vanilla. Combine the flours, baking powder, spices and salt; add to creamed mixture alternately with milk. Fold in walnuts.

Transfer to a greased 8-in. x 4-in. loaf pan. Bake at 350° for 40-45 minutes or until a toothpick inserted near the center comes out clean. Cool for 10 minutes before removing from pan to a wire rack.

Beat butter ingredients until blended; serve with bread. **Yield:** 1 loaf (12 slices) and 1/2 cup butter.

Savory Dill & Caraway Scones

PREP: 20 min. **BAKE:** 15 min.

The unique dill and caraway combination in these tender scones makes them perfect for breakfast, brunch or an afternoon tea.
—Sally Sibthorpe, Shelby Township, Michigan

2 cups all-purpose flour
4-1/2 teaspoons sugar
1 tablespoon onion powder
1 tablespoon snipped fresh dill *or* 1 teaspoon dill weed
2 teaspoons caraway seeds
1 teaspoon baking powder
3/4 teaspoon salt
1/2 teaspoon baking soda
1/2 teaspoon coarsely ground pepper
6 tablespoons cold butter
1 egg yolk
3/4 cup sour cream
1/2 cup ricotta cheese
4 teaspoons heavy whipping cream
Additional caraway seeds, optional

In a large bowl, combine the first nine ingredients. Cut in butter until mixture resembles coarse crumbs. Combine the egg yolk, sour cream and ricotta cheese; stir into crumb mixture just until moistened. Turn onto a floured surface; knead 10 times.

Pat into two 6-in. circles. Cut each into six wedges. Separate wedges and place on a greased baking sheet. Brush tops with cream; sprinkle with additional caraway seeds if desired. Bake at 400° for 15-18 minutes or until golden brown. Serve warm. **Yield:** 1 dozen.

Orange Nut Bread & Cream Cheese Spread

(Pictured below and on page 84)

PREP: 40 min. **BAKE:** 35 min. + cooling

This delectable sweet bread was my mother's favorite. Every bite gives you a burst of orange and the crunch of chopped walnuts.
—Karen Sue Garback–Pristera, Albany, New York

1/3 cup butter, softened
2/3 cup sugar
2 eggs
1/2 teaspoon orange extract
1/2 teaspoon vanilla extract
2 cups all-purpose flour
1 teaspoon baking powder
1/2 teaspoon salt
1/4 teaspoon baking soda
1 cup orange juice
1 cup chopped walnuts
SPREAD:
1 package (8 ounces) cream cheese, softened
2 tablespoons orange juice
1 tablespoon confectioners' sugar
1 teaspoon grated orange peel

In a large bowl, cream butter and sugar until light and fluffy. Add eggs, one at a time, beating well after each addition. Beat in extracts. Combine the flour, baking powder, salt and baking soda; add to creamed mixture alternately with orange juice. Fold in walnuts.

Transfer to three greased 5-3/4-in. x 3-in. x 2-in. loaf pans. Bake at 350° for 35-40 minutes or until a toothpick inserted near the center comes out clean. Cool for 10 minutes before removing from pans to wire racks.

In a small bowl, beat the cream cheese, orange juice, confectioners' sugar and peel until well blended. Chill until serving. **Yield:** 3 mini loaves (6 slices each) and 1 cup spread.

Hot Cross Buns

(Pictured below and on page 85)

PREP: 45 min. + rising **BAKE:** 15 min.

My husband's grandma used to bake a batch of these every year for Good Friday, and now I make my own version of her recipe.
—Jill Evely, Wilmore, Kentucky

  4 **packages (1/4 ounce *each*) active dry yeast**
  3 **cups warm milk (110° to 115°)**
  2 **cups canola oil**
  8 **eggs**
  4 **eggs, *separated***
1-1/3 **cups sugar**
  4 **teaspoons ground cinnamon**
  3 **teaspoons salt**
  2 **teaspoons ground cardamom**
 13 **to 15 cups all-purpose flour**
2-2/3 **cups raisins**
  2 **teaspoons water**
ICING:
  3 **cups confectioners' sugar**
  2 **tablespoons butter, melted**
  4 **to 5 tablespoons milk**

In a very large bowl, dissolve yeast in warm milk. Add oil, eggs, egg yolks, sugar, cinnamon, salt, cardamom and 10 cups flour. Beat until smooth. Stir in enough remaining flour to form a firm dough. Stir in raisins.

Turn onto a floured surface; knead until smooth and elastic, about 6-8 minutes. Place in a greased bowl, turning once to grease the top. Cover and let rise in a warm place until doubled, about 1-1/4 hours.

Punch dough down. Turn onto a lightly floured surface. Cover and let rest for 10 minutes. Divide into 72 pieces; shape each into a ball. Place 2 in. apart in four greased 15-in. x 10-in. x 1-in. baking pans. Cover and let rise in a warm place until doubled, about 40 minutes. Combine egg whites and water; brush over rolls.

Bake at 375° for 12-15 minutes or until golden brown. Remove from pans to cool on wire racks. For icing, combine the confectioners' sugar, butter and enough milk to achieve desired consistency. Pipe an "X" on top of each bun. **Yield:** 6 dozen.

Old-Fashioned Brown Bread

PREP: 20 min. + rising **BAKE:** 35 min. + cooling

This chewy, traditional bread from the Kings Landing Historical Settlement in Kings Landing, New Brunswick boasts a slightly sweet flavor that will transport you back to olden days.

☑ This recipe includes Nutrition Facts and Diabetic Exchanges.

2-1/3 **cups boiling water**
  1 **cup old-fashioned oats**
1/2 **cup butter, cubed**
1/3 **cup molasses**
5-1/2 **to 6-1/2 cups all-purpose flour**
  5 **teaspoons active dry yeast**
  2 **teaspoons salt**

In a large bowl, pour boiling water over oats. Stir in butter and molasses. Let stand until mixture cools to 120°-130°, stirring occasionally.

In another bowl, combine 3-1/2 cups flour, yeast and salt. Beat in oat mixture until blended. Stir in enough remaining flour to form a soft dough.

Turn onto a floured surface; knead until smooth and elastic, about 6-8 minutes. Place in a greased bowl, turning once to grease the top. Cover and let rise in a warm place until doubled, about 1 hour.

Punch dough down. Turn onto a lightly floured surface; divide in half. Shape into loaves. Place in two greased 9-in. x 5-in. loaf pans. Cover and let rise until doubled, about 30 minutes.

Bake at 375° for 35-40 minutes or until golden brown. Remove from pans to wire racks to cool. **Yield:** 2 loaves (16 slices each).

Nutrition Facts: 1 slice equals 124 calories, 3 g fat (2 g saturated fat), 8 mg cholesterol, 170 mg sodium, 21 g carbohydrate, 1 g fiber, 3 g protein. **Diabetic Exchange:** 1-1/2 starch.

ALL ABOUT OATS. Before either old-fashioned or quick-cooking oats are processed, the hull is removed and they are cleaned, toasted and cleaned again. At this point, they are called groats.

Old-fashioned oats are groats that are steamed and flattened with huge rollers. Quick-cooking oats are groats that have been cut into two or three pieces before being steamed and rolled. Both can be used interchangeably, although old-fashioned oats may give your recipe more texture.

let rise until doubled, about 30 minutes.

Bake at 350° for 22-28 minutes or until golden brown. Place pan on a wire rack. In a small bowl, beat the icing ingredients until smooth. Spread over rolls. Serve warm. **Yield:** 1 dozen.

Pina Colada Zucchini Bread

(Pictured below)

PREP: 25 min. **BAKE:** 45 min. + cooling

When you have a bounty of zucchini, consider this cake–like, tropical loaf. I entered the recipe at the Pennsylvania Farm Show and won first place. —*Sharon Rydbom, Tipton, Pennsylvania*

- 4 cups all-purpose flour
- 3 cups sugar
- 2 teaspoons baking powder
- 1-1/2 teaspoons salt
- 1 teaspoon baking soda
- 4 eggs
- 1-1/2 cups canola oil
- 1 teaspoon *each* coconut, rum and vanilla extracts
- 3 cups shredded zucchini
- 1 cup canned crushed pineapple, drained
- 1/2 cup chopped walnuts *or* chopped pecans

Line the bottoms of three greased and floured 8-in. x 4-in. loaf pans with waxed paper and grease the paper; set aside. In a large bowl, combine flour, sugar, baking powder, salt and baking soda. In another bowl, combine eggs, oil and extracts. Stir into dry ingredients just until moistened. Fold in zucchini, pineapple and walnuts.

Transfer to prepared pans. Bake at 350° for 45-55 minutes or until a toothpick inserted near the center comes out clean. Cool for 10 minutes before removing from pans to wire racks. Gently remove waxed paper. **Yield:** 3 loaves (12 slices each).

Cappuccino Cinnamon Rolls

(Pictured above)

PREP: 45 min. + rising **BAKE:** 25 min.

Distinctive coffee flavor accents the filling of these ooey, gooey rolls. The glaze goes on while they're still warm...and they never last long! —*Sherri Cox, Lucasville, Ohio*

- 1 package (1/4 ounce) active dry yeast
- 1 cup warm water (110° to 115°)
- 3/4 cup warm milk (110° to 115°)
- 1/2 cup buttermilk
- 3 tablespoons sugar
- 2 tablespoons butter, softened
- 1-1/4 teaspoons salt
- 5-1/2 to 6 cups all-purpose flour
FILLING:
- 1/4 cup butter, melted
- 1 cup packed brown sugar
- 4 teaspoons instant coffee granules
- 2 teaspoons ground cinnamon
ICING:
- 2 tablespoons butter, softened
- 1 to 2 tablespoons milk
- 2 teaspoons cappuccino mix
- 1-1/2 cups confectioners' sugar
- 1/2 teaspoon vanilla extract

In a large bowl, dissolve yeast in warm water. Add the warm milk, buttermilk, sugar, butter, salt and 4 cups flour. Beat on medium speed until smooth. Stir in enough remaining flour to form a soft dough (dough will be sticky).

Turn onto a floured surface; knead until smooth and elastic, about 6-8 minutes. Place in a greased bowl, turning once to grease the top. Cover and let rise in a warm place until doubled, about 1 hour.

Punch the dough down; turn onto a floured surface. Roll into an 18-in. x 12-in. rectangle; brush with butter. Combine brown sugar, coffee granules and cinnamon; sprinkle over the dough to within 1/2 in. of edges.

Roll up jelly-roll style, starting with a long side; pinch seam to seal. Cut into 12 slices. Place rolls, cut side down, in a greased 13-in. x 9-in. baking pan. Cover and

Cookies, Bars & Candies

Your family and friends won't be able to resist a cookie jar, dessert tray or gift tin filled with these goodies, from fancy Rice Krispies Treats to cute cutouts.

DELIGHTS BY THE DOZEN. Clockwise from top left: Chocolate Lover's Dream Cookies (p. 100), Peanut Butter Cup Cookies (p. 99), Chocolate Nut Bars (p. 96) and Chocolate Malt Krispie Bars (p. 103).

Chocolate Nut Bars

(Pictured above)

PREP: 20 min. **BAKE:** 15 min. + cooling

My husband loves these rich, fudgy treats chock-full of chocolate chips and three kinds of nuts. Just one bar is enough to satisfy your sweet tooth. —Lisa Darling, Rochester, New York

- 1 cup butter, softened
- 2 cups all-purpose flour
- 1/2 cup sugar
- 1/4 teaspoon salt
- 1 can (14 ounces) sweetened condensed milk
- 2 cups (12 ounces) semisweet chocolate chips, **divided**
- 1 teaspoon vanilla extract
- 1/2 cup chopped macadamia nuts
- 1/2 cup chopped walnuts
- 1/2 cup chopped pecans
- 1/2 cup milk chocolate chips

In a large bowl, beat butter until fluffy. Add the flour, sugar and salt; beat just until crumbly. Set aside 1 cup for topping. Press remaining crumb mixture into a greased 13-in. x 9-in. baking pan. Bake at 350° for 10-12 minutes or until set and edges begin to brown.

Meanwhile, in a small saucepan, combine milk and 1-1/2 cups semisweet chocolate chips. Cook and stir until chips are melted. Remove from the heat; stir in vanilla. Spread mixture over crust.

Combine the nuts and milk chocolate chips with the remaining semisweet chocolate chips and crumb mixture. Sprinkle over filling. Bake for 15-20 minutes or until center is set. Cool on a wire rack. Cut into bars. **Yield:** 3 dozen.

Colossal Batch Of Oatmeal Cookies

(Pictured below)

PREP: 20 min. **BAKE:** 10 min./batch

I divide this dough into thirds and make three different types of cookies—one with chocolate chips and nuts, one with raisins and one with butterscotch chips. —Lisa Cooper, Paris, Texas

- 2 cups butter, softened
- 3/4 cup butter-flavored shortening
- 3-1/4 cups packed brown sugar
- 1-1/4 cups sugar
- 5 eggs
- 2/3 cup buttermilk
- 4 teaspoons vanilla extract
- 6 cups quick-cooking oats
- 5-3/4 cups all-purpose flour
- 1 tablespoon baking soda
- 2-1/2 teaspoons salt
- 1 package (10 to 11 ounces) butterscotch chips
- 1 cup chopped pecans

In a very large bowl, cream the butter, shortening and sugars until light and fluffy. Add eggs, one at a time, beating well after each addition. Beat in buttermilk and vanilla.

Combine the oats, flour, baking soda and salt; gradually add to creamed mixture and mix well. Stir in chips and pecans. Drop by rounded tablespoonfuls 3 in. apart onto ungreased baking sheets.

Bake at 375° for 10-12 minutes or until golden brown. Remove to wire racks. **Yield:** about 13-1/2 dozen.

German Chocolate Brownies

PREP: 20 min. **BAKE:** 25 min. + cooling

Even as a young girl, I would page through cookbooks in search of something new to make. That's how I found these brownies. I take them to family reunions and church dinners, but they're great anytime. —Karen Grimes, Stephens City, Virginia

- 1/2 cup butter, cubed
- 1 package (4 ounces) German sweet chocolate, broken into squares
- 1/2 cup sugar
- 1 teaspoon vanilla extract
- 2 eggs, lightly beaten
- 1 cup all-purpose flour
- 1/2 teaspoon baking powder
- 1/4 teaspoon salt

TOPPING:
- 2 tablespoons butter, melted
- 1/2 cup packed brown sugar
- 1 cup flaked coconut
- 1/2 cup chopped pecans
- 2 tablespoons corn syrup
- 2 tablespoons milk

In a heavy saucepan or microwave, melt butter and chocolate; stir until smooth. Remove from the heat; cool slightly. Stir in the sugar and vanilla. Add the eggs; mix well. Combine the flour, baking powder and salt; add to chocolate mixture.

Pour into a greased 9-in. square baking pan. Bake at 350° for 18-22 minutes or a toothpick inserted near the center comes out clean.

For topping, combine butter and brown sugar in a bowl. Add coconut, pecans, corn syrup and milk; mix well. Drop by teaspoonfuls onto warm brownies; spread evenly. Broil 6 in. from the heat for 2-4 minutes or until top is browned and bubbly. Cool on a wire rack. Cut into bars. **Yield:** 16 brownies.

EDGED OUT. Follow these tips to prevent the edges of brownies from getting hard:
- Use an oven thermometer to make sure your oven temperature is accurate. Then test for doneness toward the end of the baking time.
- If the brownie springs back when lightly touched in the center and the sides have started to pull away from the pan, it is done. If your brownie recipe has a cake texture (rather than a dense fudgy consistency), it's done when a toothpick inserted in the center comes out clean.
- Avoid dark-colored baking pans, which can cause the edges to brown too fast.
- Try lowering the baking temperature by 25°.

Gooey Chocolate Cookies

(Pictured above)

PREP: 15 min. + chilling **BAKE:** 10 min./batch

These soft, chewy cookies are so yummy and couldn't be easier to make. If you like, jazz them up with a chocolate kiss in the center…or replace the chocolate cake mix with a different flavor.
—Angela Bailey, San Pierre, Indiana

☑ This recipe includes Nutrition Facts and Diabetic Exchanges.

- 1 package (8 ounces) cream cheese, softened
- 1/2 cup butter, softened
- 1 egg
- 1 teaspoon vanilla extract
- 1 package (18-1/4 ounces) chocolate cake mix

In a large bowl, beat the cream cheese and butter until light and fluffy. Beat in the egg and vanilla. Add the cake mix and mix well (dough will be sticky). Cover and refrigerate for 2 hours.

Roll rounded tablespoonfuls of the dough into balls. Place 2 in. apart on ungreased baking sheets. Bake at 350° for 9-11 minutes or until tops are cracked. Cool for 2 minutes before removing from pans to wire racks. **Yield:** 4-1/2 dozen.

Nutrition Facts: 1 cookie equals 69 calories, 4 g fat (2 g saturated fat), 13 mg cholesterol, 90 mg sodium, 8 g carbohydrate, trace fiber, 1 g protein. **Diabetic Exchanges:** 1/2 starch, 1/2 fat.

Lemon Lover's Cookies

(Pictured below)

PREP: 20 min. + chilling **BAKE:** 10 min./batch + cooling

Lemon juice and peel flavor both these light cookies and their homemade frosting. They're just the right sweet with coffee or tea.
—Virginia Dillard, Whitmire, South Carolina

    3/4 cup butter, softened
      3 tablespoons sugar
      2 teaspoons lemon juice
      1 cup all-purpose flour
    1/2 cup cornstarch
      1 teaspoon grated lemon peel
LEMON FROSTING:
    1/4 cup butter, softened
      1 cup confectioners' sugar
      2 teaspoons lemon juice
      1 teaspoon grated lemon peel
OPTIONAL GARNISH:
Additional grated lemon peel

In a small bowl, cream the butter and sugar until light and fluffy, about 5 minutes. Beat in the lemon juice. Combine the flour, cornstarch and lemon peel; gradually add to creamed mixture and mix well.

Shape the dough into a 1-1/2-in. roll; wrap in plastic wrap. Refrigerate for 1 hour or until firm. Unwrap and cut into 1/4-in. slices. Place 2 in. apart on ungreased baking sheets.

Bake at 350° for 10-12 minutes or until edges are golden brown. Cool for 3 minutes before removing to wire racks to cool completely.

In a small bowl, beat butter until fluffy. Add the confectioners' sugar, lemon juice and peel; beat until smooth. Spread over cooled cookies; sprinkle with additional lemon peel if desired. Let stand until set. Store in an airtight container. **Yield:** about 2 dozen.

Papa's Sugar Cookies

(Pictured above)

PREP: 20 min. + chilling **BAKE:** 10 min./batch

My grandchildren like these crisp sugar cookies. Flattening them with a drinking glass gives them their shape, but you could also use a cookie cutter.   *—Lee Doverspike, North Ridgeville, Ohio*

      1 cup butter, softened
      1 cup canola oil
      1 cup sugar
      1 cup confectioners' sugar
      2 eggs
      2 tablespoons butter flavoring
      1 tablespoon grated orange peel
      1 tablespoon vanilla extract
    5-1/2 cups all-purpose flour
    1/4 cup ground macadamia nuts
    1-1/2 teaspoons baking soda
      1 teaspoon salt
      1 teaspoon cream of tartar
      1 teaspoon ground cinnamon
Additional granulated sugar

In a large bowl, beat butter, oil and sugars until well blended. Add eggs, one at a time, beating well after each addition. Beat in butter flavoring, orange peel and vanilla.

Combine flour, nuts, baking soda, salt, cream of tartar and cinnamon; gradually add to butter mixture and mix well. Cover; refrigerate for 1 hour or until easy to handle.

Roll into 1-in. balls, then roll in additional sugar. Place 2 in. apart on ungreased baking sheets. Flatten with a glass dipped in additional sugar.

Bake at 350° for 10-12 minutes or until edges begin to brown. Remove to wire racks. **Yield:** 8 dozen.

Peanut Butter Cup Cookies

(Pictured below)

PREP: 20 min. + chilling **BAKE:** 15 min./batch

These drizzled treats are out of this world. Once I baked the first batch for family and friends, everyone was asking for the recipe.
—*Mary Hepperle, Toronto, Ontario*

- **1 cup butter, softened**
- **1/2 cup creamy peanut butter**
- **3/4 cup packed brown sugar**
- **1/2 cup sugar**
- **1 egg**
- **1 teaspoon vanilla extract**
- **2 cups all-purpose flour**
- **1 teaspoon baking soda**
- **1 package (13 ounces) miniature peanut butter cups**

DRIZZLE:
- **1 cup (6 ounces) semisweet chocolate chips**
- **1 tablespoon creamy peanut butter**
- **1 teaspoon shortening**

In a large bowl, cream the butter, peanut butter and sugars until light and fluffy. Beat in egg and vanilla. Combine flour and baking soda; gradually add to creamed mixture and mix well. Cover and refrigerate for 1 hour or until easy to handle.

Roll into 1-1/4-in. balls. Press a miniature peanut butter cup into each; reshape balls. Place 2 in. apart on ungreased baking sheets. Bake at 350° for 12-15 minutes or until edges are lightly browned. Cool for 2 minutes before removing from pans to wire racks.

For drizzle, in a microwave-safe bowl, melt chocolate chips, peanut butter and shortening; stir until smooth. Drizzle over cooled cookies. **Yield:** about 3 dozen.

Editor's Note: Reduced-fat or generic brands of peanut butter are not recommended for this recipe.

Java Cream Drops

(Pictured below)

PREP: 35 min. **BAKE:** 10 min./batch

My co-workers love coffee. So, whenever I bring coffee-flavored goodies to the office, they're gobbled up in a flash. These were no exception! The two-tone cookies look cute on a tray, too.
—*Maria Regakis, Somerville, Massachusetts*

- **2 tablespoons instant coffee granules**
- **1 tablespoon half-and-half cream**
- **1 cup butter, softened**
- **2/3 cup sugar**
- **2/3 cup packed brown sugar**
- **1 egg**
- **1 teaspoon vanilla extract**
- **2-1/4 cups all-purpose flour**
- **1 teaspoon baking soda**
- **1/4 teaspoon salt**
- **1/4 cup baking cocoa**
- **1/2 cup finely chopped walnuts**
- **1/2 cup miniature semisweet chocolate chips**

In a small bowl, combine coffee granules and cream; set aside. In a large bowl, cream the butter, sugar and brown sugar until light and fluffy. Beat in the egg, vanilla and reserved coffee mixture. Combine flour, baking soda and salt; gradually add to creamed mixture and mix well.

Divide dough in half. To one portion, add the cocoa and walnuts. Stir the miniature chocolate chips into the remaining dough.

To form cookies, place 1 teaspoon of each dough on an ungreased baking sheet; lightly press the doughs together to create two-tone cookies. Flatten slightly. Repeat with the remaining doughs. Bake at 375° for 8-10 minutes. Cool for 1 minute before removing from pans to wire racks. **Yield:** 5 dozen.

Chocolate Lover's Dream Cookies

(Pictured below)

PREP: 15 min. **BAKE:** 15 min./batch

When my daughter was 15 years old, she entered this recipe in the cookie division of a local chocolate festival—and ended up winning first prize. —*Paula Zsiray, Logan, Utah*

- 6 tablespoons canola oil
- 1/4 cup butter, softened
- 3/4 cup packed brown sugar
- 1/2 cup sugar
- 2 eggs
- 1 teaspoon vanilla extract
- 1-1/4 cups all-purpose flour
- 1/2 cup baking cocoa
- 1/4 teaspoon baking powder
- 1 cup vanilla *or* white chips
- 1 cup semisweet chocolate chips

In a large bowl, beat the oil, butter and sugars until well blended. Add eggs, one at a time, beating well after each addition. Beat in vanilla. Combine the flour, cocoa and baking powder; gradually add to oil mixture and mix well. Stir in chips.

Drop by rounded tablespoonfuls 2 in. apart onto ungreased baking sheets. Bake at 350° for 12-15 minutes or until edges begin to brown. Cool for 1 minute before removing from pans to wire racks. **Yield:** 3-1/2 dozen.

Florentine Cookie Bars

(Pictured above)

PREP: 1 hour + chilling **BAKE:** 20 min. + chilling

Celebrate the holiday season with these rich and chewy cookie bars. Red and green candied cherries give them a festive look for Christmas. —*Carole Sepstead, Grafton, Wisconsin*

- 1 cup butter, softened
- 2/3 cup sugar
- 1 egg
- 3 cups all-purpose flour

FILLING:

- 2 cups sugar
- 1-1/4 cups heavy whipping cream
- 3/4 cup butter, cubed
- 2/3 cup honey
- 4 cups sliced almonds
- 1-1/2 cups red *and/or* green candied cherries
- 3/4 cup dried currants

GARNISH:

- 1-1/4 pounds white candy coating

In a large bowl, cream butter and sugar until light and fluffy. Beat in egg. Gradually add flour and mix well. Refrigerate for 30 minutes or until easy to handle.

Roll dough into an ungreased 15-in. x 10-in. x 1-in. baking pan. Bake at 375° for 7-9 minutes or until lightly browned.

Meanwhile, in a large heavy saucepan, combine sugar, cream, butter and honey. Cook, stirring occasionally, until a candy thermometer reads 246° (firm-ball stage). Remove from the heat; stir in the almonds, cherries and currants. Spread evenly into crust.

Bake for 18-22 minutes or just until filling is set. Cool completely on a wire rack. Refrigerate overnight.

Remove florentine from pan. With a sharp knife, trim

edges of crust; discard the trim. Cut lengthwise into six strips; cut each strip into 16 triangles.

In a microwave-safe bowl, melt candy coating; stir until smooth. Dip the short side of each triangle into candy coating; place on waxed paper. Drizzle with additional candy coating. Let stand until set. Cover and store in the refrigerator. **Yield:** 8 dozen.

Editor's Note: We recommend that you test your candy thermometer before each use by bringing water to a boil; the thermometer should read 212°. Adjust your recipe temperature up or down based on your test.

Macadamia Nut Fudge

PREP: 15 min. + chilling

My neighbors like this fudge so much, they call me the "Candy Lady of Cleveland." If I don't have macadamia nuts, I simply substitute pecans. —Vicki Fioranelli, Cleveland, Mississippi

- 2 teaspoons plus 1/2 cup butter, *divided*
- 4-1/2 cups granulated sugar
- 1 can (12 ounces) evaporated milk
- 3 cups chopped macadamia nuts, *divided*
- 3 packages (4 ounces *each*) German sweet chocolate, chopped
- 1 package (12 ounces) semisweet chocolate chips
- 1 jar (7 ounces) marshmallow creme
- 2 teaspoons vanilla extract
- 1/2 teaspoon salt, optional

Line two 9-in. square pans with foil; butter the foil with 2 teaspoons butter. Set aside.

In a large heavy saucepan, combine the sugar, milk and remaining butter. Bring to a gentle boil. Cook for 5 minutes, stirring constantly. Remove from the heat; Stir in 2 cups nuts, chopped chocolate, chocolate chips, marshmallow creme, vanilla and salt if desired.

Pour fudge into prepared pans; sprinkle remaining nuts over top and press in lightly. Refrigerate until firm. Using foil, lift fudge out of pans. Discard foil; cut fudge into 1-in. squares. Store in an airtight container. **Yield:** about 5 pounds.

FOIL FIRST. Many fudge recipes suggest lining the pan with foil. The foil allows the fudge to be lifted out of the pan in one piece. Cutting the fudge outside of the pan prevents the pan from being scratched by the knife and also allows for more evenly cut pieces.

To prepare a foil-lined pan, line the pan with foil extending over the sides of the pan. Grease the foil with butter or coat with nonstick cooking spray. When fudge is firm, grasp the foil on opposite sides and lift the fudge out of the pan. Place it on a cutting board, remove the foil and cut.

Chocolate Coconut Slices

(Pictured below)

PREP: 25 min. + chilling **BAKE:** 10 min./batch

I love baking cookies to give away to friends and family. With a coconut center, these little goodies remind everyone of a Mounds chocolate bar. —Linda Kappelt, Linesville, Pennsylvania

- 6 tablespoons butter, softened
- 1 cup confectioners' sugar
- 1 egg
- 2 squares (1 ounce *each*) unsweetened chocolate, melted and cooled
- 3 teaspoons vanilla extract
- 1-1/2 cups all-purpose flour
- 1/2 teaspoon baking soda

FILLING:
- 1/3 cup cream cheese, softened
- 1 teaspoon vanilla extract
- 1 cup flaked coconut
- 1/2 cup finely chopped pecans

In a small bowl, cream butter and confectioners' sugar until light and fluffy. Beat in the egg, chocolate and vanilla. Combine flour and baking soda; gradually add to creamed mixture and mix well. Refrigerate for 1 hour.

In another bowl, combine cream cheese and vanilla. Stir in coconut and pecans until blended. Refrigerate for 1 hour.

Shape dough into an 8-1/2-in. x 6-in. rectangle. Shape filling into an 8-1/2-in. log; place on dough. Wrap dough around filling, sealing the seam. Wrap in plastic wrap and refrigerate for 2-3 hours or until firm.

Cut into 1/4-in. slices. Place 2 in. apart on parchment paper-lined baking sheets. Bake at 375° for 10-12 minutes or until set. Remove to wire racks. **Yield:** about 3 dozen.

It's Hip to Be Square!

REMEMBER that special taste from childhood—the crispy yet gooey goodness of Rice Krispies Treats? Why not rediscover that yummy fun with the recipes here? They'll bring back everything you loved about those classic squares...and add in a few new twists, too!

You'll want to try each playful variation—from colorful Neapolitan Krispie Bars featuring strawberry and chocolate layers to chunky Cherry & Almond Krispie Squares, which bring a bit of grown-up sophistication to a kid favorite.

If the blend of chocolate and peanut butter gets your mouth watering, check out rave-winning Chocolate Peanut Butter Treats. Or stir in some chopped candies to create Chocolate Malt Krispie Bars.

Neapolitan Krispie Bars

(Pictured below)

PREP: 15 min. **COOK:** 30 min.

Talk about a conversation piece! These festive goodies created by our Test Kitchen home economists will have your friends and family members buzzing over the multicolored layers—as well as the tempting chocolate and strawberry flavors.

  1 package (10 ounces) large marshmallows, *divided*
  3 tablespoons butter, *divided*
  2 cups Cocoa Krispies cereal
1/2 cup miniature semisweet chocolate chips
  4 cups Rice Krispies cereal, *divided*
1/2 cup strawberry preserves
  5 drops red food coloring, optional

In a large saucepan, combine a third of marshmallows (about 2 cups) and 1 tablespoon butter. Cook and stir over medium-low heat until melted. Remove from the heat; stir in Cocoa Krispies and chocolate chips. Press into a greased 11-in. x 7-in. dish.

In a large saucepan, combine a third of the marshmallows and 1 tablespoon butter. Cook and stir over medium-low heat until melted. Remove from the heat; stir in 2 cups Rice Krispies. Press into dish over chocolate layer.

In a large saucepan, combine the remaining marshmallows and butter. Cook and stir over medium-low heat until melted. Remove from the heat; stir in preserves and food coloring if desired. Stir in the remaining cereal. Press into the dish. Cool. Cut into bars. **Yield:** 1 dozen.

Chocolate Peanut Butter Treats

PREP/TOTAL TIME: 30 min.

This popular variation of classic Rice Krispies Treats is full of creamy peanut butter and rich semisweet chocolate, a flavor combination that's hard to beat. Nobody can eat just one.
—Sue McLaughlin, Onawa, Iowa

1/4 cup butter, cubed
  1 package (10 ounces) marshmallows

CRAZY FOR KRISPIES. Have fun experimenting with all sorts of different add-ins for your Rice Krispies Treats. Here are some yummy ideas:
- Raisins
- Dried chopped apples or cranberries
- M&M's miniature baking bits
- Flaked coconut
- Crushed peppermint candies
- Halved gumdrops
- Toffee bits
- Pecans, peanuts or walnuts

3/4 **cup creamy peanut butter**
5 **cups crisp rice cereal**
1 **cup butterscotch chips**
1 **cup (6 ounces) semisweet chocolate chips**

In a microwave, melt butter and marshmallows; stir until smooth. Remove from heat; stir in peanut butter until smooth. Gradually add cereal; toss to coat. Spread and press into a greased 13-in. x 9-in. pan; set aside.

In a microwave, melt chips; stir to coat. Spread over cereal mixture. Cover and freeze for 15-20 minutes or until chocolate is set. **Yield:** 12-16 servings.

Chocolate Malt Krispie Bars

(Pictured above)

PREP/TOTAL TIME: 25 min.

Our Test Kitchen coated these squares with malted milk flavor from top to bottom. Covered with whole candies, they definitely attract attention at bake sales, potlucks and parties.

4 **cups malted milk balls, *divided***
1 **package (10 ounces) large marshmallows**
3 **tablespoons butter**
5 **cups Rice Krispies cereal**
1 **cup malted milk powder, *divided***
2 **cups (12 ounces) semisweet chocolate chips**

Chop 1 cup malted milk balls; set aside. In a Dutch oven, combine marshmallows and butter. Cook and stir over medium-low heat until melted. Remove from the heat;

stir in the cereal, 3/4 cup malt powder and chopped candy. Press into a greased 13-in. x 9-in. pan.

In a microwave, melt chocolate chips; stir until smooth. Stir in remaining malt powder. Spread over cereal bars. Top with remaining malted milk balls. Let stand until set. Cut into squares. **Yield:** 2 dozen.

Cherry & Almond Krispie Squares

(Pictured above)

PREP/TOTAL TIME: 20 min.

This isn't your usual Rice Krispies Treat! Our home economists concocted a grown-up version of a childhood favorite by stirring in tangy dried cherries and crunchy roasted almonds.

1 **package (10 ounces) large marshmallows**
3 **tablespoons butter**
1 **teaspoon almond extract**
6 **cups Rice Krispies cereal**
3 **cups salted roasted almonds, *divided***
1-1/2 **cups dried cherries, *divided***

In a Dutch oven, combine marshmallows and butter. Cook and stir over medium-low heat until melted. Remove from the heat; stir in extract. Stir in the cereal, 1 cup almonds and 1 cup cherries.

Press into a greased 13-in. x 9-in. pan. Sprinkle with remaining almonds and cherries; gently press onto cereal mixture. Cool. Cut into squares. **Yield:** 2 dozen.

Lemon Cooler Cookies

(Pictured above)

PREP/TOTAL TIME: 30 min.

Baking soda helps brown these crisp, lemony, shortbread–like goodies created by our Test Kitchen home economists. If you're a fan of lemon, you're sure to love these.

   1/4 **cup butter, softened**
     2 **tablespoons canola oil**
   3/4 **cup sugar**
     1 **egg**
     1 **egg white**
   1/4 **cup thawed lemonade concentrate**
     2 **teaspoons grated lemon peel**
     2 **cups all-purpose flour**
   1/2 **teaspoon baking powder**
   1/4 **teaspoon salt**
   1/8 **teaspoon baking soda**
     1 **tablespoon yellow decorating sugar**

In a large bowl, beat the butter, oil and sugar. Beat in the egg, egg white, lemonade concentrate and lemon peel. Combine the flour, baking powder, salt and baking soda; gradually add to egg mixture.

Using a cookie press fitted with the disk of your choice, press dough 2 in. apart onto ungreased baking sheets. Sprinkle with yellow sugar. Bake at 350° for 8-10 minutes or until edges are lightly browned. Cool on wire racks. **Yield:** 3-1/2 dozen.

My Kids' Favorite Cookies

PREP: 15 min. **BAKE:** 10 min./batch

Whenever I made these cookies for my sons when they were kids, it was a challenge to keep them away from the kitchen until the cookies cooled! —*Ardys Smith, Palo Alto, California*

     1 **cup butter, softened**
   1/2 **cup sugar**
   1/2 **cup packed brown sugar**
     1 **egg**
     1 **teaspoon vanilla extract**
     2 **cups all-purpose flour**
     1 **teaspoon baking soda**
   1/2 **teaspoon salt**
1-1/2 **cups quick-cooking oats**
     1 **cup flaked coconut**
     5 **milk chocolate candy bars (1.55 ounces *each*)**

In a large bowl, cream butter and sugars until light and fluffy. Beat in egg and vanilla. Combine the flour, baking soda and salt; gradually add to creamed mixture and mix well. Beat in oats and coconut.

Roll the dough into 1-in. balls. Place 2 in. apart on ungreased baking sheets; flatten slightly. Bake at 350° for 10-12 minutes or until lightly browned. Break each candy bar into 12 pieces; press a chocolate piece into the center of each warm cookie. Remove to wire racks. **Yield:** 5 dozen.

    Editor's Note: This recipe was tested with Hershey's premier baking pieces.

Mocha Nut Balls

PREP: 20 min. **BAKE:** 15 min./batch

I always double this recipe because the cookies are so addictive— especially for anyone who likes coffee. Dotted with pecans and rolled in confectioners' sugar, the little balls are pretty, too. —*Janet Sullivan, Buffalo, New York*

     1 **cup butter, softened**
   1/2 **cup sugar**
     2 **teaspoons vanilla extract**
1-3/4 **cups all-purpose flour**
   1/3 **cup baking cocoa**
     1 **tablespoon instant coffee granules**
     1 **cup finely chopped pecans *or* walnuts**
Confectioners' sugar

In a large bowl, cream butter and sugar until light and fluffy. Beat in vanilla. Combine the flour, cocoa and coffee granules; gradually add to creamed mixture and mix well. Stir in pecans. Roll into 1-in. balls. Place 2 in. apart on ungreased baking sheets.

Bake at 325° for 14-16 minutes or until firm. Cool on pans for 1-2 minutes before removing to wire racks. Roll the warm cookies in confectioners' sugar. **Yield:** 4-1/2 dozen.

Sugar Doves

(Pictured below)

PREP: 30 min. + chilling **BAKE**: 10 min./batch

I enjoy baking and decorating these beautiful cookies as much as I do eating them. They're almost too cute to eat—but somehow always get gobbled up! —Peggy Preston, Fenton, Iowa

- 1 cup butter, softened
- 2 cups sugar
- 2 eggs
- 2 tablespoons milk
- 2 teaspoons vanilla extract
- 4-1/4 cups all-purpose flour
- 2 teaspoons baking powder
- 1/4 teaspoon salt

FROSTING:

- 1/2 cup shortening
- 3-3/4 cups confectioners' sugar
- 2 tablespoons milk
- 1 teaspoon almond extract
- 1/2 teaspoon vanilla extract
- 1 to 2 tablespoons water
- 4-1/2 cups sliced almonds
- 3-1/2 cups finely chopped walnuts
- **Miniature semisweet chocolate chips**

In a large bowl, cream butter and sugar until light and fluffy. Add eggs, one at a time, beating well after each addition. Beat in milk and vanilla. Combine the flour, baking powder and salt; gradually add to creamed mixture and mix well. Refrigerate for 2 hours or until easy to handle.

On a lightly floured surface, roll out dough to 1/8-in. thickness. Cut with a 3-in. bird-shaped cookie cutter. Place 1 in. apart on baking sheets coated with cooking spray. Bake at 350° for 7-9 minutes or until set. Remove to wire racks to cool.

For frosting, in a small bowl, combine the shortening, confectioners' sugar, milk, extracts and enough water to achieve spreading consistency. Frost the cookies. Arrange almonds over the bodies and walnuts over the heads. Add chocolate chip eyes. **Yield:** 7-1/2 dozen.

Chocolate Sauce Brownies

(Pictured above)

PREP: 20 min. **BAKE**: 20 min.

These moist, cake–like brownies are loaded with crunchy nuts and topped with a homemade chocolate frosting. No matter where I serve them, I always get the same reaction: "Mmmm!" —Vickie Overby, Wahpeton, North Dakota

- 1/2 cup butter, softened
- 1 cup sugar
- 4 eggs
- 1 can (16 ounces) chocolate syrup
- 1 teaspoon vanilla extract
- 1 cup plus 1 tablespoon all-purpose flour
- 1/2 teaspoon baking powder
- 1 cup chopped pecans *or* walnuts

FROSTING:

- 1 cup sugar
- 6 tablespoons milk
- 6 tablespoons butter
- 1/2 cup semisweet chocolate chips

In a bowl, cream butter and sugar. Add eggs, one at a time, beating well after each addition. Stir in chocolate syrup and vanilla. Combine flour and baking powder; add to the creamed mixture and mix well. Stir in nuts.

Pour into a greased 15-in. x 10-in. x 1-in. baking pan. Bake at 350° for 20-25 minutes or until a toothpick inserted near the center comes out clean. Cool on a wire rack.

For frosting, combine the sugar, milk and butter in a heavy saucepan. Bring to a boil over medium heat; boil for 1 minute. Remove from the heat. Add chocolate chips; stir or whisk for 5 minutes or until smooth. Spread over brownies. **Yield:** 5 dozen.

Cakes & Pies

Any way you slice it, the crowd-pleasing cakes and prize-worthy pies set out in this chapter are guaranteed to make eyes light up at the dinner table.

FANCY FINALES. Clockwise from top left: Frosty Coffee Pie (p. 110), Sweet Potato Pie & Maple Praline Sauce (p. 108), Blueberry Lemon Cake (p. 109), Lemon-Filled Coconut Cake (p. 116) and Lemon Delight Cake (p. 110).

In a large bowl, combine the eggs, sweet potatoes, buttermilk, butter, syrup, maple flavoring, cloves and remaining sugar. Pour over pecan layer.

Bake at 350° for 60-70 minutes or until a knife inserted near the center comes out clean. Cover edges with foil during the last 15 minutes to prevent overbrowning if necessary. Cool on a wire rack.

For sauce, in a small heavy skillet, melt butter. Add pecans; cook over medium heat until toasted, about 4 minutes. Add the sugar, syrup and maple flavoring; cook and stir for 2-4 minutes or until sugar is dissolved. Remove from the heat; stir in sour cream. Serve with pie. **Yield:** 10 servings (1-2/3 cups sauce).

Peanut Butter Cream Pie

PREP/TOTAL TIME: 30 min.

This peanut buttery dessert is a specialty I make as manager and baker at our municipal airport's cafe. Pilot friends of mine will plot their flight plan to include a stop here in rural Kansas in order to refuel their planes and enjoy a slice of pie!
—*Dolores Corke, Goodland, Kansas*

    1/2 cup semisweet chocolate chips
      1 tablespoon plus 1 cup butter, *divided*
      1 tablespoon water
    1/4 cup confectioners' sugar
      1 pastry shell (9 inches), baked
      1 cup packed brown sugar
      1 cup creamy peanut butter
      1 carton (12 ounces) frozen whipped topping, thawed
TOPPING:
    1/2 cup semisweet chocolate chips
      1 tablespoon butter
    2-1/2 teaspoons milk
    1-1/2 teaspoons light corn syrup
Whipped topping and salted peanuts

In a small saucepan, combine the chocolate chips, 1 tablespoon butter and water. Cook and stir over low heat until smooth. Whisk in the confectioners' sugar until smooth.

Spread over sides and bottom of the pastry shell. Refrigerate until set.

Meanwhile, in a saucepan, combine brown sugar and remaining butter. Cook and stir over medium heat until smooth. Transfer to a large mixing bowl. Refrigerate for 10 minutes or until cool.

Add the peanut butter and beat on medium-high speed for 1 minute. Fold in whipped topping; spoon into crust. Refrigerate.

For topping, in a small saucepan, combine chocolate chips, butter, milk and corn syrup. Cook and stir over low heat until mixture is smooth. Carefully spread over filling.

Refrigerate for at least 2 hours. Garnish with whipped topping and peanuts. **Yield:** 10-12 servings.

Sweet Potato Pie & Maple Praline Sauce

(Pictured above and on page 107)

PREP: 20 min. **BAKE:** 1 hour + cooling

With its sweet maple topping, this scrumptious pie will have your guests asking for the recipe. Spoon any leftover sauce over scoops of ice cream.   —*Rosemary Johnson, Irondale, Alabama*

Pastry for single-crust pie (9 inches)
1-1/4 cups sugar, *divided*
    1 cup chopped pecans
    1 teaspoon ground cinnamon
    4 eggs, beaten
    1 cup mashed sweet potatoes
  3/4 cup buttermilk
  1/4 cup butter, melted
  1/4 cup maple syrup
    1 teaspoon maple flavoring
  1/4 teaspoon ground cloves
SAUCE:
  1/2 cup butter, cubed
  1/2 cup chopped pecans
  1/2 cup sugar
  1/2 cup maple syrup
    1 teaspoon maple flavoring
  1/4 cup sour cream

Line a 9-in. deep-dish pie plate with pastry; trim and flute edges. In a small bowl, combine 1/4 cup sugar, pecans and cinnamon; sprinkle evenly into pastry shell. Set aside.

Blueberry Lemon Cake

(Pictured above and on page 107)

PREP: 15 min. **BAKE:** 30 min.

I always set aside some of my fresh-picked blueberries to make this quick-and-easy treat. Lemon flavor sparks the fruit layer and the tender cake. —Leona Luecking, West Burlington, Iowa

- 1/4 **cup butter, cubed**
- 1/2 **cup sugar**
- 2 **teaspoons grated lemon peel, *divided***
- 2 **cups fresh *or* frozen blueberries**
- 1 **package (9 ounces) yellow cake mix**

Whipped cream, optional

In a small saucepan, melt butter; stir in sugar until dissolved. Add 1 teaspoon lemon peel. Pour into a greased 8-in. square baking dish. Arrange blueberries in a single layer over top; set aside.

Prepare cake batter according to package directions. Stir in the remaining lemon peel. Carefully pour over blueberries.

Bake at 350° for 30-35 minutes or until a toothpick inserted near the center of cake comes out clean. Cool on a wire rack. Serve with whipped cream if desired. **Yield:** 9 servings.

Editor's Note: If using frozen blueberries, do not thaw.

Pumpkin Ice Cream Pie

PREP/TOTAL TIME: 15 min.

The holiday season is the perfect time to try this quick twist on traditional pumpkin pie. I often make it ahead of time so it can go from freezer to feast. —Marion Stoll, Dent, Minnesota

- 1 **quart vanilla ice cream, softened**
- 3/4 **cup canned pumpkin**
- 1/4 **cup honey**
- 1/2 **teaspoon ground cinnamon**
- 1/4 **teaspoon salt**
- 1/4 **teaspoon ground ginger**

Dash ground nutmeg
Dash ground cloves

- 1 **graham cracker crust (9 inches)**

Whipped topping and pecan halves, optional

In a large mixing bowl, combine the first eight ingredients; beat until smooth. Spoon into crust. Cover and freeze for 2 hours or until firm.

Remove from the freezer 15 minutes before serving. Garnish with whipped topping and pecans if desired. **Yield:** 6-8 servings.

Hot Fudge Cake

(Pictured below)

PREP: 20 min. **BAKE:** 4 hours

A cake baked in a slow cooker may seem unusual, but the smiles it gets prove how yummy it is. If you like, use butterscotch chips instead of chocolate. —Marleen Adkins, Placentia, California

- 1-3/4 **cups packed brown sugar, *divided***
- 1 **cup all-purpose flour**
- 6 **tablespoons baking cocoa, *divided***
- 2 **teaspoons baking powder**
- 1/2 **teaspoon salt**
- 1/2 **cup milk**
- 2 **tablespoons butter, melted**
- 1/2 **teaspoon vanilla extract**
- 1-1/2 **cups semisweet chocolate chips**
- 1-3/4 **cups boiling water**

Vanilla ice cream

In a bowl, combine 1 cup brown sugar, flour, 3 tablespoons cocoa, baking powder and salt.

In another bowl, combine the milk, butter and vanilla; stir into dry ingredients just until combined.

Spread evenly into a 3-qt. slow cooker coated with cooking spray. Sprinkle with chocolate chips.

In a bowl, combine remaining brown sugar and cocoa; stir in boiling water. Pour over batter (do not stir).

Cover and cook on high for 4 to 4-1/2 hours or until a toothpick inserted near the center of cake comes out clean. Serve warm with ice cream. **Yield:** 6-8 servings.

Editor's Note: This recipe does not use eggs.

Lemon Delight Cake

(Pictured below and on page 106)

PREP: 35 min. **BAKE:** 40 min. + cooling

When I needed to bring a dessert to work, I combined four different recipes into this moist cake. A boxed mix makes it easy, but the creamy filling and buttery topping make it memorable.
—Lydia Mason, Brainerd, Minnesota

- 1 package (18-1/4 ounces) lemon cake mix
- 1-1/3 cups water
- 3/4 cup egg substitute
- 1/3 cup unsweetened applesauce
- 3 tablespoons poppy seeds

FILLING:

- 1 package (8 ounces) reduced-fat cream cheese
- 1/2 cup confectioners' sugar
- 1 can (15-3/4 ounces) lemon pie filling

TOPPING:

- 1/3 cup packed brown sugar
- 1/4 cup chopped pecans
- 3 tablespoons all-purpose flour
- 4-1/2 teaspoons butter, melted
- 1/2 teaspoon ground cinnamon
- 1/8 teaspoon vanilla extract

GLAZE:

- 1/2 cup confectioners' sugar
- 4 teaspoons lemon juice

In a large bowl, combine first five ingredients; beat on low speed for 30 seconds. Beat on medium for 2 minutes. Coat a 13-in. x 9-in. baking pan with cooking spray and dust with flour; spread half of the batter into pan.

In a large bowl, beat cream cheese and confectioners' sugar until smooth. Stir in the lemon pie filling. Drop by teaspoonfuls and gently spread over batter. Top with remaining batter. Combine topping ingredients; sprinkle over batter.

Bake at 350° for 40-45 minutes or until a toothpick inserted near the center comes out clean. Cool on a wire rack. Combine glaze ingredients; drizzle over cake. Refrigerate leftovers. **Yield:** 18 servings.

Frosty Coffee Pie

(Pictured above and on page 106)

PREP: 15 min. + freezing

Cooking is my passion, and I like to come up with new recipes. This freezer treat is sure to please coffee drinkers and chocolate lovers alike. *—April Timboe, Siloam Springs, Arizona*

- 1/4 cup hot fudge ice cream topping, warmed
- 1 chocolate crumb crust (9 inches)
- 3 cups coffee ice cream, softened
- 1 package (5.9 ounces) instant chocolate pudding mix
- 1/2 cup cold strong brewed coffee
- 1/4 cup cold milk
- 1-3/4 cups whipped topping
- 1 cup marshmallow creme
- 1/4 cup miniature semisweet chocolate chips

Spread ice cream topping into crust. In a large bowl, beat the ice cream, pudding mix, coffee and milk until blended; spoon into crust.

In another bowl, combine the whipped topping and marshmallow creme; spread over top. Sprinkle with the chocolate chips. Cover and freeze until firm. **Yield:** 8 servings.

Dutch Apple Sour Cream Pie

PREP: 25 min. **BAKE:** 40 min.

With a pastry crust and crumb topping, this home-style pie is a favorite of family members and friends who come to visit. It also coordinates nicely with my apple-themed kitchen!
—Laura Thompson, Morristown, Tennessee

- 1 egg, lightly beaten
- 1-1/2 cups (12 ounces) sour cream
- 1 cup sugar
- 3 tablespoons all-purpose flour
- 1/2 teaspoon vanilla extract
- 3 cups thinly sliced peeled tart apples

1 unbaked pastry shell (9 inches)
CRUMB TOPPING:
  1/2 cup packed brown sugar
  1/2 cup all-purpose flour
  1/4 cup cold butter

In a large bowl, combine the egg, sour cream, sugar, flour and vanilla. Stir in apples. Pour into pastry shell. Bake at 375° for 30 minutes.

Meanwhile, combine brown sugar and flour. Cut in butter until mixture resembles coarse crumbs. Sprinkle over pie. Return to the oven for 10-15 minutes or until filling is set and topping is golden brown. Cool completely on a wire rack. Refrigerate leftovers. **Yield:** 6-8 servings.

Strawberry Cheesecake Pie

PREP/TOTAL TIME: 25 min.

There's a "berried" treasure at the bottom of every slice of this creamy, tangy concoction. You won't find a fresher finale to a summertime meal. —*Debbi Oeltjen, Keizer, Oregon*

  4 ounces cream cheese, softened
  1/4 cup sugar
  1/2 cup sour cream
  1 teaspoon vanilla extract
1-3/4 cups whipped topping
  1 cup strawberry glaze
  1 graham cracker crust (9 inches)
  2 pints fresh strawberries, thinly sliced
Fresh mint and additional strawberries, optional

In a small mixing bowl, beat cream cheese and sugar until smooth. Stir in sour cream and vanilla until blended. Fold in whipped topping.

Spread half of the glaze over bottom of crust; layer with strawberries. Top with remaining glaze. Spoon cream cheese mixture over the top. Refrigerate for 2-4 hours or until set. Garnish with mint and additional berries if desired. **Yield:** 6-8 servings.

Surprise Red Cupcakes

(Pictured at right)

PREP: 1 hour **BAKE:** 20 min.

You'll catch your loved ones red-handed when they snatch up these irresistible confections. My family adores the cream-filled center. —*Betty Claycomb, Alverton, Pennsylvania*

  2 cups sugar, *divided*
  3 tablespoons plus 2 cups all-purpose flour, *divided*
  1/2 cup milk
  1/2 cup plus 1/3 cup shortening, *divided*
  2 eggs
  1 bottle (1 ounce) red food coloring
  1 tablespoon white vinegar

  2 teaspoons vanilla extract, *divided*
  3 tablespoons baking cocoa
  1 teaspoon baking soda
  1 cup buttermilk
  1/2 cup butter, softened
  3 tablespoons confectioners' sugar
FROSTING:
  1 cup (6 ounces) semisweet chocolate chips
  1/3 cup plus 1 to 3 teaspoons evaporated milk, *divided*
1-1/2 cups confectioners' sugar

In a heavy saucepan, combine 1/2 cup sugar, 3 tablespoons flour and milk until smooth. Bring to a boil; cook and stir for 1-2 minutes or until thickened. Remove from the heat; cool.

In a large mixing bowl, cream 1/2 cup shortening and remaining sugar. Add eggs, one at a time, beating well after each addition. Beat in the food coloring, vinegar and 1 teaspoon vanilla. Combine the cocoa, baking soda and remaining flour; add to the creamed mixture alternately with buttermilk.

Fill paper-lined muffin cups two-thirds full. Bake at 350° for 20-25 minutes or until a toothpick comes out clean. Cool for 10 minutes before removing from pans to wire racks to cool completely.

In a small mixing bowl, beat butter and remaining shortening. Beat in the confectioners' sugar, cooled sugar mixture and remaining vanilla until light and fluffy, about 3 minutes. Insert a large round tip into a pastry or plastic bag; fill with filling. Insert the tip halfway into the center of each cupcake and fill with a small amount of filling.

For frosting, in a heavy saucepan, melt the chips with 1/3 cup evaporated milk over low heat; stir until smooth. Remove from the heat. Beat in confectioners' sugar. Add enough remaining milk to achieve spreading consistency. Frost cupcakes. **Yield:** 2 dozen.

Add cream of tartar, extracts and salt to egg whites; beat on medium speed until soft peaks form. Gradually add sugar, about 2 tablespoons at a time, beating on high until glossy peaks form and sugar is dissolved. Gradually fold in flour mixture, about 1/2 cup at a time. Fold in chocolate chips and coconut.

Gently spoon into an ungreased 10-in. tube pan. Cut through batter with a knife to remove air pockets. Bake on the lowest oven rack at 325° for 50-55 minutes or until top springs back when lightly touched and cracks feel dry. Immediately invert baking pan; cool completely.

For topping, in a large mixing bowl, beat cream until it begins to thicken. Add confectioners' sugar; beat until stiff peaks form. Serve with cake; sprinkle with coconut. Refrigerate any leftover topping. **Yield:** 12-16 servings.

Chocolate Almond Silk Pie

PREP: 20 min. **COOK:** 30 min. + cooling

This recipe is one I clipped years ago, and it was an instant hit with my husband and daughters. Because of that, it's been in my recipe file ever since! The chocolate and almond combination is absolutely heavenly. —Diane Larson, Roland, Iowa

- **2/3 cup all-purpose flour**
- **1/4 cup butter, softened**
- **3 tablespoons finely chopped almonds, toasted**
- **2 tablespoons confectioners' sugar**
- **1/8 teaspoon vanilla extract**

FILLING:
- **3/4 cup sugar**
- **3 eggs**
- **3 squares (1 ounce *each*) unsweetened chocolate, coarsely chopped**
- **1/8 teaspoon almond extract**
- **1/2 cup butter, softened**

Sweetened whipped cream and toasted sliced almonds, optional

In a small bowl, combine the first five ingredients. Beat on low speed until well combined, about 2-3 minutes. Press onto the bottom and up the sides of a greased 9-in. pie plate. Bake at 400° for 8-10 minutes or until golden. Cool on a wire rack.

For the pie filling, combine sugar and eggs in a small saucepan until well blended. Cook over low heat, stirring constantly until mixture coats the back of a metal spoon and reaches 160°. Remove from the heat. Stir in chocolate and almond extract until smooth. Cool to lukewarm (90°), stirring occasionally.

In a large bowl, cream butter until light and fluffy. Add the cooled egg mixture; beat on high speed for 5 minutes. Pour into cooled pie shell. Refrigerate for at least 6 hours before serving. Garnish with the whipped cream and almonds if desired. Refrigerate leftovers. **Yield:** 8-10 servings

Chippy Macaroon Angel Cake

(Pictured above)

PREP: 25 min. **BAKE:** 50 min.

I love to bake breads and desserts for our large family. Dotted with coconut and mini chocolate chips, this made–from–scratch angel food cake is decadent yet light as a cloud. The sweetened whipped cream "frosting" piped next to it adds elegance. —Joyce Platfoot, Wapakoneta, Ohio

- **1-1/2 cups egg whites (about 12)**
- **1-1/2 cups confectioners' sugar**
- **1 cup cake flour**
- **1-1/2 teaspoons cream of tartar**
- **1 teaspoon almond extract**
- **1 teaspoon vanilla extract**
- **1/4 teaspoon salt**
- **1 cup sugar**
- **1 cup (6 ounces) miniature semisweet chocolate chips**
- **1/2 cup flaked coconut**

TOPPING:
- **1 cup heavy whipping cream**
- **2 tablespoons confectioners' sugar**
- **1/2 cup flaked coconut, toasted**

Place egg whites in a large mixing bowl; let stand at room temperature for 30 minutes.

Sift the confectioners' sugar and flour together twice; set aside.

Minty Ice Cream Pie

(Pictured below)

PREP: 25 min. + freezing

I love ice cream desserts like this one because they can be fixed in advance and kept on hand for unexpected company. Plus, they never fail to please! This minty pie always makes a refreshing finale. —*Lorraine Darocha, Mountain City, Tennessee*

- 1 **package (3 ounces) cream cheese, softened**
- 2 **tablespoons sugar**
- 2 **cups heavy whipping cream,** *divided*
- 1/4 **cup chopped walnuts**
- 1 **chocolate crumb crust (9 inches)**
- 2 **packages (4-3/4 ounces** *each***) chocolate-covered peppermint candies,** *divided*
- 1 **pint chocolate ice cream** *or* **fudge ripple ice cream**
- 1/4 **cup hot fudge ice cream topping, warmed**
- 2 **tablespoons confectioners' sugar**
- 1 **teaspoon peppermint extract**
- 2 **to 3 drops green food coloring, optional**

In a small bowl, beat the cream cheese and sugar until smooth. Beat in 1 cup heavy whipping cream until soft peaks form. Fold in the walnuts. Spread into chocolate crumb crust. Coarsely chop 1 package peppermint candies; fold into ice cream. Spread over cream cheese mixture. Drizzle with fudge ice cream topping. Freeze for 1 hour.

In a small bowl, beat remaining cream until it begins to thicken. Add the confectioners' sugar, extract and food coloring if desired; beat until stiff peaks form. Garnish pie with whipped cream mixture and remaining candies. Freeze. Remove from the freezer 15 minutes before serving. **Yield:** 6-8 servings.

Toffee Poke Cake

(Pictured above)

PREP: 25 min. **BAKE:** 25 min. + chilling

Ice cream topping adds moistness and butterscotch flavor to this popular cake, which I like to top off with crunchy toffee candy. —*Jeanette Hoffman, Oshkosh, Wisconsin*

- 1 **package (18-1/4 ounces) chocolate cake mix**
- 1 **jar (17 ounces) butterscotch-caramel ice cream topping**
- 1 **carton (12 ounces) frozen whipped topping, thawed**
- 3 **Heath candy bars (1.4 ounces** *each***), chopped**

Prepare and bake chocolate cake according to package directions, using a greased 13-in. x 9-in. baking pan. Cool on a wire rack.

Using the handle of a wooden spoon, poke holes in the cake. Pour 3/4 cup butterscotch-caramel ice cream topping into the holes. Spoon remaining ice cream topping over cake. Top with whipped topping. Sprinkle with candy. Refrigerate for at least 2 hours before serving. **Yield:** 15 servings.

TASTE TWISTS. Feel free to experiment with the versatile, four-ingredient recipe for Toffee Poke Cake (above). For example, try a different ice cream topping in place of the butterscotch-caramel variety. You could also use another flavor of cake mix or sprinkle on different candies.

Sour Cream Peach Pecan Pie

(Pictured below)

PREP: 30 min. **BAKE:** 45 min. + cooling

When our delicious Southern peaches were in season, a friend asked me to make a peach pie. I didn't have a favorite recipe, so I looked over a few different ones and decided to come up with my own. I was thrilled when this creation won a Taste of Home recipe contest! —Sherrell Dikes, Holiday Island, Arkansas

Pastry for single-crust pie (9 inches)
>   4 cups sliced peeled peaches
>   2 tablespoons peach preserves
>   1 cup sugar
>   1 cup (8 ounces) sour cream
>   3 egg yolks
>   1/4 cup all-purpose flour
>   1 teaspoon vanilla extract

TOPPING:
>   1/2 cup all-purpose flour
>   1/2 cup packed brown sugar
>   1/4 cup sugar
>   3 tablespoons chopped pecans
>   1 teaspoon ground cinnamon
>   1/4 cup cold butter

Line a 9-in. pie plate with the pie pastry; trim and flute the edges.

In a large bowl, combine the peaches and preserves. Transfer to pastry. In a small bowl, whisk the sugar, sour cream, egg yolks, flour and vanilla. Pour over peaches.

Bake at 425° for 30 minutes. Meanwhile, in a small bowl, combine the flour, sugars, pecans and cinnamon.

Cut in butter until crumbly; sprinkle over pie. Cover edges of crust to prevent overbrowning.

Bake for 15-20 minutes or until a knife inserted in the center comes out clean and topping is golden brown. Cool on a wire rack for 1 hour. Store in the refrigerator. **Yield:** 8 servings.

Cranberry Pear Cake

(Pictured above)

PREP: 40 min. **BAKE:** 45 min.

For a change-of-pace dessert that's chock-full of autumn flavor, try this pairing of dried cranberries and ripe pears. The nutty filling and drizzled glaze make the cake even more appealing.
—Jeanne Holt, Mendota Heights, Minnesota

>   1 cup packed brown sugar
>   3/4 cup chopped pecans
>   1/3 cup chopped dried cranberries
>   1 teaspoon apple pie spice

BATTER:
>   1/2 cup butter, softened
>   1 cup sugar
>   3 eggs
>   1 teaspoon vanilla extract
>   2 cups all-purpose flour
>   2 teaspoons baking powder
>   1 teaspoon baking soda
>   1/2 teaspoon salt
>   1 cup (8 ounces) sour cream
>   2 cups chopped peeled ripe pears

GLAZE:
>   1 cup confectioners' sugar

5 teaspoons milk
4-1/2 teaspoons butter, melted
1/4 teaspoon apple pie spice
1/4 teaspoon vanilla extract

In a small bowl, combine the brown sugar, pecans, cranberries and apple pie spice; set aside.

In a large mixing bowl, cream butter and sugar until fluffy. Add eggs, one at a time, beating after each addition. Beat in vanilla. Combine the flour, baking powder, baking soda and salt; add to creamed mixture alternately with sour cream. Beat just until combined. Fold in pears.

Pour half of batter into a greased and floured 10-in. fluted tube pan. Sprinkle with half of the pecan mixture; top with remaining batter and pecan mixture.

Bake at 350° for 45-50 minutes or until a toothpick inserted near the center comes out clean. Cool for 10 minutes before removing from pan to a wire rack to cool completely. In a bowl, whisk the glaze ingredients until smooth; drizzle over cake. **Yield:** 12-14 servings.

Cherry-Topped Chocolate Cake

PREP: 30 min. BAKE: 35 min. + cooling

My husband and I love this dense, fudgy, flourless chocolate cake. Dressed up with cherry pie filling and whipped cream, it's a wonderful choice for Valentine's Day and other special occasions.
—*Bonnie Cochran, Bryson City, North Carolina*

5 teaspoons baking cocoa, *divided*
1 cup butter, cubed
9 squares (1 ounce *each*) semisweet chocolate, chopped
5 eggs
1/2 cup plus 1 tablespoon sugar, *divided*
2 teaspoons vanilla extract
1 can (21 ounces) cherry pie filling
1/2 cup heavy whipping cream, whipped

Coat a 9-in. springform pan with cooking spray; line with waxed paper and spray the paper. Dust with 2 teaspoons cocoa. Place pan on a double thickness of heavy-duty foil (about 18 in. square); securely wrap foil around pan.

In a heavy saucepan over low heat, melt butter and chocolate. Cool to lukewarm. In a large bowl, beat eggs and 1/2 cup sugar until thick and lemon-colored. Combine the remaining cocoa and sugar; beat into eggs. Add vanilla. Gradually beat in cooled chocolate mixture. Pour into prepared pan.

Place pan in a large baking pan; add 3/4 in. of hot water to larger pan. Bake at 325° for 35-40 minutes or until a toothpick inserted near the center comes out clean. Cool on a wire rack for 20 minutes.

Carefully run a knife around edge of pan; cool completely. Serve with cherry pie filling and whipped cream. Refrigerate leftovers. **Yield:** 12-14 servings.

Editor's Note: This recipe does not use flour.

California Lemon Pound Cake

(Pictured below)

PREP: 15 min. BAKE: 1 hour 10 min.

With lots of citrus flavor, this favorite pound cake makes great use of the fruit from my backyard lemon trees. My mom shared the recipe. —*Richard Killeaney, Spring Valley, California*

1 cup butter, softened
1/2 cup shortening
3 cups sugar
5 eggs
1 tablespoon grated lemon peel
1 tablespoon lemon extract
3 cups all-purpose flour
1 teaspoon salt
1/2 teaspoon baking powder
1 cup milk
FROSTING:
1/4 cup butter, softened
1-3/4 cups confectioners' sugar
2 tablespoons lemon juice
1 teaspoon grated lemon peel

In a large mixing bowl, cream the butter, shortening and sugar until light and fluffy, about 5 minutes. Add eggs, one at a time, beating well after each addition. Stir in lemon peel and extract. Combine the flour, salt and baking powder; gradually add to creamed mixture alternately with milk. Beat just until combined.

Pour into a greased 10-in. fluted tube pan. Bake at 350° for 70 minutes or until a toothpick inserted near the center comes out clean. Cool for 10 minutes before removing from pan to a wire rack to cool completely.

In a small mixing bowl, combine the frosting ingredients; beat until smooth. Spread over top of cake. **Yield:** 12-16 servings.

Lemon-Filled Coconut Cake

(Pictured above and on page 106)

PREP: 35 min. **BAKE:** 25 min. + cooling

Years ago, a co-worker of mine brought this special layer cake to a luncheon. It was so beautiful and luscious, I just had to request the recipe. I've baked it many times since—and it's always a hit!
—Jackie Bergenheier, Wichita Falls, Texas

        1 cup butter, softened
        2 cups sugar
        3 eggs
        2 teaspoons vanilla extract
   3-1/4 cups all-purpose flour
   3-1/4 teaspoons baking powder
      3/4 teaspoon salt
   1-1/2 cups milk
FILLING:
        1 cup sugar
      1/4 cup cornstarch
        1 cup water
        4 egg yolks, beaten
      1/3 cup lemon juice
        2 tablespoons butter
FROSTING:
   1-1/2 cups sugar
        2 egg whites
      1/3 cup water
      1/4 teaspoon cream of tartar
        1 teaspoon vanilla extract
        3 cups flaked coconut

In a large bowl, cream butter and sugar until light and fluffy. Add eggs, one at a time, beating well after each addition. Beat in vanilla. Combine the flour, baking powder and salt; add to creamed mixture alternately with milk.

Transfer to three greased and floured 9-in. round baking pans. Bake at 350° for 25-30 minutes or until a toothpick comes out clean. Cool for 10 minutes before removing from pans to wire racks to cool completely.

For filling, in a small saucepan, combine the sugar, cornstarch and water until smooth. Bring to a boil; cook and stir 2 minutes longer or until thickened and bubbly. Remove from the heat.

Stir a small amount of hot mixture into egg yolks; return all to the pan, stirring constantly. Bring to a gentle boil; cook and stir 2 minutes longer. Remove from the heat; gently stir in lemon juice and butter. Cool to room temperature without stirring.

Place one cake on serving plate; spread with half of the filling. Repeat layers. Top with remaining cake.

For frosting, in a large heavy saucepan, combine the sugar, egg whites, water and cream of tartar. With a portable mixer, beat on low speed for 1 minute. Continue beating on low over low heat until frosting reaches 160°, about 10 minutes.

Transfer to a large bowl; add vanilla. Beat on high until stiff peaks form, about 7 minutes. Frost top and sides of cake. Sprinkle with coconut. Store in the refrigerator. **Yield:** 16 servings.

Caramel-Pecan Cheesecake Pie

(Pictured below)

PREP: 15 min. **BAKE:** 35 min. + chilling

This nutty, rich and delicious pie is especially nice for fall and winter but is one I'm proud to serve any time of year. It looks impressive and tastes even better. —Becky Ruff, Monona, Iowa

        1 package (8 ounces) cream cheese, softened
      1/2 cup sugar
        4 eggs
        1 teaspoon vanilla extract
        1 unbaked pastry shell (9 inches)
   1-1/4 cups chopped pecans
        1 cup caramel ice cream topping

In a small bowl, beat the cream cheese, sugar, 1 egg and vanilla until smooth. Spread into pastry shell; sprinkle with pecans.

In a small bowl, whisk remaining eggs; gradually whisk in caramel topping until blended. Pour over pecans.

Bake at 375° for 35-40 minutes or until lightly browned (loosely cover with foil after 20 minutes if pie browns too quickly). Cool on a wire rack for 1 hour. Refrigerate for 4 hours or overnight before slicing. Refrigerate leftovers. **Yield:** 6-8 servings.

Heavenly Surprise Mini Cupcakes

PREP: 35 min. **BAKE:** 15 min./batch + cooling

My grandmother was an accomplished baker, and this recipe was one of her favorites. It's fun to take a bite and discover the "surprise"—a creamy filling with chocolate, nuts and coconut.
—*Jorun Meierding, Mankato, Minnesota*

FILLING:
- 1 package (8 ounces) cream cheese, softened
- 1/3 cup sugar
- 1 egg
- 1/8 teaspoon salt
- 1 cup flaked coconut
- 1 cup finely chopped walnuts
- 1 cup (6 ounces) miniature semisweet chocolate chips

BATTER:
- 2 cups sugar
- 1-1/2 cups water
- 3/4 cup canola oil
- 2 eggs
- 2 teaspoons vanilla extract
- 1 teaspoon white vinegar
- 3 cups all-purpose flour
- 1/2 cup baking cocoa
- 1 teaspoon baking soda
- 1 teaspoon salt

FROSTING:
- 1-1/3 cups semisweet chocolate chips
- 1/2 cup heavy whipping cream

For filling, in a small bowl, beat cream cheese and sugar until light and fluffy. Add egg and salt; mix well. Stir in the coconut, walnuts and chocolate chips. Set aside.

For batter, in a large bowl, beat the sugar, water, oil, eggs, vanilla and vinegar until well blended. Combine the flour, cocoa, baking soda and salt; gradually beat into oil mixture until blended.

Fill paper-lined miniature muffin cups one-third full with batter. Drop filling by teaspoonfuls into center of each. Top with additional batter, filling muffin cups three-fourths full.

Bake at 350° for 12-15 minutes or until a toothpick inserted in the cake portion of a cupcake comes out

clean. Cool for 10 minutes before removing from pans to wire racks to cool completely.

For frosting, in a small saucepan, melt chocolate with cream over low heat; stir until blended. Remove from the heat. Cool to room temperature. Frost cupcakes. Refrigerate leftovers. **Yield:** 6 dozen.

Raspberry Lemonade Pie

(Pictured above)

PREP: 10 min. + freezing

You can't beat this refreshing freezer dessert as the finale for an outdoor summer meal. The tangy fruit flavors are to-die-for combined with the chocolate crust and vanilla ice cream.
—*Sue Stewart, Hales Corners, Wisconsin*

- 1/3 cup sweetened raspberry lemonade drink mix
- 1/2 cup water
- 2 cups vanilla ice cream, softened
- 1 carton (8 ounces) frozen whipped topping, thawed
- 1 chocolate crumb crust (9 inches)

Chocolate syrup, optional

In a large bowl, combine drink mix and water. Add ice cream; beat on low speed for 2 minutes or until blended. Fold in whipped topping. Spoon into crust.

Freeze for 4 hours or until firm. Remove from the freezer 10 minutes before serving. Serve with chocolate syrup if desired. **Yield:** 8 servings.

Caramel Pecan Pie

(Pictured below)

PREP: 45 min. **BAKE:** 35 min.

Of all of the pecan pie recipes I've collected over the years and kept in my kitchen files, this is the most decadent. It simply oozes goodness! Even kids eat it slowly so they can enjoy every bite.
—*Diana Bartelings, Rock Creek, British Columbia*

- 1-2/3 **cups all-purpose flour**
- 1/4 **teaspoon salt**
- 1/2 **cup cold butter**
- 1/3 **cup sweetened condensed milk**
- 2 **egg yolks**

FILLING:
- 1-1/2 **cups sugar**
- 1/2 **cup plus 2 tablespoons butter**
- 1/3 **cup maple syrup**
- 3 **eggs**
- 3 **egg whites**
- 1/2 **teaspoon vanilla extract**
- 2 **cups ground pecans**

In a bowl, combine flour and salt; cut in butter until mixture resembles coarse crumbs. Combine milk and egg yolks; stir into the crumb mixture until dough forms a ball. Press onto the bottom and up the sides of an ungreased 9-in. deep-dish pie plate; flute the edges. Cover and refrigerate.

In a large saucepan, combine the sugar, butter and syrup; bring to a boil over medium heat, stirring constantly. Remove from the heat.

In a large mixing bowl, beat the eggs, egg whites and vanilla. Gradually add hot syrup mixture. Stir in pecans. Pour into pastry shell.

Cover edges loosely with foil. Bake at 350° for 35-40 minutes or until set. Cool on a wire rack. Refrigerate leftovers. **Yield:** 6-8 servings.

Heavenly Angel Food Cake

(Pictured above)

PREP: 20 min. **BAKE:** 35 min. + chilling

Five ingredients are all you'll need to whip up this impressive layer cake featuring a chocolaty filling. Soft and airy, each slice just melts in your mouth. —*Teri Roberts, Hilliard, Ohio*

- 1 **package (16 ounces) angel food cake mix**
- 24 **large marshmallows**
- 6 **milk chocolate candy bars with almonds (1.45 ounces *each*), chopped**
- 2/3 **cup milk**
- 1 **carton (12 ounces) frozen whipped topping, thawed, *divided***

Prepare and bake cake according to package directions, using an ungreased 10-in. tube pan. Cool.

For filling, in a small saucepan, combine the marshmallows, candy bars and milk. Cook and stir over low heat until marshmallows are melted. Transfer to a small bowl; cool to room temperature. Fold in 3/4 cup whipped topping.

Cut cake horizontally into three layers. Place bottom layer on a serving plate; spread with a third of the filling. Repeat layers twice. Refrigerate for at least 1 hour.

Frost top and sides of cake with remaining whipped topping. **Yield:** 12 servings.

ANGELIC ADVICE. When baking an angel food cake, use an oven thermometer to make sure your oven is not baking at a higher temperature than you set it at. Also, remember to place the cake pan on the lowest rack to allow sufficient air circulation over the top of this tall cake.

Mocha Chip Pie

PREP: 20 min. **BAKE:** 15 min.

This cool, coffee-flavored pie is scrumptious from top to bottom. The only difficult thing about making it is waiting for it to set—you'll want to dig right in! —Sheila Watson, Stettler, Alberta

- 1-1/2 **cups chocolate wafer crumbs**
- 1/4 **cup butter, softened**
- 1 **envelope unflavored gelatin**
- 1/2 **cup milk**
- 1/2 **cup plus 1 tablespoon sugar,** *divided*
- 1/2 **cup strong brewed coffee**
- 1/4 **cup water**
- 1/4 **teaspoon salt**
- 2 **squares (1 ounce** *each***) unsweetened chocolate, melted and cooled**
- 1 **teaspoon vanilla extract**
- 2 **cups heavy whipping cream,** *divided*

Toasted sliced almonds, optional

In a bowl, combine wafer crumbs and butter. Press onto the bottom and up the sides of a greased 9-in. pie plate. Bake at 375° for 5-7 minutes or until lightly browned. Cool on a wire rack.

In a small saucepan, sprinkle gelatin over milk; let stand for 1 minute. Cook and stir over low heat until gelatin is completely dissolved. Add 1/2 cup sugar, coffee, water and salt; cook and stir for 5 minutes or until sugar is dissolved.

Remove from the heat; stir in melted chocolate and vanilla. Transfer to a large bowl; cover and refrigerate until slightly thickened, stirring occasionally.

In a small mixing bowl, beat 1 cup cream until stiff peaks form; fold into chocolate mixture. Spread evenly into crust. Refrigerate for 4 hours or until set.

Just before serving, in a small mixing bowl, beat remaining cream until it begins to thicken. Add remaining sugar; beat until stiff peaks form. Pipe over pie. Garnish with almonds if desired. Refrigerate leftovers. **Yield:** 8 servings.

Cherry-Berry Pie

PREP: 30 min. **BAKE:** 45 min. + cooling

The red and blue fruit peeking through the lattice crust on this pie makes it festive for the Fourth of July and other summertime celebrations. —Cathi Henke, Wauwatosa, Wisconsin

- 2 **cups fresh tart cherries, pitted**
- 2 **cups fresh blueberries**
- 1 **cup chopped fresh strawberries**
- 3/4 **cup sugar**
- 3 **tablespoons cornstarch**
- 2 **teaspoons lemon juice**
- 1/2 **teaspoon almond extract**

Dash salt

- 1 **package (15 ounces) refrigerated pie pastry**
- 2 **tablespoons butter**
- 1 **egg**
- 1 **tablespoon water**

In a large bowl, combine the first eight ingredients.

Line a 9-in. pie plate with bottom crust; trim pastry even with edge. Fill with fruit mixture and dot with butter. Make a lattice crust with remaining pastry. Trim, seal and flute edges. Beat egg and water; brush over lattice top.

Bake at 400° for 45-55 minutes or until crust is golden brown and filling is bubbly. Cover edges with foil during the last 20 minutes to prevent overbrowning if necessary. Cool on a wire rack. **Yield:** 8 servings.

Basketball Cake

PREP: 20 min. **BAKE:** 1 hour

This fun cake is a slam dunk to make—no special pan is needed. It scored big points at a dinner held for the church basketball team my husband coached. —Lonna Liccini, Clifton, Virginia

- 1 **package (18-1/4 ounces) chocolate cake mix**
- 1-1/2 **cups vanilla frosting**

Orange paste food coloring

- 4 **pieces black shoestring licorice**

Prepare the cake batter according to the package directions. Pour into a greased and floured 2-1/2-qt. ovenproof bowl.

Bake at 350° for 60-70 minutes or until a toothpick inserted near the center comes out clean. Cool for 10 minutes before removing from bowl to a wire rack to cool completely.

In a small bowl, combine frosting and food coloring. Place cake on a serving plate. Spread with frosting. Gently press a meat mallet into frosting so texture resembles a basketball. For seams, gently press licorice into frosting. **Yield:** 12-16 servings.

Just Desserts

From holiday feasts to busy weekday dinners, meals are sure to end on a delectable note when you top them off with the sweet sensations here.

FANCY FINALES. Clockwise from top left: Cranberry Angel Parfaits (p. 128), Layered Turtle Cheesecake (p. 122), Peach Melba Cheesecake (p. 124) and Pina Colada Cheesecake (p. 128).

Place a greased 9-in. springform pan on a double thickness of heavy-duty foil (about 18 in. square). Securely wrap foil around pan.

In a small bowl, combine the flour, brown sugar and pecans; cut in the butter until crumbly. Press onto the bottom of prepared pan. Place pan on a baking sheet. Bake at 325° for 12-15 minutes or until set. Cool on a wire rack.

In a large bowl, beat cream cheese and sugars until smooth. Beat in 1/4 cup flour, cream and vanilla. Add eggs; beat on low speed just until combined. Remove 1 cup batter to a small bowl; stir in melted chocolate until blended. Spread over crust.

Combine caramel topping and remaining flour; stir in pecans. Drop by tablespoonfuls over chocolate batter. Top with remaining batter. Place springform pan in a large baking pan; add 1 in. of hot water to larger pan.

Bake at 325° for 1-1/4 to 1-1/2 hours or until center is just set and top appears dull. Remove springform pan from water bath. Cool on a wire rack for 10 minutes. Carefully run a knife around edge of pan to loosen; cool 1 hour longer. Refrigerate overnight.

For ganache, place chips in a small bowl. In a small saucepan, bring cream just to a boil. Pour over chips; whisk until smooth. Cool slightly, stirring occasionally. Spread over cheesecake. Sprinkle with chopped pecans. Refrigerate until set. Garnish with pecan halves and additional caramel topping if desired. **Yield:** 12 servings.

Layered Turtle Cheesecake

(Pictured above and on page 121)

PREP: 40 min. **BAKE:** 1-1/4 hours + chilling

After receiving a request for a turtle cheesecake and not finding a good recipe, I created my own. Everyone has been thrilled with the results.   —*Sue Gronholz, Beaver Dam, Wisconsin*

>   1 cup all-purpose flour
>   1/3 cup packed brown sugar
>   1/4 cup finely chopped pecans
>   6 tablespoons cold butter
> **FILLING:**
>   4 packages (8 ounces *each*) cream cheese, softened
>   1 cup sugar
>   1/3 cup packed brown sugar
>   1/4 cup plus 1 teaspoon all-purpose flour, *divided*
>   2 tablespoons heavy whipping cream
> 1-1/2 teaspoons vanilla extract
>   4 eggs, lightly beaten
>   1/2 cup milk chocolate chips, melted and cooled
>   1/4 cup caramel ice cream topping
>   1/3 cup chopped pecans
> **GANACHE:**
>   1/2 cup milk chocolate chips
>   1/4 cup heavy whipping cream
>   2 tablespoons chopped pecans
> **Optional garnish: pecan halves and additional caramel ice cream topping**

Dipped Ice Cream Cones

PREP: 20 min. + standing

Dress up waffle cones or bowls with this fun-filled, party-worthy idea from our Test Kitchen home economists. It'll make a plain scoop of ice cream extra special.

>   1 cup (6 ounces) semisweet chocolate chips, vanilla *or* white chips
>   1 teaspoon shortening
>   12 ice cream waffle cones *or* bowls
> **Optional toppings: assorted sprinkles, chopped nuts, flaked coconut and small jelly beans**

In a microwave, melt chips and shortening; stir until smooth. Dip top of each cone into chocolate, allowing excess to drip off; roll in toppings of your choice. Place on waxed paper; let stand until set. **Yield:** 1 dozen.

IS IT DONE YET? Our Test Kitchen determines the doneness of a cheesecake by tapping the side of the pan with a wooden spoon to measure the center of the cheesecake's "jiggle." As a general rule, it should be about the size of a walnut. Keep in mind that cheesecakes do not set up completely until they are thoroughly cooled or chilled.

Aunt Ruth's Famous Butterscotch Cheesecake

(Pictured below)

PREP: 30 min. **BAKE:** 65 min. + chilling

My Aunt Ruth prepared this often, many times after I got home from school so I could help her. The cheesecake chills overnight but is definitely worth the wait! —Trisha Kruse, Eagle, Idaho

- **1-1/2 cups graham cracker crumbs**
- **1/3 cup packed brown sugar**
- **1/3 cup butter, melted**
- **1 can (14 ounces) sweetened condensed milk**
- **3/4 cup cold milk**
- **1 package (3.4 ounces) instant butterscotch pudding mix**
- **3 packages (8 ounces *each*) cream cheese, softened**
- **1 teaspoon vanilla extract**
- **3 eggs, lightly beaten**
- **Whipped cream and crushed butterscotch candies, optional**

Place a greased 9-in. springform pan on a double thickness of heavy-duty foil (about 18 in. square). Securely wrap foil around pan. In a small bowl, combine the cracker crumbs and sugar; stir in butter. Press onto the bottom of prepared pan. Place pan on a baking sheet. Bake at 325° for 10 minutes. Cool on a wire rack.

In a small bowl, whisk the milks and pudding mix for 2 minutes. Let stand for 2 minutes or until soft-set.

Meanwhile, in a large bowl, beat cream cheese until smooth. Beat in pudding and vanilla. Add eggs; beat on low speed just until combined. Pour over crust. Place springform pan in a large baking pan; add 1 in. of hot water to larger pan.

Bake at 325° for 65-75 minutes or until center is almost set and top appears dull. Remove springform pan from water bath. Cool on a wire rack for 10 minutes. Carefully run a knife around edge of pan to loosen; cool 1 hour longer. Refrigerate overnight. Garnish with whipped cream and candies if desired. **Yield:** 12 servings.

Lime Tartlets

(Pictured above)

PREP: 30 min. **BAKE:** 10 min./batch + cooling

Made with refrigerated pie pastry, these little sweet–tart treats are perfect for parties. I like to serve them with a slice of melon for color. —Billie Moss, Walnut Creek, California

☑ This recipe includes Nutrition Facts and Diabetic Exchanges.

- **2 packages (15 ounces *each*) refrigerated pie pastry**
- **1 package (8 ounces) cream cheese, softened**
- **1 cup (8 ounces) plain yogurt**
- **3 tablespoons confectioners' sugar**
- **1 jar (10 ounces) lime curd, *divided***
- **Whipped cream and lime slices, optional**

Roll out each pastry on a lightly floured surface. Using a 2-1/2-in. round cookie cutter, cut out 12 circles from each pastry. Press rounds onto the bottoms and up the sides of greased miniature muffin cups. Prick bottoms with a fork.

Bake at 450° for 8-10 minutes or until golden brown. Cool for 5 minutes before removing from the pans to wire racks.

In a large bowl, beat the cream cheese, yogurt and confectioners' sugar until smooth. Stir in 1/2 cup lime curd. Spoon into the tart shells; top with the remaining lime curd. Garnish with whipped cream and lime slices if desired. **Yield:** 4 dozen.

Nutrition Facts: 1 tartlet equals 121 calories, 7 g fat (3 g saturated fat), 14 mg cholesterol, 86 mg sodium, 13 g carbohydrate, 0 fiber, 1 g protein. **Diabetic Exchanges:** 1 starch, 1 fat.

Peach Melba Cheesecake

(Pictured below and on page 121)

PREP: 30 min. **BAKE:** 55 min. + chilling

My high school English teacher gave me the recipe for this pretty cheesecake, and my family loved it. It's an impressive dessert to make for guests, too. —Hope Gonzalez, Lancaster, California

  1-3/4　**cups crushed gingersnap cookies (about 35 cookies)**
    1/3　**cup butter, melted**
      1　**egg white, beaten**
      3　**packages (8 ounces *each*) reduced-fat cream cheese**
      1　**cup sugar**
      1　**cup (8 ounces) sour cream**
    1/2　**cup all-purpose flour**
      1　**teaspoon vanilla extract**
    1/2　**cup egg substitute**
      1　**cup frozen unsweetened sliced peaches, thawed and chopped**
    1/2　**cup raspberry preserves, warmed**
Optional garnish: Fresh raspberries and additional peaches and sugar

In a large bowl, combine the cookie crumbs, butter and egg white. Press onto the bottom of a greased 9-in. springform pan; set aside.

In a large bowl, beat cream cheese and sugar until smooth. Beat in sour cream, flour and vanilla. Add egg substitute; beat on low speed just until combined. Stir in peaches. Pour over crust. Place pan on a baking sheet.

Bake at 325° for 55-65 minutes or until center is almost set. Cool on a wire rack for 10 minutes. Carefully run a knife around edge of pan to loosen; cool 1 hour longer. Refrigerate overnight. Spread preserves over the top. Garnish with raspberries and additional peaches if desired; sprinkle with sugar. **Yield:** 12 servings.

Editor's Note: You may use two whole eggs instead of egg substitute if desired. Beat the eggs before adding them to the batter.

Spiced Apple-Cranberry Crepes

(Pictured above)

PREP: 30 min. + chilling **COOK:** 45 min.

I'm a newlywed and enjoy coming up with recipes. I created this creamy dessert when I invited friends over for a winter brunch. —Shannon Oetter, Chicago, Illinois

      6　**cups chopped peeled tart apples**
      1　**cup fresh cranberries**
    3/4　**cup sugar**
      1　**tablespoon apple pie spice**
  1-1/2　**teaspoons grated orange peel**
    1/2　**teaspoon dried lavender flowers**
    1/4　**cup butter**
CREPES:
      2　**eggs, beaten**
      2　**cups milk**
      2　**tablespoons butter, melted**
      1　**teaspoon vanilla extract**
  1-1/2　**cups all-purpose flour**
      1　**tablespoon sugar**
    1/2　**teaspoon salt**
    1/2　**teaspoon baking powder**
      1　**carton (8 ounces) Mascarpone cheese**
Confectioners' sugar, optional

In a large skillet, saute the apples, cranberries, sugar, pie spice, orange peel and lavender in butter until fruit is tender. Set aside.

In a large bowl, combine the eggs, milk, butter and vanilla. Combine the flour, sugar, salt and baking powder; add to egg mixture and mix well. Cover and refrigerate for 1 hour.

Heat a lightly greased 8-in. nonstick skillet; pour 2 tablespoons batter into the center of skillet. Lift and tilt pan to evenly coat bottom. Cook until top appears dry; turn and cook 15-20 seconds longer. Remove to a wire rack. Repeat with remaining batter, greasing skillet as needed. When cool, stack crepes with waxed paper or paper towels in between.

Spread each crepe with 2 teaspoons cheese; top with

3 tablespoons apple mixture and roll up. Dust with confectioners' sugar if desired. Serve immediately.
Yield: 11 servings.

Editor's Note: Dried lavender flowers are available from Penzeys Spices. Call 1-800/741-7787 or visit *www.penzeys.com.*

Pumpkin Creme Brulee

PREP: 20 min. **BAKE:** 25 min. + chilling

I've never met a creme brulee I didn't like! I'm not a big fan of pumpkin, but the rich flavor of this spiced custard is fantastic.
—Tamara Leonard Merritt, Raleigh, North Carolina

 8 **egg yolks**
 1/3 **cup plus 1/2 cup sugar, *divided***
 3 **cups heavy whipping cream**
 3/4 **cup canned pumpkin**
 1-1/2 **teaspoons vanilla extract**
 1/2 **teaspoon ground cinnamon**
 1/4 **teaspoon *each* ground ginger, nutmeg and cloves**

In a small bowl, whisk egg yolks and 1/3 cup sugar. In a small saucepan, heat cream over medium heat until bubbles form around sides of pan. Remove from the heat; stir a small amount of hot cream into egg yolk mixture. Return all to the pan, stirring constantly. Stir in the pumpkin, vanilla and spices.

Transfer to eight 6-oz. ramekins or custard cups. Place ramekins in a baking pan; add 1 in. of boiling water to pan. Bake, uncovered, at 325° for 25-30 minutes or until centers are just set (mixture will jiggle). Remove ramekins from water bath; cool for 10 minutes. Cover and refrigerate for at least 4 hours.

If using a creme brulee torch, sprinkle with remaining sugar. Heat sugar with the torch until caramelized. Serve immediately.

If broiling the custards, place ramekins on a baking sheet; let stand at room temperature for 15 minutes. Sprinkle with remaining sugar. Broil 8 in. from the heat for 4-7 minutes or until sugar is caramelized. Refrigerate for 1-2 hours or until firm. **Yield:** 8 servings.

PUMPKIN PLAN. Homegrown pumpkin may be used cup-for-cup in place of canned pumpkin. "Pie pumpkins" are the most flavorful variety for use in baking. Pick when they are fully ripened— the color will be deep orange, and the stem will easily break loose when ready to harvest.

Wash, peel and remove the seeds from the pumpkin. Cut it into chunks and steam until soft. Puree using a food mill or processor. Cool, then pack it into freezer bags or containers in the amounts needed for your recipes.

Apple-Raisin Bread Pudding

(Pictured below)

PREP: 20 min. **BAKE:** 40 min.

Our six children request this for breakfast on chilly mornings, and it's a yummy dessert as well. It makes the kitchen smell warm and homey. —*Janelle Fahnestock, Lititz, Pennsylvania*

 3 **tablespoons butter, melted**
 1 **loaf (1 pound) day-old cinnamon-raisin bread, cubed**
 3 **cups chopped peeled tart apples**
 7 **eggs**
 2-1/2 **cups milk**
 3/4 **cup sugar**
 3 **teaspoons vanilla extract**
VANILLA SAUCE:
 2/3 **cup sugar**
 1 **tablespoon cornstarch**
 1/8 **teaspoon salt**
 1 **cup cold water**
 1 **tablespoon butter**
 1 **teaspoon vanilla extract**

Pour butter into a 13-in. x 9-in. baking dish. Combine bread cubes and apples; sprinkle over butter. In a large bowl, whisk eggs, milk, sugar and vanilla. Pour over bread.

Bake, uncovered, at 325° for 40-45 minutes or until a knife inserted near the center comes out clean.

In a small saucepan, combine the sugar, cornstarch, salt and water until smooth. Bring to a boil over low heat, stirring constantly. Cook and stir for 1-2 minutes or until thickened. Remove from the heat; stir in the butter and vanilla. Serve with warm bread pudding.
Yield: 12 servings (1-1/4 cups sauce).

Oh-So-Tempting Trifles

LAYER upon layer, a trifle treats you to a bountiful blend of delights. From cake to cream, a multitude of sweet ingredients combine for one delectable dessert.

Why not whip up one today? Here, we've featured Brownie Mocha Trifle, made in a large bowl...as well as three recipes served in individual dishes. Plus, you'll find ideas for setting up a trifle bar (see the box at right).

Brownie Mocha Trifle

PREP: 15 min. + chilling **BAKE:** 25 min. + cooling

Because you use instant pudding and a convenient box mix to prepare this trifle, there's nothing to it. The result is moist and chewy. —Louise Fauth, Foremost, Alberta

 1 package fudge brownie mix (8-inch square pan size)
1-3/4 cups cold milk
 2 packages (3.4 ounces *each*) instant vanilla pudding mix
 1/4 cup cold brewed coffee
 2 cups whipped topping
 1 Heath candy bar (1.4 ounces), crushed

Prepare brownie batter and bake according to package directions. Cool; cut into 1-in. pieces.

In a large bowl, beat the milk and pudding mixes for 2 minutes or until thickened. Stir in coffee. Fold in whipped topping.

In a trifle bowl or 2-qt. glass bowl, layer a third of the brownie pieces, pudding mixture and crushed candy. Repeat layers twice. Chill until serving. **Yield:** 8 servings.

Mandarin Trifles

(Pictured at left in photo at far right)

PREP/TOTAL TIME: 15 min.

With their sunny color, these layered treats from our Test Kitchen staff will brighten up any meal. Mandarin oranges and papaya give them a refreshingly tropical taste.

 1/2 cup heavy whipping cream
 2 teaspoons honey
 1/4 cup dried papaya
 1 can (11 ounces) mandarin oranges, drained

In a large bowl, beat cream until it begins to thicken. Add honey; beat until stiff peaks form. Set aside.

Place 1 tablespoon dried papaya in each of two cocktail glasses or dessert dishes; layer each with 1/4 cup whipped cream. Top with the oranges and remaining papaya; dollop with remaining whipped cream. Serve immediately. **Yield:** 2 servings.

Build Your Own Trifle Bar

WHAT a luscious idea! Let friends and family make their own dessert at a trifle bar. Set out an array of ingredients to layer and include a glass for each guest. You could mix and match glassware of different shapes to add to the fun.

Our Test Kitchen staff came up with this list of ingredient ideas. Try these, or create your own!

CAKES
Angel food
Pound cake
Sponge cake
Quick breads (pumpkin, blueberry, etc.)
Cut-up doughnuts or doughnut holes
Macaroons

FILLINGS
Instant puddings
Whipped cream
Gelatin
Lemon or lime curd
Mousse
Pie fillings
Whipped cream cheeses

FRUITS
Blueberries
Mandarin oranges
Blackberries
Strawberries
Raspberries

Kiwi
Pineapple
Star fruit
Cherries
Dried fruit
Mango

TOPPINGS
Plain or flavored whipped cream (add chocolate, lime zest, etc.)
Syrups
Caramel sauce
Miniature marshmallows
Cocoa powder
Toasted coconut

EXTRAS
Chocolate leaves
Mini cookies
Red Hots
Nuts
Granola
Candied ginger
Pirouette cookies
Chocolate coffee beans

Kiwi-Pistachio Trifles

(Pictured above center)

PREP/TOTAL TIME: 20 min.

Serving these individual trifles in wine glasses brings a touch of elegance to your table. Our Test Kitchen home economists added pistachios for a pleasantly crunchy contrast.

> **1 cup lime curd**
> **3/4 cup pistachios, chopped, *divided***
> **4 cups cubed angel food cake**
> **4 medium kiwifruit, peeled, quartered and sliced**
> **1-1/2 cups prepared vanilla pudding**

Spoon lime curd into six wine glasses or dessert dishes; sprinkle each with 1 tablespoon pistachios. Layer with cake cubes, kiwi and pudding. Sprinkle with remaining pistachios. Chill until serving. **Yield:** 6 servings.

Raspberry Lemon Trifles

(Pictured above right)

PREP/TOTAL TIME: 15 min.

Make plain vanilla pudding for the kids, then use the rest of it to create these layered desserts for the adults. You'll need only two additional ingredients! With fresh raspberries and lemon curd, our staff gave the little trifles tongue-tingling flavor.

> **1-1/4 cups prepared vanilla pudding**
> **1/4 cup lemon curd**
> **3 cups fresh raspberries**

In a small bowl, combine vanilla pudding and lemon curd. Spoon 2 tablespoons pudding mixture into each of four wine glasses or dessert dishes; sprinkle each with 1/4 cup raspberries. Repeat layers twice. Chill until serving. **Yield:** 4 servings.

heat, stirring until gelatin is completely dissolved. Stir in the cream, cranberry puree and yogurt.

Place 2 tablespoons gelatin mixture in each of four parfait glasses; top each with 1/4 cup cake cubes. Repeat layers. Top with remaining gelatin mixture. Cover and refrigerate for at least 4 hours. Just before serving, garnish with whipped topping and reserved berries. **Yield:** 4 servings.

Pina Colada Cheesecake

(Pictured below and on page 120)

PREP: 40 min. **BAKE:** 1-1/4 hours + cooling

I came across this cheesecake recipe several years ago and knew I'd found a keeper. I love anything with coconut and pineapple!
—*Peggy Key, Grant, Alabama*

  15 **shortbread cookies, crushed**
    1 **cup flaked coconut, toasted**
    3 **tablespoons butter, melted**
FILLING:
    3 **packages (8 ounces** *each***) reduced-fat cream cheese**
  3/4 **cup sugar**
  3/4 **cup cream of coconut**
    3 **tablespoons milk**
  3/4 **teaspoon rum extract**
    3 **eggs, lightly beaten**
TOPPING:
  1/2 **fresh pineapple, peeled and cored**
    3 **tablespoons apple jelly**
Edible blossoms, optional

Place a greased 9-in. springform pan on a double thickness of heavy-duty foil (about 18 in. square). Securely wrap foil around pan.

In a small bowl, combine the shortbread cookie crumbs and coconut; stir in butter. Press onto bottom of prepared pan. Place pan on a baking sheet. Bake at

Cranberry Angel Parfaits

(Pictured above and on page 120)

PREP: 50 min. + chilling

With cranberries and spices, this is a light and luscious finale for the Christmas holiday season. Using a purchased angel food cake speeds up the preparation. —*Ruth Lee, Troy, Ontario*

1-1/4 **cups plain yogurt**
    3 **cups fresh** *or* **frozen cranberries**
  3/4 **cup sugar**
  1/2 **cup plus 2 tablespoons cold water,** *divided*
  1/8 **teaspoon ground cinnamon**
  1/8 **teaspoon ground nutmeg**
    1 **teaspoon unflavored gelatin**
    3 **tablespoons half-and-half cream**
    2 **cups cubed angel food cake**
  1/2 **cup whipped topping**

Line a strainer with four layers of cheesecloth or one coffee filter; place over a bowl. Add yogurt to strainer; fold edges of cheesecloth over yogurt. Refrigerate for 8 hours or overnight.

In a large saucepan, combine the cranberries, sugar and 1/2 cup water. Cook over medium heat until the berries pop, about 15 minutes. Set aside 1/3 cup berries for garnish; cover and refrigerate until serving. Mash and strain remaining cranberry mixture, discarding pulp; stir in cinnamon and nutmeg. Set aside.

Remove yogurt from cheesecloth and discard liquid from bowl. In a small saucepan, sprinkle gelatin over remaining water; let stand for 1 minute. Cook over low

325° for 8-10 minutes or until set and lightly browned. Cool on a wire rack.

In a large bowl, beat cream cheese and sugar until smooth. Beat in the cream of coconut, milk and extract. Add eggs; beat on low speed just until combined. Pour over crust. Place springform pan in a large baking pan; add 1 in. of hot water to larger pan.

Bake at 325° for 1-1/4 to 1-1/2 hours or until center is just set and top appears dull. Remove springform pan from water bath. Cool on a wire rack for 10 minutes. Carefully run a knife around edge of pan to loosen; cool 1 hour longer. Refrigerate overnight.

Thinly slice pineapple; arrange on cheesecake. Warm apple jelly; brush over pineapple. Refrigerate until chilled. Just before serving, garnish with blossoms if desired. **Yield:** 12 servings.

Editor's Note: Verify that flowers are edible and have not been treated with chemicals.

Royal Icing

PREP/TOTAL TIME: 25 min.

Our Test Kitchen home economists shared their recipe for this classic decorating icing that sets up and dries quickly. It's especially nice to use for cookies that will be stacked on a plate.

- **3-3/4 to 4 cups confectioners' sugar**
- **3 tablespoons meringue powder**
- **5 to 6 tablespoons warm water**

In a bowl, combine all ingredients. Beat on high speed with a portable mixer for 10-12 minutes or on low speed with a stand mixer for 7-10 minutes or until peaks form. **Yield:** 3 cups.

Chocolate-Dipped Strawberry Cheesecake

(Pictured above right)

PREP: 45 min. + chilling

What a combination—rich cheesecake and chocolate–covered strawberries! Present this at your next party and prepare to hear oohs and aahs. —Kathy Berger, Dry Ridge, Kentucky

☑ This recipe includes Nutrition Facts and Diabetic Exchanges.

- **1-3/4 cups chocolate graham cracker crumbs (about 9 whole crackers)**
- **1/4 cup butter, melted**
- **1 pound fresh or frozen strawberries, thawed**
- **2 envelopes unflavored gelatin**
- **1/2 cup cold water**
- **2 packages (8 ounces each) fat-free cream cheese, cubed**
- **1 cup (8 ounces) fat-free cottage cheese**

Sugar substitute equivalent to 3/4 cup sugar
- **1 carton (8 ounces) frozen reduced-fat whipped topping, thawed, divided**

- **13 medium fresh strawberries**
- **4 squares (1 ounce each) semisweet chocolate**

In a small bowl, combine cracker crumbs and butter. Press onto the bottom and 1 in. up the sides of a 9-in. springform pan coated with cooking spray. Place on a baking sheet. Bake at 350° for 10 minutes or until set. Cool on a wire rack.

Hull strawberries if necessary; puree in a food processor. Remove and set aside. In a small saucepan, sprinkle gelatin over cold water; let stand for 1 minute. Heat over low heat, stirring until gelatin is completely dissolved. Transfer to the food processor; add cream cheese, cottage cheese and sugar substitute. Cover and process until smooth.

Add strawberry puree; cover and process until blended. Transfer to a large bowl; fold in 2 cups whipped topping. Pour into crust. Cover and refrigerate for 2-3 hours or until set.

For garnish, wash strawberries and gently pat with paper towels until completely dry. Cut tops off berries. In a microwave-safe bowl, melt chocolate at 50% power; stir until smooth. Dip each berry tip until half of the berry is coated, allowing excess to drip off. Place with tips pointing up on a waxed paper-lined baking sheet; refrigerate for at least 30 minutes.

Carefully run a knife around edge of springform pan to loosen; remove sides of pan. Arrange berries, chocolate tips up, around edge of cheesecake and place one in the center. Garnish with remaining whipped topping. Refrigerate leftovers. **Yield:** 12 servings.

Nutrition Facts: 1 slice equals 245 calories, 11 g fat (7 g saturated fat), 14 mg cholesterol, 377 mg sodium, 26 g carbohydrate, 2 g fiber, 10 g protein. **Diabetic Exchanges:** 2 starch, 2 fat.

Pumpkin Walnut Cheesecake

(Pictured below)

PREP: 40 min. **BAKE:** 1-1/2 hours + chilling

When it comes to autumn desserts, you just can't beat this deluxe cheesecake! One of my Bunco friends gave me the recipe, and it's now a family favorite.   —Susan Garoutte, Georgetown, Texas

> 2 **cups graham cracker crumbs**
> 1/4 **cup sugar**
> 6 **tablespoons butter, melted**

FILLING:

> 3 **packages (8 ounces *each*) cream cheese, softened**
> 3/4 **cup sugar**
> 3/4 **cup packed dark brown sugar**
> 1 **can (15 ounces) solid-pack pumpkin**
> 1/4 **cup heavy whipping cream**
> 1 **teaspoon ground cinnamon**
> 1 **teaspoon ground cloves**
> 5 **eggs, lightly beaten**

TOPPING:

> 6 **tablespoons butter, softened**
> 1 **cup packed dark brown sugar**
> 1 **cup chopped walnuts**

Place a greased 9-in. springform pan on a double thickness of heavy-duty foil (about 18 in. square). Securely wrap foil around pan. In a small bowl, combine cracker crumbs and sugar; stir in butter. Press onto the bottom and 1 in. up the sides of prepared pan.

In a large bowl, beat cream cheese and sugars until smooth. Beat in the pumpkin, cream, cinnamon and cloves until blended. Add eggs; beat on low speed just until combined. Pour over crust. Place springform pan in a large baking pan; add 1 in. of hot water to larger pan.

Bake at 325° for 1 hour. For topping, in a small bowl, combine butter and brown sugar. Stir in walnuts. Carefully sprinkle over hot cheesecake. Bake 30 minutes longer or until center is just set. Remove springform pan from water bath. Cool on a wire rack for 10 minutes. Carefully run a knife around edge of pan to loosen; cool 1 hour longer. Refrigerate overnight. **Yield:** 12 servings.

Turtle Praline Tart

PREP: 35 min. + chilling

This chocolate–drizzled tart is my own creation. With just five ingredients, it's simple enough to fix anytime but nice enough to serve guests.   —Kathy Specht, Cambria, California

> 1 **refrigerated pie pastry**
> 36 **caramels**
> 1 **cup heavy whipping cream, *divided***
> 3-1/2 **cups pecan halves**
> 1/2 **cup semisweet chocolate chips**

On a lightly floured surface, unroll pastry. Transfer to an 11-in. fluted tart pan with removable bottom; trim edges. Line unpricked pastry with a double thickness of heavy-duty foil. Bake at 450° for 8 minutes. Remove foil; bake 5-7 minutes longer or until lightly golden brown.

In a large saucepan, combine caramels and 1/2 cup cream. Cook and stir over medium-low heat until caramels are melted. Stir in pecans. Spread filling evenly into crust.

In a small microwave-safe bowl, melt chips; drizzle over filling. Cover and refrigerate for 30 minutes or until set. Whip remaining cream; serve with tart. **Yield:** 16 servings.

Apple Dessert Sauce

PREP/TOTAL TIME: 10 min.

Spooned over vanilla ice cream, this sauce gives you the taste of warm apple pie without all the fuss. The recipe is so easy, even kids can make it.   —Jacqueline Graves, Cumming, Georgia

> 3/4 **cup chopped peeled tart apple**
> 1 **tablespoon water**
> 1 **cup packed brown sugar**
> 1 **cup (8 ounces) sour cream**
> 1/4 **teaspoon ground cinnamon**

Vanilla ice cream

A SMOOTH MOVE. To avoid lumps in Pumpkin Walnut Cheesecake (recipe above left) or other cheesecakes, be sure to soften the cream cheese at room temperature for about 30 minutes before mixing. If the cream cheese is not softened before mixing, it won't be smoothed after blending.

Transfer puree to a 13-in. x 9-in. dish. Freeze for 1 hour or until the edges begin to firm. Stir and return to freezer. Freeze 2 hours longer or until firm.

Just before serving, transfer the sorbet to a food processor; cover and process for 2-3 minutes or until smooth. **Yield:** 1 quart.

Nutrition Facts: 2/3 cup equals 254 calories, trace fat (trace saturated fat), 0 cholesterol, 4 mg sodium, 59 g carbohydrate, 2 g fiber, 1 g protein.

Candied-Almond Chocolate Strawberries

(Pictured below)

PREP: 35 min. + standing

For a special presentation, I sprinkle a serving tray with crushed almonds, lay these strawberries on top and garnish them with mint leaves.   —Laura McAllister, Morganton, North Carolina

> 60 **fresh strawberries (about 2 pounds)**
> 2 **cups honey-roasted almonds**
> 1 **package (11-1/2 ounces) 60% cacao bittersweet chocolate baking chips**
> 1/4 **cup butter, cubed**
> **Dash cayenne pepper**

Wash strawberries and gently pat with paper towels until completely dry. Place almonds in a food processor; cover and process to desired fineness. Transfer to a shallow bowl; set aside.

In a microwave, melt chocolate chips and butter; add cayenne and stir until smooth. Dip strawberries in chocolate mixture; allow excess to drip off. Roll berries in almonds; place on waxed paper and let stand until set. Serve immediately. **Yield:** 5 dozen.

In a 1-qt. microwave-safe dish, combine apple and water. Cover and microwave on high for 1 minute. Stir in brown sugar. Cover and cook 1 minute longer.

Stir in sour cream and cinnamon. Cover and cook at 50% power for 1-1/2 to 1-3/4 minutes or until brown sugar is melted, stirring once. Stir until blended. Serve warm with ice cream. **Yield:** 1-3/4 cups.

Editor's Note: This recipe was tested in a 1,100-watt microwave.

Strawberry & Wine Sorbet

(Pictured above)

PREP: 20 min. + freezing

Bright and refreshing, this grown-up treat may remind you of a just-picked strawberry. White wine and lemon juice enhance its not-too-sweet flavor.   —Donna Lamano, Olathe, Kansas

✓ **This recipe includes Nutrition Facts.**

> 3/4 **cup sugar**
> 1/2 **cup water**
> 1-1/2 **pounds fresh strawberries, hulled**
> 1 **cup white wine**
> 1/2 **cup honey**
> 1/4 **cup lemon juice**

In a small saucepan, bring sugar and water to a boil. Cook and stir until sugar is dissolved; set aside to cool.

Place the remaining ingredients in a food processor; add sugar syrup. Cover and process for 2-3 minutes or until smooth. Strain and discard seeds and pulp.

Potluck Pleasers

Want to wow the crowd? It's easy!
Just bring any of the popular salads,
casseroles, bars and other group-size
foods set out in this chapter.

BUFFET-TABLE BEST. Clockwise from upper left: Grilled Greek Potato Salad (p. 135), The Firehouse Special (p. 142), Double-Cheese Macaroni (p. 138) and Make Once, Eat Twice Lasagna (p. 140).

Cinnamon Biscuit Peach Cobbler

(Pictured above)

PREP: 30 min. **BAKE:** 20 min.

The first time I made this yummy spiced cobbler, it was a big hit. Now, it's expected to appear at every family gathering we have!
—Fawna Eastman, Evanston, Wyoming

1-1/2 **cups all-purpose flour**
   1 **tablespoon plus 1/3 cup packed brown sugar,** *divided*
   2 **teaspoons baking powder**
 1/4 **teaspoon salt**
 1/4 **teaspoon baking soda**
   6 **tablespoons cold butter**
 1/2 **cup milk**
   2 **tablespoons butter, melted**
 3/4 **cup chopped walnuts**
 3/4 **teaspoon ground cinnamon**
FILLING:
   1 **cup packed brown sugar**
   2 **tablespoons cornstarch**
 3/4 **teaspoon grated lemon peel**
   1 **cup water**
   9 **cups sliced peeled peaches**

Combine flour, 1 tablespoon brown sugar, baking powder, salt and baking soda; cut in butter until mixture resembles coarse crumbs. Stir in milk just until blended. Transfer to floured surface; knead 10-12 times. Pat into a 12-in. square. Brush with melted butter. Combine walnuts, cinnamon and remaining brown

sugar; sprinkle over dough to within 1/2 in. of edge. Roll up jelly-roll style. Seal dough; set aside.

In a large saucepan, combine brown sugar, cornstarch and lemon peel; stir in water until blended. Add peaches. Bring to a boil. Cook and stir for 2 minutes or until thickened and bubbly. Transfer to a greased 13-in. x 9-in. baking dish.

Cut biscuit dough into twelve 1-in. slices; arrange biscuits over filling. Bake, uncovered, at 400° for 20-25 minutes or until golden brown. **Yield:** 12 servings.

Sloppy Joes for 8 Dozen

(Pictured below)

PREP: 20 min. **COOK:** 1-1/2 hours

We raised three hungry boys, and I had to cook and bake huge amounts of everything. This sloppy joe recipe is terrific when you're feeding a crowd. —Wanieta Penner, Assaria, Kansas

 15 **pounds ground beef**
  6 **medium onions, chopped**
  1 **gallon ketchup**
 3/4 **cup Worcestershire sauce**
 1/2 **cup packed brown sugar**
 1/2 **cup prepared yellow mustard**
 1/4 **cup white vinegar**
  1 **tablespoon chili powder**
 96 **hamburger buns, split**

In two soup kettles over medium heat, cook and stir beef and onions until meat is no longer pink; drain.

Stir in the ketchup, Worcestershire sauce, brown sugar, mustard, vinegar and chili powder. Bring to a boil. Reduce the heat; simmer, uncovered, for 1 hour to allow flavors to blend. Spoon 1/3 cup onto each bun. **Yield:** 96 servings.

Brenda's Lemon Bars

PREP: 20 min. **BAKE:** 30 min.

These simple but luscious bars rank among my most-requested recipes. They're great as a contribution to potlucks and parties, but I never need a reason to whip up a pan of these tangy treats.
—Brenda Hamilton, Nelson, British Columbia

- 2-1/4 **cups all-purpose flour,** *divided*
- 1/2 **cup plus 1 tablespoon confectioners' sugar,** *divided*
- 1 **cup cold butter**
- 4 **eggs**
- 2 **cups sugar**
- 2/3 **cup lemon juice**
- 1/2 **teaspoon baking powder**

In a large bowl, combine 2 cups flour and 1/2 cup confectioners' sugar; cut in butter until crumbly. Press into an ungreased 13-in. x 9-in. x 2-in. baking dish. Bake at 350° for 12-15 minutes or until lightly browned. Place on a wire rack to cool slightly.

Meanwhile, in a small mixing bowl, beat the eggs, sugar, lemon juice, baking powder and remaining flour until frothy. Pour over the warm crust. Bake for 18-22 minutes or until lightly browned. Cool on a wire rack.

Dust with remaining confectioners' sugar. Cut into bars. Store in the refrigerator. **Yield:** 2 dozen.

Hot Italian Roast Beef Sandwiches

PREP: 10 min. **COOK:** 3 hours 30 min.

A line tends to form whenever these flavorful, tender roast beef sandwiches show up on a buffet table. Try them for all of your special occasions, from graduation parties to family reunions.
—Betty Claycomb, Alverton, Pennsylvania

- 1 **boneless beef sirloin tip roast (5 pounds)**
- 1 **tablespoon butter**
- 1 **can (28 ounces) diced tomatoes, undrained**
- 1/3 **cup water**
- 3 **teaspoons dried thyme**
- 1 **to 3 teaspoons crushed red pepper flakes**
- 1 **teaspoon salt**
- 20 **sandwich buns, split**

In a Dutch oven over medium heat, brown the beef roast in butter on all sides. Stir in the tomatoes, water, thyme, crushed red pepper flakes and salt. Bring to a boil. Reduce the heat; cover and simmer for 3-1/2 to 4 hours or until the meat is tender, adding more water if necessary.

Remove the roast and reserve the cooking juices. Let the roast stand for 15 minutes; trim any fat and thinly slice the meat. To serve, reheat the sliced beef in the cooking juices. Serve sliced beef on sandwich buns. **Yield:** 20 sandwiches.

Grilled Greek Potato Salad

(Pictured above and on page 132)

PREP: 30 min. **GRILL:** 20 min.

Colorful and fresh-tasting, this is my most popular summer side dish. It's perfect for outdoor gatherings and can be served warm or cold.
—Robin Jungers, Campbellsport, Wisconsin

☑ **This recipe includes Nutrition Facts and Diabetic Exchanges.**

- 3 **pounds small red potatoes, halved**
- 2 **tablespoons olive oil**
- 1/2 **teaspoon salt**
- 1/4 **teaspoon pepper**
- 1 **large sweet yellow pepper, chopped**
- 1 **large sweet red pepper, chopped**
- 1 **medium red onion, halved and sliced**
- 1 **medium cucumber, chopped**
- 1-1/4 **cups grape tomatoes, halved**
- 1/2 **pound fresh mozzarella cheese, cubed**
- 3/4 **cup Greek vinaigrette**
- 1/2 **cup halved Greek olives**
- 1 **can (2-1/4 ounces) sliced ripe olives, drained**
- 2 **tablespoons minced fresh oregano** *or* **1 teaspoon dried oregano**

Drizzle potatoes with oil and sprinkle with salt and pepper; toss to coat. Grill potatoes, covered, over medium heat for 20-25 minutes or until tender. Place in a large bowl. Add remaining ingredients; toss to coat. Serve warm or cold. **Yield:** 21 servings (3/4 cup each).

Nutrition Facts: 3/4 cup equals 142 calories, 8 g fat (2 g saturated fat), 8 mg cholesterol, 248 mg sodium, 14 g carbohydrate, 2 g fiber, 4 g protein. **Diabetic Exchanges:** 1-1/2 fat, 1 starch.

Stamp-of-Approval Spaghetti Sauce

(Pictured below)

PREP: 30 min. **COOK:** 8 hours

My father has strong opinions, especially when it comes to good food. The first time he tasted this meaty, from-scratch spaghetti sauce made in the slow cooker, he enthusiastically gave it his stamp of approval. So I knew the recipe was a keeper!
—Melissa Taylor, Higley, Arizona

- 2 pounds ground beef
- 3/4 pound bulk Italian sausage
- 4 medium onions, finely chopped
- 8 garlic cloves, minced
- 4 cans (14-1/2 ounces *each*) diced tomatoes, undrained
- 4 cans (6 ounces *each*) tomato paste
- 1/2 cup water
- 1/4 cup sugar
- 1/4 cup Worcestershire sauce
- 1 tablespoon canola oil
- 1/4 cup minced fresh parsley
- 2 tablespoons minced fresh basil *or* 2 teaspoons dried basil
- 1 tablespoon minced fresh oregano *or* 1 teaspoon dried oregano
- 4 bay leaves
- 1 teaspoon rubbed sage
- 1/2 teaspoon salt
- 1/2 teaspoon dried marjoram
- 1/2 teaspoon pepper

Hot cooked spaghetti

In a Dutch oven, cook the ground beef, Italian sausage, onions and garlic over medium heat until the meat is no longer pink; drain.

Transfer to a 5-qt. slow cooker. Stir in the tomatoes, tomato paste, water, sugar, Worcestershire sauce, oil and seasonings. Cover and cook on low for 8 hours or until bubbly. Discard bay leaves. Serve with spaghetti. **Yield:** 12 servings (3 quarts).

Raspberry Patch Crumb Bars

(Pictured above)

PREP: 30 min. **BAKE:** 35 min.

Everyone will want to indulge when they see a fresh-baked pan of these scrumptious raspberry bars. To give the tangy treats even more crunch, add a sprinkling of nuts to the crumb topping.
—Leanna Thorne, Lakewood, Colorado

- 3 cups all-purpose flour
- 1-1/2 cups sugar, *divided*
- 1 teaspoon baking powder
- 1/4 teaspoon salt
- 1/4 teaspoon ground cinnamon
- 1 cup shortening
- 2 eggs, lightly beaten
- 1 teaspoon almond extract
- 1 tablespoon cornstarch
- 4 cups fresh *or* frozen raspberries

In a large bowl, combine the flour, 1 cup sugar, baking powder, salt and cinnamon. Cut in shortening until mixture resembles coarse crumbs. Stir in eggs and extract. Press two-thirds of the mixture into a greased 13-in. x 9-in. x 2-in. baking dish.

In a large bowl, combine cornstarch and remaining sugar; add raspberries and gently toss. Spoon over crust. Sprinkle with remaining crumb mixture.

Bake at 375° for 35-45 minutes or until bubbly and golden brown. Cool on a wire rack. Cut into bars. Store in the refrigerator. **Yield:** 3 dozen.

Editor's Note: If using frozen raspberries, do not thaw before tossing with cornstarch mixture.

Citrus Cider Punch

PREP/ TOTAL TIME: 5 min.

I share this refreshing punch recipe with people who visit our apple cider mill. It's the perfect beverage for autumn and winter gatherings. —Carolyn Beck, St. Johns, Michigan

- **1 gallon apple cider, chilled**
- **1 can (12 ounces) frozen lemonade concentrate, thawed**
- **1 medium lemon, sliced**
- **4 spiced apple rings**

In a large punch bowl, combine the apple cider and lemonade. Garnish with lemon slices and apple rings.
Yield: 25 servings (4-3/4 quarts).

Mediterranean Salad

(Pictured below)

PREP/TOTAL TIME: 20 min.

This crisp, big-batch salad is a welcome accompaniment to any grilled entree. The recipe's homemade dressing is just the right finishing touch. —Pat Stevens, Granbury, Texas

☑ This recipe includes Nutrition Facts and Diabetic Exchanges.

- **18 cups torn romaine (about 2 large bunches)**
- **1 medium cucumber, sliced**
- **1 cup crumbled feta cheese**
- **1 cup cherry tomatoes, quartered**
- **1 small red onion, thinly sliced**
- **1/2 cup julienned roasted sweet red peppers**
- **1/2 cup pitted Greek olives, halved**
- **DRESSING:**
- **2/3 cup olive oil**
- **1/4 cup red wine vinegar**
- **1 garlic clove, minced**
- **1 teaspoon Italian seasoning**
- **1/4 teaspoon salt**
- **1/4 teaspoon pepper**

In a very large salad bowl, combine the first seven ingredients. In a jar with a tight-fitting lid, combine the remaining ingredients; shake well. Drizzle over salad and toss to coat. Serve immediately. **Yield:** 28 servings (3/4 cup each).
   Nutrition Facts: 3/4 cup equals 69 calories, 6 g fat (1 g saturated fat), 2 mg cholesterol, 117 mg sodium, 2 g carbohydrate, 1 g fiber, 1 g protein. **Diabetic Exchanges:** 1 vegetable, 1 fat.

Calico Beans

(Pictured above)

PREP: 30 min. **BAKE:** 1 hour

These saucy beans aren't overly sweet like some versions I've tried. Bring them to a picnic, and the bowl will be empty before you know it! —Pat Price Cook, Mission Viejo, California

- **4 medium onions, halved and sliced**
- **5 bacon strips, diced**
- **2 garlic cloves, minced**
- **1 cup packed dark brown sugar**
- **1/2 cup cider vinegar**
- **1/4 teaspoon ground mustard**
- **2 cans (15-1/4 ounces *each*) lima beans, rinsed and drained**
- **2 cans (15 ounces *each*) pork and beans**
- **1 can (16 ounces) kidney beans, rinsed and drained**

In a Dutch oven, saute the onions, bacon and garlic until onions are tender. Add brown sugar, vinegar and mustard; bring to a boil. Reduce heat; simmer, uncovered, for 20 minutes. Stir in beans. Transfer to a 3-qt. baking dish. Cover and bake at 350° for 1 hour or until heated through. **Yield:** 12 servings (3/4 cup each).

Casseroles for the Crowd

WHAT goes over better at a potluck supper than a creamy, cheesy pasta casserole? Warm and gooey, the one-dish wonders here will have young and old alike coming back for second helpings—and even thirds!

Double-Cheese Macaroni

(Pictured below and on page 133)

PREP: 25 min. **BAKE:** 20 min.

I make this comforting mac–and–cheese often, and I have yet to encounter anyone who doesn't love it. For a garnish, sprinkle on a little parsley.   —Sabrina Dewitt, Cumberland, Maryland

- 1 package (16 ounces) elbow macaroni
- 3 cups (24 ounces) 4% cottage cheese
- 1/2 cup butter, cubed
- 1/2 cup all-purpose flour
- 1 teaspoon salt
- 1/2 teaspoon white pepper
- 1/4 teaspoon garlic salt
- 3 cups half-and-half cream
- 1 cup milk
- 4 cups (16 ounces) shredded cheddar cheese

TOPPING:
- 1 cup dry bread crumbs
- 1/4 cup butter, melted

Cook the macaroni according to the package directions. Meanwhile, place cottage cheese in a food processor; cover and process until smooth. Set aside.

In a large saucepan, melt the butter. Stir in the flour, salt, pepper and garlic salt until smooth. Gradually add the cream and milk. Bring to a boil; cook and stir for 2 minutes or until thickened.

Drain macaroni; transfer to a large bowl. Add cheddar cheese, cottage cheese and sauce; toss to coat. Transfer to a greased 13-in. x 9-in. baking dish. (Dish will be full.)

Combine bread crumbs and butter; sprinkle over top. Bake, uncovered, at 400° for 20-25 minutes or until bubbly. **Yield:** 12 servings (1 cup each).

Creamy Chicken Noodle Bake

(Pictured above)

PREP: 25 min. **BAKE:** 40 min. + standing

This ever–popular casserole is loaded with noodles and tender chunks of chicken. Don't be surprised if you end up bringing home an empty dish!   —Shirley Unger, Bluffton, Ohio

- 4 cups uncooked egg noodles
- 1/2 cup butter, *divided*
- 1/4 cup all-purpose flour
- 1/2 teaspoon salt
- 1/8 teaspoon white pepper
- 3-1/2 cups milk
- 4 cups cubed cooked chicken
- 2 jars (12 ounces *each*) chicken gravy
- 1 jar (2 ounces) diced pimientos, drained
- 1/2 cup cubed process cheese (Velveeta)
- 1/2 cup dry bread crumbs
- 4 teaspoons butter, melted

Cook the noodles according to the package directions. Meanwhile, in a Dutch oven, melt 6 tablespoons butter. Stir in the flour, salt and pepper until smooth. Gradually add milk. Bring to a boil; cook and stir for 1-2 minutes or until thickened. Remove from the heat. Stir in chicken, gravy and pimientos.

Drain noodles; toss with remaining butter. Stir into chicken mixture. Transfer to a greased 13-in. x 9-in. baking dish. Cover and bake at 350° for 30-35 minutes or until bubbly.

Combine the cheese, bread crumbs and melted butter.

Sprinkle around edges of casserole. Bake, uncovered, for 10 minutes or until golden brown. Let stand for 10 minutes before serving. **Yield:** 12 servings (1 cup each).

Ham & Shells Casserole

(Pictured below)

PREP: 40 min. **BAKE:** 25 min.

Caramelized onions and rosemary add subtle seasoning to this meal–in–one bake. It's a grown–up treatment for pasta shells that kids like, too. —Genise Krause, Sturgeon Bay, Wisconsin

- 1 **package (16 ounces) medium pasta shells**
- 3 **large onions, halved and sliced**
- 1 **tablespoon olive oil**
- 1 **package (9 ounces) fresh spinach, torn**
- 1 **tablespoon minced fresh rosemary or**
  1 teaspoon dried rosemary, crushed
- 1/4 **cup butter, cubed**
- 1/3 **cup all-purpose flour**
- 1/4 **teaspoon pepper**
- 3-1/2 **cups fat-free milk**
- 1 **cup part-skim ricotta cheese**
- 1 **cup (4 ounces) crumbled goat cheese**
- 2 **cups cubed fully cooked ham**
- 1/3 **cup grated Parmesan cheese**

Cook the pasta according to the package directions. Meanwhile, in a large skillet over medium heat, cook and stir onions in oil for 15-20 minutes or until golden brown. Add spinach and rosemary; cook 1-2 minutes longer or until spinach is wilted.

Meanwhile, in a large saucepan, melt butter. Stir in flour and pepper until smooth. Gradually add milk. Bring to a boil; cook and stir for 2 minutes or until thickened. Remove from the heat. Stir in ricotta and goat cheeses until blended.

Drain pasta; place in a large bowl. Add the ham, onion mixture and sauce; toss to coat. Transfer to a greased 13-in. x 9-in. baking dish; sprinkle with Parmesan cheese. Bake, uncovered, at 350° for 25-30 minutes or until bubbly. **Yield:** 12 servings (1 cup each).

Roasted Veggie Pasta

(Pictured above)

PREP: 40 min. **BAKE:** 25 min.

My sister gave me this recipe years ago, and it's become a favorite company meal. The roasted vegetables provide wonderful flavor and color. —Robyn Baney, Lexington Park, Maryland

- 4 **small zucchini, halved lengthwise and cut into**
  1-inch slices
- 2 **large onions, cut into wedges**
- 2 **medium yellow summer squash, halved**
  lengthwise and cut into 1-inch slices
- 2 **large sweet yellow peppers, cut into 1-inch**
  pieces
- 1 **cup fresh baby carrots, halved lengthwise**
- 2 **tablespoons olive oil**
- 3-1/2 **cups uncooked fusilli pasta**
- 2 **cups (8 ounces) shredded fontina cheese**
- 1-1/2 **cups heavy whipping cream**
- 1/2 **cup canned diced tomatoes in sauce**
- 1/2 **cup grated Parmesan cheese, *divided***
- 2 **garlic cloves, minced**
- 1/2 **teaspoon salt**
- 1/4 **teaspoon pepper**

In a large bowl, combine the first six ingredients. Transfer to two greased 15-in. x 10-in. x 1-in. baking pans. Bake at 450° for 20-25 minutes or until crisp-tender; set aside. Reduce heat to 350°.

Cook pasta according to package directions; drain. Add the fontina cheese, cream, tomatoes, 1/4 cup Parmesan cheese, garlic, salt and pepper. Stir in vegetable mixture.

Transfer to a greased 13-in. x 9-in. baking dish (dish will be full). Sprinkle with remaining Parmesan cheese. Bake, uncovered, for 25-30 minutes or until bubbly. **Yield:** 16 servings (3/4 cup each).

45 minutes. Uncover; bake 10 minutes longer or until bubbly. Let stand for 10 minutes before cutting.

To use frozen lasagna: Thaw in the refrigerator overnight. Remove from the refrigerator 30 minutes before baking. Cover and bake at 375° for 60-70 minutes or until heated through. Uncover; bake 10 minutes longer or until bubbly. Let stand for 10 minutes before cutting. **Yield:** 2 lasagnas (12 servings each).

Pink Rhubarb Punch

PREP: 20 min. **COOK:** 10 min.

Here's a pretty punch for spring or summer luncheons, bridal showers or other gatherings. It has a crisp, tangy taste everyone enjoys. —*Rebecca Mininger, Jeromesville, Ohio*

- 8 **cups chopped fresh *or* frozen rhubarb**
- 8 **cups water**
- 2-1/2 **cups sugar**
- 2 **tablespoons strawberry gelatin powder**
- 2 **cups boiling water**
- 2 **cups pineapple juice**
- 1/4 **cup lemon juice**
- 6 **cups ginger ale, chilled**

In a Dutch oven, bring the rhubarb and water to a boil. Reduce heat; simmer, uncovered, for 10 minutes. Drain, reserving liquid (save rhubarb for another use).

In a large bowl, dissolve the sugar and gelatin powder in boiling water. Add the pineapple and lemon juices; mix well. Stir in rhubarb liquid; refrigerate until chilled. Just before serving, pour into a punch bowl and stir in ginger ale. **Yield:** about 5 quarts.

Tangy Watermelon Salad

PREP/ TOTAL TIME: 35 min.

This refreshing blend of watermelon, red onions and a splash of citrus always does me proud at picnics and potlucks. I like to prepare it a day ahead so the flavors have a chance to blend, and I use the melon rind as a colorful serving bowl. If you're short on time, simply substitute any bottled citrus vinaigrette.
—*Alisha Duncan, Blanchard, Oklahoma*

- 14 **cups cubed seedless watermelon**
- 1 **medium red onion, halved and thinly sliced**
- 1 **cup chopped green onions**
- 3/4 **cup orange juice**
- 5 **tablespoons red wine vinegar**
- 2 **tablespoons plus 1-1/2 teaspoons honey**
- 1 **tablespoon finely chopped sweet red pepper**
- 1/2 **teaspoon salt**
- 1/4 **teaspoon onion powder**
- 1/4 **teaspoon garlic powder**
- 1/4 **teaspoon ground mustard**
- 1/4 **teaspoon pepper**
- 3/4 **cup vegetable oil**

Make Once, Eat Twice Lasagna

(Pictured above and on page 132)

PREP: 35 min. **BAKE:** 50 min. + standing

Our family loves this beefy lasagna served with a green salad and garlic bread. It's so handy to have an extra, ready-made pan in the freezer for lazy days or when we're expecting company.
—*Geri Davis, Prescott, Arizona*

- 1 **package (16 ounces) lasagna noodles**
- 3 **pounds ground beef**
- 3 **jars (26 ounces *each*) spaghetti sauce**
- 2 **eggs, beaten**
- 1-1/2 **pounds ricotta cheese**
- 6 **cups (24 ounces) shredded part-skim mozzarella cheese, *divided***
- 1 **tablespoon dried parsley flakes**
- 1 **teaspoon salt**
- 1/2 **teaspoon pepper**
- 1 **cup grated Parmesan cheese**

Cook the noodles according to the package directions. Meanwhile, in a Dutch oven, cook beef over medium heat until no longer pink; drain. Remove from the heat; stir in spaghetti sauce. In a large bowl, combine the eggs, ricotta cheese, 4-1/2 cups mozzarella cheese, parsley, salt and pepper.

Drain noodles. Spread 1 cup meat sauce in each of two greased 13-in. x 9-in. baking dishes. Layer each with three noodles, 1 cup ricotta mixture and 1-1/2 cups meat sauce. Repeat layers twice. Top with Parmesan cheese and remaining mozzarella cheese.

Cover and freeze one lasagna for up to 3 months. Cover and bake the remaining lasagna at 375° for

In a large bowl, combine the watermelon and onions. In a small bowl, combine the orange juice, vinegar, honey, red pepper and seasonings; slowly whisk in the oil. Pour over watermelon mixture; toss gently.

Cover the salad and refrigerate for at least 2 hours, stirring occasionally. Serve with a slotted spoon. **Yield:** 16 servings.

Peanut Butter Brownie Bars

(Pictured below)

PREP: 20 min. **BAKE:** 25 min.

A packaged brownie mix creates the base for these simple but yummy treats. Creamy peanut butter, crunchy nuts and crisp cereal make the bars fun to bite into—and quick to disappear!
—*Radelle Knappenberger, Oviedo, Florida*

   1 **package fudge brownie mix (13-inch x 9-inch pan size)**
  12 **peanut butter cups, chopped**
 1/2 **cup salted peanuts, chopped**
   2 **cups (12 ounces) semisweet chocolate chips**
1-1/4 **cups creamy peanut butter**
   1 **tablespoon butter**
 1/8 **teaspoon salt**
   1 **teaspoon vanilla extract**
1-1/2 **cups crisp rice cereal**

Prepare the brownie batter according to the package directions. Spread into a greased 13-in. x 9-in. x 2-in. baking pan. Bake at 350° for 20-25 minutes or until a toothpick inserted near the center comes out with moist crumbs.

Sprinkle with peanut butter cups and peanuts. Bake 4-6 minutes longer or until chocolate is melted. Cool on a wire rack.

Meanwhile, in a large saucepan, combine the chocolate chips, peanut butter, butter and salt. Cook and stir until chips are melted and mixture is smooth.

Remove from the heat; stir in vanilla and cereal. Carefully spread over brownies. Cover and refrigerate for at least 2 hours before cutting. **Yield:** 3 dozen.

Loaded Vegetable Beef Stew

(Pictured above)

PREP: 40 min. **COOK:** 8-1/2 hours

I first tasted this chunky stew during a trip to Argentina a few years ago, and I was inspired to try re-creating it at home. It's delicious and filling. —*Kari Caven, Post Falls, Idaho*

 8 **bacon strips, diced**
 3 **pounds beef stew meat, cut into 1-inch cubes**
 6 **medium carrots, cut into 1-inch pieces**
 6 **medium tomatoes, peeled and cut into wedges**
 4 **medium potatoes, peeled and cubed**
 3 **cups cubed peeled butternut squash**
 2 **medium green peppers, chopped**
 2 **teaspoons dried thyme**
 2 **garlic cloves, minced**
 2 **cans (14-1/2 ounces *each*) beef broth**
 6 **cups chopped cabbage**
1/2 **teaspoon pepper**

In a large skillet, cook bacon over medium heat until crisp. Using a slotted spoon, remove to paper towels to drain. In the bacon drippings, brown beef in batches. Refrigerate the bacon until serving.

In a 6-qt. slow cooker, combine the carrots, tomatoes, potatoes, squash, green peppers, thyme and garlic. Top with beef. Pour broth over the top. Cover and cook on low for 8 hours.

Stir in cabbage and pepper. Cover and cook on high for 30 minutes or until cabbage is tender. Sprinkle each serving with bacon. **Yield:** 12 servings (1-1/3 cups each).

The Firehouse Special

(Pictured below and on page 133)

PREP: 45 min.   **BAKE:** 55 min.

As good as this casserole is straight out of the oven, it tastes even better the second day. I think it's best topped with a dollop of sour cream and salsa.   —*Darrell Alvord, Boise, Idaho*

- **2 cans (14-1/2 ounces *each*) chicken broth**
- **3 cups uncooked instant rice**
- **4 tablespoons butter, *divided***
- **2 pounds ground beef**
- **2 packages (12 ounces *each*) bulk spicy pork sausage**
- **1 pound sliced fresh mushrooms**
- **3 garlic cloves, minced**
- **2 packages (10 ounces *each*) frozen chopped spinach, thawed and squeezed dry**
- **2 cups (16 ounces) 4% cottage cheese**
- **8 eggs, beaten**
- **1 envelope onion soup mix**
- **1 envelope leek soup mix**
- **2 teaspoons garlic powder**
- **1 teaspoon Creole seasoning**
- **1/4 cup grated Parmesan cheese**

In a large saucepan, bring the chicken broth to a boil. Stir in rice; cover and remove from the heat. Let stand for 5 minutes. Stir in 2 tablespoons butter; set aside.

Meanwhile, in a large skillet, cook beef and sausage over medium heat until no longer pink; drain. Transfer to a large bowl.

In the same skillet, saute mushrooms and garlic in remaining butter until tender; add to meat mixture. Stir in the spinach, cottage cheese, eggs, soup mixes, garlic powder, Creole seasoning and reserved rice mixture.

Divide between two greased 13-in. x 9-in. baking dishes; sprinkle with Parmesan cheese. Cover and bake at 350° for 45 minutes. Uncover; bake 10-15 minutes longer or until heated through. **Yield:** 2 casseroles (10 servings each.)

Editor's Note: The following spices may be substituted for 1 teaspoon Creole seasoning: 1/4 teaspoon each salt, garlic powder and paprika; and a pinch each of dried thyme, ground cumin and cayenne pepper.

Mexican Lasagna

PREP: 25 min.   **BAKE:** 40 min.

Tortillas replace the noodles in this beefy lasagna. The salsa, enchilada sauce, chilies and refried beans create a real fiesta of flavors.   —*Tina Newhauser, Peterborough, New Hampshire*

- **1-1/4 pounds ground beef**
- **1 medium onion, chopped**
- **4 garlic cloves, minced**
- **2 cups salsa**
- **1 can (16 ounces) refried beans**
- **1 can (15 ounces) black beans, rinsed and drained**
- **1 can (10 ounces) enchilada sauce**
- **1 can (4 ounces) chopped green chilies**
- **1 envelope taco seasoning**
- **1/4 teaspoon pepper**
- **6 flour tortillas (10 inches)**
- **3 cups (12 ounces) shredded Mexican cheese blend, *divided***
- **2 cups broken tortilla chips**
- **Sour cream, sliced ripe olives, guacamole and chopped tomatoes, optional**

In a large skillet, cook beef, onion and garlic over medium heat until meat is no longer pink; drain. Stir in salsa, beans, enchilada sauce, chilies, taco seasoning and pepper; heat through.

Spread 1 cup sauce in a greased 13-in. x 9-in. x 2-in. baking dish. Layer with two tortillas, a third of the meat mixture and 1 cup cheese. Repeat layers. Top with remaining tortillas and meat mixture.

Cover and bake at 375° for 30 minutes. Uncover; sprinkle with remaining cheese and top with tortilla chips. Bake 10-15 minutes more or until cheese is melted. Let stand 10 minutes before serving. Garnish with sour cream, olives, guacamole and tomatoes if desired. **Yield:** 12 servings.

PARMESAN POINTER. Finely grated Parmesan works well in lasagna and casseroles. To grate your own, use the finest section on your grating tool. Or cut 1-inch cubes and process 1 cup of them at a time on high in your blender or food processor until finely grated.

Caprese Tomato Bites

(Pictured above)

PREP/TOTAL TIME: 30 min.

I like the classic combination of tomatoes, mozzarella and basil in these bite–size appetizers. The juicy burst you get when you pop one in your mouth is the genuine taste of summertime.
—Crystal Williams, Brooklyn, New York

- 1 **pint cherry tomatoes, halved**
- 3 **tablespoons heavy whipping cream**
- 1/2 **pound fresh mozzarella cheese, sliced**
- 6 **fresh basil leaves**
- 1 **garlic clove, minced**
- 1 **tablespoon balsamic vinegar**

Scoop out and discard pulp of cherry tomatoes. Invert tomatoes onto paper towels to drain.

In a food processor, combine the cream, mozzarella cheese, basil and garlic; cover and process until blended. Transfer to a heavy-duty resealable plastic bag; cut a small hole in a corner of bag.

Turn tomato halves over; drizzle with vinegar. Pipe cheese mixture into tomatoes. Refrigerate until serving. **Yield:** about 3-1/2 dozen.

Texas-Style Beef Brisket

(Pictured at right)

PREP: 25 min. + marinating **COOK:** 6-1/2 hours

A friend introduced me to this recipe, and my husband loved the tender sliced brisket with its homemade barbecue sauce. Now, I make it all the time. —Vivian Warner, Elkhart, Kansas

- 3 **tablespoons Worcestershire sauce**
- 1 **tablespoon chili powder**
- 2 **bay leaves**
- 2 **garlic cloves, minced**
- 1 **teaspoon celery salt**
- 1 **teaspoon pepper**
- 1 **teaspoon Liquid Smoke, optional**
- 1 **fresh beef brisket (6 pounds)**
- 1/2 **cup beef broth**

BARBECUE SAUCE:
- 1 **medium onion, chopped**
- 2 **tablespoons canola oil**
- 2 **garlic cloves, minced**
- 1 **cup ketchup**
- 1/2 **cup molasses**
- 1/4 **cup cider vinegar**
- 2 **teaspoons chili powder**
- 1/2 **teaspoon ground mustard**

In a large resealable plastic bag, combine Worcestershire sauce, chili powder, bay leaves, garlic, celery salt, pepper and Liquid Smoke if desired. Cut the beef brisket in half; add to the bag. Seal the bag and turn to coat. Refrigerate overnight.

Transfer beef brisket to a 5- or 6-qt. slow cooker; add the beef broth. Cover and cook on low for 6-8 hours or until tender.

For sauce, in a small saucepan, saute onion in oil until tender. Add garlic; cook 1 minute longer. Stir in the remaining ingredients; heat through.

Remove the brisket from the slow cooker; discard the bay leaves. Place 1 cup cooking juices in a measuring cup; skim fat. Add to the barbecue sauce. Discard the remaining juices.

Return brisket to the slow cooker; top with sauce mixture. Cover and cook on high for 30 minutes to allow flavors to blend. Thinly slice across the grain; serve with sauce. **Yield:** 12 servings.

Brunch Egg Bake

(Pictured above)

PREP: 15 min. **COOK:** 35 min.

I was raised in Pennsylvania Dutch country, where family often gathers around food. This colorful, hearty egg casserole makes entertaining easy and is perfect for a Mother's Day brunch.
　　　　　　　　—Gloria Rohlfing, York, Pennsylvania

- **3 cups (12 ounces) shredded cheddar cheese**
- **3 cups (12 ounces) shredded part-skim mozzarella cheese**
- **1 jar (4-1/2 ounces) sliced mushrooms, drained**
- **1/2 cup chopped sweet red pepper**
- **1/3 cup sliced green onions**
- **2 tablespoons butter**
- **2 cups diced fully cooked ham**
- **1/2 cup all-purpose flour**
- **1-3/4 cups milk**
- **8 eggs, beaten**
- **2 tablespoons minced fresh parsley**
- **1/2 teaspoon salt**
- **1/2 teaspoon dried basil**
- **1/4 teaspoon pepper**

Combine the cheeses; place 3 cups in an ungreased 13-in. x 9-in. x 2-in. baking dish and set aside.

In a large skillet, saute the mushrooms, red pepper and onions in butter until tender; drain. Spoon into baking dish. Sprinkle with ham and remaining cheeses.

In a large bowl, whisk flour and milk until smooth; stir in the eggs, parsley, salt, basil and pepper until blended. Slowly pour over cheeses.

Bake, uncovered, at 350° for 35-40 minutes or until a knife inserted near the center comes out clean. Let stand for 10 minutes before cutting. **Yield:** 12 servings.

Taco Pasta Salad

PREP: 15 min. **COOK:** 15 min.

I've taken this dish to 4-H potlucks, church functions and my parents' 50th anniversary party. It's a salad with a little spunk!
　　　　　　　　—Mary Bergen, Winnipegosis, Manitoba

- **3 cups uncooked spiral pasta**
- **1 pound ground beef**
- **1 envelope taco seasoning**
- **1-1/4 cups mayonnaise**
- **2 to 3 tablespoons milk**
- **3-3/4 teaspoons cider vinegar**
- **3-3/4 teaspoons sugar**
- **1 tablespoon ground mustard**
- **7 cups torn iceberg lettuce**
- **1 to 2 medium tomatoes, chopped**
- **2 cups (8 ounces) shredded cheddar cheese**
- **1 to 2 cups crushed nacho tortilla chips**

Cook the pasta according to the package directions. Meanwhile, in a large skillet, cook beef over medium heat until no longer pink; drain. Stir in taco seasoning; heat through.

In a small bowl, combine mayonnaise, milk, vinegar, sugar and mustard; set aside. Drain pasta; place in a large bowl. Add beef and mayonnaise mixture; toss to coat. Add the lettuce, tomatoes and cheese; toss to combine. Sprinkle with chips. **Yield:** 12-14 servings.

Blueberry-Rhubarb Crumble

(Pictured below)

PREP: 15 min. **BAKE:** 45 min. + cooling

Sometimes I drizzle flavored coffee creamer on top of this yummy dessert instead of using whipped cream. Either way, this crumble is oh-so-good.　　　*—Nancy Sousley, Lafayette, Indiana*

- **6 cups fresh *or* frozen unsweetened blueberries**
- **4 cups diced fresh *or* frozen rhubarb**
- **1 cup sugar**
- **1/4 cup all-purpose flour**

TOPPING:
- 1 cup quick-cooking oats
- 1 cup packed brown sugar
- 1/2 cup all-purpose flour
- 1/2 teaspoon ground nutmeg
- 1/2 teaspoon ground cinnamon
- 1/2 cup cold butter

Whipped cream, optional

Combine blueberries, rhubarb, sugar and flour. Transfer to a greased 13-in. x 9-in. baking dish.

For the topping, combine the oats, brown sugar, flour, nutmeg and cinnamon; cut in the butter until crumbly. Sprinkle over fruit mixture.

Bake at 350° for 45-55 minutes or until fruit is bubbly and topping is golden brown. Let cool 10 minutes. Serve warm; dollop with whipped cream if desired. **Yield:** 12 servings.

Triple-Chocolate Brownie Cookies

(Pictured above)

PREP: 25 min. **BAKE:** 10 min.

Our family of chocolate lovers gets three times as excited when these irresistible treats come out of the oven. They have the taste and texture of fudge brownies and a drizzle of melted chocolate on top.   —*Linda Robinson, New Braunfels, Texas*

- 3/4 cup butter, cubed
- 4 squares (1 ounce *each*) unsweetened chocolate
- 2 cups sugar
- 4 eggs
- 1-1/2 cups all-purpose flour
- 1/2 cup baking cocoa
- 2 teaspoons baking powder
- 1/2 teaspoon salt
- 2 cups (12 ounces) semisweet chocolate chips, *divided*
- 2 teaspoons shortening

In a small saucepan over low heat, melt butter and unsweetened chocolate; cool. Transfer to a large mixing bowl; add sugar and eggs. Beat until smooth.

Combine the flour, cocoa, baking powder and salt; gradually add to chocolate mixture. Stir in 1-1/2 cups chocolate chips. Cover and refrigerate for 2 hours or until easy to handle.

Drop by tablespoonfuls 2 in. apart onto greased baking sheets. Bake at 350° for 7-9 minutes or until edges are set and tops are slightly cracked. Cool for 2 minutes before removing from pans to wire racks to cool completely.

In a microwave-safe bowl, heat shortening and remaining chocolate chips on high for 1 minute or until chips are melted; stir until smooth. Drizzle over cookies. Let stand for 30 minutes or until chocolate is set. Store in an airtight container. **Yield:** 6 dozen.

Cooking for One or Two

When just a single or double serving is the order of the day, turn to this chapter. You'll make down-sized breakfasts, lunches and dinners extra special.

SIZED JUST RIGHT. Clockwise from top left: Pepperoni Caesar Salad (p. 154), Omelet Croissants (p. 154), Lemony Shrimp Sandwiches (p. 148) and Spanish-Style Brunch Wraps (p. 149).

Lemony Shrimp Sandwiches

(Pictured above and on page 147)

PREP/TOTAL TIME: 20 min.

After one bite of these mouth-watering seafood sandwiches, you'll likely find yourself turning to them time and time again. The effortless citrus spread perfectly complements the shrimp. Plus, there's an added bonus—the recipe is on the lighter side.
—*Catherine Fontana, Fox Lake, Illinois*

☑ This recipe includes Nutrition Facts.

- 1/3 **cup fat-free mayonnaise**
- 1 **teaspoon lemon juice**
- 3/4 **teaspoon grated lemon peel**
- 1/4 **teaspoon ground coriander**
- 1/8 **teaspoon salt**
- 1/8 **teaspoon pepper**
- 2 **slices sourdough bread (1/2 inch thick)**
- 2 **Boston lettuce leaves**
- 1 **medium tomato, cut into 1/4-inch slices**
- 6 **cooked large shrimp, peeled and deveined, butterflied**
- 1/2 **medium ripe avocado, peeled and sliced**
- 2 **thin slices red onion**

In a small bowl, combine the mayonnaise, lemon juice, lemon peel, coriander, salt and pepper. Spread over both slices of bread. Layer each with lettuce, tomato, shrimp, avocado and onion. **Yield:** 2 servings.

Nutrition Facts: 1 sandwich equals 321 calories, 11 g fat (2 g saturated fat), 36 mg cholesterol, 907 mg sodium, 46 g carbohydrate, 6 g fiber, 11 g protein.

Chocolate Banana Smoothies

PREP/TOTAL TIME: 10 min.

Looking to add more calcium to your diet? Consider these frothy, chocolaty smoothies our Test Kitchen home economists whipped up using both milk and yogurt.

- 1 **cup chocolate milk**
- 1/2 **cup plain yogurt**
- 1 **medium banana, peeled, cut into chunks and frozen**
- 1 **teaspoon honey**
- 1/2 **teaspoon vanilla extract**
- 1 **cup ice cubes**

In a blender, combine the milk, yogurt, banana, honey and vanilla; cover and process until smooth. Add ice cubes; cover and process until blended. Pour into chilled glasses; serve immediately. **Yield:** 2 servings.

Thyme Chicken Marsala

PREP: 15 min. **BAKE:** 15 min.

Here's a quick recipe with restaurant style and flavor—perfect for entertaining. Sauteed chicken breasts are served in a wine sauce atop julienned veggies. —*Dorothy Smith, El Dorado, Arkansas*

☑ This recipe includes Nutrition Facts and Diabetic Exchanges.

- 2 **boneless skinless chicken breast halves (4 ounces *each*)**
- 1 **tablespoon all-purpose flour**
- 1/8 **teaspoon plus 1/4 teaspoon salt, *divided***
- 1/8 **teaspoon plus 1/4 teaspoon pepper, *divided***
- 1 **medium carrot, julienned**
- 1 **small sweet yellow *or* red pepper, julienned**
- 3 **teaspoons olive oil, *divided***
- 2 **garlic cloves, minced**
- 1/3 **cup marsala wine *or* reduced-sodium chicken broth**
- 1 **tablespoon minced fresh thyme *or* 1 teaspoon dried thyme**

Place chicken in a large resealable plastic bag; flatten to 1/4-in. thickness. Add flour and 1/8 teaspoon each salt and pepper; shake to coat. Set aside.

In a large skillet, saute the carrot and yellow pepper in 1-1/2 teaspoons oil for 3 minutes. Add the garlic and remaining salt and pepper; cook and stir until the vegetables are crisp-tender. Transfer to two serving plates; keep warm.

In the same skillet, heat remaining oil over medium heat. Cook chicken for 3-4 minutes on each side or until a meat thermometer reads 170°; place over vegetables. Add the wine or broth and thyme to the pan; cook for 1 minute, stirring to loosen browned bits. Serve with chicken. **Yield:** 2 servings.

Nutrition Facts: 1 chicken breast half equals 285 calories, 10 g fat (2 g saturated fat), 63 mg cholesterol,

365 mg sodium, 15 g carbohydrate, 2 g fiber, 24 g protein.
Diabetic Exchange: 3 lean meat, 1 starch, 1 fat.

Spanish-Style Brunch Wraps

(Pictured below and on page 146)

PREP/TOTAL TIME: 25 min.

Made with a tapenade (a traditional Spanish spread) or a bruschetta topping, this meatless wrap is a fun blend of tastes, colors and textures. —Roxanne Chan, Albany, California

- 3 **eggs**
- 1 **tablespoon shredded Manchego cheese**
- 2 **teaspoons minced fresh oregano** *or*
  1/2 **teaspoon dried oregano**
- 1/4 **teaspoon pepper**
- 1 **tablespoon chopped green onion**
- 1 **tablespoon chopped roasted sweet red pepper**
- 1-1/2 **teaspoons olive oil**
- 2 **sun-dried tomato tortillas (10 inches), warmed**
- 1/4 **cup tapenade** *or* **ripe olive bruschetta topping**

TOPPING:
- 1-1/2 **teaspoons minced fresh parsley**
- 1-1/2 **teaspoons lemon juice**
- 1-1/2 **teaspoons olive oil**
- 1 **garlic clove, minced**
- 1/2 **teaspoon capers, drained**

In a small bowl, whisk the eggs, Manchego cheese, oregano and pepper; set aside.

In a small skillet over medium heat, cook onion and red pepper in oil until tender. Add egg mixture; cook and stir until eggs are completely set.

Spread tortillas with tapenade. Spoon egg mixture off-center onto tortillas; roll up tightly. Cut wraps in half. Combine topping ingredients; drizzle over wraps. Serve at once. **Yield:** 2 servings.

Carolina Crab Cakes

(Pictured above)

COOK: 10 min. **PREP:** 10 min. + chilling

I think these little rounds are spiced just right, and the mustard sauce is the ideal accent. If you're a fan of crab cakes, these are a must-try! —Katie Sloan, Charlotte, North Carolina

- 1 **egg, lightly beaten**
- 1/2 **cup soft bread crumbs**
- 1/4 **cup mayonnaise**
- 1 **teaspoon grated onion**
- 1/2 **teaspoon minced fresh parsley**
- 1/2 **teaspoon Worcestershire sauce**
- 1/8 **teaspoon seafood seasoning**
- 1/8 **teaspoon ground mustard**

Dash pepper
Dash hot pepper sauce
- 1 **can (6 ounces) crabmeat, drained, flaked and cartilage removed**
- 1 **tablespoon canola oil**

MUSTARD SAUCE:
- 2 **tablespoons mayonnaise**
- 2 **tablespoons sour cream**
- 1 **tablespoon Dijon mustard**
- 1/2 **teaspoon lemon juice**
- 1/2 **teaspoon Worcestershire sauce**

In a small bowl, combine the first 10 ingredients. Fold in crab. Refrigerate for 30 minutes. Meanwhile, combine sauce ingredients.

In a large skillet, heat oil over medium heat. Drop crab mixture by 1/4 cupfuls into the pan; cook for 3-5 minutes on each side or until golden brown. Serve with sauce. **Yield:** 2 servings.

Sailor Sandwiches With Caesar Mayo

(Pictured below)

PREP: 25 min. **BROIL:** 10 min.

These were inspired by the sandwiches in Patricia Cornwall's detective novels. Don't be fooled by the list of ingredients—the recipe goes together quickly. —Lesley Pew, Lynn, Massachusetts

- 1/4 **cup milk**
- 1/4 **cup cornmeal**
- 2 **tablespoons all-purpose flour**
- 1 **tablespoon grated Parmesan cheese**
- 1/2 **teaspoon dried oregano**
- 1/4 **teaspoon garlic powder**
- 1/4 **teaspoon salt**
- 1/4 **teaspoon pepper**
- 2 **cod** *or* **haddock fillets (6 ounces** *each***)**
- 1 **tablespoon butter, melted**

CAESAR MAYO:
- 4 **teaspoons grated Parmesan cheese**
- 4 **teaspoons mayonnaise**
- 4 **teaspoons olive oil**
- 1 **tablespoon lemon juice**
- 1 **tablespoon Worcestershire sauce**
- 3/4 **teaspoon garlic powder**
- 1/2 **teaspoon ground mustard**
- 1/4 **teaspoon hot pepper sauce**

SANDWICHES:
- 2 **kaiser rolls, split and toasted**
- 2 **lettuce leaves**
- 1 **small tomato, thinly sliced**
- 2 **slices sweet onion**

Place milk in a shallow bowl. In another shallow bowl, combine cornmeal, flour, cheese and seasonings. Dip fish in milk, then cornmeal mixture. Place on a greased broiler pan; drizzle with butter. Broil 4 in. from the heat for 8-10 minutes or until fish flakes easily with a fork.

Combine the mayonnaise ingredients; spread over rolls. On roll bottoms, layer the fish, lettuce, tomato and onion. Replace tops. **Yield:** 2 servings.

Creamy Bow Tie Pasta

(Pictured above)

PREP/TOTAL TIME: 25 min.

Bring a little zip to your dinnertime routine with this saucy, seasoned pasta. It's a great accompaniment to almost any main course. —Kathy Kittell, Lenexa, Kansas

- 1 **cup uncooked bow tie pasta**
- 1-1/2 **teaspoons butter**
- 2-1/4 **teaspoons olive oil**
- 1-1/2 **teaspoons all-purpose flour**
- 1/2 **teaspoon minced garlic**

Dash salt
Dash dried basil
Dash crushed red pepper flakes
- 3 **tablespoons milk**
- 2 **tablespoons chicken broth**
- 1 **tablespoon water**
- 2 **tablespoons shredded Parmesan cheese**
- 1 **tablespoon sour cream**

Cook pasta according to package directions. Meanwhile, in a small saucepan, melt butter. Stir in the oil, flour, garlic and seasonings until blended. Gradually add the milk, broth and water. Bring to a boil; cook and stir for 2 minutes or until slightly thickened.

Remove from the heat; stir in cheese and sour cream. Drain pasta; toss with sauce. **Yield:** 2 servings.

Meatballs with Vegetable Sauce

PREP: 15 min. **BAKE:** 25 min.

With these easy meatballs, you don't have the mess of frying and turning each one. Best of all, they can be made ahead and frozen, then added to the tangy, vegetable-rich sauce and served over noodles or rice. —Dorothy Stegall, Appleton, Wisconsin

- 1 **egg yolk, lightly beaten**
- 1 **tablespoon milk**
- 3 **tablespoons soft bread crumbs**

2 tablespoons finely chopped onion
1/4 teaspoon salt
1/2 pound ground beef
SAUCE:
   1/4 cup sliced fresh mushrooms
   1/4 cup chopped celery
    3 tablespoons chopped onion
    3 tablespoons chopped green pepper
    1 teaspoon butter
   1/2 cup tomato sauce
    2 tablespoons brown sugar
    2 tablespoons beef broth
    4 teaspoons lemon juice
   1/8 teaspoon garlic powder
Hot cooked noodles

In a bowl, combine the first five ingredients. Crumble beef over mixture and mix well. Shape into 1-in. balls. Place 1 in. apart on a greased baking pan. Bake, uncovered, at 425° for 10-12 minutes or until no longer pink. Drain on paper towels.

   Meanwhile, in a saucepan, saute the mushrooms, celery, onion and green pepper in butter. Add the tomato sauce, brown sugar, broth, lemon juice and garlic powder. Bring to a boil. Reduce heat; add the meatballs. Cover and simmer for 15 minutes or until heated through. Serve over noodles. **Yield:** 2 servings.

Turkey Reubens

PREP: 5 min. **BAKE:** 10 min.

I've had this recipe in my kitchen collection for a long time, and it's still a lunchtime favorite. I recommend draining the canned cabbage well so the sandwiches don't become soggy.
—*Chris Boshoven, Hebron, Indiana*

☑ This recipe includes Nutrition Facts and Diabetic Exchanges.

   1 tablespoon butter, softened
   4 slices rye bread
   2 tablespoons mayonnaise
   4 ounces thinly sliced deli turkey
   2/3 cup canned sweet-and-sour red cabbage
   2 slices (1/2 ounce *each*) Monterey Jack cheese

Spread butter over one side of each slice of bread; spread mayonnaise over the other side. On the mayonnaise side of two slices, layer the turkey, cabbage and cheese; top with remaining bread, buttered side up.

   On a griddle or in a skillet, toast sandwiches over medium heat for 3 minutes on each side or until golden brown. **Yield:** 2 servings.

   Nutrition Facts: 1 sandwich (prepared with reduced-fat butter, fat-free mayonnaise and reduced-fat cheese) equals 352 calories, 9 g fat (4 g saturated fat), 47 mg cholesterol, 1,530 mg sodium, 49 g carbohydrate, 4 g fiber, 21 g protein. **Diabetic Exchanges:** 2-1/2 starch, 2 very lean meat, 1-1/2 fat, 1 vegetable.

Garden Chickpea Salad

(Pictured below)

PREP/TOTAL TIME: 25 min.

Looking for something different on a hot summer's day? This refreshing salad makes a terrific cold side dish or even an entree.
—*Sally Sibthorpe, Shelby Township, Michigan*

   3 cups spring mix salad greens
   3/4 cup canned chickpeas *or* garbanzo beans, rinsed and drained
   1/2 cup packed fresh parsley sprigs, coarsely chopped
   1 medium carrot, julienned
   1 small zucchini, julienned
   2 green onions, thinly sliced
   1/4 cup crumbled feta cheese
   1/4 cup thinly sliced radishes
   3 tablespoons chopped walnuts
TOMATO VINAIGRETTE:
   1/4 cup lemon juice
   1/4 cup olive oil
   1/4 cup chopped tomato
   1 garlic clove, minced
   1/2 teaspoon cumin seeds, toasted
   1/4 teaspoon salt
   1/4 teaspoon cayenne pepper

Divide greens between two salad plates. Combine the chickpeas, parsley, carrot, zucchini, onions, cheese, radishes and walnuts.

   In a small bowl, combine the vinaigrette ingredients. Pour 1/3 cup over chickpea mixture and toss to coat. Spoon chickpea mixture over greens. Drizzle salads with remaining vinaigrette. Serve immediately. **Yield:** 2 servings.

Crunchy Marinated Vegetables

(Pictured above)

PREP/TOTAL TIME: 25 min.

I never worry about getting enough veggies when this crisp and colorful salad is on the menu. My mother gave me the recipe for this eye–catching medley, and it always disappears in a hurry.
—Mrs. Lynn Blosser, Lynnwood, Washington

- 1/2 **cup fresh cauliflowerets**
- 1/2 **cup fresh broccoli florets**
- 1 **small carrot, sliced**
- 2 **tablespoons chopped peeled kohlrabi**
- 2 **tablespoons chopped celery**
- 2 **tablespoons sliced ripe olives**
- 1 **large radish, sliced**
- 1 **tablespoon chopped green pepper**
- **MARINADE:**
- 1/4 **cup sugar**
- 4-1/2 **teaspoons white vinegar**
- 1/4 **teaspoon salt**
- 1/4 **teaspoon ground mustard**
- 4-1/2 **teaspoons vegetable oil**
- 1 **tablespoon finely chopped onion**
- 1/8 **teaspoon celery seed**
- **Dash Italian seasoning**

In a small bowl, combine the first eight ingredients; set aside. In a small saucepan, combine the sugar, vinegar, salt and mustard; cook and stir over low heat just until sugar is dissolved. Pour into a bowl; cool slightly.

Add the oil, onion, celery seed and Italian seasoning; whisk until well combined. Pour over the vegetables and toss to coat. Cover and refrigerate for 4 hours or overnight. Serve with a slotted spoon. **Yield:** 2 servings.

Stuffed Iceberg Salad

PREP/TOTAL TIME: 15 min.

For a refreshing side salad or light summer meal, try this iceberg lettuce stuffed with ham salad. Add breadsticks or rolls to round out the menu.   —Della Biddiscombe, Lewiston, Idaho

- 1 **medium head iceberg lettuce**
- 2 **tablespoons mayonnaise**
- 1/8 **teaspoon curry powder**
- 1/2 **cup shredded cheddar cheese**
- 1/4 **cup sliced deli ham, julienned**
- 2 **tablespoons finely chopped celery**
- 2 **tablespoons minced fresh parsley**
- 1 **tablespoon diced pimientos**
- 1/4 **cup salad dressing of your choice**

Remove and discard core from lettuce. Place lettuce core side down and cut in half with a plastic lettuce knife from top to bottom (save one half for another use). With knife, remove enough leaves from the center of the cut side of lettuce to create a 2-in. circle, about 1-1/4 in. deep.

In a bowl, combine mayonnaise and curry powder. Stir in the cheese, ham, celery, parsley and pimientos. Spoon into center of lettuce. Wrap tightly in plastic wrap; refrigerate for 30 minutes or until serving. Cut in half, forming two wedges. Serve with salad dressing. **Yield:** 2 servings.

Peanutty Candy Bars

PREP: 15 min. **BAKE:** 15 min. + chilling

You can be sure that a batch of these chewy, gooey bars won't last long. It's a good thing they're so quick and easy to make!
—Mary Schmittinger, Colgate, Wisconsin

- 4 **cups quick-cooking oats**
- 1 **cup packed brown sugar**
- 2/3 **cup butter, melted**
- 1/2 **cup plus 2/3 cup peanut butter,** *divided*
- 1/2 **cup light corn syrup**
- 1 **teaspoon vanilla extract**
- 1 **package (11 ounces) butterscotch chips**
- 1 **cup (6 ounces) semisweet chocolate chips**
- 1 **cup chopped salted peanuts**

In a large bowl, combine the oats, brown sugar, butter, 1/2 cup peanut butter, corn syrup and vanilla. Press into a greased 13-in. x 9-in. baking pan. Bake at 375° for 12-14 minutes or until mixture is bubbly around the edges.

In a microwave-safe bowl, melt butterscotch and chocolate chips; stir until smooth. Stir in the peanuts and remaining peanut butter; spread over the oat mixture. Refrigerate for at least 1 hour before cutting. **Yield:** 2 dozen.

Editor's Note: Reduced-fat or generic brands of peanut butter are not recommended for this recipe.

Pork Tenderloin With Fruit Sauce

(Pictured below)

PREP/TOTAL TIME: 30 min.

My husband hates leftovers and there are just the two of us at the table, so I always try to pare down recipes in both quantity and fat content. This sweet–and–sour pork is a favorite...and my husband is more than happy to finish any leftovers for lunch the next day! —Linda Brown, Columbus, North Carolina

- 1 **cup chicken broth**
- 1/4 **cup uncooked brown rice**
- 4-1/2 **teaspoons cornstarch**
- 2 **tablespoons water**
- 1 **can (8 ounces) unsweetened pineapple chunks, undrained**
- 1/2 **cup 100% raspberry spreadable fruit**
- 2 **tablespoons reduced-sodium soy sauce**
- 1/2 **teaspoon garlic powder**
- 1/4 **teaspoon ground ginger**
- 1 **pork tenderloin (3/4 pound)**

In a small saucepan, bring broth and rice to a boil. Reduce heat; cover and simmer for 30 minutes or until rice is tender.

Meanwhile, in a small bowl, combine cornstarch and water until smooth; set aside. In a saucepan, combine the pineapple and spreadable fruit; cook and stir until spreadable fruit is dissolved. Stir in the soy sauce, garlic powder and ginger. Bring to a boil. Stir cornstarch mixture and stir into pineapple mixture; cook and stir for 2 minutes or until thickened. Keep warm.

Cut pork into 3/4-in.-thick slices. In a nonstick skillet

coated with cooking spray, cook pork for 2-3 minutes on each side or until browned. Pour fruit sauce over meat. Reduce heat; cover and simmer for 10-12 minutes or until a meat thermometer reads 160°. Serve with rice. **Yield:** 2 servings.

Macadamia-Crusted Custards

(Pictured above)

PREP: 10 min. **BAKE:** 25 min.

Sized just right for a twosome, these elegant nut–crusted custards make a simple but scrumptious finale for any meal. Best of all, they whip up in a flash when you're craving something sweet on a busy weeknight. —Anna Erickson, Terrebonne, Oregon

- 2 **egg yolks**
- 1 **egg**
- 3/4 **cup half-and-half cream**
- 4-1/2 **teaspoons sugar**
- 1/2 **teaspoon rum extract**
- 1/8 **teaspoon salt**
- 1/4 **cup finely chopped macadamia nuts, walnuts *or* pecans**

In a small mixing bowl, beat the egg yolks, egg, half-and-half cream, sugar, rum extract and salt until blended. Pour into two ungreased 6-oz. custard cups. Sprinkle with nuts.

Place cups in a baking pan; add 1 in. of boiling water to pan. Bake, uncovered, at 350° for 25-30 minutes or until a knife inserted near the center comes out clean. Remove from the pan to a wire rack; cool for 15 minutes. Refrigerate until chilled. **Yield:** 2 servings.

Omelet Croissants

(Pictured below and on page 147)

PREP/TOTAL TIME: 30 min.

You'll make an ordinary morning memorable with these special sandwiches, which are cooked on a panini maker or indoor grill. With ranch salad dressing, Muenster cheese, arugula and tomato on croissants, bacon and eggs never tasted so good!
—Edna Coburn, Tucson, Arizona

    3 eggs
    1 tablespoon water
    1 teaspoon chicken bouillon granules
    1 green onion, finely chopped
    2 tablespoons finely chopped sweet red pepper
 1/4 teaspoon lemon-pepper seasoning
 1/2 teaspoon butter
    2 croissants, split
4-1/2 teaspoons ranch salad dressing
    4 slices Canadian bacon
    4 slices Muenster cheese
 1/2 cup fresh arugula
    4 thin slices tomato

In a small bowl, whisk the eggs, water and chicken bouillon granules; set aside.

In a small nonstick skillet over medium heat, cook the green onion, red pepper and lemon-pepper seasoning in butter until tender.

Add egg mixture. As eggs set, push the cooked edges toward the center, letting the uncooked portion flow underneath. When eggs are completely set, fold omelet

in half and cut into two wedges.

Spread croissants with salad dressing. On croissant bottoms, layer the bacon, omelet, cheese, arugula and tomato. Replace croissant tops.

Cook on a panini maker or indoor grill for 2-4 minutes or until cheese is melted. **Yield:** 2 servings.

Pepperoni Caesar Salad

(Pictured above and on page 146)

PREP/TOTAL TIME: 10 min.

I like to share this unique Caesar salad with friends and family. Pepperoni, avocado and hard-cooked egg are unconventional ingredients that add a punch to a traditional favorite.
—Nancy Stock, Minonk, Illinois

☑ This recipe includes Nutrition Facts.

1-1/2 cups torn leaf lettuce
    8 slices pepperoni, halved
 1/2 small tomato, seeded and chopped
 1/4 cup cubed avocado
    1 hard-cooked egg, sliced
 1/3 cup salad croutons
    2 tablespoons prepared creamy Caesar salad dressing
    2 teaspoons shredded Parmesan cheese

On a salad plate, arrange lettuce, pepperoni, tomato, avocado, egg and croutons. Drizzle with salad dressing; sprinkle with Parmesan cheese. **Yield:** 2 servings.

Nutrition Facts: 1 serving (prepared with fat-free salad dressing) equals 356 calories, 22 g fat (7 g saturated fat), 229 mg cholesterol, 968 mg sodium, 27 g carbohydrate, 5 g fiber, 15 g protein.

Sausage Potato Supper

PREP: 5 min. **BAKE:** 20 min.

One Saturday night a few years ago, I came up with this recipe on the spur of the moment. The skillet supper has been a hit ever since. —Nancy Russell, Englewood, Colorado

> 2 **small red potatoes, cubed**
> 1 **small zucchini, cut into 1/4-inch slices**
> 1/4 to 1/2 **teaspoon garlic salt**
> 1 **tablespoon butter**
> 1/2 **pound smoked sausage, cut into 1/2-inch slices**
> 4 **tablespoons grated Parmesan cheese,** *divided*
> 1/8 to 1/4 **teaspoon pepper**

Place potatoes in a small saucepan and cover with water. Bring to a boil. Reduce heat; cover and cook for 15-20 minutes or until tender.

Meanwhile, sprinkle the zucchini with garlic salt. In a small skillet, stir-fry the zucchini in butter until crisp-tender. Add sausage; cook until browned.

Drain the potatoes; add to skillet. Sprinkle with 2 tablespoons Parmesan and pepper; heat through. Sprinkle with remaining cheese. **Yield:** 2 servings.

Tex-Mex Scramble

PREP: 10 min. **COOK:** 15 min.

This hearty combination of scrambled eggs, corn tortilla strips, roast beef and other savory ingredients is a favorite. Our Test Kitchen added jalapeno pepper for a Southwestern kick.

> 3 **corn tortillas (6 inches), cut into thin strips**
> 4 **teaspoons olive oil,** *divided*
> 2 **tablespoons chopped onion**
> 1 **jalapeno pepper, seeded and chopped**
> 4 **eggs, beaten**
> 1 **plum tomato, diced**
> 1/4 **cup shredded cooked roast beef**
> 1/8 **teaspoon salt**
> 1/8 **teaspoon pepper**
> 1/4 **cup shredded Monterey Jack cheese**

In a large nonstick skillet, cook the corn tortilla strips in 2 teaspoons oil for 5 minutes or until lightly golden but not crisp. Add the onion, jalapeno pepper and remaining oil; cook 2 minutes longer.

Add the eggs, tomato, beef, salt and pepper; cook and stir until eggs are almost set. Sprinkle with Monterey Jack cheese; cover and let stand for 2-3 minutes until cheese is melted. **Yield:** 2 servings.

Editor's Note: When cutting hot peppers, disposable gloves are recommended. Avoid touching your face.

Swiss Pear Sandwiches

(Pictured below)

PREP/TOTAL TIME: 10 min.

I'm always on the lookout for a quick meal that'll fit the lifestyle of a very busy retired couple, and this recipe really fills the bill. It uses the microwave, so you don't need to dirty a pan. Also, any kind of nuts will work in this pleasant-tasting sandwich.
—Janet Akey, Presque Isle, Wisconsin

☑ **This recipe includes Nutrition Facts.**

> 4 **slices whole wheat bread**
> 4 **teaspoons honey mustard**
> 4 **slices (3/4 ounce** *each***) reduced-fat Swiss cheese**
> 1 **large pear, sliced**
> 2 **slices red onion**
> 2 **tablespoons chopped pecans**

Spread two slices of bread with mustard. Layer each with cheese, pear, onion slices and pecans; top with remaining cheese and bread.

Place the sandwiches on a microwave-safe plate. Cover and microwave on high for 20-30 seconds or until cheese is melted. **Yield:** 2 servings.

Nutrition Facts: 1 sandwich equals 399 calories, 17 g fat (5 g saturated fat), 21 mg cholesterol, 441 mg sodium, 50 g carbohydrate, 7 g fiber, 21 g protein.

ZUCCHINI ZIP. Zucchini is one of the most common varieties of summer squash, which have edible thin skins and soft seeds. Choose firm summer squash with a brightly colored skin free from spots and bruises. Generally, the smaller the squash, the more tender it will be.

Refrigerate summer squash in a plastic bag for up to 5 days. Before using, wash squash and trim both ends. When using sliced summer squash in a salad or stir-fry such as Sausage Potato Supper (above), blot the squash dry with a paper towel.

Holiday and Seasonal Celebrations

Christmas, Thanksgiving, Mother's Day, the Fourth of July…special occasions call for special menus. In this chapter, we've featured scrumptious, festive recipes sure to dazzle your family and friends at get-togethers all year long.

TIMELY TREATS. Clockwise from upper left: Sand Art Brownie Mix (p. 183), 1-2-3 Blackberry Sherbet (p. 167), Spiced Christmas Cookies (p. 185), Oatmeal Brulee with Ginger Cream (p. 164) and Ham & Cheese Breakfast Strudels (p. 163).

Chocolate for Your Valentine

ALWAYS IRRESISTIBLE, chocolate is the perfect treat to give someone special on February 14. And you don't have to purchase prepackaged confections at the store when you have fuss-free recipes you can whip up in your own kitchen.

Here, we've put together an assortment of decadent delights that go together in a heartbeat. From smooth Dark Chocolate Pudding Sundaes and layered Raspberry Chocolate Cake to Wonderful Candies Two Ways, these rich temptations are sure to thrill even the most discerning of sweet tooths.

With all of these heavenly sensations featuring chocolate, you won't need a Valentine's Day card to say "I love you" in an unforgettable way!

Raspberry Chocolate Cake

(Pictured at left)

PREP: 45 min. + standing **BAKE:** 35 min. + cooling

Whenever I bake this beautiful, made-from-scratch cake, it gets rave reviews. The creamy raspberry filling is wonderful! For an attractive finishing touch, garnish each slice with fresh berries.
—Marlene Sanders, Paradise, Texas

       3 **cups sugar**
  2-3/4 **cups all-purpose flour**
       1 **cup baking cocoa**
       2 **teaspoons baking soda**
  1-1/2 **teaspoons salt**
     3/4 **teaspoon baking powder**
  1-1/4 **cups buttermilk**
     3/4 **cup canola oil**
       3 **teaspoons vanilla extract**
       3 **eggs**
  1-1/2 **cups strong brewed coffee, room temperature**
FILLING:
       3 **tablespoons all-purpose flour**
       6 **tablespoons milk**
       6 **tablespoons shortening**
       3 **tablespoons butter, softened**
       3 **cups confectioners' sugar**
       2 **tablespoons raspberry liqueur**
     1/4 **teaspoon salt**
       2 **drops red food coloring, optional**
       4 **tablespoons seedless raspberry jam, melted**
FROSTING:
       1 **package (8 ounces) cold cream cheese**
     1/3 **cup butter, softened**
     1/2 **cup baking cocoa**
       1 **tablespoon raspberry liqueur**
       4 **cups confectioners' sugar**

Line three greased 9-in. round baking pans with waxed paper and grease the paper; set aside. In a large bowl, combine the first six ingredients. Combine buttermilk, oil and vanilla; add to the dry ingredients. Add eggs, one at a time, beating well after each addition; beat for 2 minutes. Gradually add coffee (batter will be thin).

Pour batter into prepared pans. Bake at 350° for 35-40 minutes or until a toothpick inserted near the center comes out clean. Cool for 10 minutes before removing from pans to wire racks to cool completely; discard the waxed paper.

For the filling, in a small saucepan, whisk together flour and milk until smooth. Cook over medium heat for 1 minute or until thickened, stirring constantly. Remove from the heat and let stand until cool. In a large bowl, cream the shortening and butter. Gradually add the confectioners' sugar; mix well. Gradually add the cooled milk mixture; beat for 4 minutes or until light and fluffy. Beat in liqueur, salt and food coloring if desired.

Level tops of cakes if necessary. Place one layer on a serving plate; spread with about 2 tablespoons jam. Place remaining layers on waxed paper; spread one of the remaining layers with remaining jam. Let stand for 30 minutes. Spread 1/2 cup filling over cake on plate to within 1/4 in. of edges. Top with jam-covered cake, then spread with remaining filling. Top with remaining layer.

In a large bowl, beat cream cheese and butter until smooth. Add cocoa and liqueur; mix well. Gradually beat in confectioners' sugar until light and fluffy. Frost top and sides of cake. Store in refrigerator. **Yield:** 16 servings.

CHOCOLATE CHECKLIST. Keep the following tips in mind when working with chocolate:
• In most recipes, semisweet and bittersweet chocolate can be substituted for each other.
• Baking chocolate may be stored up to 1 year in a cool, dry place.
• Humidity can affect how chocolate acts. Try to avoid working with chocolate on rainy, foggy or hot summer days.
• Sometimes chocolate develops white or gray "blooms" on its surface. This just means that the cocoa butter has separated. While it doesn't look pretty, the chocolate is still fine to use.
• Chocolate can scorch over high heat (generally above 115°). It's better to melt chocolate slowly in the microwave or over low-heat in a double boiler.
• When microwaving chocolate, remember—chips and chunks may appear formed and unmelted after heating but will be fluid upon stirring.

Chocolate Cookie Cheesecake

(Pictured above)

PREP: 30 min. **BAKE:** 50 min. + chilling

Both cheesecake lovers and chocolate fans go wild when I present this rich dessert sprinkled with cream-filled cookies. It's always gone in a flash. —Lisa Varner, Greenville, South Carolina

1-1/2 **cups cream-filled chocolate sandwich cookie crumbs (about 16 cookies)**
   3 **tablespoons butter, melted**
   4 **packages (8 ounces *each*) cream cheese, softened**
   1 **cup sugar**
1-1/2 **cups semisweet chocolate chips, melted and cooled**
   3 **teaspoons vanilla extract**
   4 **eggs, lightly beaten**
 20 **cream-filled chocolate sandwich cookies, coarsely chopped**

In a small bowl, combine the cookie crumbs and butter. Press onto the bottom of a greased 9-in. springform pan. Refrigerate while preparing filling.

In a large bowl, beat cream cheese and sugar until smooth. Beat in chocolate and vanilla. Add the eggs; beat on low speed just until combined. Fold in half of the chopped cookies. Pour over crust. Sprinkle with the remaining cookies. Place pan on a baking sheet.

Bake at 325° for 50-60 minutes or until the center is almost set and the top appears dull. Cool on a wire rack for 10 minutes. Carefully run a knife around the edge of pan to loosen; cool 1 hour longer. Refrigerate overnight. **Yield:** 12 servings.

Chocolate Walnut Tart

PREP: 15 min. **BAKE:** 25 min. + cooling

This pecan pie–like tart is absolutely heavenly and so simple to fix using ready-made pie pastry. There's no hassle, no fuss—and no leftovers! —Sue Shank, Harrisonburg, Virginia

Pastry for single-crust pie (9 inches)
   1 **cup coarsely chopped walnuts**
   1 **cup (6 ounces) semisweet chocolate chips**
   3 **eggs**
3/4 **cup dark corn syrup**
1/2 **cup packed brown sugar**
1/4 **cup butter, melted**
   1 **teaspoon vanilla extract**

Press pastry onto the bottom and up the sides of an ungreased 9-in. fluted tart pan with removable bottom; trim edges. Sprinkle walnuts and chocolate chips into crust. In a small bowl, combine the eggs, corn syrup, brown sugar, butter and vanilla. Pour into crust.

Bake at 350° for 25-30 minutes or until top is bubbly and crust is golden brown. Cool tart on a wire rack. Refrigerate leftovers. **Yield:** 12 servings.

Dark Chocolate Pudding Sundaes

(Pictured below)

PREP: 10 min. **COOK:** 10 min. + chilling

You can't beat this homemade pudding for fabulous flavor and smooth, silky texture. Dress it up as a sundae with your family's favorite toppings. —Julie Power, Chandler, Texas

2-3 minutes or until chocolate is softened.

Spread chocolate over crust; sprinkle with nuts. Cool on a wire rack for 15 minutes. Refrigerate for 1-2 hours or until set. **Yield:** 16 slices.

Wonderful Candies Two Ways

(Pictured below)

PREP/TOTAL TIME: 2-1/2 hours

This recipe makes a big batch of two different kinds of delectable candies. They're great not only for Valentine's Day, but also for Christmas. —Jeannie Trudell, Del Norte, Colorado

- 1 cup butter, melted
- 1 can (14 ounces) sweetened condensed milk
- 3 pounds confectioners' sugar

COOKIES AND CREME BONBONS:
- 1/2 cup cream-filled chocolate sandwich cookie crumbs
- 1 pound white candy coating, chopped

CHOCOLATE-COVERED CHERRIES:
- 54 maraschino cherries, patted dry (about two 10-ounce jars)
- 1 pound milk chocolate candy coating, chopped

In a large bowl, combine butter and milk. Gradually beat in confectioners' sugar until a smooth dough is formed. Divide in half; cover with plastic wrap.

For bonbons, stir the cookie crumbs into one portion. Shape into 1-in. balls. In a microwave-safe bowl or heavy saucepan, melt white candy coating; stir until smooth. Dip balls in coating, allowing excess to drip off; place on waxed paper-lined baking sheets. Chill until firm.

For chocolate-covered cherries, shape one portion into 1-in. balls; flatten to 2-in. circles. Wrap each circle around a cherry and gently shape into a ball. Place on waxed paper. Melt chocolate candy coating; stir until smooth. Dip balls in chocolate, allowing excess to drip off; place on waxed paper-lined baking sheets. Chill until firm. Store in an airtight container. **Yield:** 9 dozen.

Ingredients (left column)

- 1/2 cup sugar
- 1/2 cup dark baking cocoa *or* baking cocoa
- 1 tablespoon cornstarch
- 1/8 teaspoon salt
- 2-1/4 cups evaporated milk
- 2 egg whites, beaten
- 1-1/2 teaspoons vanilla extract

TOPPINGS:
Whipped topping, chocolate syrup, slivered almonds and maraschino cherries

In a small heavy saucepan, combine the sugar, cocoa, cornstarch and salt. Stir in milk until smooth. Cook and stir over medium-high heat until thickened and bubbly.

Remove from the heat. Stir a small amount of the hot mixture into the egg whites; return all to the pan, stirring constantly. Bring to a gentle boil; cook and stir for 2 minutes. Remove from the heat; stir in vanilla. Cool for 15 minutes, stirring occasionally.

Transfer pudding to individual dessert dishes. Cover and refrigerate for 1 hour. Just before serving, garnish with whipped topping, chocolate syrup, almonds and cherries. **Yield:** 5 servings.

Chocolate Lover's Pizza

(Pictured above)

PREP: 10 min. **BAKE:** 10 min. + chilling

My dad suggested dark chocolate and pecans for this pizza...but you can easily customize it by using whatever types of chocolate and nuts you like. —Kathy Rairigh, Milford, Indiana

- 2-1/2 cups graham cracker crumbs
- 2/3 cup butter, melted
- 1/2 cup sugar
- 2 packages Dove dark chocolate candies (9-1/2 ounces *each*)
- 1/2 cup chopped pecans

Combine the graham cracker crumbs, butter, and sugar; press onto a greased 12-in. pizza pan. Bake at 375° for 7-9 minutes or until lightly browned. Top the graham cracker crust with the dark chocolate candies; bake for

Bright Mother's Day Brunch

ANY MOM will feel like a queen when you start off Mother's Day with the treats here. And because these recipes are easy on the cook, you won't have to rise at the crack of dawn to create a beautiful menu.

Dress up blueberry pancakes with a scrumptious cream-cheese topping...bake a pan of ooey-gooey breakfast buns...toss together a refreshing fruit salad... no matter which sunrise sensations you choose, they'll make Mom's day one to remember.

Ham & Cheese Breakfast Strudels

(Pictured at left and on page 156)

PREP: 25 min. **BAKE:** 15 min.

These savory pastries bring a special touch to any morning. The recipe includes directions for making the strudels in advance and freezing them individually. —Jo Groth, Plainfield, Iowa

- 3 tablespoons butter, *divided*
- 2 tablespoons all-purpose flour
- 1 cup milk
- 1/3 cup shredded Swiss cheese
- 2 tablespoons grated Parmesan cheese
- 1/4 teaspoon salt
- 5 eggs, beaten
- 1/4 pound ground fully cooked ham (about 3/4 cup)
- 6 sheets phyllo dough
- 1/2 cup butter, melted
- 1/4 cup dry bread crumbs

TOPPING:
- 2 tablespoons grated Parmesan cheese
- 2 tablespoons minced fresh parsley

In a small saucepan, melt 2 tablespoons butter. Stir in flour until smooth; gradually add milk. Bring to a boil; cook and stir for 2 minutes or until thickened. Stir in cheeses and salt. Set aside.

In a large nonstick skillet, melt remaining butter over medium heat. Add eggs to the pan; cook and stir until almost set. Stir in ham and reserved cheese sauce; heat through. Remove from the heat.

Place one sheet of phyllo dough on a work surface. (Keep remaining phyllo covered with plastic wrap and a damp towel to prevent it from drying out.) Brush with melted butter. Sprinkle with 2 teaspoons bread crumbs. Fold in half lengthwise; brush again with butter. Spoon 1/2 cup filling onto phyllo about 2 in. from a short side. Fold side and edges over filling and roll up.

Brush with butter. Repeat. Place desired number of strudels on a greased baking sheet; sprinkle each with 1 teaspoon cheese and 1 tsp. parsley. Bake at 375° for 10-15 minutes or until golden brown. Serve immediately.

To freeze and bake strudels: Individually wrap uncooked strudels in waxed paper and foil. Freeze for up to 1 month. Place 2 in. apart on a greased baking sheet; sprinkle with cheese and parsley. Bake at 375° for 30-35 minutes or until golden brown. **Yield:** 6 servings.

Sunny Morning Doughnuts

PREP: 30 min. + chilling **COOK:** 5 min./batch

I absolutely love doughnuts, but buying them can get expensive. This recipe is economical and so yummy. It beats store-bought doughnuts hands down! —Sherry Flaquel, Cutler Bay, Florida

- 4-1/2 to 5 cups all-purpose flour
- 1-1/4 cups sugar
- 4 teaspoons baking powder
- 1 teaspoon salt
- 3 eggs, beaten
- 1 cup milk
- 1/4 cup canola oil
- 2 tablespoons orange juice
- 4 teaspoons grated orange peel
- Oil for deep-fat frying
- Confectioners' sugar

In a large bowl, combine 4-1/2 cups flour, sugar, baking powder and salt. Combine the eggs, milk, oil, orange juice and peel; stir into the dry ingredients just until moistened. Stir in enough remaining flour to form a soft dough. Cover and refrigerate for at least 1 hour.

Turn onto a floured surface; roll to 1/2-in. thickness. Cut with a floured 2-1/2-in. doughnut cutter. In an electric skillet or deep-fat fryer, heat oil to 375°. Fry doughnuts, a few at a time, until golden brown on both sides. Drain on paper towels. Dust with confectioners' sugar. **Yield:** 20 doughnuts.

PHYLLO FACTS. Handling phyllo dough quickly is key. Follow the package directions for thawing phyllo in the unopened package. When ready to use the dough, count out the number of phyllo sheets required for your recipe, place them on a smooth, dry surface and immediately cover them with plastic wrap and a damp towel. Gently pull sheets from the stack as you need them, keeping the remaining ones covered until needed.

the heat; strain and discard the solids. Stir in the maple syrup and nutmeg; set aside.

In a large saucepan over medium heat, bring the water to a boil. Add the oats, apricots, cherries and salt; cook and stir for 5 minutes. Remove from the heat; stir in brown sugar and 1/4 cup ginger cream. Cover and let stand for 2 minutes.

Grease four 10-ounces ramekins with butter; add the raspberries. Spoon oatmeal over the top; sprinkle with sugar. Place on a baking sheet. Broil 4-6 in. from the heat for 7-9 minutes or until sugar is caramelized. Serve with remaining ginger cream. **Yield:** 4 servings.

Fruit Salad with O.J. Reduction

PREP: 15 min. **COOK:** 25 min.

The eye-catching colors and refreshing taste of this fruit medley always bring on the wows. It's best prepared an hour or two before serving. —Roger Eberlin, Baltimore, Maryland

✓ This recipe includes Nutrition Facts and Diabetic Exchanges.

    2 medium red apples, cubed
    1 medium green apple, cubed
    2 medium peaches, cubed
    2 tablespoons lemon juice
    1 cup orange juice
  1/3 cup sugar
    2 medium navel oranges, peeled, sectioned and
      chopped
    2 cups fresh blueberries

Place the apples, peaches and lemon juice in a large bowl. Cover with water; set aside.

In a small saucepan, combine orange juice and sugar. Bring to a boil; cook until the liquid is reduced to about 1/2 cup. Drain apple mixture. Add oranges, blueberries and orange juice mixture; toss to coat. **Yield:** 12 servings (3/4 cup each).

Nutrition Facts: 3/4 cup equals 75 calories, trace fat (trace saturated fat), 0 cholesterol, 1 mg sodium, 19 g carbohydrate, 2 g fiber, 1 g protein. **Diabetic Exchange:** 1 fruit.

Oatmeal Brulee with Ginger Cream

(Pictured above and on page 156)

PREP: 30 min. **BROIL:** 10 min.

This is such a yummy, comforting breakfast, especially on chilly mornings. I love the crispy, caramelized top and raspberry surprise at the bottom. —Yvonne Starlin, Portland, Tennessee

GINGER CREAM:
  1/2 cup heavy whipping cream
    2 slices fresh gingerroot (about 3/4-inch
      diameter)
    1 cinnamon stick (3 inches)
    1 tablespoon grated orange peel
    3 tablespoons maple syrup
  1/8 teaspoon ground nutmeg
OATMEAL:
    4 cups water
    2 cups old-fashioned oats
  1/4 cup chopped dried apricots
  1/4 cup dried cherries, chopped
  1/2 teaspoon salt
    3 tablespoons brown sugar
    2 tablespoons butter
    1 cup fresh *or* frozen unsweetened raspberries,
      thawed
  1/4 cup sugar

In a small saucepan, bring the heavy whipping cream, ginger, cinnamon and orange peel to a boil. Reduce the heat; cover and simmer for 10 minutes. Remove from

Petite Sticky Buns

(Pictured above right)

PREP: 30 min. + rising **BAKE:** 15 min.

Start off your day on a sweet note with these tender, maple sticky buns baked in muffin cups. They're light, airy and irresistible! —Lisa Naugle, Fayetteville, Pennsylvania

    3 to 3-1/4 cups all-purpose flour
  1/4 cup sugar
    1 package (1/4 ounce) active dry yeast
    1 teaspoon salt

1-1/4 cups milk
1/4 cup butter, cubed
1 egg
TOPPING:
1 cup packed brown sugar
3/4 cup butter, cubed
3/4 cup chopped pecans, toasted
2 tablespoons honey
1 teaspoon ground cinnamon
1/2 teaspoon maple flavoring

In a large bowl, combine 2 cups flour, sugar, yeast and salt. In a small saucepan, heat the milk and butter to 120°-130°. Add to the dry ingredients; beat just until moistened. Add egg; beat until smooth. Stir in enough remaining flour to form a firm dough (dough will be sticky). Do not knead. Cover and let rise in a warm place until doubled, about an hour.

In a small saucepan over low heat, cook topping ingredients until butter is melted. Drop by rounded teaspoonfuls into 24 well-greased muffin cups.

Stir dough down. Fill greased muffin cups half full. Cover and let rise in a warm place until doubled, about 30 minutes.

Place muffin cups on foil-lined baking sheets. Bake at 375° for 12-15 minutes or until golden brown. Cool for 2 minutes before inverting onto baking sheets. Transfer to serving platters. Serve warm. **Yield:** 2 dozen.

Blueberry Cheesecake Flapjacks

(Pictured at right)

PREP: 30 min. **COOK:** 5 min./batch

These golden, berry-dotted cakes are so pretty, it's tempting to just gaze at them. But as good as they are to look at, they're even better to eat!
—Donna Cline, Pensacola, Florida

1 package (3 ounces) cream cheese, softened
3/4 cup whipped topping
1 cup all-purpose flour
1/2 cup graham cracker crumbs
1 tablespoon sugar
1 teaspoon baking powder
1/2 teaspoon baking soda
1/4 teaspoon salt
2 eggs, lightly beaten
1-1/4 cups buttermilk
1/4 cup butter, melted
1 cup fresh *or* frozen blueberries
3/4 cup maple syrup, warmed
Additional blueberries, optional

For the topping, in a small bowl, beat cream cheese and whipped topping until smooth. Chill until serving.

In a large bowl, combine the flour, cracker crumbs, sugar, baking powder, baking soda and salt. Combine the eggs, buttermilk and butter; add to dry ingredients just until moistened. Fold in blueberries.

Pour the batter by 1/4 cupfuls onto a greased hot griddle; turn when bubbles form on top. Cook until the second side is golden brown. Spread the topping over pancakes. Top with warm maple syrup; sprinkle with additional blueberries if desired. **Yield:** 12 pancakes (3/4 cup topping).

Editor's Note: If using frozen blueberries, do not thaw them before adding to the pancake batter. Be sure to thaw any berries used in the optional garnish.

'Berry' Good Fourth of July

WHEN FARMERS MARKETS, roadside stands and orchards are bursting with pailfuls of fresh-picked blueberries, strawberries and more, make the most of it by adding them to your seasonal menus. Here, you'll find those juicy gems featured in six delectable desserts—all sure to brighten July 4th events and other summer celebrations.

From star-shaped Lemon Blueberry Shortcakes to cool 1-2-3 Blackberry Sherbet, these treats will top off a picnic or party in a tongue-tingling way. Chances are, your berry-packed spread will get just as many oohs and aahs as the fireworks do!

Berry Cheese Torte

(Pictured at left)

PREP: 40 min. + chilling

We love this red, white and blue dessert not only for July 4th, but for any summertime gathering when berries are abundant. The torte looks fancy but is actually super-easy to prepare.
—*Deborah Hitchcock, Granite Falls, Washington*

- 1 **cup crushed gingersnap cookies (about 20 cookies)**
- 3/4 **cup crushed vanilla wafers (about 25 wafers)**
- 1/4 **cup finely chopped walnuts**
- 1/3 **cup butter, melted**
- 1 **envelope unflavored gelatin**
- 1-3/4 **cups white grape juice**
- 1 **package (8 ounces) cream cheese, softened**
- 1/4 **cup sugar**
- 1 **teaspoon vanilla extract**
- 2-1/2 **cups fresh blueberries**
- 1-1/2 **cups sliced fresh strawberries**

For the crust, combine the gingersnap cookie crumbs, vanilla wafer crumbs, walnuts and butter; press onto the bottom and 1-1/2 in. up the sides of a greased 9-in. springform pan. Bake at 350° for 8-10 minutes or until set. Cool on a wire rack.

In a small saucepan, sprinkle gelatin over grape juice; let stand for 1 minute. Heat over low heat, stirring until gelatin is completely dissolved. Cover and refrigerate until partially set, about 45 minutes.

Meanwhile, in a large bowl, beat the cream cheese, sugar and vanilla until smooth. Spread mixture over the cooled crust.

Place the berries in a large bowl. Gently stir in the gelatin mixture. Spoon over the cream cheese layer. Refrigerate for 2 hours before serving. Carefully run a knife around edge of pan to loosen. Remove sides of pan. **Yield:** 12 servings.

1-2-3 Blackberry Sherbet

(Pictured below and on page 156)

PREP: 10 min. + freezing

My mother gave me this recipe, which was a favorite when I was young. Now, when I make it myself, my mouth is watering before I'm finished! —*Lisa Eremia, Irwin, Pennsylvania*

☑ This recipe includes Nutrition Facts.

- 4 **cups fresh *or* frozen blackberries, thawed**
- 2 **cups sugar**
- 2 **cups buttermilk**

In a food processor, combine blackberries and sugar; cover and process until smooth. Strain and discard seeds and pulp. Stir in buttermilk. Transfer puree to a 13-in. x 9-in. dish. Freeze for 1 hour or until edges begin to firm. Stir and return to freezer. Freeze 2 hours longer or until firm.

Just before serving, transfer the sherbet to a food processor; cover and process for 2-3 minutes or until smooth. **Yield:** 1 quart.

Nutrition Facts: 1/2 cup equals 249 calories, 1 g fat (trace saturated fat), 2 mg cholesterol, 65 mg sodium, 60 g carbohydrate, 4 g fiber, 3 g protein.

In a large bowl, cream the shortening and sugar until light and fluffy. Add the eggs, one at a time, beating well after each addition. Beat in the food coloring, vinegar and vanilla. Combine the flour, cocoa, salt and baking soda; add to the creamed mixture alternately with the buttermilk.

Pour into a greased 13-in. x 9-in. baking pan. Bake at 350° for 30-35 minutes or until a toothpick inserted near the center comes out clean. Cool on a wire rack.

For the sauce, in a small saucepan, combine sugar and cornstarch. Stir in the orange juice until smooth. Add the blueberries, nutmeg and salt; cook and stir over medium-high heat until thickened and bubbly. Reduce heat; cook and stir 2 minutes longer. Cool.

In a small bowl, whip the cream and confectioners' sugar until stiff peaks form. Serve cake with sauce and whipped cream. **Yield:** 15 servings.

Berry Splash Smoothies

PREP/TOTAL TIME: 10 min.

These fruity smoothies are loaded with calcium and antioxidants, and they taste great on a hot day. My mom and I like to make these together. —Elayna Ask, Cogan Station, Pennsylvania

☑ This recipe includes Nutrition Facts.

   1/4 **cup fat-free milk**
     1 **cup (8 ounces) cherry yogurt**
     2 **cups frozen unsweetened mixed berries**
   1/4 **cup fresh blueberries,** *divided*
Sugar, optional
     3 **tablespoons vanilla yogurt**

In a blender, combine the milk, cherry yogurt, mixed berries, half of the blueberries and sugar if desired; cover and process until smooth. Stir if necessary. Pour smoothies into chilled glasses. Spoon vanilla yogurt over the top; sprinkle with the remaining blueberries. **Yield:** 3 servings.

Nutrition Facts: 3/4 cup equals 157 calories, 1 g fat (1 g saturated fat), 6 mg cholesterol, 59 mg sodium, 32 g carbohydrate, 2 g fiber, 5 g protein.

America's Birthday Cake

(Pictured above)

PREP: 25 min. **BAKE:** 30 min. + cooling

I created this red, white and blue cake to celebrate my birthday on July 3rd. Of course, it suits America's birthday just as well! —Darlene Brenden, Salem, Oregon

   1/2 **cup shortening**
 1-1/2 **cups sugar**
     2 **eggs**
   1/4 **cup red food coloring**
     1 **teaspoon white vinegar**
     1 **teaspoon vanilla extract**
 2-1/4 **cups cake flour**
     2 **tablespoons baking cocoa**
     1 **teaspoon salt**
     1 **teaspoon baking soda**
     1 **cup buttermilk**
SAUCE:
   3/4 **cup sugar**
     2 **tablespoons cornstarch**
     1 **cup orange juice**
     2 **cups fresh** *or* **frozen blueberries**
   1/8 **teaspoon ground nutmeg**
Dash salt
CREAM:
 1-1/2 **cups heavy whipping cream**
     3 **tablespoons confectioners' sugar**

PATRIOTIC PIZZAZZ. Want another way to give your Fourth of July picnics some berry flair?

• Turn your favorite strawberry shortcake into a red, white and blue dessert by adding blueberries and whipped cream.

• Enhance a bowl of fruit punch with strawberries and blueberries. Or, freeze the berries in ice cubes and add the cubes to the punch.

• Decorate dishes of strawberry or blueberry ice cream with candy stars, star-shaped sugar cookies or red and blue sprinkles.

Lemon Blueberry Shortcakes

(Pictured below)

PREP: 25 min. + freezing **BAKE:** 10 min.

This recipe combines three summer favorites—lemonade, berries and ice cream—into one luscious confection. The star shape makes it fun for parties, too. —Jackie Pressinger, Stuart, Florida

- 1 pint vanilla ice cream
- 3 tablespoons sweetened lemonade drink mix
- 2 cups all-purpose flour
- 6 tablespoons sugar
- 2 teaspoons baking powder
- 2 teaspoons poppy seeds
- 1-1/2 teaspoons grated lemon peel
- 1/2 teaspoon salt
- 1/4 cup cold butter
- 1 egg
- 1/2 cup heavy whipping cream
- 1/4 cup frozen unsweetened blueberries

Confectioners' sugar

In a small bowl, combine ice cream and drink mix; cover and freeze for at least 1 hour.

In a large bowl, combine flour, sugar, baking powder, poppy seeds, peel and salt. Cut in butter until mixture resembles coarse crumbs. Whisk egg and cream; stir into dry ingredients just until moistened. Stir in berries.

Turn dough onto a lightly floured surface; knead 8-10 times. Pat into a 3/4-in. thickness; cut with a floured 3-in. star-shaped cutter. Place 2 in. apart on a greased baking sheet. Bake at 400° for 8-10 minutes or until golden brown around edges.

To assemble, gently split the cakes horizontally with a serrated knife. Top each bottom layer with a scant 1/4 cup of ice cream mixture; replace tops. Sprinkle with confectioners' sugar. **Yield:** 10 servings.

Cream Cheese Pound Cake

(Pictured above)

PREP: 25 min. **BAKE:** 1-1/4 hours + cooling

I regularly make desserts for family gatherings, church suppers and get-togethers at work. Fresh fruit and whipped cream dress up this tender cake. —Richard Hogg, Anderson, South Carolina

- 1-1/2 cups butter, softened
- 1 package (8 ounces) cream cheese, softened
- 3 cups sugar
- 6 eggs
- 2 teaspoons vanilla extract
- 1 teaspoon lemon extract
- 3 cups all-purpose flour
- 1/2 teaspoon baking powder
- 1/4 teaspoon salt

Confectioners' sugar, sliced fresh strawberries and whipped cream, optional

In a large bowl, cream the butter, cream cheese and sugar until light and fluffy. Add eggs, one at a time, beating well after each addition. Beat in the extracts. Combine the flour, baking powder and salt; beat into creamed mixture until blended.

Pour batter into a greased and floured 10-in. fluted tube pan. Bake at 325° for 1-1/4 to 1-1/2 hours or until a toothpick inserted near the center comes out clean. Cool for 10 minutes before removing from pan to a wire rack to cool completely. Garnish with confectioners' sugar, strawberries and whipped cream if desired. **Yield:** 16 servings.

Halloween High Jinks

WHAT'S THE TRICK to making October 31 parties as fun as can be? The answer is simple—the creepy but clever treats here!

You'll get rave reviews from witches, ghosts and goblins alike when you serve sweets such as Sugar Ghost Cupcakes and crunchy Jack-o'-Lantern Popcorn Balls. Your guests are sure to scream for glasses of Swamp Juice a la Slime, Arach-namole and other snacks, too.

Just beware—these monstrous morsels and terrifying tidbits will disappear in a flash!

Sugar Ghost Cupcakes

(Pictured at left)

PREP: 3 hours **BAKE:** 20 min. + cooling

I had 10 neighborhood kids stop over to help me make these cupcakes for a bake sale. I have no doubt that most of the treats never made it that far! —Mysie Sabin, Franklin, Wisconsin

1 package (18-1/4 ounces) chocolate cake mix
FONDANT:
    1 package (16 ounces) miniature marshmallows
    4 to 5 tablespoons water
    1 package (2 pounds) confectioners' sugar
    1/2 cup shortening
DECORATING:
    1 can (16 ounces) vanilla frosting
Blue, orange and green paste food coloring
Miniature peanut butter cups
Malted milk balls
Clear vanilla extract

Prepare and bake the chocolate cake mix according to the package directions for cupcakes; cool completely on wire racks.

In a large microwave-safe bowl, combine miniature marshmallows and 2 tablespoons water. Microwave, uncovered, on high for 1-1/2 to 2 minutes or until melted, stirring every 30 seconds. Stir in three-fourths of the sugar; turn onto a work surface coated with 3 tablespoons shortening.

Knead until smooth and pliable, gradually adding remaining sugar and shortening. If necessary, moisten with remaining water. Wrap fondant in plastic wrap to prevent it from drying out.

To decorate, set aside 1/4 cup frosting. Tint remaining frosting blue; frost cupcakes.

For ghosts: Invert two peanut butter cups and stack, securing together with a small amount of the reserved frosting. Top with a malted milk ball, attaching with frosting. Repeat, forming 24 stacks.

On a work surface lightly sprinkled with confectioners'

sugar, roll a 1-1/4-in. ball of fondant into a 4-in. circle; drape over a stack. For eyes and mouth, gently cut out shapes using pastry tips. Repeat for remaining ghosts.

For pumpkins, stems and tendrils: Tint desired amount of fondant orange. Wrap fondant around malted milk balls; shape into pumpkins. Add imprint lines with a veining tool or toothpick.

For stems and tendrils, tint a small amount of fondant green. Shape into stems; attach to the pumpkins using vanilla. For tendrils, roll out remaining green fondant; using a pizza cutter, cut into thin strips. Gently wrap strips around toothpicks; set aside to dry. (Tightly wrap any remaining fondant in plastic wrap and store in a resealable plastic bag for another use.)

To finish cupcakes: Place a small amount of the reserved frosting on top of each cupcake; top with a prepared ghost. Carefully remove the tendrils from the toothpicks and attach to the pumpkins using vanilla. Attach the pumpkins to the cupcakes as desired. **Yield:** 2 dozen.

Editor's Note: This recipe was tested in a 1,100-watt microwave. This recipe was tested with Kraft brand marshmallows.

HAUNTING HOW-TOS. Follow these steps when making Sugar Ghost Cupcakes (above left):

1. Stack two peanut butter cups and top them with a malted milk ball. Use frosting to hold the candies together.

2. Roll a 1-1/4-inch ball of white fondant into a 4-inch circle and drape it over a candy stack. Use pastry tips to carefully cut out the ghost's eyes and mouth.

place in a heavy-duty resealable plastic bag. Cut a small hole in corner of the bag. Pipe four legs on each side of spider body. Pipe a black line around outer edge of the web. Serve with chips. **Yield:** 2-1/2 cups.

Jack-o'-Lantern Popcorn Balls

PREP: 30 min. **COOK:** 30 min. + cooling

These popcorn balls get dressed up for Halloween with orange color, chocolate faces and leaves to resemble carved pumpkins.
—Melissa Hayes, Hundred, West Virginia

> 4 **quarts popped popcorn**
> 2 **cups sugar**
> 1-1/2 **cups water**
> 1/2 **cup light corn syrup**
> 1 **teaspoon white vinegar**
> 1/2 **teaspoon salt**
> 1 **teaspoon vanilla extract**
>
> **Yellow and red food coloring**
> 2 **to 3 milk chocolate candy bars (1.55 ounces** *each***)**
> 1/4 **cup vanilla frosting**
> 8 **candy spearmint leaves**

Place popcorn in a roasting pan; keep warm in a 200° oven. In a large heavy saucepan, combine sugar, water, corn syrup, vinegar and salt. Cook over medium heat until a candy thermometer reads 250° (hard-ball stage).

Remove from the heat. Stir in the vanilla and food coloring (about 1 teaspoon yellow and 9 drops red) until blended. Immediately pour over popcorn and stir until coated. When mixture is cool enough to handle, quickly shape into 3-1/2-in. balls, dipping hands in cold water to prevent sticking.

Cut triangles and rectangles from the candy bars for the pumpkin eyes, noses and mouths. In a small bowl, combine the frosting with 5 drops of yellow and 3 drops of red food coloring; attach the pumpkin facial features with frosting. Attach a spearmint leaf to the top of each. **Yield:** 8 servings.

Leg Bones

PREP/TOTAL TIME: 30 min.

Kids can help out with these bone-chilling breadsticks because they're so simple to create. Enjoy them with soup, stew or chili.
—Summer Jones, Pleasant Grove, Utah

✓ **This recipe includes Nutrition Facts and Diabetic Exchanges.**

> 2 **tubes (11 ounces** *each***) refrigerated breadsticks**
> 3 **tablespoons butter, melted**
> 1/2 **teaspoon seasoned salt**
> 1/2 **teaspoon pepper**

Unroll and separate the breadsticks; tie each end into a knot. Place on ungreased baking sheets. Brush with butter and sprinkle with seasoned salt and pepper.

Arach-namole

(Pictured above)

PREP/TOTAL TIME: 30 min.

Everyone will get caught up in this appetizing web eaten with tortilla chips. Feel free to substitute your favorite homemade or purchased guacamole. —*Kenna Jo Lambertsen, Traer, Iowa*

> 3 **medium ripe avocados, peeled and pitted,** *divided*
> 2 **plum tomatoes, quartered and seeded**
> 1 **small onion, cut into wedges**
> 2 **tablespoons lime juice**
> 1 **tablespoon taco seasoning**
> 1 **garlic clove, peeled and halved**
> 3/4 **cup sour cream,** *divided*
> 1 **large ripe olive**
> 1 **colossal ripe olive**
>
> **Black paste food coloring**
> **Tortilla chips**

In a food processor, combine two avocados, tomatoes, onion, lime juice, taco seasoning and garlic. Cover and process until smooth.

In a small bowl, mash the remaining avocado with a fork. Stir into pureed mixture. Spread onto a 10-in. plate.

Place 1/2 cup sour cream in a heavy-duty resealable plastic bag; cut a small hole in corner of bag. Pipe thin concentric circles 1 in. apart over guacamole. Beginning with the center circle, gently pull a toothpick through the circles toward outer edges. Wipe toothpick clean. Repeat to complete web pattern.

Pipe small dots for eyes on the large olive; place near center of the spider web. Place colossal olive behind the face. Add food coloring to the remaining sour cream;

Bake at 375° for 10-15 minutes or until golden brown.
Yield: 1 dozen

Nutrition Facts: 1 breadstick equals 83 calories, 3 g fat (2 g saturated fat), 4 mg cholesterol, 227 mg sodium, 13 g carbohydrate, trace fiber, 2 g protein. **Diabetic Exchange:** 1 starch.

Pizza Snake

(Pictured below)

PREP: 20 min. **BAKE:** 25 min.

Once this snake is filled, rolled and shaped, let the kids "paint" it with food coloring. The bread will bake up just creepy enough to satisfy the boys and ghouls! —*Jen Spaeth, Ozark, Missouri*

- 1 tube (11 ounces) refrigerated crusty French loaf dough
- 1 jar (14 ounces) pizza sauce, *divided*
- 1 cup (4 ounces) shredded part-skim mozzarella cheese
- 1 cup sliced fresh mushrooms
- 25 slices pepperoni
- 1 egg, beaten

Assorted food coloring
New paintbrushes

Unroll the French loaf dough into a large rectangle; spread with 1 cup pizza sauce to within 1 in. of edges. Sprinkle with cheese and mushrooms. Cut a forked tongue from a pepperoni slice; refrigerate until serving. Layer remaining pepperoni over cheese and mushrooms.

Roll up jelly-roll style, starting with a long side; pinch seam to seal and tuck ends under. Place seam side down on a greased baking sheet and shape like an "S." Divide egg among several small bowls; tint with food coloring as desired. Paint snake as desired with egg wash.

Bake at 350° for 25-30 minutes or until golden brown. Cut a small hole for the mouth; insert tongue. Warm remaining sauce; serve on the side. **Yield:** 5 servings.

Swamp Juice a la Slime

(Pictured above)

PREP: 25 min. + freezing

The green "goo" oozing down the sides of the glasses makes this cool beverage a frightfully fun addition to any Halloween party. —*Melisa Ann Beier, Howell, Michigan*

☑ **This recipe includes Nutrition Facts.**

- 1/2 cup light corn syrup

Green paste food coloring

- 5 cups unsweetened pineapple juice
- 2 cups white grape juice
- 2 drops yellow food coloring, optional
- 1 cup club soda, chilled

Fresh pineapple slices, optional

Refrigerate 10 champagne flutes or cocktail glasses until chilled. In a small bowl, combine corn syrup and green food coloring; dip the rims of chilled glasses into mixture. Turn glasses upright, allowing the mixture to slightly run down sides of glasses. Freeze until firm.

In a pitcher, combine pineapple juice, grape juice and yellow food coloring if desired. Refrigerate until chilled.

Just before serving, stir the club soda into the juice mixture. Pour juice into prepared glasses; garnish with pineapple if desired. **Yield:** 10 servings (2 quarts).

Nutrition Facts: 3/4 cup equals 142 calories, trace fat (trace saturated fat), 0 cholesterol, 21 mg sodium, 36 g carbohydrate, trace fiber, 1 g protein.

Thanksgiving Day Dinner

THE HOUSE is full of loved ones...rooms are decorated with autumn flair...the table is set in a festive way. On Thanksgiving, you want your feast to be every bit as special as the holiday itself. And it will be when you start with exceptional Brined Grilled Turkey Breast as the main course.

For complementary side dishes, choose from "Everything" Stuffing, Winter Squash Souffle Bake, Honey and Cherry Chutney, Taste-of-Fall Salad and Kelsey's Favorite Cranberry Bread. No matter which accompaniments you present to your family, your Turkey Day dinner is sure to get a cornucopia of compliments!

Brined Grilled Turkey Breast

(Pictured at left)

PREP: 20 min. + chilling **GRILL:** 1-1/4 hours + standing

Once you taste this mouth-watering bird, you'll never want to oven-roast a turkey again! It's so moist and tender, and it slices with ease. —Tina Repak-Mirilovich, Johnstown, Pennsylvania

- 2 **quarts cold water,** *divided*
- 1/2 **cup kosher salt**
- 1/2 **cup packed brown sugar**
- 1 **tablespoon whole peppercorns**
- 1 **boneless skinless turkey breast half (2 to 3 pounds)**

BASTING SAUCE:
- 1/4 **cup canola oil**
- 1/4 **cup sesame oil**
- 1/4 **cup reduced-sodium soy sauce**
- 3 **tablespoons lemon juice**
- 2 **tablespoons honey**
- 3 **garlic cloves, minced**
- 1/4 **teaspoon dried thyme**
- 1/4 **teaspoon crushed red pepper flakes**

In a large saucepan, combine 1 quart water, salt, brown sugar and peppercorns. Bring to a boil. Cook and stir until salt and sugar are dissolved. Remove from the heat. Add the remaining cold water to cool the brine to room temperature.

Place a large resealable plastic bag inside a second plastic bag; add turkey breast. Carefully pour cooled brine into bag. Squeeze out as much air as possible; seal bags and turn to coat. Place in a pan. Refrigerate for 4-6 hours or overnight.

Prepare the grill for indirect heat, using a drip pan. Meanwhile, combine basting sauce ingredients. Place turkey over drip pan and grill, covered, over indirect medium heat for 1-1/4 to 1-1/2 hours or until a meat thermometer reads 170°, basting occasionally with sauce. Cover and let stand for 10 minutes before slicing. **Yield:** 6 servings.

Editor's Note: This recipe was tested with Morton brand kosher salt. It is best not to use a prebasted turkey breast for this recipe. However, if you do, omit the salt in the recipe.

"Everything" Stuffing

(Pictured at far left)

PREP: 30 min. **COOK:** 3 hours

My husband and father go crazy for this superb sausage stuffing. It "bakes" in a slow cooker to keep your oven free for the turkey, and it freezes well, too. —Bette Votral, Bethlehem, Pennsylvania

- 1/2 **pound bulk Italian sausage**
- 4 **cups seasoned stuffing cubes**
- 1-1/2 **cups crushed corn bread stuffing**
- 1/2 **cup chopped toasted chestnuts** *or* **pecans**
- 1/2 **cup minced fresh parsley**
- 1 **tablespoon minced fresh sage** *or* **1 teaspoon rubbed sage**
- 1/8 **teaspoon salt**
- 1/8 **teaspoon pepper**
- 1-3/4 **cups sliced baby portobello mushrooms**
- 1 **package (5 ounces) sliced fresh shiitake mushrooms**
- 1 **large onion, chopped**
- 1 **medium apple, peeled and chopped**
- 1 **celery rib, chopped**
- 3 **tablespoons butter**
- 1 **can (14-1/2 ounces) chicken broth**

In a large skillet, cook sausage over medium heat until no longer pink; drain. Place in a large bowl. Stir in the stuffing cubes, corn bread stuffing, chestnuts, parsley, sage, salt and pepper.

In the same skillet, saute the mushrooms, onion, apple and celery in butter until tender. Stir into stuffing mixture. Add enough broth to reach desired moistness. Transfer to a 5-qt. slow cooker. Cover and cook on low for 3 hours, stirring once. **Yield:** 9 servings.

SAGE ADVICE. Sage adds a distinctive flavor to "Everything" Stuffing (recipe above). To freeze fresh sage leaves, remove the leaves from the stems and pack the leaves loosely in freezer bags for up to 1 year. Freezing will intensify the flavor.

Taste-of-Fall Salad

(Pictured above)

PREP/TOTAL TIME: 25 min.

When my parents visited over the holidays, I served them this wonderful green salad one night. They enjoyed it so much that it became the first course every night during their entire stay!
—Kristin Kossak, Bozeman, Montana

- **2/3 cup pecan halves**
- **1/4 cup balsamic vinegar, divided**
- **Dash cayenne pepper**
- **Dash ground cinnamon**
- **3 tablespoons sugar, divided**
- **1 package (5 ounces) spring mix salad greens**
- **1/4 cup olive oil**
- **1 teaspoon Dijon mustard**
- **1/8 teaspoon salt**
- **1 medium pear, thinly sliced**
- **1/4 cup shredded Parmesan cheese**

In a large heavy skillet, cook the pecans, 2 tablespoons vinegar, cayenne and cinnamon over medium heat until the nuts are toasted, about 4 minutes. Sprinkle with 1 tablespoon sugar. Cook and stir for 2-4 minutes or until sugar is melted. Spread on foil to cool.

Place salad greens in a large bowl. Combine the oil, mustard, salt and remaining vinegar and sugar; drizzle over greens and toss to coat. Arrange the greens, pear slices and pecans on six salad plates. Sprinkle with cheese. **Yield:** 6 servings.

Kelsey's Favorite Cranberry Bread

PREP: 25 min. **BAKE:** 55 min. + cooling

My granddaughter, Kelsey, and I saw this recipe and decided to bake it together. She and her sister don't like nuts, so I replaced them with golden raisins. —Annette Grahl, Midway, Kentucky

- **2 cups all-purpose flour**
- **3/4 cup sugar**

1-1/2 teaspoons baking powder
   1 teaspoon salt
 1/2 teaspoon baking soda
 1/4 cup cold butter
   1 egg
 3/4 cup orange juice
   2 teaspoons grated orange peel
   1 cup chopped fresh *or* frozen cranberries
 1/2 cup golden raisins
STREUSEL:
 1/3 cup packed brown sugar
   3 tablespoons all-purpose flour
   2 tablespoons cold butter
GLAZE:
 1/2 cup confectioners' sugar
   2 teaspoons orange juice

In a large bowl, combine the first five ingredients; cut in butter until crumbly. In a small bowl, whisk the egg, orange juice and peel. Stir into dry ingredients just until moistened. Fold in cranberries and raisins. Transfer to a greased 8-in x 4-in. loaf pan.

Combine brown sugar and flour; cut in butter until crumbly. Sprinkle over batter. Bake at 350° for 55-65 minutes or until a toothpick inserted near the center comes out clean. Cool for 10 minutes before removing from pan to a wire rack to cool completely.

For the glaze, combine the confectioners' sugar and orange juice until smooth. Drizzle over the bread. **Yield:** 1 loaf (12 slices).

Honey & Cherry Chutney

PREP/TOTAL TIME: 30 min.

This rich relish is a nice change of pace from the usual cranberry sauce and complements turkey so well. Be prepared with extra copies of the recipe—one bite and everyone will be asking for it!
— *Kitty Stout, Madison, Ohio*

   1 can (14-1/2 ounces) pitted tart cherries, undrained
 1/2 cup raisins
 1/2 cup honey
 1/4 cup packed brown sugar
 1/4 cup cider vinegar
 1/2 teaspoon ground cinnamon
 1/8 teaspoon ground cloves
 1/2 cup chopped walnuts
   1 tablespoon cornstarch
   1 tablespoon water

In a small saucepan, bring the first seven ingredients to a boil. Reduce heat; simmer, uncovered, for 15 minutes or until slightly thickened. Stir in walnuts.

Combine cornstarch and water until smooth. Stir into the pan. Bring to a boil; cook and stir for 2 minutes or until thickened. **Yield:** 2 cups.

Winter Squash Souffle Bake

(Pictured below)

PREP: 15 min. **BAKE:** 55 min.

With its beautiful golden color and hint of citrus, this side-dish souffle is a feast for the eyes as well as the taste buds. It's perfect for your Thanksgiving table…or any other autumn occasion.
— *Christine Omar, Harwich Port, Massachusetts*

   4 eggs
   2 packages (12 ounces *each*) frozen cooked winter squash, thawed
 1/4 cup butter, melted
   2 tablespoons brown sugar
 1/2 teaspoon salt
 1/2 teaspoon grated orange peel
 1/8 teaspoon ground nutmeg
 1/8 teaspoon pepper

Separate eggs. Let the eggs and squash stand at room temperature for 30 minutes. Grease a 1-1/2-qt. souffle dish and lightly sprinkle with flour; set aside.

In a large bowl, combine the egg yolks, squash, butter, brown sugar, salt, orange peel, nutmeg and pepper.

In a large bowl with clean beaters, beat egg whites until stiff peaks form. With a spatula, stir a fourth of the egg whites into squash mixture until no white streaks remain. Fold in remaining egg whites until combined. Transfer to prepared dish.

Bake at 350° for 55-60 minutes or until the top of the souffle is puffed and the center appears set. Serve immediately. **Yield:** 5 servings.

Fantasyland of Cupcakes

THE BEST-SELLING AUTHORS of the book *Hello, Cupcake!*, Karen Tack and Alan Richardson, spent a few days in the Taste of Home Test Kitchen whipping up one-of-a-kind goodies for Christmas and winter get-togethers. And what a wonderland they created!

You can make their four Winter Fantasy cupcake designs right in your own kitchen—no special tools or talents are required. Just start with either Perfect Cake-Mix Cupakes or from-scratch Chocolate Cupcakes, the two basic cupcake recipes included here…or use your own favorite recipe. Then follow any of the other four recipes and have fun decorating!

Winter Fantasy Snowman Cupcakes

(Pictured at bottom left)

PREP: 1 hour

Who doesn't love a snowman? You'll melt the hearts of children and grown-ups alike when you build these frosty fellows.
—Karen Tack, Riverside, Connecticut

1 to 2 cans vanilla frosting (16 ounces *each*)
Cupcakes of your choice
SNOWMEN:
Coarse sugar
Chocolate wafers
Semisweet chocolate chips and miniature semisweet chocolate chips
Orange candy slices
Additional vanilla frosting
Blue food coloring, pearl dragees, blue jumbo diamond sprinkles and edible glitter, optional

Frost cupcakes, reserving some frosting for decorating as desired.

For snowman cupcakes: Dip the top of each cupcake in coarse sugar; gently shake off excess sugar. For stovepipe hats, microwave chocolate wafers for a few seconds to slightly soften as needed. Use a serrated knife to cut two narrow strips from opposite sides of each wafer. (Large center piece will form crown of hat; one strip will form the brim.)

Add chips and mini chips to cupcake to form eyes and mouth. Cut a small piece of orange slice to form the nose.

Stick the brim of hat, rounded side up, into top of cupcake; insert the hat crown into the top edge. Secure with additional frosting. Color the frosting if desired; place in a resealable plastic bag. Cut a small hole in the corner of bag. Pipe a decorative hat band; add dragees and sprinkles if desired. Sprinkle cupcakes with glitter if desired. **Yield:** varies.

Winter Fantasy Snowflake Cupcakes

(Pictured below)

PREP: 1 hour + chilling

These elegant confections are easier to make than they appear. Delicate and shimmery, the snowflakes are as eye-catching as Mother Nature's!
—Karen Tack, Riverside, Connecticut

1 to 2 cans vanilla frosting (16 ounces *each*)
Cupcakes of your choice
SNOWFLAKES:
Clear decorating sugar
Pencil, paper, scissors and waxed paper
White candy coating
Blue decorating sugar and edible glitter

Frost cupcakes, reserving some frosting for decorating as desired.

For snowflake cupcakes: Place clear decorating sugar in a small shallow bowl; roll top edge of each cupcake in sugar to form a decorative rim. Set aside.

With a pencil and paper, draw assorted snowflake designs. Cut into individual patterns. Melt candy coating in a microwave-safe bowl; stir until smooth. Transfer to a resealable plastic bag; cut a small hole in corner of bag. Place waxed paper over the drawings and pipe candy coating over designs. Sprinkle with blue decorating sugar and edible glitter. Refrigerate until set.

Gently lift flakes from waxed paper and arrange on cupcakes. Sprinkle with additional glitter. **Yield:** varies.

Winter Fantasy
Poinsettia Cupcakes

(Pictured above)

PREP: I hour

Let your creativity blossom with these beautiful Christmastime blooms. Your guests may find it hard to believe that the flower petals are chewing gum. —Karen Tack, Riverside, Connecticut

1 to 2 cans vanilla frosting (16 ounces *each*)
Cupcakes of your choice
POINSETTIAS:
Clear decorating sugar
Winterfresh chewing gum
Additional vanilla frosting
Yellow candy-coated sunflower kernels

Frost cupcakes, reserving some frosting for decorating as desired.

For poinsettia cupcakes: Place decorating sugar in a small shallow bowl; roll top edge of each cupcake in sugar to form a decorative rim. Set aside.

Using clean kitchen scissors or a small sharp knife, cut gum into leaf shapes of various sizes. Pinch the base end of each leaf, forming a curved leaf shape. Add frosting to a small resealable plastic bag; cut a small hole in the corner.

Arrange leaves in a circular pattern over top of each cupcake, working from the outer leaves in. Press outer leaves into top of cupcake; secure with additional frosting as needed. Continue adding leaves and securing with frosting to form a poinsettia. Gently press sunflower kernels into the center. **Yield:** varies.

Perfect Cake-Mix Cupcakes

PREP: IO min. **BAKE:** I5 min. + cooling

When you're busy as can be, use a convenient cake mix to whip up cupcakes in a flash. Then spend more time doing the fun part—dressing them up! —Karen Tack, Riverside, Connecticut

> 1 package (18-1/4 ounces) white cake mix
> 1 cup buttermilk
> 4 eggs
> 1/3 cup canola oil

In a large bowl, combine all ingredients. Beat on low speed until moistened; increase speed to high and beat 2 minutes longer.

Spoon half of the batter into a large resealable plastic bag; cut a 1/4-in. hole in corner of bag. Fill paper-lined muffin cups two-thirds full. Repeat with the remaining batter. Bake at 350° for 15-20 minutes or until a toothpick inserted near the center comes out clean.

Cool for 10 minutes before removing from pans to wire racks to cool completely. Frost and decorate as desired. **Yield:** 2 dozen.

Chocolate Cupcakes

PREP: 20 min. **BAKE:** 15 min. + cooling

If you love chocolate, you're going to adore these from–scratch cupcakes. No matter how I top them, they get snatched up fast.
—*Marlene Martin, Country Harbour Mines, Nova Scotia*

> 1/2 cup butter, softened
> 1 cup sugar
> 1 egg
> 1 teaspoon vanilla extract
> 1-1/2 cups all-purpose flour
> 1/2 cup baking cocoa
> 1 teaspoon baking soda
> 1/4 teaspoon salt
> 1/2 cup water
> 1/2 cup buttermilk

In a small bowl, cream butter and sugar until light and fluffy. Beat in egg and vanilla. Combine the flour, cocoa, baking soda and salt; gradually add to creamed mixture alternately with water and buttermilk, beating well after each addition.

Fill paper-lined muffin cups two-thirds full. Bake at 375° for 12-15 minutes or until a toothpick inserted near the center comes out clean. Cool for 10 minutes before removing from pans to wire racks to cool completely. Frost and decorate as desired. **Yield:** 16 cupcakes.

Winter Fantasy Star Cupcakes

(Pictured at right)

PREP: 1 hour + cooling

Shine the light on cupcake fun with these star–trimmed goodies. The elegant decorations on top are surprisingly easy to make using melted hard candies, frosting, sugar, dragees and a cookie cutter.
—*Karen Tack, Riverside, Connecticut*

> 1 to 2 cans vanilla frosting (16 ounces *each*)
> **Cupcakes of your choice**

STARS:
> **Clear decorating sugar**
> **Miniature silver dragees, optional**
> **Nonstick foil *or* parchment paper**
> **Blue, clear *and/or* white hard candies**
> **Additional vanilla frosting**
> **Blue decorating sugar**

Frost cupcakes, reserving some frosting for decorating as desired.

For star cupcakes: Place clear decorating sugar in a small shallow bowl; stir in miniature dragees if desired. (Dragees are not edible and are for decorative use only.) Roll top edge of each cupcake in sugar to form a decorative rim. Set aside.

Line a 15-in. x 10-in. x 1-in. baking pan with nonstick foil. Crush candies in desired color to yield about 1 cup. Place in prepared pan, spreading candy to about 1/4-in. thickness. Bake at 350° for 3-5 minutes or until melted. Meanwhile, coat 6-8 metal star-shaped cookie cutters with cooking spray.

Remove the pan from the oven; press the prepared cutters into melted candy. Let stand until just before candy is set; remove cutters. (Reheat scraps in the oven if desired.)

Add frosting to a small resealable plastic bag; cut a small hole in corner of the bag. Pipe frosting around the edges of the stars; top with decorating sugars and miniature dragees as desired. Press stars onto the top of cupcake; secure with additional frosting if needed. **Yield:** varies.

Merry Gifts in Good Taste

WHAT SPREADS holiday cheer faster than something scrumptious from the kitchen? No matter how many names are on your Christmas gift list, you're sure to find a treat here to please.

Pack some Spiced Christmas Cookies or Gingerbread People in a festive tin...wrap up Chocolate-Dipped Beverage Spoons or Spiced Chai Mix for the person who loves hot beverages...or give colorful Fruitcake Loaves tied with holiday ribbon.

Or share that classic favorite—the gift of a mix in a jar, so friends can make their own fresh-baked treats!

Sand Art Brownie Mix

(Pictured at left and on page 156)

PREP: 15 min. **BAKE:** 25 min. + cooling

Keep a few jars of this brownie mix on hand, and you'll have a wonderful treat to put in Christmas gift baskets or to use as a hostess gift.   —Claudia Temple, Sutton, West Virginia

    1 **cup plus 2 tablespoons all-purpose flour**
  1/2 **teaspoon salt**
  2/3 **cup packed brown sugar**
  2/3 **cup sugar**
  1/3 **cup baking cocoa**
  1/2 **cup semisweet chocolate chips**
  1/2 **cup vanilla *or* white chips**
  1/2 **cup chopped pecans**
ADDITIONAL INGREDIENTS:
    3 **eggs**
  2/3 **cup canola oil**
    1 **teaspoon vanilla extract**

In a small bowl, combine flour and salt. In a 1-qt. glass container, layer the flour mixture, brown sugar, sugar, cocoa, chips and pecans. Cover; store in a cool dry place for up to 6 months. **Yield:** 1 batch (about 4 cups total).

To prepare brownies: In a large bowl, whisk the eggs, oil and vanilla. Add the brownie mix; stir until blended. Spread into a greased 9-in. square baking pan. Bake at 350° for 25-30 minutes or until a toothpick inserted near the center comes out clean (do not overbake). Cool on a wire rack. **Yield:** 16 servings.

Fruitcake Loaves

(Pictured at right)

PREP: 25 min. **BAKE:** 1 hour + cooling

I received this holiday recipe from my husband's aunt. Everyone who's sampled it has liked it—even I do, and I've never been a big fan of fruitcake!   —JoAnn Huhn, Cleveland, Wisconsin

    2 **packages (8 ounces *each*) pitted dates, chopped**
    1 **pound chopped candied pineapple**
    1 **pound red candied cherries**
  1/2 **pound walnut halves**
  1/2 **pound Brazil nuts**
    1 **cup all-purpose flour**
    1 **cup sugar**
    2 **teaspoons baking powder**
Dash salt
    4 **eggs, *separated***
    1 **teaspoon vanilla extract**

In a large bowl, combine the dates, pineapple, cherries and nuts. Combine the flour, sugar, baking powder and salt; stir into fruit mixture until well coated.

In a small bowl, whisk the egg yolks until slightly thickened. In another bowl, beat egg whites and vanilla until stiff peaks form. With a spatula, stir a fourth of the egg whites into egg yolk mixture until no white streaks remain. Fold in remaining egg whites until combined. Add to fruit mixture; gently fold until blended. Pour into two well-greased and floured 8-in. x 4-in. loaf pans.

Bake at 300° for 1 to 1-1/2 hours or until a toothpick inserted near the center comes out clean. Cool for 20 minutes before removing from pans to wire racks. Cool completely. Wrap tightly and store in a cool dry place. Using a serrated knife, cut into slices. **Yield:** 2 loaves (12 slices each).

On a lightly floured surface, roll out each portion to 1/4-in. thickness. Cut with a floured 4-in. gingerbread boy cookie cutter. Place 2 in. apart on baking sheets coated with cooking spray. Reroll scraps.

Bake at 350° for 7-9 minutes or until edges are firm. Remove to wire racks to cool completely. Decorate as desired. **Yield:** 2-1/2 dozen.

Chocolate-Dipped Beverage Spoons

(Pictured below)

PREP: 45 min. + chilling

These make a delightful gift when tied with ribbon and displayed in a holiday mug. To set the chocolate quickly, chill the dipped spoons in the freezer. —*Marcy Boswell, Menifee, California*

  1 **cup milk chocolate chips,** *divided*
 24 **metal** *or* **plastic spoons**
  1 **cup vanilla** *or* **white chips,** *divided*
Coarse sugar *or* **chocolate sprinkles, optional**

In a microwave-safe bowl, melt 3/4 cup milk chocolate chips; stir until smooth. Dip half of the spoons into chocolate, tapping spoon handles on the edge of the bowl to remove excess chocolate. Place on a waxed paper-lined baking sheet. Chill for 5 minutes or until set. Repeat with 3/4 cup vanilla chips and remaining spoons.

Melt remaining milk chocolate chips; stir until smooth. Pipe or drizzle over the vanilla-dipped spoons. Decorate with sugar if desired. Repeat with the remaining vanilla chips and chocolate-dipped spoons. Chill for 5 minutes or until set. **Yield:** 2 dozen.

Gingerbread People

(Pictured above)

PREP: 25 min. + chilling
BAKE: 10 min./batch + cooling

Soft and chewy, these nicely spiced cookies are favorites of my grandchildren. They love to help me decorate them with icing and candies. —*Joan Truax, Pittsboro, Indiana*

    6 **tablespoons butter, softened**
  3/4 **cup packed dark brown sugar**
  1/2 **cup molasses**
    1 **egg**
    2 **teaspoons vanilla extract**
    1 **teaspoon grated lemon peel**
    3 **cups all-purpose flour**
    3 **teaspoons ground ginger**
1-1/2 **teaspoons baking powder**
1-1/4 **teaspoons ground cinnamon**
  3/4 **teaspoon baking soda**
  1/4 **teaspoon salt**
  1/4 **teaspoon ground cloves**
Icing and candies of your choice

In a large bowl, cream butter and brown sugar until light and fluffy. Beat in the molasses, egg, vanilla and lemon peel. Combine the flour, ginger, baking powder, cinnamon, baking soda, salt and cloves; gradually add to creamed mixture and mix well. Divide dough in half. Refrigerate for 30 minutes or until easy to handle.

with a floured 2-1/4-in. round cookie cutter. Place 1 in. apart on ungreased baking sheets. Bake at 350° for 10-12 minutes or until bottoms are lightly browned. Remove to wire racks to cool.

Beat frosting ingredients until smooth. Frost cookies; decorate with cherries. Store in an airtight container. **Yield:** 7-1/2 dozen.

Spiced Chai Mix

(Pictured below)

PREP/TOTAL TIME: 15 min.

This hot beverage shared by my sister–in–law is wonderful all by itself, but I think it's best with a cozy blanket and a good book!
—Dee Falk, Stromsburg, Nebraska

✓ This recipe includes Nutrition Facts and Diabetic Exchanges.

- 3 cups nonfat dry milk powder
- 1-1/2 cups sugar
- 1 cup unsweetened instant tea
- 3/4 cup vanilla powdered nondairy creamer
- 1-1/2 teaspoons ground ginger
- 1-1/2 teaspoons ground cinnamon
- 1/2 teaspoon ground cardamom
- 1/2 teaspoon ground cloves

OPTIONAL GARNISH:

Whipped cream

In a food processor, combine all dry ingredients; cover and process until powdery. Store the mix in an airtight container in a cool dry place for up to 6 months.

To prepare 1 serving: Dissolve 3 tablespoons of mix in 3/4 cup boiling water; stir well. Dollop with whipped cream if desired. **Yield:** about 5 cups mix (26 servings).

Nutrition Facts: 1 serving equals 114 calories, 1 g fat (1 g saturated fat), 3 mg cholesterol, 75 mg sodium, 21 g carbohydrate, trace fiber, 5 g protein. **Diabetic Exchange:** 1-1/2 starch.

Spiced Christmas Cookies

(Pictured above and on page 156)

PREP: 45 min. + chilling **BAKE:** 10 min./batch

Brought to America from Germany in 1846, this recipe has been passed down through six generations! It's a timeless treat for the holiday season. —Tanya Juhasz, Newberry, Florida

- 2 cups molasses
- 1 cup butter, melted
- 1 cup (8 ounces) sour cream
- 1 tablespoon lemon juice
- 8 cups all-purpose flour
- 1 cup packed brown sugar
- 3 teaspoons *each* ground cinnamon, nutmeg and cloves
- 2-1/4 teaspoons baking soda
- 1 teaspoon grated lemon peel
- 3/4 teaspoon salt
- 3 cups chopped walnuts
- 1-2/3 cups raisins
- 1/4 cup chopped candied lemon peel
- 1/4 cup chopped candied orange peel

FROSTING:

- 4-1/2 cups confectioners' sugar
- 1 cup heavy whipping cream
- 2 tablespoons lemon juice

GARNISH:

- 2 cups red *and/or* green candied cherries, cut as desired

In a large bowl, beat the molasses, butter, sour cream and lemon juice until well blended. Combine flour, brown sugar, spices, baking soda, lemon peel and salt. Gradually add to butter mixture; mix well. Stir in walnuts, raisins and candied peels. Cover; refrigerate for 30 minutes or until easy to handle.

Divide dough into four portions. On a lightly floured surface, roll out each portion to 1/4-in. thickness. Cut

'Mom's Best'

Six family cooks fondly recall their
mothers' cooking...and share
the recipes for their favorite
made-by-mom meals and more.

UNFORGETTABLE FARE. Clockwise from upper left:
Home-Style Chicken Dinner (p. 188), Cooking by the
Campfire (p. 204), Casual Summer Spread (p. 200) and
Crowd-Pleasing Feast (p. 196).

Roast Chicken with
Oyster Stuffing

POTATO VEGETABLE MEDLEY   CHERRY GELATIN SALAD   CHOCOLATE RING CAKE

Always made from scratch with plenty of love, her mother's good cooking on the dinner table was the family's reward after a long, hard day's work on the farm.

By Joann Jensen, Lowell, Indiana

I GREW UP in a hardworking farm family full of big appetites. When the six of us gathered at the table, the first thing we did was say grace. Other than that, we didn't talk much...unless it was to ask someone to pass the chicken!

Our only concern was whether or not Mom made enough for second helpings. And everyone wanted seconds of her wonderful meals. There never seemed to be any leftovers.

My mom, Edna Hoffman (above, at left) of Hebron, Indiana, was raised on a farm, too. I don't think she ever prepared a recipe using a boxed cake mix or heated a frozen dinner. She cooked from scratch. And she's never been afraid to try something new.

Her meals weren't extravagant, but boy, were they good! Hard work, especially at harvesttime, made Mom's cooking taste even better.

While my two brothers helped our dad, Marty, with farm work, my sister and I helped Mom with canning, freezing and tending our huge garden. We both learned from Mom in the kitchen, but I also picked up many skills in 4-H and at school. Now I cook for my husband, Steve. We have two grown daughters, Jamie and Kellie.

Mom's been a *Taste of Home* field editor since the first issue. Many of her recipes have been showcased in the magazine, in addition to this favorite meal of mine featuring Cherry Gelatin Salad, Roast Chicken with Oyster Stuffing, Potato Vegetable Medley and Chocolate Ring Cake. I hope you'll give it a try!

Cherry Gelatin Salad

PREP: 15 min. + chilling

✓ This recipe includes Nutrition Facts and Diabetic Exchanges.

- **1 can (15 ounces) pitted dark sweet cherries**
- **1 package (3 ounces) cherry gelatin**
- **1 cup cold water**
- **1 tablespoon lemon juice**
- **2 medium bananas, sliced**
- **1/4 cup chopped pecans**

Additional sliced banana and chopped pecans, optional

Drain cherries, reserving liquid in a 1-cup measuring cup; add enough water to measure 1 cup. In a small saucepan, bring mixture to a boil. Remove from the heat; stir in gelatin until dissolved. Stir in cold water and lemon juice.

Cover and refrigerate until syrupy, about 40 minutes. Fold in bananas, pecans and cherries. Transfer to a 6-cup mold coated with cooking spray. Refrigerate until firm. Unmold onto a serving platter. Garnish with additional banana and pecans if desired. **Yield:** 6 servings.

Nutrition Facts: 1/2 cup equals 169 calories, 4 g fat (trace saturated fat), 0 cholesterol, 35 mg sodium, 34 g carbohydrate, 3 g fiber, 3 g protein. **Diabetic Exchanges:** 1 starch, 1 fruit, 1 fat.

BREAK THE MOLD. To unmold gelatin, loosen it from the top edge of the mold by gently pulling the gelatin away from the edge with a moistened finger. Then dip the mold up to its rim in a sink or pan of warm water for a few seconds or until the edges begin to release from the side of the mold. Next, place a platter over the mold, invert and carefully lift the mold from the salad.

When unmolding a large gelatin salad, rinse the platter with cold water before turning the gelatin out. The moisture will allow the unmolded salad to be easily centered on the platter.

drippings. (Cover loosely with foil if the chicken browns too quickly.)

Cover the chicken and let stand for 10 minutes before removing the stuffing and carving chicken. Skim fat and thicken pan juices if desired. **Yield:** 6 servings (4 cups stuffing).

Potato Vegetable Medley

PREP: 10 min. **BAKE:** 40 min.

☑ This recipe includes Nutrition Facts and Diabetic Exchanges.

  6 **small red potatoes, quartered**
 16 **baby carrots, halved lengthwise**
  1 **small onion, cut into wedges**
 1/2 **cup chicken broth**
1-1/4 **teaspoons seasoned salt,** *divided*
  2 **medium zucchini, chopped**
  2 **tablespoons minced fresh parsley**

In a 2-qt. baking dish coated with cooking spray, combine the potatoes, carrots, onion, chicken broth and 1 teaspoon seasoned salt. Cover and bake at 400° for 30 minutes.

Stir in zucchini and remaining seasoned salt. Bake 10-15 minutes longer or until vegetables are tender. Sprinkle with parsley. **Yield:** 6 servings.

Nutrition Facts: 3/4 cup equals 59 calories, trace fat (trace saturated fat), trace cholesterol, 424 mg sodium, 13 g carbohydrate, 2 g fiber, 2 g protein. **Diabetic Exchanges:** 1 vegetable, 1/2 starch.

Roast Chicken with Oyster Stuffing

PREP: 35 min. **BAKE:** 2 hours + standing

  1 **can (8 ounces) whole oysters**
 1/4 **cup butter, cubed**
  1 **celery rib, chopped**
  1 **small onion, chopped**
  2 **tablespoons minced fresh parsley**
 1/2 **teaspoon Italian seasoning**
  3 **cups cubed bread, lightly toasted**
  1 **roasting chicken (6 pounds)**
 1/4 **cup butter, melted**
  1 **to 2 teaspoons paprika**

Drain the oysters, reserving the liquid; coarsely chop the oysters. Set aside. In a small skillet, melt the butter. Add the celery and onion; saute until tender. Stir in parsley and Italian seasoning. Place bread cubes in a large bowl; add the butter mixture, oysters and 1/4 cup reserved oyster liquid.

Just before baking, loosely stuff chicken with stuffing. Place breast side up on a rack in a roasting pan; tie drumsticks together. Combine melted butter and paprika; brush over chicken.

Bake, uncovered, at 350° for 2 to 2-1/2 hours or until a meat thermometer reads 180° for the chicken and 165° for the stuffing, basting occasionally with the pan

Chocolate Ring Cake

PREP: 30 min. + cooling BAKE: 40 min. + cooling

- **3 squares (1 ounce *each*) unsweetened chocolate, chopped**
- **1/2 cup boiling water**
- **1 cup shortening**
- **1-3/4 cups sugar**
- **4 eggs**
- **2 teaspoons vanilla extract**
- **2-1/4 cups all-purpose flour**
- **1-1/2 teaspoons salt**
- **1 teaspoon baking soda**
- **1/2 teaspoon baking powder**
- **1 cup buttermilk**
- **1-1/2 cups black walnuts**

FROSTING:

- **6 tablespoons butter, cubed**
- **1/3 cup milk**
- **1/3 cup sugar**
- **2 squares (1 ounce *each*) unsweetened chocolate, chopped**
- **1 tablespoon light corn syrup**
- **1/4 teaspoon salt**
- **1 teaspoon vanilla extract**

In a small bowl, stir chocolate and boiling water until chocolate is melted; cool for 10 minutes. In a large bowl, cream shortening and sugar until light and fluffy. Add eggs, one at a time, beating well after each addition. Stir in vanilla and chocolate mixture.

Combine the flour, salt, baking soda and baking powder; add to the creamed mixture alternately with buttermilk, beating well after each addition. Stir in the walnuts.

Pour into a greased and floured 10-in. fluted tube pan. Bake at 350° for 40-50 minutes or until a toothpick inserted near the center comes out clean. Cool for 10 minutes before removing from pan to a wire rack to cool completely.

For frosting, in a small saucepan, combine the butter, milk, sugar, chocolate, corn syrup and salt. Cook and stir over low heat until blended. Remove from the heat; stir in vanilla. Beat with a mixer for 15 minutes or until mixture begins to thicken. Refrigerate until frosting reaches spreading consistency. Frost top and sides of cake. Refrigerate leftovers. **Yield:** 12 servings.

**Crown Roast with
Wild Rice Stuffing**

PEAS A LA FRANCAISE

SOUR CREAM YEAST ROLLS

JUBILEE SUNDAES

She grew up craving her mother's mouth-watering, crowd-pleasing cooking...and now, there's nothing better than returning to her mom's table for a special meal with the whole family.

By Christine Frazier, Auburndale, Florida

WHEN IT COMES to special-occasion meals, my mom, Louise Precourt (above, at left), has been an inspiration. While I was growing up, she relished hosting large family gatherings after church.

My mouth waters as I recall one particular dinner featuring crown roast of pork with a savory wild rice stuffing. Mom served it with Peas a la Francaise (a favorite), tender Sour Cream Yeast Rolls and yummy Jubilee Sundaes.

This impressive menu is perfect for Easter or other festive occasions. Easter has always been very special for our family, and Mom hosts the best egg hunts for her grandchildren and great-grandchildren.

Our family—Mom, Dad, my sister, three brothers and me—moved a lot because my dad was an aerospace engineer. Mom was a teacher. Now, my parents are retired and live in Winter Haven, Florida.

Mom still cooks but no longer does it all when we get together. Instead, everyone chips in...and there's always lots of laughter!

I am who I am because of my mom, and cooking is our shared passion. I am proud to say that she is both my mother and my best friend.

I'm happy to share this meal with fellow *Taste of Home* readers—it's one of her best!

YEAST DOUGH IN THE FREEZER. Yeast dough is best frozen after it is kneaded and before the first rise. To freeze dough, divide it into the desired amounts and flatten it into disks that are about 1 inch thick. Place the flattened dough on baking sheets and freeze it for 1 hour.

When dough is frozen, remove it from the freezer and wrap it tightly with either plastic wrap or aluminum foil. Then place it in resealable plastic bags and return it to the freezer. Dough can be kept frozen for up to 4 weeks.

For even thawing, put dough in the refrigerator overnight. When ready to use it, place the dough on your kitchen counter; cover it lightly and let it come to room temperature (first rise). Punch the dough down, then proceed as usual with shaping and the second rising.

Sour Cream Yeast Rolls

PREP: 35 min. + rising **BAKE:** 25 min.

2-1/2 to 3 cups all-purpose flour
   2 tablespoons sugar
   1 package (1/4 ounce) active dry yeast
   1 teaspoon salt
   1 cup sour cream
 1/4 cup water
   3 tablespoons butter, *divided*
   1 egg

In a large bowl, combine 1-1/2 cups flour, sugar, yeast and salt. In a small saucepan, heat the sour cream, water and 2 tablespoons butter to 120°-130°; add to dry ingredients. Beat on medium speed for 2 minutes. Add egg and 1/2 cup flour; beat 2 minutes longer. Stir in enough remaining flour to form a soft dough.

Turn onto a floured surface; knead until smooth and elastic, about 6-8 minutes. Place in a greased bowl, turning once to grease the top. Cover and let rise in a warm place until doubled, about 1 hour.

Punch down dough. Turn onto a lightly floured surface; divide into 12 pieces. Shape each into a ball. Place in a greased 13-in. x 9-in. baking pan. Cover and let rise until doubled, about 30 minutes.

Bake at 375° for 25-30 minutes or until golden brown. Melt remaining butter; brush over rolls. Remove from pan to a wire rack. **Yield:** 1 dozen.

For stuffing, in a large saucepan, bring the water, wild rice and salt if desired to a boil. Reduce heat; cover and simmer for 45-60 minutes or until tender.

In a large skillet, saute the fresh mushrooms and onions in the butter until tender. Transfer to a large bowl. In the same skillet, cook the pork sausage over medium heat until no longer pink; drain. Drain the rice; add the rice and sausage to the mushroom mixture and stir until blended.

Transfer the roast to a serving platter; let stand for 15 minutes. Remove foil. Spoon the stuffing into center of roast. Garnish the platter with kale and beets if desired. Cut between ribs to serve. **Yield:** 15 servings (12 cups stuffing).

Peas a la Francaise

PREP/TOTAL TIME: 30 min.

☑ This recipe includes Nutrition Facts and Diabetic Exchanges.

- 1-1/2 **cups pearl onions**
- 1/4 **cup butter, cubed**
- 1/4 **cup water**
- 1 **tablespoon sugar**
- 1 **teaspoon salt**
- 1/4 **teaspoon dried thyme**
- 1/4 **teaspoon dried chervil**
- 1/4 **teaspoon pepper**
- 2 **packages (16 ounces *each*) frozen peas, thawed**
- 2 **cups shredded lettuce**

In a large saucepan, bring 6 cups water to a boil. Add the pearl onions; boil for 5 minutes. Drain and rinse the

Crown Roast with Wild Rice Stuffing

PREP: 15 min. **BAKE:** 2-3/4 hours + standing

- 1 **teaspoon dried thyme**
- 1 **teaspoon fennel seed, crushed**
- 1 **teaspoon salt**
- 1/2 **teaspoon pepper**
- 1 **pork crown roast (about 9 pounds)**
- 1 **cup unsweetened apple juice**

STUFFING:
- 2 **quarts water**
- 2 **cups uncooked wild rice**
- 2 **teaspoons salt, optional**
- 1/2 **pound sliced fresh mushrooms**
- 2 **medium onions, chopped**
- 2 **tablespoons butter**
- 2 **pounds seasoned bulk pork sausage**

OPTIONAL GARNISH:
Fresh kale and pickled whole beets

Combine the thyme, fennel, salt and pepper; sprinkle over roast. Place on a rack in a large shallow roasting pan. Cover rib ends with foil. Bake, uncovered, at 350° for 2-3/4 to 3-1/4 hours or until a meat thermometer reads 160°, basting occasionally with apple juice.

pearl onions in cold water; peel.

In the same saucepan, melt butter over medium heat. Stir in the onions, water, sugar and seasonings. Add peas and lettuce; stir until blended. Cover and cook for 6-8 minutes or until tender. Serve with a slotted spoon. **Yield:** 12 servings (1/2 cup each).

Nutrition Facts: 1/2 cup equals 112 calories, 4 g fat (2 g saturated fat), 10 mg cholesterol, 315 mg sodium, 15 g carbohydrate, 4 g fiber, 4 g protein. **Diabetic Exchanges:** 1 starch, 1 fat.

Jubilee Sundaes

PREP: 10 min. COOK: 10 min. + cooling

✓ This recipe includes Nutrition Facts and Diabetic Exchanges.

- **1/3 cup sugar**
- **2 tablespoons cornstarch**
- **1/8 teaspoon salt**
- **1 can (14-1/2 ounces) pitted tart cherries**
- **2 teaspoons lemon juice**
- **1/4 teaspoon grated lemon peel**
- **1/4 teaspoon almond extract**
- **Vanilla ice cream**

In a large saucepan, combine the sugar, cornstarch and salt. Drain cherries, reserving juice; set cherries aside. Stir cherry juice into cornstarch mixture until smooth. Bring to a boil over medium heat, stirring constantly. Cook and stir for 1-2 minutes or until thickened.

Remove from the heat; stir in the lemon juice and peel, extract and reserved cherries. Cool to room temperature. Serve with ice cream. **Yield:** 2 cups sauce.

Nutrition Facts: 3 tablespoons sauce (calculated without ice cream) equals 64 calories, trace fat (trace saturated fat), 0 cholesterol, 33 mg sodium, 16 g carbohydrate, trace fiber, trace protein. **Diabetic Exchange:** 1 starch.

Coconut Cream
Angel Pie

FRIED CHICKEN WITH PAN GRAVY   GARDEN COLESLAW   CREAMED POTATOES & PEAS

She fondly recalls her mother's skills in the kitchen—and her abillity to create wholesome, tasty meals for a huge family without using the latest cooking conveniences.

By Ginny Werkmeister, Tilden, Nebraska

FOR MOST of her life, my mom, Enoth Bratten (above, at right), made do with whatever was on hand. Yet she could transform the simplest ingredients into a delicious meal for our family of nine. She rarely used recipes, and many dishes came from the huge garden she cultivated when we lived in Oklahoma.

During those years, my dad, Ulis, farmed but also worked in the aircraft industry to make ends meet. Mom stayed home and helped with the finances by raising chickens and turkeys, selling eggs and canning everything her garden produced. We kids helped her with gardening and cooking.

By age 8, I was already whipping up batches of brownies, corn bread and biscuits. "A really good biscuit makes a slim meal more pleasing," Mom would say, and I have to agree!

On Sundays, Mom often served Fried Chicken with Pan Gravy, Garden Coleslaw, Creamed Potatoes & Peas and Coconut Cream Angel Pie. For years, she made this marvelous meal with antiquated kitchen tools and an old stove.

My parents gave up the farm when I was 13, and Mom became a beautician. Our lives changed again when we moved to southern California, where Mom cut hair for young starlets. I went to high school in East Los Angeles.

When I married my husband, Marvin, we decided to return to the land and ended up on a Nebraska farm, where we raised three children. I ran a small greenhouse business and loved every minute because I am my mother's daughter. I love gardening, canning and cooking as much as she did.

I have many wonderful memories of my mom, filled with love...and mouth-watering meals. I hope you enjoy the unforgettable one here!

Fried Chicken with Pan Gravy

PREP: 15 min. **COOK:** 30 min.

- 1 cup all-purpose flour
- 3/4 teaspoon salt
- 1/4 teaspoon dried thyme
- 1/4 teaspoon rubbed sage
- 1/4 teaspoon pepper
- 1 broiler/fryer chicken (3-1/2 to 4 pounds), cut up

Oil for frying

GRAVY:
- 2 tablespoons all-purpose flour
- 1/8 teaspoon salt
- 1-1/3 cups milk

In a large resealable plastic bag, combine the first five ingredients. Add chicken, a few pieces at a time, and shake to coat.

In a large skillet over medium-high heat, heat 1/4 in. of oil; fry chicken until browned on all sides. Reduce heat; cover and cook for 30-35 minutes or until juices run clear, turning occasionally. Uncover and cook 5 minutes longer. Remove chicken to paper towels and keep warm.

For gravy, pour off excess fat from skillet, reserving the browned bits and 2 tablespoons drippings. Stir in the flour and salt until blended; gradually add the milk. Bring to a boil; cook and stir for 1-2 minutes or until thickened. Serve gravy with chicken. **Yield:** 6 servings (1-1/2 cups gravy).

Coconut Cream Angel Pie

PREP: 30 min. **BAKE:** 20 min. + chilling

1/2 cup sugar
1/4 cup cornstarch
1/4 teaspoon salt
2 cups milk
3 egg yolks, lightly beaten
1/2 cup flaked coconut
1 tablespoon butter
1-1/2 teaspoons vanilla extract
1 pastry shell (9 inches), baked
MERINGUE:
3 egg whites
1/4 teaspoon cream of tartar
1/4 teaspoon vanilla extract
6 tablespoons sugar
1/4 cup flaked coconut

In a small heavy saucepan, combine the sugar, cornstarch and salt. Add the milk; stir until smooth. Cook and stir over medium-high heat until thickened and bubbly. Reduce heat to low; cook and stir for 2 minutes longer.

Remove from the heat. Stir a small amount of the hot filling into the egg yolks; return all to the pan, stirring constantly. Bring to a gentle boil; cook and stir 2 minutes longer. Remove from the heat; stir in the

coconut, butter and vanilla. Pour into the prepared pastry shell.

In a small bowl, beat the egg whites, cream of tartar and vanilla on medium speed until soft peaks form. Gradually beat in the sugar, 1 tablespoon at a time, on high until stiff peaks form. Spread the meringue over the hot filling, sealing the edges to the crust. Sprinkle with coconut.

Bake at 350° for 20 minutes or until golden brown. Cool on a wire rack for 1 hour; refrigerate for 1-2 hours before serving. **Yield:** 8 servings.

Creamed Potatoes & Peas

PREP: 10 min. **COOK:** 25 min.

1 pound small red potatoes
2-1/2 cups frozen peas
1/4 cup butter, cubed
1 green onion, sliced
1/4 cup all-purpose flour
1/2 teaspoon salt
Dash pepper
2 cups milk

Scrub and quarter the red potatoes; place in a large saucepan and cover with water. Bring to a boil. Reduce heat; cover and simmer for 10 minutes. Add the peas; cook 5 minutes longer or until the potatoes and peas are tender.

Meanwhile, in another large saucepan, melt butter.

Add onion; saute until tender. Stir in the flour, salt and pepper until blended; gradually add the milk. Bring to a boil. Cook and stir for 1-2 minutes or until thickened. Drain potatoes and peas; toss with sauce. **Yield:** 6 servings.

Garden Coleslaw

PREP/TOTAL TIME: 10 min.

```
  3  cups shredded cabbage
1/4  cup chopped green pepper
  1  green onion, thinly sliced
1/4  cup mayonnaise
1/4  cup heavy whipping cream
  1  teaspoon sugar
  1  teaspoon cider vinegar
1/4  teaspoon salt
```

In a small bowl, combine the cabbage, green pepper and green onion. Combine the remaining ingredients; add to the cabbage mixture and toss to coat. **Yield:** 4 servings.

CABBAGE CLUES. Keep these tips in mind when using cabbage for Garden Coleslaw (at left) or other recipes:

• When buying a head of cabbage, look for those with crisp-looking leaves that are firmly packed. The head should feel heavy for its size.

• Store cabbage tightly wrapped in a plastic bag in the refrigerator for up to 2 weeks.

• Remove the core, rinse the cabbage and blot it dry just before using.

• To core a cabbage, cut it in half or quarters. Then make a V-shaped cut around the core and remove it.

• To shred cabbage by hand, cut it into wedges. Place the cut side down on a cutting board. With a large sharp knife, cut it into thin slices.

• A 1-1/2-pound cabbage will yield appoximately 8 cups shredded—more than enough for making a batch of Garden Coleslaw.

Shredded Beef
Au Jus

MOM'S SPECIAL POTATO SALAD   RHUBARB SLUSH   OLD-FASHIONED CHERRY TORTE

Her mother's passion for cooking and entertaining resulted in a homemade meal on the table every night, plus plenty of picnics and other get-togethers for family and friends.

By Danielle Brandt, Ruthton, Minnesota

FOR SOME COOKS, preparing meals for a family of five is enough. Not for my mom, Darla Bakker (above, at left). When she wants something fun to do, she entertains. She especially enjoys hosting Sunday brunches, picnics and dinner parties at our farm.

One year, she fixed a Mother's Day brunch for a few girlfriends and their moms, setting the table with pretty, pansy-decorated dishes and yellow accents. Each guest received a potted pansy.

Mom has earned a reputation as a great cook and baker in our small community. But my dad, Jeff; my sisters, Andrea and Laura; and I have always known it. When we were growing up, she put well-balanced meals on the table every night—always cooking from scratch while working full-time as a nurse.

She often relied on her slow cooker and microwave to have dinner ready on time. Mom would try a few new recipes every week to keep cooking and eating fun and interesting.

She encouraged us girls to try new recipes, too, and see how much fun reading a cookbook can be. Mom even published a cookbook, which has sold over 1,800 copies. It started as a computer folder of recipes she wanted to pass on to us and grew to over 300 recipes.

As a part-time registered nurse, I use her cookbook almost daily to provide nutritious meals for my husband, Dean, and our children, Garret and Elena.

This meal of Rhubarb Slush, Shredded Beef Au Jus, Mom's Special Potato Salad and Old-Fashioned Cherry Torte is one of our favorites. Enjoy!

Rhubarb Slush

PREP: 40 min. + freezing

- 8 **cups diced fresh *or* frozen rhubarb**
- 1 **package (16 ounces) frozen unsweetened strawberries**
- 3 **cups sugar**
- 8 **cups water**
- 1 **package (3 ounces) strawberry gelatin**
- 1/2 **cup lemon juice**
- 11 **cups ginger ale, chilled**

Rhubarb curls, optional

In a Dutch oven, bring the rhubarb, strawberries, sugar and water to a boil. Reduce heat; simmer, uncovered,

for 5-8 minutes or until rhubarb is tender. Press through a sieve; discard pulp. Stir in gelatin and lemon juice until dissolved.

Transfer mixture to a freezer container and freeze, stirring occasionally, until firm. May be frozen for up to 3 months.

To use frozen rhubarb mixture: In a punch bowl or several pitchers, combine equal amounts of rhubarb mixture and ginger ale. Or for one serving, combine 1/2 cup rhubarb mixture and 1/2 cup ginger ale in a glass. Garnish with rhubarb curls if desired. Serve immediately. **Yield:** 22 servings (1 cup each).

Editor's Note: If using frozen rhubarb, measure rhubarb while still frozen, then thaw completely. Drain in a colander, but do not press liquid out.

Mom's Special Potato Salad

PREP: 30 min. **COOK:** 20 min. + chilling

DRESSING:
- 3 eggs
- 1/2 cup sugar
- 1/2 cup cider vinegar
- 3 tablespoons heavy whipping cream
- 2 teaspoons butter
- 1 teaspoon ground mustard

Dash salt
- 2 cups mayonnaise

SALAD:
- 6 pounds potatoes, peeled and cubed (about 10 large)
- 5 celery ribs, thinly sliced
- 1 large onion, chopped

Pepper to taste, optional

In a double boiler or metal bowl over simmering water, constantly whisk the eggs, sugar, cider vinegar, heavy whipping cream, butter, mustard and salt until mixture reaches 160° or is thick enough to coat the back of a metal spoon. Remove from the heat; cool to room temperature. Fold in the mayonnaise. Chill until preparing salad.

For salad, place potatoes in a large saucepan and cover with water. Bring to a boil. Reduce heat; cover and cook for 10-15 minutes or until tender. Drain and cool to room temperature. In a large bowl, combine the potatoes, celery and onion. Add prepared dressing and pepper if desired; stir until blended. Chill until serving.
Yield: 18 servings (3/4 cup each).

Shredded Beef Au Jus

PREP: 10 min. **COOK:** 6 hours

- 1 boneless beef chuck roast (3 pounds)
- 2 cups water
- 2 teaspoons beef bouillon granules
- 1-1/2 teaspoons dried oregano
- 1 teaspoon garlic salt
- 1 teaspoon seasoned salt
- 1/4 teaspoon dried rosemary, crushed
- 8 hamburger buns, split

Cut roast in half and place in a 4- or 5-quart slow cooker. Combine the water, bouillon granules and seasonings; pour over the beef.

Cover and cook on low for 6-8 hours or until meat is tender. Remove beef; cool slightly. Meanwhile, skim fat from the cooking liquid.

Shred meat with two forks; return to the cooking liquid and heat through. Using a slotted spoon, place 1/2 cup meat on each hamburger bun. Serve the sandwiches with additional cooking liquid on the side.
Yield: 8 servings.

Old-Fashioned Cherry Torte

PREP: 30 min. + chilling

- **1 cup crushed saltines**
- **1/2 cup butter, melted**
- **4 egg whites**
- **1 teaspoon white vinegar**
- **1 teaspoon vanilla extract**
- **1/2 cup sugar**
- **1 can (21 ounces) cherry pie filling**
- **1-3/4 cups heavy whipping cream, whipped**

Combine cracker crumbs and butter; press onto the bottom of a greased 13-in. x 9-in. baking dish.

In a large bowl, beat egg whites, vinegar and vanilla on medium speed until soft peaks form. Gradually beat in sugar, 1 tablespoon at a time, on high until stiff glossy peaks form and sugar is dissolved. Spread meringue evenly over crust. Bake at 400° for 10 minutes or until golden brown. Cool completely on a wire rack.

Spread cherry pie filling over meringue. Top with whipped cream. Refrigerate for at least 2 hours. **Yield:** 12 servings.

MARVELOUS MERINGUE. Remember these hints when making the meringue for Old-Fashioned Cherry Torte (at left):

• Because humidity is the most critical factor in making a successful meringue, choose a dry day. Meringues can absorb moisture on a humid day and become limp or sticky.

• Separate the eggs while they are still cold from the refrigerator, then allow the egg whites to stand at room temperature for 30 minutes before beating them.

• For the greatest volume, place the egg whites in a small clean metal or glass mixing bowl. Even a drop of fat from the egg yolk or a film sometimes found on plastic bowls will prevent egg whites from foaming. For this reason, be sure to use clean beaters.

• After stiff peaks form, check that the sugar is dissolved. It should feel silky smooth when rubbed between your thumb and index finger.

Dutch Oven
Pork Roast

BRIQUETTE SCALLOPED
POTATOES

POT OF S'MORES

CAKE & BERRY CAMPFIRE COBBLER

Whether the family was sitting around the dinner table at home or gathered around the fire on a camping trip, her outdoorsy mom's cooking made everyone feel extra special.

By Nicole Underwood, Boise, Idaho

MY MOM, June Dress (above, at left), loves to cook and bake for others...and always has. Whether it's preparing my brother Scott's favorite meals when he's on leave from the Air Force, or cooking Dutch oven specialties while camping with all the relatives, Mom shows her love through cooking.

When Mom was a child, she'd watch my grandmother preparing food in the kitchen. So Grandma put her to work baking cookies, cakes and pies for neighborhood gatherings.

I was a little older when the cooking bug hit me, and Mom had me baking bread, brownies and cinnamon rolls. Funny how history repeats itself!

Mom got into Dutch oven cooking when I was a teenager. She and my dad, Mike, love camping and instilled that love in us kids—Scott, my sister, Junell, and me. The whole family looked forward to our camping trips (six to eight times a year!).

Sometimes, aunts, uncles and cousins joined us. We'd fish with Dad and Grandpa while Mom and Grandma fixed dinner.

Once Mom realized that it didn't take a professional chef to cook over coals in a Dutch oven, she went Dutch-oven crazy! It became a featured part of our cookouts during camping trips.

Here, I've shared our all-time favorite recipes—Cake & Berry Campfire Cobbler, Dutch Oven Pork Roast, Briquette Scalloped Potatoes and Pot of S'mores (a fun, eat-with-a-spoon twist on the traditional handheld favorite). No one can resist second helpings of these outdoor treats.

We still camp as a family. My husband, Cody, and daughters, Karly and Krystal, are always ready to go. We love making memories in the great outdoors—and eating Mom's wonderful meals.

Maybe it's the fresh mountain air that makes the food taste so good...but I'm more inclined to think it's because Mom is such a great cook!

Cake & Berry Campfire Cobbler

PREP: 10 min. **GRILL:** 30 min.

2 cans (21 ounces *each*) raspberry pie filling
1 package (18-1/4 ounces) yellow cake mix

1-1/4 cups water
1/2 cup canola oil
Vanilla ice cream, optional

Prepare the grill or campfire for low heat, using 16-20 charcoal briquettes or large wood chips.

Line a Dutch oven with heavy-duty aluminum foil; add the raspberry pie filling. In a large bowl, combine the yellow cake mix, water and oil. Spread over raspberry pie filling.

Cover Dutch oven. When briquettes or wood chips are covered with white ash, place Dutch oven directly on top of 8-10 of them. Using long-handled tongs, place remaining briquettes on pan cover.

Cook for 30-40 minutes or until the filling is bubbly and a toothpick inserted in the topping comes out clean. To check for doneness, use the tongs to carefully lift the cover. Serve with vanilla ice cream if desired. **Yield:** 12 servings.

Editor's Note: This recipe does not use eggs.

Briquette Scalloped Potatoes

PREP: 20 min.   **GRILL:** 70 min.

5 pounds potatoes (about 6 large), peeled and thinly sliced
3 cups (12 ounces) shredded cheddar cheese
1 large onion, chopped
1/4 cup butter, cubed
6 garlic cloves, minced
2 teaspoons onion salt
1/2 teaspoon salt
1/2 teaspoon pepper
1 cup milk

Prepare grill or campfire for low heat, using 20-24 charcoal briquettes or large wood chips.

Line a Dutch oven with heavy-duty aluminum foil; add half of the potatoes. Top with 1-1/2 cups cheddar cheese, onion, butter, garlic, onion salt, salt and pepper. Top with remaining potatoes and cheddar cheese. Pour milk over the top.

Cover Dutch oven. When briquettes or wood chips are covered with white ash, place Dutch oven directly on top of 10 of them. Using long-handled tongs, place remaining briquettes on pan cover.

Cook for 70-80 minutes or until bubbly and potatoes are tender. To check for doneness, use the tongs to carefully lift the cover. **Yield:** 16 servings (3/4 cup each).

Dutch Oven Pork Roast

PREP: 10 min.   **GRILL:** 1-1/4 hours

✓ This recipe includes Nutrition Facts and Diabetic Exchanges.

1 boneless whole pork loin roast (3 to 4 pounds)
1 jar (16 ounces) salsa
1 can (16 ounces) kidney beans, undrained
1/4 teaspoon salt
1/4 teaspoon pepper

Prepare the grill or campfire for low heat, using 20-24 charcoal briquettes or large wood chips.

Line a Dutch oven with heavy-duty aluminum foil; add the pork. Combine the salsa, kidney beans, salt and pepper; pour over pork.

Cover Dutch oven. When briquettes or wood chips are covered with white ash, place Dutch oven directly on top of 10-12 of them. Using long-handled tongs, place remaining briquettes on pan cover.

Cook 1-1/4 to 1-1/2 hours or until a meat thermometer reads 160°. To check for doneness, use the tongs to carefully lift the cover. **Yield:** 9 servings (3 cups sauce).

Nutrition Facts: 4 ounces cooked pork with 1/3 cup sauce equals 248 calories, 7 g fat (3 g saturated fat), 75 mg cholesterol, 445 mg sodium, 11 g carbohydrate, 2 g fiber, 32 g protein. **Diabetic Exchanges:** 4 lean meat, 1 starch.

Pot of S'mores

PREP/TOTAL TIME: 25 min.

- **1 package (14-1/2 ounces) whole graham crackers, crushed**
- **1/2 cup butter, melted**
- **1 can (14 ounces) sweetened condensed milk**
- **2 cups (12 ounces) semisweet chocolate chips**
- **1 cup butterscotch chips**
- **2 cups miniature marshmallows**

Prepare grill or campfire for low heat, using 16-18 charcoal briquettes or large wood chips.

Line a Dutch oven with heavy-duty aluminum foil. Combine the graham cracker crumbs and butter; press onto the bottom of the pan. Pour the sweetened condensed milk over the crust and sprinkle with the chocolate and butterscotch chips. Top with miniature marshmallows.

Cover Dutch oven. When briquettes or wood chips are covered with white ash, place Dutch oven directly on top of six of them. Using long-handled tongs, place remaining briquettes on pan cover.

Cook for 15 minutes or until chips are melted. To check for doneness, use the tongs to carefully lift the cover. **Yield:** 12 servings.

S'MORE FUN. Feel free to change up the recipe for Pot of S'mores (at left):
- Replace the semisweet chocolate and butterscotch chips with milk chocolate, peanut butter or vanilla (white) chips.
- Use chocolate- or cinnamon-flavored graham crackers instead of the regular kind.
- Try tossing in some caramels to add a bit of extra, ooey-gooey goodness.

Dipped Lemon Spritz

DATE PINWHEELS   PECAN ROLL-UPS   MACAROON KISSES

Her mother has been a phenomenal cookie baker, especially during the holiday season...but she wonders if her mom realized how many cookies never made it into a tin!

By Hannah Roberts, Racine, Wisconsin

FOR MY MOM, Lee Roberts (above, at left), the holidays wouldn't be complete without cookie baking. She's been making cookies with her friend, Sandy Devlin, longer than I can remember. Together, they whip up at least 20 different kinds each year to serve at holiday gatherings and give as gifts to friends and neighbors... even the mailman and newspaper carrier.

When I was in elementary school, I'd go to Sandy's house after school to help sort cookies into tins and sprinkle on confectioners' sugar. I liked my job because I could sneak cookies. I don't think my mother realized how many I ate instead of packed!

My mother grew up in Somerset, New Jersey and learned to cook from my grandmother. Mom definitely passed on a lot of her culinary wisdom to me, but I also learned from my dad, his mother and Sandy. It takes a village to raise a chef!

As I got older and Mom went back to work full-time (she's a newspaper feature writer), cookie-baking day moved to a Saturday, and I helped all day. This was a serious cookie operation, and I started small, rolling the dough balls for the jelly thumbprints. But I was soon introducing new recipes into the mix. I jokingly got the title "apprentice."

I remember Mom using the spritzer to make Dipped Lemon Spritz; I was fascinated with this strange device that only saw daylight once a year. A tangy version of a holiday favorite, these cookies combine two of my favorite flavors—citrus and dark chocolate—and feature a homemade lemon sugar.

I was always sneaking little bites of dough for the Date Pinwheels and Pecan Roll-Ups. When I started making the tender, old-fashioned pinwheels years ago, it took a little practice to get the hang of it. But they're definitely worth the effort!

The original Pecan Roll-Ups recipe called for whole dates, but we found the pecan half was an even better complement to the cream cheese dough. They puff up during baking like little pastries.

The Macaroon Kisses came along later in the game but are one of my favorites. The chocolate kisses make them taste like a Mounds candy bar.

I was sad to leave cookie baking behind when I left for Arizona State University. I'm now living in an apartment and enjoy having my own kitchen. But I hope to get back to Wisconsin in time for cookie-baking day this year and resume my post rolling thumbprint balls!

Pecan Roll-Ups

PREP: 45 min. **BAKE:** 15 min./batch + cooling

☑ This recipe includes Nutrition Facts and Diabetic Exchanges.

- 1 cup butter, softened
- 1 package (8 ounces) cream cheese, softened
- 2 cups all-purpose flour
- 1/4 teaspoon salt
- 2 cups pecan halves
- 1 cup confectioners' sugar

In a large bowl, beat butter and cream cheese until light and fluffy. Combine flour and salt; gradually add to the butter mixture and mix well. Cover and refrigerate for 1-2 hours or until easy to handle.

Divide dough in half. On a lightly floured surface, roll out one portion into an 18-in. x 8-in. rectangle. Cut widthwise into six 3-in. sections; cut each section into 3-in. x 1-in. strips. Roll each strip around a pecan half; place 1 in. apart on ungreased baking sheets. Repeat.

Bake at 350° for 12-15 minutes or until the bottoms are lightly browned. Remove to wire racks to cool completely. Roll in confectioners' sugar. Store in an airtight container at room temperature, or freeze for up to 3 months. **Yield:** 8 dozen.

Nutrition Facts: 1 cookie equals 55 calories, 4 g fat (2 g saturated fat), 8 mg cholesterol, 27 mg sodium, 4 g carbohydrate, trace fiber, 1 g protein. **Diabetic Exchange:** 1 fat.

Dipped Lemon Spritz

PREP: 50 min.   **BAKE:** 10 min./batch + cooling

☑ This recipe includes Nutrition Facts and Diabetic Exchanges.

- 2/3 cup plus 2 tablespoons sugar
- 2 teaspoons grated lemon peel
- 1 cup unsalted butter, softened
- 1 egg
- 2 teaspoons lemon juice
- 1 teaspoon vanilla extract
- 2-1/2 cups all-purpose flour
- 1/4 teaspoon baking powder

Dash salt

- 1 package (12 ounces) dark chocolate chips

In a small food processor, combine sugar and lemon peel; cover and process until blended. In a large bowl, cream butter and 2/3 cup lemon-sugar until light and fluffy. Beat in the egg, lemon juice and vanilla. Combine the flour, baking powder and salt; gradually add to the creamed mixture and mix well.

Using a cookie press fitted with a 1-1/2-in. bar disk, form the dough into long strips on ungreased baking sheets. Cut each strip into squares (there is no need to separate the pieces). Bake at 350° for 8-10 minutes or until set (do not brown). Remove to wire racks to cool completely.

In a microwave, melt chocolate; stir until smooth. Dip cookies diagonally in chocolate, allowing the excess to drip off. Place on waxed paper; sprinkle chocolate with remaining lemon-sugar. Let stand until set. Store in an airtight container at room temperature, or freeze for up to 3 months. **Yield:** 6 dozen.

Nutrition Facts: 1 cookie equals 83 calories, 5 g fat (3 g saturated fat), 10 mg cholesterol, 5 mg sodium, 10 g carbohydrate, trace fiber, 1 g protein. **Diabetic Exchanges:** 1 fat, 1/2 starch.

Macaroon Kisses

PREP: 45 min. + chilling   **BAKE:** 10 min./batch + cooling

☑ This recipe includes Nutrition Facts and Diabetic Exchanges.

- 1/3 cup butter, softened
- 1 package (3 ounces) cream cheese, softened
- 3/4 cup sugar
- 1 egg yolk
- 2 teaspoons almond extract
- 1-1/2 cups all-purpose flour
- 2 teaspoons baking powder
- 1/2 teaspoon salt
- 5 cups flaked coconut, *divided*
- 48 milk chocolate kisses

Coarse sugar

In a large bowl, cream the butter, cream cheese and sugar until light and fluffy. Beat in egg yolk and extract. Combine the flour, baking powder and salt; gradually add to creamed mixture and mix well. Stir in 3 cups coconut. Cover and refrigerate for 1 hour or until dough is easy to handle.

Roll into 1-in. balls and roll in the remaining coconut. Place 2 in. apart on ungreased baking sheets.

Bake at 350° for 10-12 minutes or until lightly browned. Immediately press a chocolate kiss into the center of each cookie; sprinkle with coarse sugar. Cool on pan for 2-3 minutes or until chocolate is softened. Remove to wire racks to cool completely. **Yield:** 4 dozen.

Nutrition Facts: 1 cookie equals 120 calories, 7 g fat (5 g saturated fat), 11 mg cholesterol, 85 mg sodium, 14 g carbohydrate, 1 g fiber, 1 g protein. **Diabetic Exchanges:** 1 starch, 1 fat.

Date Pinwheels

PREP: 45 min. + chilling **BAKE:** 10 min./batch

☑ This recipe includes Nutrition Facts and Diabetic Exchanges.

- 1 cup butter, softened
- 2 cups packed brown sugar
- 3 eggs
- 1 teaspoon vanilla extract
- 4 cups all-purpose flour
- 1/2 teaspoon salt
- 1/2 teaspoon baking soda

FILLING:

- 2-1/2 cups chopped dates
- 1 cup sugar
- 1 cup water
- 1 cup finely chopped pecans

In a large bowl, cream butter and brown sugar until light and fluffy. Beat in eggs and vanilla. Combine the flour, salt and baking soda; gradually add to creamed mixture and mix well. Divide dough into four portions. Refrigerate until chilled.

In a large saucepan, bring the dates, sugar and water to a boil. Reduce heat to medium; cook until mixture is thickened, about 15 minutes. Cool completely. Stir in the pecans.

On a baking sheet, roll out each portion of dough between two sheets of waxed paper into a 12-in. x 9-in. rectangle. Refrigerate for 30 minutes.

Remove waxed paper; spread with the date mixture. Tightly roll up each portion jelly-roll style, starting with a long side; wrap in plastic wrap. Refrigerate for 2 hours or until firm.

Unwrap and cut into 1/4-in. slices. Place 1 in. apart on greased baking sheets. Bake at 350° for 10-12 minutes or until set. Remove to wire racks to cool. Store cookies in an airtight container at room temperature, or freeze for up to 3 months. **Yield:** 16 dozen.

Nutrition Facts: 1 cookie equals 43 calories, 2 g fat (1 g saturated fat), 6 mg cholesterol, 18 mg sodium, 7 g carbohydrate, trace fiber, trace protein. **Diabetic Exchange:** 1/2 starch.

Field Editor Favorites

Taste of Home is edited by 1,000 cooks across North America. Here, you'll "meet" six of them and see their family-favorite recipes.

SIGNATURE DISHES. Clockwise from top left: Queen of the Grill (p. 230), Cooking on the Move (p. 214), A Taste for Tex-Mex (p. 222), Keeping an Italian Accent (p. 226) and Fresh from the Oven (p. 218).

**Brown Sugar
Glazed Salmon**

CURRIED SWEET POTATO LATKES   BISCUIT-Y BELL PEPPER MUFFINS   CINNAMON PEACH KUCHEN

Cooking on the Move

Relocating around the U.S. with the Army has shaped the way
this journalist and mom cooks for her family.

By Rachel Garcia, Arlington, Virginia

MY HUSBAND, Jamie, is an Army officer, and we currently reside in the Washington, D.C. area with our son Jacob and dog "Chloe." But we've lived in many different places over the years due to Jamie's career. And it has definitely influenced my cooking!

In the military community, food is really integrated into life. Potlucks and teas are opportunities to get to know people. The stories you hear over meals and the variety of food shared are incredible. At neighborhood luaus in Hawaii, we made many friends we still keep in touch with today.

When I was growing up, my mother cooked traditional Jewish food. Now, I learn new cooking styles wherever we happen to be living—Georgia, Colorado, Hawaii, Louisiana or Virginia. The most novel food was in Hawaii, influenced by Asian culture and abundant fresh produce.

I work as a journalist, and in my spare time I enjoy traveling, hiking, gardening and getting to know new communities and neighbors. I am continually inspired by the fabulous, strong military families we meet.

I also find it very relaxing to create different meals and put a new spin on old favorites. I love to bake cookies and breads, too.

The recipes I'm sharing here—Cinnamon Peach Kuchen, Brown Sugar Glazed Salmon, Curried Sweet Potato Latkes and Biscuit-y Bell Pepper Muffins—have all gotten great feedback from friends and family. I've tweaked these dishes a bit over the years, but I keep going back to them time and time again.

I hope you enjoy this menu as much as we have!

Cinnamon Peach Kuchen

PREP: 25 min. **BAKE:** 45 min. + cooling

- 2 **cups all-purpose flour**
- 2 **tablespoons sugar**
- 1/2 **teaspoon salt**
- 1/4 **teaspoon baking powder**
- 1/2 **cup cold butter**
- 2 **cans (15-1/4 ounces *each*) peach halves, drained and patted dry**
- 1 **cup packed brown sugar**
- 1 **teaspoon ground cinnamon**
- 2 **egg yolks, beaten**
- 1 **cup heavy whipping cream**

In a small bowl, combine the flour, sugar, salt and baking powder; cut in butter until crumbly. Press onto the bottom and 1-1/2 in. up the sides of a greased 9-in. springform pan.

Place pan on a baking sheet. Arrange peach halves, cut side up, in the crust. Combine brown sugar and cinnamon; sprinkle over peaches.

Bake at 350° for 20 minutes. Combine egg yolks and cream; pour over peaches. Bake 25-30 minutes longer or until the top is set. Cool on a wire rack. Refrigerate leftovers. **Yield:** 10 servings.

20-25 minutes or until fish flakes easily with a fork. **Yield:** 8 servings.

Curried Sweet Potato Latkes

PREP: 20 min. **COOK:** 10 min./batch

- 1/2 **cup all-purpose flour**
- 2 **teaspoons sugar**
- 2 **teaspoons curry powder**
- 1 **teaspoon baking powder**
- 1 **teaspoon brown sugar**
- 1 **teaspoon ground cumin**
- 3/4 **teaspoon salt**
- 1/2 **teaspoon cayenne pepper**
- 1/4 **teaspoon pepper**
- 2 **eggs, lightly beaten**
- 1/2 **cup milk**
- 4 **cups grated peeled sweet potatoes**

Oil for frying

In a small bowl, combine the first nine ingredients. Stir in eggs and milk until blended. Add sweet potatoes; toss to coat.

Heat oil in a large nonstick skillet over medium heat. Drop batter by heaping tablespoonfuls into oil; press lightly to flatten. Fry for 3-5 minutes on each side or until golden brown, adding oil as needed. Drain on paper towels. **Yield:** 24 latkes.

Brown Sugar Glazed Salmon

PREP: 15 min. **BAKE:** 20 min.

- 1 **tablespoon brown sugar**
- 2 **teaspoons butter**
- 1 **teaspoon honey**
- 1 **tablespoon olive oil**
- 1 **tablespoon Dijon mustard**
- 1 **tablespoon soy sauce**
- 1/2 **to 3/4 teaspoon salt**
- 1/4 **teaspoon pepper**
- 1 **salmon fillet (2-1/2 pounds)**

In a small saucepan over medium heat, cook and stir the brown sugar, butter and honey until melted. Remove from the heat; whisk in the oil, mustard, soy sauce, salt and pepper. Cool for 5 minutes.

Place salmon in a large foil-lined baking pan; brush with brown sugar mixture. Bake, uncovered, at 350° for

SWEET SECRETS. Keep these hints in mind when cooking with sweet potatoes:

• Select sweet potatoes that are firm with no cracks or bruises.

• If stored in a cool, dark, well-ventilated place, they'll remain fresh for about 2 weeks. If the temperature is above 60°, they'll sprout sooner or become woody.

• Once cooked, sweet potatoes can be stored for up to 1 week in the refrigerator.

Biscuit-y Bell Pepper Muffins

PREP: 15 min. **BAKE:** 20 min.

1/2 **cup butter, cubed**
1/3 **cup finely chopped green onions**
1/3 **cup finely chopped sweet red pepper**
1/4 **cup finely chopped sweet yellow pepper**
   2 **eggs**
2/3 **cup sour cream**
1-1/2 **cups all-purpose flour**
   2 **tablespoons sugar**
1-1/2 **teaspoons baking powder**
3/4 **teaspoon salt**

1/2 **teaspoon dried basil**
1/4 **teaspoon baking soda**
1/4 **teaspoon dried tarragon**

In a small skillet, melt butter. Add onions and peppers; saute until tender. Remove from the heat; cool for 5 minutes.

In a small bowl, whisk eggs and sour cream. Stir in onion mixture until blended. In a large bowl, combine the remaining ingredients. Stir in sour cream mixture just until moistened.

Fill greased or paper-lined muffin cups two-thirds full. Bake at 350° for 20-25 minutes or until a toothpick comes out clean. Serve warm. **Yield:** 10 muffins.

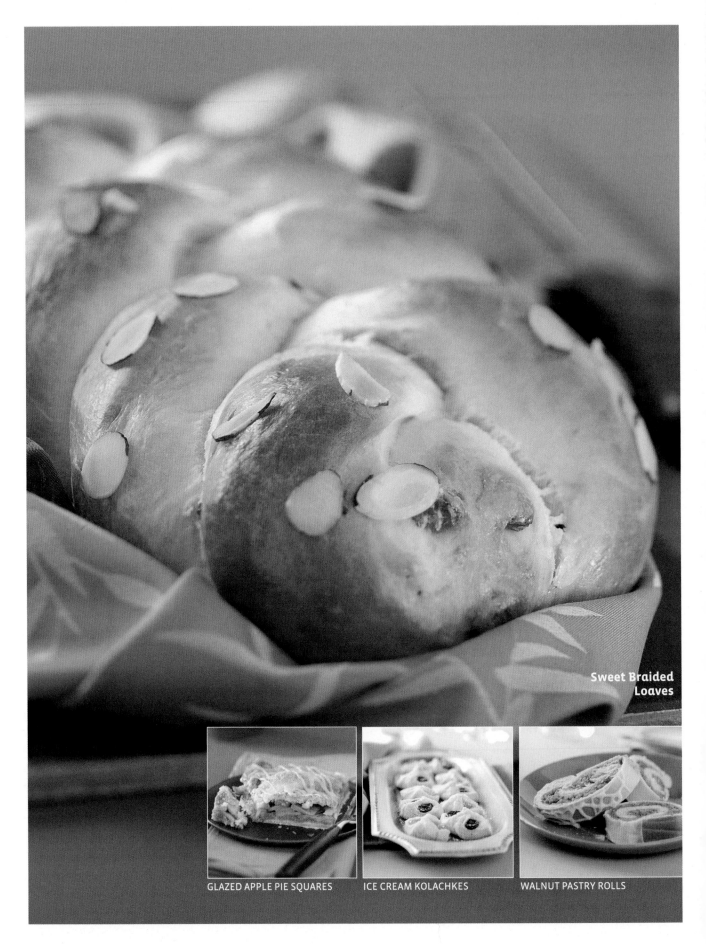

Sweet Braided
Loaves

GLAZED APPLE PIE SQUARES   ICE CREAM KOLACHKES   WALNUT PASTRY ROLLS

Fresh from the Oven

Baking is an art and craft for this field editor, who loves to share her masterpieces with family and friends.

By Diane Turner, Brunswick, Ohio

I THINK of baking as an art form, and it's definitely a creative outlet for me. I like to bake when I'm happy, sad, stressed, nervous—really all the time!

I learned to bake the same way many people have—by watching family members. For me, it was my mom and grandmother. Grandma was a cake decorator, and she taught me a lot of fancy tips and tricks. I also learned how to make wonderful nut rolls from a woman at a local bakery.

I live in Brunswick, Ohio with my husband, John; sons Austin and Sean; daughter Kristin; and dog "Charlie." The kids love to help with my baking, especially when it comes to decorating cookies!

I run a licensed wholesale bakery out of my kitchen, and I've also gone back to school to study court reporting. In my spare time, I enjoy volunteering at school, writing, reading and, of course, baking goodies for my family.

My breads are among my most popular creations, and I also get a lot of orders for my nut and poppy-seed rolls around the holidays, especially for Easter.

Here, I've shared some of my favorite recipes—Ice Cream Kolachkes, Sweet Braided Loaves, Walnut Pastry Rolls and Glazed Apple Pie Squares.

Although I sell much of what I make, I also give a lot away as gifts to neighbors and friends. It's nice to hear that they enjoy my baked treats.

Ice Cream Kolachkes

PREP: 1 hour + chilling **BAKE:** 10 min./batch

☑ This recipe includes Nutrition Facts and Diabetic Exchanges.

- 2 **cups butter, softened**
- 1 **pint vanilla ice cream, softened**
- 4 **cups all-purpose flour**
- 2 **tablespoons sugar**
- 2 **cans (12 ounces *each*) apricot *and/or* raspberry cake and pastry filling**
- 1 **to 2 tablespoons confectioners' sugar, optional**

In the bowl of a heavy-duty stand mixer, beat butter and ice cream until blended (mixture will appear curdled). Add flour and sugar; mix well. Divide dough into four portions; cover and refrigerate for 2 hours or until easy to handle.

On a lightly floured surface, roll one portion of dough into a 12-in. x 10-in. rectangle; cut into 2-in. squares. Place a teaspoonful of filling in the center of each square. Overlap two opposite corners of dough over filling; pinch tightly to seal. Place 2 in. apart on ungreased baking sheets. Repeat with remaining dough and filling.

Bake at 350° for 11-14 minutes or until bottoms are lightly browned. Cool for 1 minute before removing from pans to wire racks. Sprinkle with confectioners' sugar if desired. **Yield:** 10 dozen.

Nutrition Facts: 1 cookie equals 60 calories, 3 g fat (2 g saturated fat), 9 mg cholesterol, 27 mg sodium, 7 g carbohydrate, trace fiber, 1 g protein. **Diabetic Exchanges:** 1/2 starch, 1/2 fat.

Sweet Braided Loaves

PREP: 45 min. + rising **BAKE:** 25 min. + cooling

☑ This recipe includes Nutrition Facts and Diabetic Exchanges.

- 1 package (1/4 ounce) active dry yeast
- 1/4 cup warm water (110° to 115°)
- 1 cup warm milk (110° to 115°)
- 1/2 cup sugar
- 1/2 cup butter, softened
- 3 eggs
- 1/2 teaspoon salt
- 5-1/2 to 6 cups all-purpose flour
- 1 cup golden raisins

GARNISH:
- 1 egg, beaten
- 2 tablespoons sliced almonds

In a large bowl, dissolve yeast in warm water. Add the milk, sugar, butter, eggs, salt and 3 cups flour; beat until smooth. Stir in enough remaining flour to form a soft dough. Stir in raisins.

Turn onto a floured surface; knead until smooth and elastic, about 6-8 minutes. Place in a greased bowl, turning once to grease the top. Cover and let rise in a warm place until doubled, about 1 hour.

Punch dough down. Turn onto a lightly floured surface; divide dough into six portions. Shape each into a 12-in. rope. Place three ropes on a greased baking sheet and braid; pinch ends to seal and tuck under. Repeat with remaining ropes. Cover and let rise until doubled, about 45 minutes.

Brush with egg; sprinkle with almonds. Bake at 350° for 25-30 minutes or until golden brown. Cool on wire racks. **Yield:** 2 loaves (12 slices each).

Nutrition Facts: 1 slice equals 194 calories, 6 g fat (3 g saturated fat), 46 mg cholesterol, 93 mg sodium, 32 g carbohydrate, 1 g fiber, 5 g protein. **Diabetic Exchanges:** 2 starch, 1/2 fat.

Walnut Pastry Rolls

PREP: 2 hours + chilling **BAKE:** 20 min. + cooling

- 1-1/2 cups plus 1/3 cup sugar, *divided*
- 1 can (12 ounces) evaporated milk, *divided*
- 6 cups ground walnuts (1-1/2 pounds)
- 1-1/2 teaspoons honey
- 3 eggs, *separated*
- 2 packages (1/4 ounce *each*) active dry yeast
- 3/4 cup warm water (110° to 115°)
- 4 to 4-1/2 cups all-purpose flour
- 1 teaspoon salt
- 1/2 cup cold butter
- 3 to 4 tablespoons milk, *divided*
- 1 to 2 cups confectioners' sugar, optional

In a small saucepan, cook and stir 1-1/2 cups sugar and 1 cup evaporated milk until mixture comes to a boil. Transfer to a large bowl; stir in walnuts and honey. In a small bowl, beat egg whites until stiff peaks form. Fold into walnut mixture. Cover and refrigerate filling for at least 2 hours.

For dough, in a small bowl, dissolve yeast in warm water. In a large bowl, combine 3 cups flour, salt and remaining sugar; cut in butter until crumbly. Add the yeast mixture, egg yolks and remaining evaporated milk; beat until smooth. Stir in enough remaining flour to form a firm dough.

Turn onto a floured surface; knead until smooth and elastic, about 6-8 minutes. Place in a greased bowl, turning once to grease the top. Cover and let rise in a warm place until doubled, about 1 hour.

Turn onto a floured surface. Punch dough down; divide into four portions. Roll each portion into a 15-in. x 11-in. rectangle. Spread prepared walnut filling to

within 1/2 in. of edges. Roll up jelly-roll style, starting with a long side; pinch seams to seal and tuck ends under. Place seam side down on greased baking sheets. Cover and let rise in a warm place until doubled, about 30 minutes.

Brush 2 tablespoons milk over tops and sides of rolls. Bake at 350° for 20-25 minutes or until golden brown. Cool on wire racks.

For the glaze, combine the confectioners' sugar and remaining milk; drizzle over the rolls. **Yield:** 4 rolls (15 slices each).

Glazed Apple Pie Squares

PREP: 1 hour **BAKE:** 45 min. + cooling

☑ This recipe includes Nutrition Facts and Diabetic Exchanges.

- **2-1/2 cups all-purpose flour**
- **1 teaspoon salt**
- **1 cup cold butter**
- **1 egg,** *separated*
- **3 to 4 tablespoons milk**
- **1 cup crushed cornflakes**
- **9 cups thinly sliced peeled tart apples (about 10 medium)**
- **1 cup plus 2 tablespoons sugar,** *divided*
- **2 teaspoons ground cinnamon,** *divided*
- **1/2 teaspoon ground nutmeg**

GLAZE:
- **1 cup confectioners' sugar**
- **1/2 teaspoon vanilla extract**
- **1 to 2 tablespoons milk**

In a large bowl, combine flour and salt; cut in butter until mixture resembles coarse crumbs. In a measuring cup, combine egg yolk and enough milk to measure 1/3 cup. Gradually add to the flour mixture, tossing with a fork until dough forms a ball.

Divide dough in half. Roll one portion into a thin 15-in. x 10-in. rectangle. Transfer to the bottom of an ungreased 15-in. x 10-in. x 1-in. baking pan. Sprinkle with cornflakes. In a large bowl, combine the apples, 1 cup sugar, 1-1/2 teaspoons cinnamon and nutmeg; toss to coat. Spoon over crust.

Roll remaining dough into a thin 15-in. x 10-in. rectangle; place over apple filling. Beat egg white; brush over pastry. Combine remaining sugar and cinnamon; sprinkle over the top. Bake at 350° for 45-50 minutes or until golden brown.

For the glaze, combine confectioners' sugar, vanilla and enough milk to achieve a drizzling consistency. Drizzle over warm pastry. Cool completely on a wire rack. Cut into squares. **Yield:** 2 dozen.

Nutrition Facts: 1 square equals 209 calories, 8 g fat (5 g saturated fat), 29 mg cholesterol, 183 mg sodium, 33 g carbohydrate, 1 g fiber, 2 g protein. **Diabetic Exchanges:** 2 starch, 1 fat.

El Sombrero
Corn Bread

ENCHILADAS VERDES

MEXICAN LAYERED SALAD

VANILLA RING CAKE

A Taste for Tex-Mex

This Texan loves sharing recipes—such as the festive Cinco de Mayo feast here—as much as preparing them.

By Joan Hallford, North Richland Hills, Texas

HAVING LIVED in Texas most of my life, I enjoy eating and preparing Mexican food. The recipes here, all shared by friends, create a terrific meal that I make for my family and guests.

The menu consists of Enchiladas Verdes as the meaty main course, with golden El Sombrero Corn Bread and Mexican Layered Salad as sides. Drizzled Vanilla Ring Cake always makes a yummy dessert.

My husband, Joe, and I live in North Richland Hills, not far from our son Jonathan and daughter-in-law Sara. Now retired, I worked as a government printing specialist and special education teacher.

These days, I enjoy traveling by land, air or sea. On trips, I like to pick up cookbooks as souvenirs. I'm a self-taught cook but had fun taking a cooking class in Tuscany on a visit to Italy.

At home, I love entertaining on holidays and hosting friends for summer barbecues. Joe, who was a cook in the Marines, likes to fire up his smoker for briskets and ribs. As for me, I don't really have a specialty—I'll cook anything and everything!

I get a kick out of entering recipe contests and once won a trip to Hawaii. Also, an ice cream cake of mine was a runner-up in a *Taste of Home* contest.

Being a *Taste of Home* field editor has allowed me to share recipes with so many people—and I firmly believe a good recipe shouldn't be kept a secret! I've enjoy meeting cooks from all over through the *Taste of Home* Web site (*tasteofhome.com*) and at gatherings of field editors and readers in this area, too.

The next time you have a taste for Tex-Mex, consider the menu here. I think you'll love it!

Vanilla Ring Cake

PREP: 15 min. **BAKE:** 55 min. + cooling

- 1 cup shortening
- 2 cups sugar
- 4 eggs
- 2 tablespoons vanilla extract
- 3 cups all-purpose flour
- 1 teaspoon baking powder
- 1/2 teaspoon baking soda
- 1 cup buttermilk

DRIZZLE:
- 1 cup confectioners' sugar
- 1 to 2 tablespoons milk
- 1/2 teaspoon vanilla extract

In a large bowl, cream shortening and sugar until light and fluffy, about 5 minutes. Add eggs, one at a time, beating well after each addition. Beat in vanilla. Combine the flour, baking powder and baking soda; add to the creamed mixture alternately with buttermilk, beating well after each addition.

Pour into a greased and floured 10-in. fluted tube pan. Bake at 350° for 55-65 minutes or until a toothpick inserted in the center comes out clean. Cool for 10 minutes before removing from pan to a wire rack to cool completely.

Combine the drizzle ingredients; drizzle over cake. **Yield:** 12 servings.

cream and oil. Stir into dry ingredients just until moistened. Fold in 1 cup cheese and jalapenos.

Transfer to a greased 9-in. square baking pan. Sprinkle with remaining cheese. Bake at 350° for 35-40 minutes or until a toothpick inserted near the center comes out clean. Serve warm. **Yield:** 9 servings.

Editor's Note: When cutting or seeding hot peppers, use rubber or plastic gloves to protect your hands. Avoid touching your face.

Mexican Layered Salad

PREP/TOTAL TIME: 20 min.

  4 cups torn romaine
  1 large cucumber, peeled, halved and sliced
  3 medium tomatoes, chopped
  2 medium ripe avocados, peeled and sliced
  2 large green peppers, chopped
1-1/2 cups mayonnaise
  1/4 cup canned chopped green chilies
  2 teaspoons chili powder
  1/2 teaspoon onion powder
  1/4 teaspoon salt
  1/4 teaspoon garlic powder
  1 cup crushed tortilla chips
  1/2 cup shredded cheddar cheese

In a 2-qt. trifle bowl or glass serving bowl, layer the first five ingredients. Combine the mayonnaise, chilies and seasonings; spread over the top. Sprinkle with chips and cheese. Serve immediately. **Yield:** 10 servings.

El Sombrero Corn Bread

PREP: 10 min. **BAKE:** 35 min.

1-1/2 cups cornmeal
  3 teaspoons baking powder
  1/2 teaspoon salt
  2 eggs
  1 can (14-3/4 ounces) cream-style corn
  1 cup (8 ounces) sour cream
  1/2 cup canola oil
1-1/2 cups shredded cheddar cheese, *divided*
  3 jalapeno peppers, seeded and finely chopped

In a large bowl, combine the cornmeal, baking powder and salt. In another bowl, whisk the eggs, corn, sour

GOOD AS GOLD. Here are some hints for making the best corn bread:

• Before using cornmeal, make sure it's fresh. It should have a slightly sweet smell. Rancid cornmeal will smell stale and musty.

• To avoid overmixing, stir the batter by hand just until moistened. Lumps in the batter are normal and desired.

• Don't let the mixed batter stand before baking. Have the oven preheated and the skillet or pan ready to go.

• Corn bread tastes best fresh from the oven. If that's not possible, serve it the same day it's made.

• If you like a more crusty corn bread, use a dark pan or skillet instead of one with a light finish.

Enchiladas Verdes

PREP: 45 min. **BAKE:** 25 min.

- **1 pound lean ground beef**
- **1 large onion, chopped**
- **1 small garlic clove, minced**
- **1/4 teaspoon salt**
- **2 cups (8 ounces) shredded cheddar cheese**
- **1 can (10-3/4 ounces) condensed cream of chicken soup, undiluted**
- **1 package (8 ounces) process cheese (Velveeta), cubed**
- **3/4 cup evaporated milk**
- **1 can (4 ounces) chopped green chilies, drained**
- **1 jar (2 ounces) diced pimientos, drained**
- **12 corn tortillas (6 inches)**
- **1/4 cup canola oil**

In a large skillet, cook the beef, onion, garlic and salt over medium heat until meat is no longer pink; drain. Stir in cheddar cheese; set aside.

Meanwhile, in a large saucepan, cook and stir the soup, process cheese and milk over medium heat until cheese is melted. Stir in chilies and pimientos.

In a large skillet, fry tortillas, one at a time, in oil for 5 seconds on each side or until golden. Drain on paper towels. Place a scant 1/4 cup of reserved meat mixture down the center of each tortilla. Roll up and place seam side down in greased 13-in. x 9-in. baking dish. Pour cheese sauce over the top. Cover and bake at 350° for 25-30 minutes or until heated through. **Yield:** 6 servings.

Roasted Tomato Soup
With Fresh Basil

FLOUNDER WITH
SHRIMP STUFFING

ARUGULA SUMMER SALAD

ITALIAN COOKIES

Keeping an Italian Accent

This East Coast cook looks to her heritage and traditional tastes to create a marvelous summertime meal.

By Marie Forte, Raritan, New Jersey

BEING ITALIAN, my family tends to crave traditional Italian dishes and the ingredients that are often prominently featured in them.

For example, we love tomatoes, and they're a big part of the dinner menu I've shared here: Arugula Summer Salad, Roasted Tomato Soup with Fresh Basil, Flounder with Shrimp Stuffing and coconut-topped Italian Cookies.

I think these recipes perfectly reflect my style of cooking. They're also among my favorites for summertime. Our family and guests especially enjoy the main course of stuffed flounder.

My husband, Frank, and I live in Raritan, New Jersey. We've been married for over 40 years and have two grown sons. I'm a homemaker, and Frank is a government inspector of materials and equipment.

Both of us are active in our church. We also like to travel to historic places and attend symphony concerts whenever we have the chance.

But I love to cook, too, so I make plenty of time to spend in the kitchen! I often come up with my own recipes or improvise based on what I see in cookbooks. I have hundreds of them and also collect salt-and-pepper shakers and refrigerator magnets.

Because the boys are now out of the house, I don't make as many big dishes as I used to. When I do prepare larger quantities, I freeze a portion or share the food with a friend or relative.

My passion for cooking began when I was still a girl. In high school, I entered a cooking contest sponsored by the local gas company—and, to my surprise and delight, ended up winning.

My prize was a trip to Atlantic City, where winners from all over the state prepared their special dishes. Mine was a tuna macaroni ring! I came home with a ribbon and a plate that still has a place of honor in my china cabinet today.

I think a great place to begin learning your way around the kitchen is to seek out family members or friends who are good cooks. Just ask if you can help prepare their favorite recipes.

I'm happy to share some of my own best-loved dishes with fellow *Taste of Home* fans. I hope you enjoy them as much as we have!

Arugula Summer Salad

PREP/TOTAL TIME: 15 min.

✓ This recipe includes Nutrition Facts and Diabetic Exchanges.

- 4 **cups fresh arugula *or* baby spinach**
- 1 **large sweet onion, thinly sliced**
- 2 **medium tomatoes, cut into wedges**

DRESSING:
- 2 **tablespoons olive oil**
- 1 **tablespoon lemon juice**
- 1 **tablespoon red wine vinegar**

Salt and pepper to taste

In a salad bowl, combine the arugula, onion and tomatoes. Whisk the dressing ingredients; drizzle over salad and gently toss to coat. Serve immediately. **Yield:** 6 servings.

Nutrition Facts: 3/4 cup equals 63 calories, 5 g fat (1 g saturated fat), 0 cholesterol, 7 mg sodium, 5 g carbohydrate, 1 g fiber, 1 g protein. **Diabetic Exchanges:** 1 vegetable, 1 fat.

Flounder with Shrimp Stuffing

PREP: 30 min. **BAKE:** 20 min.

STUFFING:
- 6 tablespoons butter, cubed
- 1 small onion, finely chopped
- 1/4 cup finely chopped celery
- 1/4 cup finely chopped green pepper
- 1 pound uncooked shrimp, peeled, deveined and chopped
- 1/4 cup beef broth
- 1 teaspoon diced pimientos, drained
- 1 teaspoon Worcestershire sauce
- 1/2 teaspoon dill weed
- 1/2 teaspoon minced chives
- 1/8 teaspoon salt
- 1/8 teaspoon cayenne pepper
- 1-1/2 cups soft bread crumbs

FISH:
- 6 flounder fillets (3 ounces *each*)
- 5 tablespoons butter, melted
- 2 tablespoons lemon juice
- 1 teaspoon minced fresh parsley
- 1/2 teaspoon paprika

Salt and pepper to taste

In a large skillet, melt the butter. Add the onion, celery and green pepper; saute until tender. Add shrimp; cook and stir until shrimp turn pink. Add the beef broth, pimientos, Worcestershire sauce, dill, chives, salt and cayenne pepper; heat through. Remove from the heat; stir in bread crumbs.

Spoon about 1/2 cup stuffing onto each flounder

fillet; roll up. Place seam side down in a greased 13-in. x 9-in. baking dish. Drizzle with butter and lemon juice. Sprinkle with seasonings. Bake, uncovered, at 375° for 20-25 minutes or until the fish flakes easily with a fork. **Yield:** 6 servings.

Roasted Tomato Soup With Fresh Basil

PREP: 40 min. **COOK:** 5 min.

☑ This recipe includes Nutrition Facts and Diabetic Exchanges.

- 3-1/2 pounds tomatoes (about 11 medium), halved
- 1 small onion, quartered
- 2 garlic cloves, peeled and halved
- 2 tablespoons olive oil
- 2 tablespoons fresh thyme leaves
- 1 teaspoon salt
- 1/4 teaspoon pepper
- 12 fresh basil leaves

Salad croutons and additional fresh basil leaves, optional

Place the tomatoes, onion and garlic in a greased 15-in. x 10-in. x 1-in. baking pan; drizzle with the oil. Sprinkle with the thyme, salt and pepper; toss to coat. Bake at 400° for 25-30 minutes or until tender, stirring once. Cool slightly.

In a blender, process the tomato mixture and basil in batches until blended. Transfer to a large saucepan and heat through. Garnish each serving with croutons and additional basil if desired. **Yield:** 6 servings.

Nutrition Facts: about 1 cup (calculated without garnish) equals 107 calories, 5 g fat (1 g saturated fat), 0 cholesterol, 411 mg sodium, 15 g carbohydrate, 4 g fiber, 3 g protein. **Diabetic Exchanges:** 3 vegetable, 1 fat.

Italian Cookies

PREP: 20 min. **BAKE:** 10 min./batch + cooling

✓ This recipe includes Nutrition Facts and Diabetic Exchanges.

- 1/2 **pound butter, softened**
- 1/2 **cup sugar**
- 6 **eggs**
- 2 **teaspoons vanilla** *or* **anise extract**
- 4 **cups all-purpose flour**
- 4 **teaspoons baking powder**

ICING:
- 3-3/4 **cups confectioners' sugar**
- 5 **to 6 tablespoons milk**
- 2 **teaspoons vanilla extract**

DECORATIONS:
Flaked coconut *or* **assorted sprinkles**

In a large bowl, cream the butter and sugar until light and fluffy. Beat in the eggs and extract. Combine flour and baking powder; gradually add to creamed mixture and mix well.

Drop by rounded teaspoonfuls onto ungreased baking sheets. Bake at 350° for 9-11 minutes or until bottoms are lightly browned. Remove to wire racks to cool completely.

For icing, in a small bowl, combine the confectioners' sugar, milk and vanilla until smooth. Dip the cookies, allowing the excess icing to drip off. Place cookies on waxed paper; decorate as desired. Let stand until set.
Yield: 7 dozen.

Nutrition Facts: 1 cookie (calculated without decorations) equals 73 calories, 3 g fat (2 g saturated fat), 21 mg cholesterol, 40 mg sodium, 11 g carbohydrate, trace fiber, 1 g protein. **Diabetic Exchanges:** 1/2 starch, 1/2 fat.

KEEPING COCONUT. To soften shredded coconut that's turned hard, soak it in milk 30 minutes to soften it. Drain it and pat it dry on paper towels before using. The leftover coconut-flavored milk can be used within 5 days in baked goods or blended with fresh fruit for a tasty beverage.

Low Country Grill

T-BONES FOR TWO

TERIYAKI PINEAPPLE &
PORK CHOPS

GRILLED SNAPPER WITH
CAPER SAUCE

Queen of the Grill

This Low Country cook fires up the grill at least once a week all year long. Why? The fabulous flavor!

By Alaina Showalter, Clover, South Carolina

IN MY FAMILY, grilling isn't just a summertime activity. It's a great way of making delicious meals on a weekly basis year-round.

I grill for special occasions, but I'll also grill just because it's Tuesday! When we entertain or have weekend guests, you can bet the grill will be fired up.

I live in Clover, South Carolina with my husband, Tim, and have three stepchildren and a granddaughter. We also have two dogs, two cats, chickens and a stocked pond.

After serving 10 years in the Navy, I got my master's degree in education and now teach seventh-grade science. Tim is a pilot ground school instructor.

Traveling, camping, boating, fishing and gardening top our list of favorite pastimes. We also have a greenhouse for year-round herbs and a vegetable garden. These come in very handy for our cookouts!

I grill not only every meat I can think of, but also most vegetables and fruits. We devour grilled garden veggies several times a week in summer.

My main grill is a Perfect Flame gas model. For smoking/grilling, I use a Brinkmann Electric Smoker/Grill. I use a Weber Smokey Joe when we're camping or in the mood for charcoal.

One of the things I love about grilling is that it's so versatile. Your menu can be anything from quick and simple to decadent and elegant. The four main dishes here—Teriyaki Pineapple & Pork Chops, Low Country Grill, T-Bones for Two and Grilled Snapper with Caper Sauce—are among my favorites.

Whenever someone asks if I have any grilling tips, here's what I tell them:

• Get to know your grill and have patience. It takes a while to get it seasoned and learn to control the heat. A fancy grill does not mean quality...technique and practice are much more important.

• Try grilling things other than meat—portobellos, veggies (such as squash and eggplant) and fruit.

• Olive oil and cooking spray are your friends—they prevent sticking and help with seasoning the grill; just learn how to control flare-ups!

• If using charcoal, don't rush the coals...this just leads to food that tastes like lighter fluid.

• Don't wait for a holiday or special event to grill!

Teriyaki Pineapple & Pork Chops

PREP: 15 min. + marinating **GRILL:** 10 min.

- 1 cup unsweetened pineapple juice
- 4 bone-in pork loin chops (8 ounces *each*)
- 1 tablespoon minced fresh rosemary *or* 1 teaspoon dried rosemary, crushed
- 1 teaspoon garlic powder
- 1/2 teaspoon salt
- 1/4 teaspoon pepper
- 1 fresh pineapple
- 1/2 cup teriyaki sauce
- 1 package (9 ounces) fresh baby spinach

Place pineapple juice in a large resealable plastic bag; add the pork chops. Seal bag and turn to coat; refrigerate for up to 2 hours. Drain pork chops and discard marinade. Combine the rosemary, garlic powder, salt and pepper; sprinkle over chops.

Peel and core the pineapple; cut into eight spears. Grill chops and pineapple, covered, over medium heat for 4-6 minutes on each side or until a meat thermometer reads 160° and pineapple is tender, basting occasionally with teriyaki sauce.

Arrange spinach on a serving platter; top with pineapple and chops. **Yield:** 4 servings.

T-Bones for Two

PREP: 10 min. + standing GRILL: 10 min.

- **2 beef T-bone steaks (1 inch thick and 12 ounces *each*)**
- **2 tablespoons olive oil**
- **1/2 cup packed brown sugar**
- **1/2 teaspoon seasoned salt**
- **1/2 teaspoon lemon-pepper seasoning**
- **1/2 teaspoon lime-pepper seasoning *or* additional lemon-pepper seasoning**
- **1/4 teaspoon garlic powder**

Brush steaks with oil. Combine the remaining ingredients; rub over steaks. Let stand for 10 minutes before grilling.

Grill the steaks, covered, over medium heat for 5-7 minutes on each side or until meat reaches desired doneness (for medium-rare, a meat thermometer should read 145°; medium, 160°; well-done, 170°). **Yield:** 2 servings.

GETTING SOAKED. Wood (bamboo) skewers are inexpensive, disposable and widely available in lengths from 4 to 10 inches. Also, they don't absorb heat, so they can go from the grill to your guests' plates when desired. But wood skewers may ignite over a hot flame. To avoid this, first soak them in water for about 30 minutes.

Low Country Grill

PREP: 20 min. GRILL: 50 min.

- **2 tablespoons olive oil**
- **1 teaspoon salt, *divided***
- **1 teaspoon garlic powder, *divided***
- **1 teaspoon seafood seasoning, *divided***
- **12 small red potatoes, quartered**
- **1/3 cup butter, melted**
- **1 pound smoked kielbasa**
- **3 medium ears sweet corn, cut in half**
- **1-1/2 pounds uncooked medium shrimp, peeled and deveined**

In a large bowl, combine the oil with 1/4 teaspoon each of salt, garlic powder and seafood seasoning. Add potatoes; toss to coat. Spoon onto a greased double thickness of heavy-duty foil (about 18 in. square).

Fold foil around potatoes and seal tightly. Grill, covered, over medium heat for 30-35 minutes or until tender, turning once. Set aside and keep warm.

In a small bowl, combine butter with remaining salt, garlic powder and seafood seasoning. Grill kielbasa and corn, covered, over medium heat for 10-12 minutes or until kielbasa is heated through and corn is tender, turning occasionally and basting corn with half of the butter mixture. Keep warm.

Thread shrimp onto four metal or soaked wooden skewers; grill shrimp, covered, over medium heat for 3-4 minutes on each side or until shrimp turn pink, basting with remaining butter mixture. Slice kielbasa into six pieces before serving. Carefully open foil from the potatoes to allow steam to escape. **Yield:** 6 servings.

Grilled Snapper With Caper Sauce

PREP: 20 min. + marinating **GRILL:** 10 min.

☑ This recipe includes Nutrition Facts and Diabetic Exchanges.

- **1/3 cup lime juice**
- **1 jalapeno pepper, seeded**
- **3 garlic cloves, peeled**
- **1-1/4 teaspoons fresh thyme leaves *or* 1/4 teaspoon dried thyme**
- **1 teaspoon salt**
- **1 teaspoon pepper**
- **4 red snapper fillets (6 ounces *each*)**

SAUCE:
- **3 tablespoons lime juice**
- **3 tablespoons olive oil**
- **2 tablespoons water**
- **2 teaspoons red wine vinegar**
- **1/2 cup fresh cilantro leaves**
- **1 shallot, peeled**
- **1 tablespoon capers, drained**
- **1-1/2 teaspoons chopped seeded jalapeno pepper**
- **1 garlic clove, peeled and halved**
- **1/4 teaspoon pepper**

For marinade, in a small food processor, combine the first six ingredients; cover and process until blended. Pour into a large resealable plastic bag. Add the fish fillets; seal the bag and turn to coat. Refrigerate for 30 minutes.

Coat grill rack with cooking spray before starting the grill. Drain and discard marinade. Grill fillets, covered, over medium heat for 3-5 minutes on each side or until fish flakes easily with a fork.

Meanwhile, combine sauce ingredients in a small food processor. Cover and process until blended. Serve with fish. **Yield:** 4 servings.

Nutrition Facts: 1 fillet with 3 tablespoons sauce equals 272 calories, 12 g fat (2 g saturated fat), 60 mg cholesterol, 435 mg sodium, 5 g carbohydrate, 1 g fiber, 34 g protein. **Diabetic Exchanges:** 5 very lean meat, 2 fat.

Easy Pumpkin Pie

MARINATED SALAD

SCALLOPED OYSTERS

SWEET POTATOES & APPLES

Gathering on Thanksgiving

There's always room for one more at her Thanksgiving table, which features these special dishes to complement a turkey main course.

By Marty Rummel, Trout Lake, Washington

WE HAVE always seen Thanksgiving Day as a chance to reach out to those who may have no family, have no way to cook or are just in need of a hug. Through the years, I've served about 25 Thanksgiving dinners and seated as many as 40 people at once in our home.

My friend, Sue Steward, and I joined forces for Thanksgiving dinner in the 1980s when the Stewards began pastoring our small community church. We've done this for so many years that now we can put together our menu with a five-minute conversation. We only need to know if we're feeding 10 or 40!

Here, I've shared some of our favorite Thanksgiving dishes. The Marinated Salad and Sweet Potatoes & Apples are recipes Sue shared with me.

I live in Trout Lake, Washington with my husband, Darrol (he builds custom homes) and my father-in-law. Our son and daughter are both married and live out of state. I work as a bookkeeper for our construction company and volunteer in the community as a R.N.

I love the outdoors—hiking, huckleberry picking, snowmobiling, cross-country skiing and, in recent years, rock-climbing (I have the bruises to prove it!). I also lead a women's Bible study group.

On Thanksgiving, it's easiest to divide up the cooking chores. I always prepare the turkey, dressing and gravy. In fact, I roast it the day before, then debone and arrange the meat on a platter to reheat the next day. I make the gravy in advance and reheat it in a slow cooker. From there, the traditional recipes get handed out to our guests to bring from their homes.

To keep Thanksgiving as easy as can be, I keep these guidelines in mind:

• Set the tables the day before.

• If you need more seating, move some of the living room furniture into the dining room and set up more tables in the living room. A sheet of plywood on saw horses will never be noticed under a nice tablecloth!

• Use card tables for the kids, and set up a buffet table for second servings.

• Be flexible. The mashed potatoes may have a few lumps, but your guests won't remember that. I have had many tell me years later how much it meant to have dinner with our "extended family."

Scalloped Oysters

PREP: 10 min. **BAKE:** 25 min.

- 6 **eggs, beaten**
- 1 **quart half-and-half cream**
- 1/4 **teaspoon pepper**
- 4 **cans (8 ounces *each*) whole oysters, drained**
- 2 **cups crushed butter-flavored crackers (about 50 crackers)**

In a large bowl, combine the eggs, half-and-half cream and pepper. Stir in the oysters and crackers. Pour into 12 greased 6-ounce ramekins or custard cups; place on a baking sheet. Bake at 350° for 25-30 minutes or until a knife inserted near the center comes out clean. **Yield:** 12 servings.

Editor's Note: Scalloped Oysters may also be baked in a 13-in. x 9-in. baking dish for 55-65 minutes or until a knife inserted near the center comes out clean.

leaf-shaped cookie cutters. With a sharp knife, score leaf veins on cutouts.

Place the pastry cutouts on an ungreased baking sheet. Bake at 400° for 6-8 minutes or until golden brown. Remove to a wire rack to cool. Arrange around edge of pie. Garnish with whipped cream if desired. **Yield:** 8 servings.

Sweet Potatoes & Apples

PREP: 50 min. + cooling **BAKE:** 40 min.

☑ This recipe includes Nutrition Facts and Diabetic Exchanges.

>   5 **medium sweet potatoes**
>   5 **medium tart apples, peeled and thinly sliced**
> 1/2 **cup sugar**
>   1 **tablespoon cornstarch**
>   1 **cup cold water**
>   1 **teaspoon lemon juice**
> 1/4 **cup butter, cubed**
> 1/4 **teaspoon ground cinnamon**
> 1/8 **teaspoon salt**

Place the sweet potatoes in a Dutch oven and cover with water. Bring to a boil. Reduce heat; cover and cook for 20 minutes or just until tender.

Drain the sweet potatoes and cool slightly. Peel and cut into 1/4-in. slices. In a greased 13-in. x 9-in. baking dish, layer half of the apples and sweet potatoes. Repeat layers.

In a small saucepan, combine the sugar, cornstarch, water and lemon juice until smooth. Bring to a boil;

Easy Pumpkin Pie

PREP: 10 min. **BAKE:** 50 min. + cooling

>   3 **eggs**
>   1 **cup canned pumpkin**
>   1 **cup evaporated milk**
> 1/2 **cup sugar**
> 1/4 **cup maple syrup**
>   1 **teaspoon ground cinnamon**
> 1/2 **teaspoon salt**
> 1/2 **teaspoon ground nutmeg**
> 1/2 **teaspoon maple flavoring**
> 1/2 **teaspoon vanilla extract**
>   1 **unbaked pastry shell (9 inches)**

Additional pie pastry, optional
Whipped cream, optional

In a large bowl, beat the first 10 ingredients until smooth; pour into the pastry shell. Cover the edges loosely with foil. Bake at 400° for 10 minutes. Reduce heat to 350°; bake 40-45 minutes longer or until a knife inserted near the center comes out clean. Remove the foil. Cool on a wire rack.

If decorative cutouts are desired, roll additional pastry to 1/8-in. thickness; cut out with 1-in. to 1-1/2-in.

cook and stir for 2 minutes or until thickened. Remove from the heat; stir in the butter, cinnamon and salt. Pour over sweet potatoes and apples.

Cover and bake at 350° for 30 minutes. Uncover; bake 10 minutes longer or until the apples are tender. **Yield:** 12 servings.

Nutrition Facts: 3/4 cup equals 143 calories, 4 g fat (2 g saturated fat), 10 mg cholesterol, 56 mg sodium, 27 g carbohydrate, 2 g fiber, 1 g protein. **Diabetic Exchanges:** 1 starch, 1 fat, 1/2 fruit.

Marinated Salad

PREP: 25 min. + marinating

- 4 **cups fresh cauliflowerets**
- 4 **cups fresh broccoli florets**
- 1 **medium red onion, halved and sliced**
- 1 **can (8 ounces) sliced water chestnuts, drained**
- 1 **can (6 ounces) pitted ripe olives, drained**
- 1 **jar (4-1/2 ounces) sliced mushrooms, drained**
- 1 **bottle (16 ounces) Italian salad dressing**

In a large bowl, combine the first six ingredients. Drizzle with the Italian salad dressing and toss to coat. Cover the salad and refrigerate overnight. **Yield:** 16 servings (3/4 cup each).

CAULIFLOWER CLUES. When purchasing fresh cauliflower for Marinated Salad (at left) or another recipe, look for a head with compact florets that are free from yellow or brown spots. The leaves should be crisp and green, not withered or discolored.

Tightly wrap an unwashed head and refrigerate it for up to 5 days. Before using, wash and remove the leaves at the base and trim the stem.

Meals in Minutes

In this time-saving chapter, you'll find 12 complete, family friendly menus that get on the table in just 30 minutes...or less. Even your busiest days will be no match for these in-a-hurry recipes!

MADE-IN-MOMENTS MAINSTAYS. Clockwise from top left: Take a Quick Trip to the Tropics (p. 252), Casual Combo Fits Lunchtime or Later (p. 242), Fresh-Tasting Fare Has Summer Flavor (p. 244) and Bundle Up a Special Seafood Dinner (p. 240).

Bundle Up a Special Seafood Dinner

IS IT POSSIBLE to enjoy restaurant-worthy meals at home—even on busy weeknights? The answer is, absolutely! All you need is a quick but special menu, such as the one featured here.

Our Test Kitchen home economists put together this speedy meal using favorite recipes from two great cooks. It's not only delicious, but also ready to serve in just 30 minutes.

"My main course is a fast and easy way to showcase salmon fillets," says Larissa Farnam of Myrtle Beach, South Carolina. "It's nice enough to serve company."

From Emily Paluszak of Spartanburg, South Carolina, Balsamic Vegetable Salad has terrific flavor and couldn't be easier to prepare. "Feel free to customize it with your favorite veggies," Emily notes.

Spinach Salmon Bundles

PREP/TOTAL TIME: 30 min.

- 2 tubes (8 ounces *each*) refrigerated crescent rolls
- 4 salmon fillets (6 ounces *each*)
- 1/4 teaspoon salt
- 1/4 teaspoon pepper
- 1/3 cup garlic-herb cheese spread
- 1 package (10 ounces) frozen chopped spinach, thawed and squeezed dry

Unroll the crescent roll dough and separate into four rectangles; seal perforations. Place a salmon fillet in the center of each rectangle; sprinkle with salt and pepper. Spoon cheese spread over each; top with spinach. Fold dough over filling and pinch edges to seal.

Place on an ungreased baking sheet. Bake at 400° for 20-25 minutes or until golden brown. Serve bundles immediately. **Yield:** 4 servings.

Editor's Note: This recipe was tested with Alouette Garlic-Herb Cheese Spread.

A BIT ON BALSAMIC. Balsamic vinegar is made from sweet white grapes and aged in wooden barrels for at least 10 years (that explains why it can have a hefty price!). You can substitute cider vinegar or a mild red wine vinegar. White wine vinegar is much stronger and sharper, and it should be used sparingly if it's your only substitute.

Balsamic Vegetable Salad

PREP/TOTAL TIME: 10 min.

- 3 large tomatoes, cut into wedges
- 3 medium cucumbers, peeled, halved and sliced
- 1/2 cup olive oil
- 1/4 cup balsamic vinegar
- 3 tablespoons water
- 1 envelope Italian salad dressing mix

In a salad bowl, combine the tomatoes and cucumbers. In a small bowl, whisk the oil, vinegar, water and dressing mix. Pour over the vegetables and toss to coat. **Yield:** 6 servings.

Casual Combo Fits Lunchtime or Later

WHETHER you're looking for a wholesome lunch to get you through the rest of the afternoon or a quick but filling supper on a busy weeknight, consider the terrific twosome featured here. It goes together in a flash and is sure to satisfy.

In her Levittown, Pennsylvania kitchen, Rhonda Wilkinson likes to fix speedy Spinach Pastrami Wraps. "With minimal ingredients, these roll-ups make a fuss-free meal at noon or after work," she notes. "And with pastrami and cheddar cheese, they're substantial and won't leave you hungry."

Eileen Korecko of Hot Springs Village, Arkansas has just a few requirements for recipes. "I like to make foods that are quick, easy and great-tasting," she says. "My Oh-So-Easy Tomato Cream Soup is all three."

Spinach Pastrami Wraps

PREP/TOTAL TIME: 20 min.

- 4 flour tortillas (10 inches), room temperature
- 4 ounces cream cheese, softened
- 3/4 cup shredded cheddar cheese
- 1/4 cup chopped red onion
- 1/4 cup sliced Greek olives
- 1/2 pound thinly sliced deli pastrami
- 1-1/2 cups fresh baby spinach

Spread tortillas with cream cheese; sprinkle with cheddar cheese, onion and olives. Top with pastrami and spinach. Roll up tightly; secure with toothpicks. **Yield:** 4 servings.

Oh-So-Easy Tomato Cream Soup

PREP/TOTAL TIME: 20 min.

- 2 cups milk
- 1 can (14-1/2 ounces) diced tomatoes, undrained
- 1 package (8 ounces) cream cheese, softened
- 1/4 cup coarsely chopped fresh basil
- 1/2 teaspoon salt
- 1/8 teaspoon pepper

Place all ingredients in a blender; cover and process until smooth. Transfer to a large saucepan; heat through. **Yield:** 4 servings.

MEALTIME TWISTS. Vary the recipes in this meal in any of the following ways to suit your taste:
- Use a savory-flavored cream cheese for Spinach Pastrami Wraps.
- If you don't have spinach on hand for the wraps, just substitute any other lettuce.
- Use whole wheat tortillas for the wraps to triple the fiber content.
- Roll the tortillas tightly, then thinly slice the wraps for an effortless appetizer.
- Try making Oh-So-Easy Tomato Cream Soup with Italian-flavored diced tomatoes. Just remember to reduce the amount of basil.
- If you'd prefer more heat in your soup, use a can of diced tomatoes and green chilies.

Fresh-Tasting Fare Has Summer Flavor

WHEN something refreshing is the order of the day, turn to the tongue-tingling menu here. The entire three-course meal—sandwich, side salad and dessert—can be prepared and ready to enjoy in a flash.

Stacey Johnson of Tacoma, Washington often whips up Fresh Mozzarella Sandwiches. "We love these, especially when it's too warm to use the oven," she says.

Our Test Kitchen staff picked Sweet Onion, Tomato & Cuke Salad as a complement to the sandwiches. "It's a terrific way to use your garden-grown veggies," notes Mickey Turner of Grants Pass, Oregon.

For the finale, try the yummy sundaes from Kristin Kossak of Bozeman, Montana. "This is my number one option when I don't have much time to prepare dessert but still want to wow my guests," she says. "Smiling, satisfied faces are guaranteed!"

Fresh Mozzarella Sandwiches

PREP/TOTAL TIME: 15 min.

- 8 slices sourdough bread, toasted
- 1/4 cup wasabi mayonnaise
- 1/2 pound fresh mozzarella cheese, sliced
- 2 medium tomatoes, sliced
- 4 thin slices sweet onion
- 8 fresh basil leaves

Spread toast with wasabi mayonnaise. On four slices, layer the mozzarella cheese, tomatoes, onion and basil leaves; top with remaining toast. **Yield:** 4 servings.

Sweet Onion, Tomato & Cuke Salad

PREP/TOTAL TIME: 15 min.

- 3 large tomatoes, chopped
- 3 large cucumbers, peeled, halved, seeded and sliced
- 1 large sweet onion, halved and thinly sliced
- 1/2 cup olive oil
- 3 tablespoons mayonnaise
- 2 tablespoons rice vinegar
- 1 tablespoon Dijon mustard
- 1 garlic clove, minced
- 1/2 teaspoon salt
- 1/4 teaspoon pepper
- 1/4 cup crumbled feta cheese

In a large bowl, combine the tomatoes, cucumbers and onion. In a small bowl, combine the oil, mayonnaise, vinegar, mustard, garlic, salt and pepper. Pour over tomato mixture and toss to coat. Sprinkle with cheese. **Yield:** 10 servings.

Banana Colada Sundaes

PREP/TOTAL TIME: 20 min.

- 6 tablespoons butter, cubed
- 1/3 cup packed brown sugar
- 1/3 cup orange juice
- 2 teaspoons ground cinnamon
- 4 medium bananas, sliced
- 1/2 teaspoon rum extract
- 3 pints vanilla ice cream
- 1/2 cup flaked coconut, toasted

In a small saucepan, combine the butter, brown sugar, juice and cinnamon. Cook and stir over medium heat for 4-5 minutes or until sauce is smooth. Stir in bananas; heat through. Remove from the heat; stir in extract.

Serve warm over ice cream. Sprinkle with coconut. **Yield:** 8 servings.

Pasta Dinner Gets On the Table Pronto

GOOD FOOD travels fast in Marilyn Janssen's kitchen in Dawson Creek, British Columbia. In order for her supply to keep pace with the demand, it has to!

"With six grown children and lots of grandkids, I often have company for dinner," Marilyn shares. "My quick recipes allow me to visit with my family without worrying about how the meal will turn out."

The seconds Marilyn spares are often spent serving second helpings of the winning meal shown here, which requires only about half an hour of prep time.

"I always have frozen chicken breasts on hand for making Chicken with Fettuccine," Marilyn says. "But leftover chicken or turkey also works fine.

"My greens-and-beans salad is packed with tasty surprises," she adds. "It's dressed before serving, so it's ideal for a help-yourself buffet."

Marilyn tops off her speedy supper with a dessert recipe passed along by her mother. "I get the cake in the oven first so it can bake while we're eating," she relates. "It's wonderful served warm."

Chicken with Fettuccine

PREP: 10 min. **COOK:** 20 min.

- 6 boneless skinless chicken breast halves
- 1 tablespoon butter
- 1 tablespoon vegetable oil
- 1 medium onion, coarsely chopped
- 1/2 cup minced fresh basil *or* 1 tablespoon dried basil
- 4 garlic cloves, minced
- 1/2 teaspoon salt
- 1/4 teaspoon pepper
- 3/4 cup chicken broth
- 1/2 cup whipping cream
- 2 tablespoons dried parsley flakes
- 2 large tomatoes, diced
- 1 pound fettuccine

Flatten chicken to 1/2-in. thickness. In a skillet, brown chicken on both sides in butter and oil; remove and set aside. In the same skillet, saute onion until tender. Add basil, garlic, salt and pepper; cook and stir for 2-3 minutes. Stir in broth, cream, parsley and tomatoes. Return chicken to pan. Cover and simmer for 15 minutes or until chicken juices run clear. Meanwhile, cook the fettuccine according to the package directions; drain. Arrange the chicken over fettuccine; top with sauce. **Yield:** 6 servings.

Tomato Bean Salad

PREP/TOTAL TIME: 10 min.

- 1 cup canned kidney beans, rinsed and drained
- 1 large tomato, diced
- 1 celery rib, sliced
- 4 green onions, sliced
- 1/2 cup mayonnaise *or* salad dressing
- 1/4 cup ranch salad dressing
- 1 teaspoon dill weed
- 1/4 teaspoon garlic powder
- 3 cups torn leaf lettuce

In a bowl, combine the first four ingredients. In another bowl, combine the mayonnaise, ranch salad dressing, dill and garlic powder. Pour over the vegetables and toss to coat. Place the leaf lettuce in a serving bowl; add the vegetable mixture. Toss just before serving. **Yield:** 6 servings.

Saucy Chocolate Cake

PREP: 15 min. **BAKE:** 25 min.

- 1 cup sugar, *divided*
- 3 tablespoons baking cocoa, *divided*
- 1-1/2 cups boiling water
- 2 tablespoons butter, softened
- 1 teaspoon vanilla extract
- 1 cup all-purpose flour
- 2 teaspoons baking powder
- 1/2 teaspoon salt
- 1/2 cup milk
Ice cream *or* whipped topping
Maraschino cherries, optional

In a saucepan, combine 1/2 cup sugar and 1 tablespoon cocoa. Stir in boiling water until smooth. Simmer, uncovered, for 5 minutes.

Meanwhile, in a mixing bowl, cream butter, vanilla and remaining sugar. Combine flour, baking powder, salt and remaining cocoa; add to creamed mixture alternately with milk. Beat well. Pour the chocolate sauce into a greased 1-1/2-qt. baking dish. Drop batter by rounded teaspoonfuls onto sauce.

Bake, uncovered, at 375° for 25 minutes or until a toothpick inserted in the center comes out clean. Serve warm with ice cream. Garnish with cherries if desired. **Yield:** 4-6 servings.

Italian-Style Spread Pleases Everyone

DURING the hustle and bustle of the Christmas season, most cooks are ready to take a holiday from time-consuming dinner preparations. But rather than resort to takeout or frozen meals, try the recipes here. You can put the menu together in a mere 30 minutes.

C.C. Yeats of Lewiston, Idaho gets Pepperoni Pizza Bake to the table pronto. "On nights my husband works late or our children have after-school commitments, I rely on this one-dish wonder," she says.

"The egg noodles make a great 'crust' and don't require the time it takes from-scratch pizza dough to rise. Often, I use my food processor to chop up the ingredients quickly. Or, I'll buy presliced and shredded veggies and cheese."

From Bellville, Ohio, Gayle Parker shares a snappy recipe for Italian Tossed Salad that pressed-for-time cooks can squeeze into any menu. "Simple and colorful, it complements everything from a casual lunch to a fancy holiday dinner," she relates.

"It's a little different from plain old iceberg lettuce and tomatoes. Canned kidney beans add protein and texture, and the pepperoni and other fixings give it a fresh zesty taste."

One of Tricia Moore's favorite desserts comes together as quick as 1-2-3. "It uses just three ingredients that I always have on hand—ice cream, honey and nuts," she relates from her home in Somersworth, New Hampshire.

"Feel free to vary the measurements and use as much of each ingredient as you like. To change things up, sprinkle on walnuts instead of almonds. And adding pecans will make you think you're eating pralines."

Pepperoni Pizza Bake

PREP: 15 min. BAKE: 15 min.

  1 package (16 ounces) wide egg noodles
2-1/4 cups pizza sauce, *divided*
  1 cup sliced fresh mushrooms
  1 can (2-1/4 ounces) sliced ripe olives, drained
  1 package (3-1/2 ounces) sliced pepperoni
  2 cups (8 ounces) shredded part-skim mozzarella cheese

Cook noodles according to package directions; drain. In a bowl, combine noodles and 3/4 cup pizza sauce. Transfer to a greased 13-in. x 9-in. x 2-in. baking dish. Top with remaining pizza sauce.

Layer with the mushrooms, olives and pepperoni. Sprinkle with cheese. Bake, uncovered, at 375° for 15-18 minutes or until heated through and cheese is melted. **Yield:** 8 servings.

Italian Tossed Salad

PREP/TOTAL TIME: 10 min.

  1 package (12 ounces) ready-to-serve salad greens
  1 cup (4 ounces) shredded part-skim mozzarella cheese
  1 cup canned kidney beans, drained
  1 cup diced pepperoni
1/4 cup chopped onion
  2 medium tomatoes, diced
1/4 to 1/2 cup Italian salad dressing

In a salad bowl, combine the first six ingredients. Drizzle with dressing; toss to coat. **Yield:** 8 servings.

Honey-Nut Ice Cream

PREP/TOTAL TIME: 5 min.

1-1/2 quarts ice cream
1/2 cup honey
  3 tablespoons slivered almonds, toasted

Scoop ice cream into serving dishes; drizzle with honey and sprinkle with almonds. **Yield:** 8 servings.

MORE ON MUSHROOMS. Fresh mushrooms are best used within a few days of purchase. If that's not possible, you can blanch or saute them, then freeze them for up to 1 month.
• To blanch mushrooms, slice larger mushrooms or use small whole mushroom caps. Bring 1 quart of water to a boil; add mushrooms and 1 tablespoon lemon juice to prevent darkening. Cook in boiling water 3 minutes for slices or 4 minutes for caps. Immediately remove mushrooms with a slotted spoon and cool in ice water for 3 to 4 minutes. Drain well and pack into freezer containers.
• To saute sliced mushrooms, melt butter in a skillet over medium heat; cook and stir mushrooms for 3 minutes. Remove them to a bowl to cool, then pack them into freezer containers.

Summery Home Cooking is a Breeze

AS MUCH as Nella Parker loves to cook, she doesn't want to be stuck in the kitchen when the sun and fun are outdoors.

"During summer, you'll find me river rafting or tending my garden," she relates from Hersey, Michigan. Luckily, she can still fit in quick meals that celebrate the flavors of the season.

In fact, Nella has a sizzling strategy for making summer cooking easy. The convenient menu she shares here is ready in 30 minutes or less.

Nella's garden offers up a treasure trove of fresh vegetables to spark her imagination. "When I toss my spinach with Swiss cheese and bacon, the salad tastes like quiche lorraine...without the effort," she says.

"It goes well with Orange Beef Teriyaki, my favorite anytime stir-fry. When my family comes to visit me, it satisfies them fast. Plus, it's special enough to serve party guests."

Want to change things up? "Try making the Orange Beef Teriyaki with chicken or pork," Nella suggests. "For a fruitier flavor, add pineapple tidbits. Or sprinkle some crispy Chinese noodles on top."

You could also vary the salad by replacing the Caesar dressing with an oil-and-vinegar version. "I like to shake some up with homegrown herbs," she adds.

When it comes to dessert, Nella has a sweet solution. "A cool comfort food is Pink Lemonade Pie," she says. "On very hot days, I serve it straight from the freezer. That way, it's slightly frosty and extra refreshing.

"If you're in the mood for somethng different, replace the pink lemonade with another frozen drink to make orange- or grape-flavored pie. Then garnish it with citrus slices or grapes. A graham cracker crust would also work in place of the shortbread variety."

The minutes Nella saves in the kitchen are dedicated to her work with disabled adults, volunteering for Meals on Wheels and entertaining the "neighbors" that share her woodsy rural acreage.

"I enjoy fixing quick meals for wildlife, too," she laughs. "Hungry 'customers' fly into my butterfly garden, and rabbits and deer often stop by to snack in the rows of greens and veggies I plant especially for them."

Orange Beef Teriyaki

PREP: 5 min. **COOK:** 15 min.

- **1 can (11 ounces) mandarin oranges**
- **1 tablespoon cornstarch**
- **1-1/2 pounds boneless beef sirloin steak, thinly sliced**
- **2 tablespoons vegetable oil**
- **1/2 cup soy sauce**
- **2 tablespoons honey**
- **1-1/2 teaspoons ground ginger**
- **1 garlic clove, minced**
- **Hot cooked rice**

Drain oranges, reserving juice; set oranges aside. In a small bowl, combine cornstarch and 2 tablespoons reserved juice until smooth; set aside.

In a large skillet or wok, stir-fry beef in oil. Add the soy sauce, honey, ginger, garlic and remaining juice. Cover and cook over medium heat for 5-10 minutes or until meat is tender.

Stir cornstarch mixture; stir into beef mixture. Bring to a boil; cook and stir for 2 minutes or until thickened. Stir in the oranges. Serve over rice. **Yield:** 4-6 servings.

Swiss Spinach Salad

PREP/TOTAL TIME: 10 min.

- **1 package (6 ounces) fresh baby spinach**
- **1 cup (4 ounces) shredded Swiss cheese**
- **3 tablespoons crumbled cooked bacon**
- **1/2 cup Caesar salad dressing**
- **Salad croutons**

In a large bowl, combine the spinach, cheese and bacon. Drizzle with dressing and toss to coat. Top with croutons. Serve immediately. **Yield:** 4-6 servings.

Pink Lemonade Pie

PREP/TOTAL TIME: 10 min.

- **1 package (8 ounces) cream cheese, softened**
- **3/4 cup pink lemonade concentrate**
- **4 drops red food coloring, optional**
- **1 carton (8 ounces) frozen whipped topping, thawed**
- **1 shortbread pie crust (9 inches)**
- **Lemon slices and additional whipped topping, optional**

In a large mixing bowl, beat the cream cheese until smooth. Beat in lemonade and food coloring if desired. Fold in whipped topping. Spoon into pie crust. Freeze for 20 minutes. Refrigerate until serving. Garnish with lemon and additional whipped topping if desired. **Yield:** 6-8 servings.

Take a Quick Trip to the Tropics

FIXING FOOD on the double is simple for Gail Hutton of Bremerton, Washington. She simply relies on this refreshing meal that's ready in just half an hour.

Moist and tender, Aloha Chicken gets fruitful flavor from pineapple, peaches and a zesty lemon glaze. To complement that main course, Gail quickly stirs up Curried Confetti Corn as a spicy side.

For a fast dessert, Baby Orange Babas are a yummy option. Using a muffin pan allows Gail to create fun individual-size cakes—without requiring extra time.

Aloha Chicken

PREP: 15 min. **BAKE:** 15 min.

- 4 boneless skinless chicken breast halves
- 4 tablespoons butter, *divided*
- 1 teaspoon cornstarch
- 1/3 cup pineapple juice
- 1/4 cup lemon juice
- 1 teaspoon grated lemon peel
- 1 teaspoon soy sauce
- 1/4 teaspoon dried thyme
- 2 tablespoons chopped onion
- 1 can (15-1/4 ounces) peach halves, drained
- 1 cup pineapple tidbits, drained

Hot cooked rice, optional

In a large skillet, brown the chicken breast halves on both sides in 2 tablespoons butter. Transfer to a shallow microwave-safe dish. Cover and microwave on high for 4-5 minutes or until juices run clear.

In a small bowl, combine cornstarch and pineapple juice until smooth. Stir in the lemon juice, lemon peel, soy sauce and thyme. In the same skillet, saute onion in remaining butter until tender. Stir juice mixture and add to the skillet. Bring to a boil; cook and stir for 2 minutes or until thickened.

Arrange peaches and pineapple over chicken; baste with sauce. Cover and microwave for 1 minute or until sauce is bubbly. Serve over rice with remaining sauce if desired. **Yield:** 4 servings.

Editor's Note: This recipe was tested in a 1,100-watt microwave.

Curried Confetti Corn

PREP: 10 min. **COOK:** 5 min.

- 3 tablespoons chopped onion
- 2 tablespoons chopped sweet red pepper
- 2 tablespoons chopped green pepper
- 3 tablespoons butter
- 2 cans (11 ounces *each*) Mexicorn, drained
- 3/4 teaspoon curry powder
- 1/2 teaspoon salt
- 1/4 teaspoon pepper
- 3/4 cup sour cream

In a small skillet, saute the onion and peppers in butter. Add the corn, curry powder, salt and pepper. Cook over low heat until vegetables are heated through. Stir in the sour cream. Cook 1 minute longer or until heated through. **Yield:** 4 servings.

Baby Orange Babas

PREP: 15 min. **BAKE:** 15 min.

- 1 package (9 ounces) yellow cake mix
- 1/2 cup sugar
- 1/2 cup water
- 1/2 cup orange juice
- 2 teaspoons finely grated orange peel

Whipped topping and maraschino cherries

Prepare cake batter according to package directions. Fill greased muffin cups two-thirds full. Bake at 375° for 15 minutes or until a toothpick comes out clean. Cool for 10 minutes.

Meanwhile, in a saucepan, combine the sugar, water, orange juice and orange peel. Cook and stir for 5 minutes over medium heat until the sugar is dissolved. Invert cupcakes onto a platter; immediately drizzle with the hot orange syrup. Freeze for 10 minutes. Serve with whipped topping and cherries. **Yield:** 9 servings.

Give Weekday Dinners a Taste Twist

WANT to bring a breath of fresh air into your spring cooking routine—but don't have the time to try something new? Relax! Making a deliciously different meal doesn't have to mean hours of effort, thanks to the fuss-free dishes here.

Ready in only 30 minutes, this menu features recipes from three cooks who are determined to get in and out of the kitchen in a hurry.

Kay Bell of Palestine, Texas relies on her Oven-Fried Catfish. "Being a grade school teacher and minister's wife, I find that quick recipes are a necessity," she says.

Her golden baked fillets have the appealing crunch of batter-fried catfish—without the additional calories or preparation time.

"Often, I put the fish and crumb mixture into a plastic bag and shake on the coating, which is a great no-mess technique," Kay adds. "A dash of lemon juice or salsa complements the mild fish nicely."

In Somersworth, New Hampshire, Tricia Moore likes to round out meals with Orange Broccoli, a winning partner for any entree.

"My husband can be a picky eater, but he always enjoys this side dish," Tricia says. "It's nearly effortless to fix—and sure to please even finicky family members who aren't fond of green veggies.

"A buttery hint of citrus comes through wonderfully in the sauce, and slivered almonds add taste and texture," Tricia adds.

Jean Komlos of Plymouth, Michigan serves Praline Snackers when she needs a snappy dessert or sweet munchies for company.

"The ladies in my card club rave about these simple treats, and I've even brought a batch of them to a cookie exchange," Jean says. "Adults seem to think they taste like pecan pie, while children often compare them to s'mores."

Either way, these dressed-up graham crackers are an instant cure for the "hungries" any time of day. "Try them as a late-night snack with a big glass of ice-cold milk," Jean adds. "You'll love it!"

Oven-Fried Catfish

PREP: 10 min. **BAKE:** 25 min.

- 1 cup crushed cornflakes
- 3/4 teaspoon celery salt
- 1/4 teaspoon onion powder
- 1/4 teaspoon paprika
- 1/8 teaspoon pepper
- 6 catfish fillets (6 ounces *each*)
- 1/3 cup butter, melted

In a shallow bowl, combine the cornflakes, celery salt, onion powder, paprika and pepper. Brush the fish fillets with butter; coat with crumb mixture.

Place in a greased 13-in. x 9-in. x 2-in. baking dish. Bake, uncovered, at 350° for 25 minutes or until fish flakes easily with a fork. **Yield:** 6 servings.

Orange Broccoli

PREP: 5 min. **COOK:** 15 min.

- 2 pounds fresh broccoli florets
- 5 tablespoons butter, cubed
- 1/4 cup orange juice
- 1 teaspoon grated orange peel
- 1/2 teaspoon salt
- 1/3 cup slivered almonds

Place 1 in. of water in a saucepan; add broccoli. Bring to a boil. Reduce heat; cover and simmer for 5-8 minutes or until crisp-tender. Drain and keep warm.

In the same pan, combine the butter, orange juice, orange peel and salt; heat until butter is melted. Return the broccoli to the saucepan; toss to coat. Transfer to a serving bowl; sprinkle with almonds. **Yield:** 6 servings.

Praline Snackers

PREP: 15 min. **BAKE:** 10 min.

- 24 graham cracker squares
- 1/2 cup butter, cubed
- 1/2 cup packed brown sugar
- 1/2 teaspoon vanilla extract
- 1/2 cup chopped pecans
- 1 cup miniature marshmallows
- 1/4 cup chocolate syrup

Arrange graham crackers in a single layer in a foil-lined 15-in. x 10-in. x 1-in. baking pan. In a saucepan, bring butter and brown sugar to a boil; cook and stir just until sugar is dissolved. Remove from the heat; add vanilla. Pour evenly over crackers; sprinkle with nuts.

Bake at 350° for 5 minutes. Sprinkle with miniature marshmallows; bake 3-5 minutes longer or until top is bubbly and marshmallows are lightly browned. Drizzle with chocolate syrup. Cool for 10 minutes. Break into squares. **Yield:** 2 dozen.

Stovetop Supper Is Ready in a Snap

GOOD NEWS travels fast for Karalee Reinke of Omaha, Nebraska. And, being a busy mom, so does she... particularly around mealtime.

"It's not unusual for me to be chasing my son one minute and working at my home-based computer job the next—before heading to a church meeting with my husband, Tony. So I need to fix time-saving meals that fit my family's busy schedule."

Happily, streamlined recipes such as the ones featured here help Karalee get cooking. It's a 30-minute meal she can always rely on in a pinch.

"The simple sauce in my Angel Hair Alfredo is delicious reheated," she relates. "In fact, I often keep a couple servings in the freezer.

"To make that main dish heartier, I sometimes add grilled chicken, shrimp or steamed vegetables," Karalee adds. "I've also varied the type of pasta, using fettuccini, tortellini or lasagna."

The dressing for her Creamy Italian Salad calls for on-hand ingredients and complements any kind of greens—from pre-bagged salad to fresh lettuce from the garden. "Plus, it stays tasty for several days in the refrigerator," Karalee notes.

"When you're in the mood for different flavors in the salad, simply vary the ingredients. For example, add parsley, black pepper or blue cheese."

With convenient pudding mix, Karalee can prepare a picture-perfect dessert in an instant. "Chocolate Mint Parfaits are so light and refreshing, especially after the zesty pasta entree," she notes.

"For a fun finishing touch, top them with shaved chocolate, nuts or crumbled cookies. Or, substitute vanilla or banana pudding for the chocolate."

Angel Hair Alfredo

PREP: 10 min. **COOK:** 15 min.

 8 to 12 ounces angel hair pasta
 2 garlic cloves, minced
 2 tablespoons olive *or* vegetable oil
 2 tablespoons all-purpose flour
 1 tablespoon cornstarch
 1/4 teaspoon garlic salt
 1/4 teaspoon pepper
 1/4 teaspoon dried basil
 1-1/2 cups milk
 4 ounces cream cheese, cubed
 1/4 cup grated Parmesan cheese
 1/3 to 1/2 cup diced fully cooked ham, optional

Cook the pasta according to the package directions. Meanwhile, in a large skillet, saute garlic in oil until lightly browned. Stir in the flour, cornstarch, garlic salt, pepper and basil until blended. Gradually stir in milk. Bring to a boil; cook and stir for 2 minutes or until thickened. Reduce heat; whisk in cream cheese and Parmesan cheese until smooth. Add ham if desired; heat through. Drain pasta; add to sauce and toss to coat. **Yield:** 4-6 servings.

Creamy Italian Salad

PREP/TOTAL TIME: 10 min.

 4 to 6 cups mixed salad greens
Sliced plum tomatoes *or* halved cherry tomatoes
 1/4 cup mayonnaise
 1 tablespoon milk
 1 tablespoon cider vinegar
 1/2 teaspoon dried oregano
 1/2 teaspoon dried basil
 1/4 teaspoon sugar
 1/8 teaspoon garlic powder
 1/8 teaspoon garlic salt
Pepper to taste

Divide the salad greens and tomatoes among salad plates. In a jar with a tight-fitting lid, combine the remaining ingredients; shake well. Drizzle over salads. **Yield:** 4-6 servings.

Chocolate Mint Parfaits

PREP/TOTAL TIME: 15 min.

 2 cups plus 1 tablespoon cold milk, *divided*
 1 package (3.9 ounces) instant chocolate pudding mix
 4 ounces cream cheese, softened
 1 tablespoon sugar
 1/4 teaspoon peppermint extract
 1 cup whipped topping
 4 to 6 mint Andes candies, optional

In a bowl, whisk 2 cups milk and the pudding mix for 2 minutes; set aside. In a small mixing bowl, beat the cream cheese, sugar, extract and remaining milk. Fold in whipped topping. In parfait or dessert glasses, layer the pudding and cream cheese mixtures. Garnish with mint candies if desired. **Yield:** 4-6 servings.

Salmon Feast Will Have 'Em Hooked

SUPPER TIME often finds Florine Bruns with a whole herd of hungry mouths to feed. So it's no wonder this Texas ranch wife and grandmother has a knack for keeping food moving.

"My husband, Alton, and I raise cattle and a few sheep and goats," she notes from their home near rural Fredericksburg. "After hours spent penning and feeding livestock, we've worked up quite an appetite—for something tasty, nutritious and quick."

Luckily, Florine has corralled plenty of ideas for flavorful, no-fuss fare, including the three recipes featured here. Her entire seafood supper is ready to serve in just 20 minutes.

"The crusty fish fillets always bake up moist and golden brown," Florine relates. "Our grown daughters and grandsons like their food on the spicy side, so I knew Creole seasoning would make this salmon entree a family favorite.

"Feel free to season the salmon with a blend of your favorite herbs and spices, or even just a sprinkle of paprika," Florine suggests. "Fresh lemon would give it a tangy twist. You could also add a dollop of tartar sauce or some melted garlic butter."

Being in a pickle with prolific cucumbers one summer, Florine was inspired to toss together a cool side dish. "Tomato Cucumber Salad is a nice complement to zesty entrees like my salmon fillets, as well as barbecued meats and poultry," she notes.

To add even more color and crunch to the salad, toss in some bell pepper strips and croutons just before serving, Florine suggests. Or, whip up an easy homemade vinaigrette ahead of time to give the vegetable medley extra zip.

For dessert, the convenience of canned fruit often comes in handy. "Our part of Texas is famous for its juicy peaches, so I use fresh fruit when I can," Florine notes. "But when I'm crunched for time, canned fruit is a welcome option. A Mixed Fruit Cup is a pretty and refreshing way to end a meal.

"A dollop of real whipped cream and a cherry on top make the cups look and taste extra special. For a switch, try dressing up the dessert with a sprinkling of nutmeg or a scoop of ice cream."

You could even serve these cups as a sweet side dish for breakfast or brunch, Florine adds. "Or, use the recipe to top off an angel food trifle."

In her free time, Florine enjoys performing with a local church chorus in concerts all around the community. And that seems only natural for a busy cook who always keeps things humming in the kitchen!

Creole Salmon Fillets

PREP: 10 min. **BROIL:** 10 min.

- 4 **teaspoons Creole seasoning**
- 2 **garlic cloves, minced**
- 2 **teaspoons pepper**
- 4 **salmon fillets (6 ounces *each*)**
- 1/4 **cup minced fresh parsley**

In a large resealable plastic bag, combine the first three ingredients. Add salmon; shake to coat. Place salmon on a broiler pan or baking sheet.

Broil 6 in. from the heat for 10-14 minutes or until the fish flakes easily with a fork. Sprinkle with fresh parsley. **Yield:** 4 servings.

Tomato Cucumber Salad

PREP/TOTAL TIME: 10 min.

- 2 **medium cucumbers, cut into 1/4-inch slices**
- 1 **large tomato, cut into wedges**
- 1 **small red onion, cut into thin strips**
- 1/4 **cup creamy Italian, ranch *or* salad dressing of your choice**

In a bowl, combine the vegetables. Add dressing; toss to coat. **Yield:** 4 servings.

Mixed Fruit Cup

PREP/TOTAL TIME: 5 min.

- 1 **can (15-1/4 ounces) sliced peaches, drained**
- 1 **can (15 ounces) fruit cocktail, drained**

Whipped cream

Spoon peaches and fruit cocktail into individual dishes. Top with whipped cream. **Yield:** 4 servings.

FRUIT FLEXIBILITY. Feel free to experiment with whatever types of canned fruit your family prefers when you're preparing Mixed Fruit Cup (recipe above). For example, try canned pears, pineapple or mandarin oranges. Or, if you have a little extra time on your hands, cut up and mix in any fresh fruit you may have in the kitchen.

Skillet Dish Makes For a Filling Meal

IF YOU CAN fix a fast meal at a moment's notice, you have the makings of a farm wife, Rose Purrington of Windom, Minnesota says.

"When we're especially busy, dinner can be anytime between 6 p.m. and 3 o'clock in the morning," she relates from the soybean and corn farm she runs with her husband, Doug.

"My shopping list usually includes things like tires, plugs and tractor parts in one column—and ingredients for speedy suppers in the other!"

Luckily, Rose is outstanding in her field when it comes to creating family-pleasing menus such as the one featured here. Half an hour is all you'll need to get this filling main dish, slaw side and yummy dessert on the dinner table.

"The mix of ground beef, beans and barbecue sauce in Bean and Beef Skillet is a mainstay for us," Rose notes. "Often, I'll brown the meat with the sauce and freeze it in a resealable bag. Later, I thaw it, add the beans, cook and serve.

"My favorite way of eating this skillet is scooping it up with tortilla chips. Or, you could crumble corn chips over the top."

If your family prefers burritos, Rose adds, simply mix the meat and beans with taco sauce, spoon it onto tortillas and roll them up.

However you serve the main dish, Rose's Tangy Cabbage Slaw makes a great accompaniment. "It's always in demand at home and for potluck functions," she notes. "People often comment on the crunchy texture and the sweet-and-sour zip. Plus, the recipe can easily be prepared ahead of time."

To give the cabbage salad a different twist, Rose adds, use beef ramen noodles and toss in some sesame or sunflower seeds.

Her Pudding Parfaits recipe, a comfortingly creamy dessert, is literally "kid stuff." "Our daughters, Erin and Shannon, who are now grown, have always adored these make-your-own treats," Rose relates.

"With layers of vanilla pudding, cherry pie filling and crunchy granola, they're a fun way to end a meal. You could also make the parfaits with a different flavor of pudding, such as chocolate or butterscotch. And in place of the granola, try adding cookie crumbs or your favorite nuts."

In her time off from chores at home and around the farm, Rose is cultivating a career as a substitute teacher. "I'm also a collector of stamps, rocks, angels, Depression glass, Santas," she lists, "and quick recipes for family-filling food, of course!"

Bean and Beef Skillet

PREP: 5 min. **COOK:** 15 min.

- 1 **pound ground beef**
- 1 **medium onion, chopped**
- 1 **can (28 ounces) baked beans**
- 1/4 **cup barbecue sauce *or* ketchup**
- 1 **cup (4 ounces) shredded cheddar cheese**

In a large skillet, cook beef and onion over medium heat until meat is no longer pink; drain. Stir in the beans and sauce; heat through. Sprinkle with cheese; cover and cook on low until cheese is melted. **Yield:** 4 servings.

Tangy Cabbage Slaw

PREP/TOTAL TIME: 10 min.

- 1 **package (3 ounces) chicken ramen noodles**
- 3-3/4 **cups coleslaw mix**
- 1/3 **cup slivered almonds**
- 3 **tablespoons sliced green onions**
- 1/2 **cup vegetable oil**
- 1/3 **cup white wine vinegar *or* cider vinegar**
- 3 **tablespoons sugar**

In a large bowl, break noodles into small pieces; set seasoning packet aside. Add the coleslaw mix, almonds and onions. In a small bowl, combine the oil, vinegar, sugar and contents of seasoning packet. Pour over coleslaw mixture and toss to coat; serve immediately. Refrigerate leftovers. **Yield:** 4-6 servings.

Pudding Parfaits

PREP/TOTAL TIME: 15 min.

- 2 **cups cold milk**
- 1 **package (3.4 ounces) instant vanilla pudding mix**
- 1 **can (21 ounces) cherry pie filling**
- 1 **cup granola cereal**
- **Whipped topping, optional**

In a mixing bowl, beat milk and pudding mix on low speed for 2 minutes or until thickened. Refrigerate for 10 minutes. Spoon half of the pudding into four parfait glasses. Top each with 3 tablespoons pie filling and 2 tablespoons granola. Repeat layers. Garnish with whipped topping if desired. **Yield:** 4 servings.

Stir Up a Super-Fast Family Supper

SPEEDING tasty meals to the table is child's play for Carly Carter of Nashville, Tennessee. In fact, she could probably write the book on it!

"In addition to my number-one job as a wife and mother, I write articles on children and family life," she relates. "I love to cook, so a favorite topic of mine is fun and family time in the kitchen."

It's evident by the fast-to-fix dinner featured here that Carly's recipes are every bit as good as her words. The complete menu she shares from her collection is ready to eat in just half an hour.

Her Chicken Stir-Fry Bake took shape on the spur of the moment. "One night, while trying to tend to both supper and our young son, I opted to use frozen vegetables in my chicken stir-fry," Carly relates.

"Not wanting to stand watch next to the stovetop, I baked the entree in the oven instead. Guests say it tastes like it's hot from the skillet."

For more color, you could quickly brown turkey or chicken strips in a skillet before baking the stir-fry, Carly notes. "Or, if you want a special touch for guests, add red pepper as a pretty garnish."

Carly also makes it easy to add a homemade touch to salad. "As a switch from bottled dressing, I whisk together my own sweet and tangy, honey-mustard concoction," she says. "I love the flavor it brings to ordinary salad greens and tomatoes.

"If you like, adjust the dressing by substituting yellow mustard for the Dijon. You could also add extra zip with a sprinkling of ground pepper."

When it comes to putting together a fast but family-pleasing dessert, Carly relies on convenience products. Instant pudding mix is the "secret ingredient" that makes her delightful Chocolate Fudge Mousse such a breeze to prepare.

"It's so much quicker and easier to whip up than a traditional mousse," she notes. "But it's equally fluffy and luscious, so it satisfies even my husband David's rather large sweet tooth!"

To make this decadent treat even more tempting, add chocolate chips or raspberries as a finishing touch, Carly suggests. Or, if you want to cut back on calories, choose low-fat pudding.

Carly's done-in-a-dash dinner offers another big advantage for busy cooks—make-ahead convenience. And she often takes advantage of it.

"Because our son is an early riser, I frequently assemble this entire meal in the morning and pop it in the refrigerator. Then, at dinnertime, it's just a matter of baking the main course and serving."

Chicken Stir-Fry Bake

PREP: 5 min. **COOK:** 25 min.

- 2 cups uncooked instant rice
- 1 can (8 ounces) sliced water chestnuts, drained
- 2 cups cubed cooked chicken
- 1 package (16 ounces) frozen stir-fry vegetables, thawed
- 1 can (14-1/2 ounces) chicken broth
- 1/4 cup soy sauce
- 1 garlic clove, minced
- 1/2 to 3/4 teaspoon ground ginger

Place rice in an 11-in. x 7-in. x 2-in. baking dish. Layer with water chestnuts, chicken and vegetables. Combine the remaining ingredients; pour over chicken and vegetables. Cover and bake at 375° for 25 minutes or until rice is tender. **Yield:** 4 servings.

Honey-Mustard Tossed Salad

PREP/TOTAL TIME: 15 min.

- 1/4 cup buttermilk
- 1/4 cup sour cream
- 2 tablespoons Dijon mustard
- 2 tablespoons honey
- 1-1/2 teaspoons dried minced onion
- 1 teaspoon dried parsley flakes

Torn salad greens and tomato wedges

For the salad dressing, in a small bowl, whisk together the first six ingredients. Serve dressing over the salad greens and tomatoes. Refrigerate leftover dressing. **Yield:** 3/4 cup dressing.

Chocolate Fudge Mousse

PREP/TOTAL TIME: 10 min.

- 2 cups cold milk
- 1 package (3.9 ounces) instant chocolate pudding mix
- 1/4 cup hot fudge ice cream topping
- 3 cups whipped topping

In a mixing bowl, beat milk and pudding mix on low speed for 2 minutes. Stir in the hot fudge topping. Fold in whipped topping until blended. Pour mousse into dessert dishes. Chill until serving. **Yield:** 6 servings.

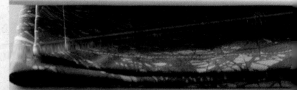

Cooking Lighter

Whether you're following a special diet or just trying to eat healthier, this trimmed-down chapter is the one for you. You'll find lightened-up dishes that will take you all the way from breakfast to dinner—deliciously!

✓ **All recipes in this chapter include Nutrition Facts. Most include Diabetic Exchanges.**

GUILT-FREE FARE. Clockwise from top left: Lentil Soup (p. 270), Wild Rice Salad (p. 274), Calico Pepper Frittata (p. 270), Fresh Asparagus with Pecans (p. 278) and Seafood Salad Pitas (p. 267).

Cashew Turkey Salad Sandwiches

(Pictured above)

PREP/TOTAL TIME: 15 min.

One bite and you're sure to be hooked on this sweet and savory sandwich. It's protein-packed, so you can feel good about it while you munch. —Mary Wilhelm, Sparta, Wisconsin

> 1-1/2 **cups cubed cooked turkey breast**
> 1/4 **cup thinly sliced celery**
> 2 **tablespoons chopped dried apricots**
> 2 **tablespoons chopped unsalted cashews**
> 1 **green onion, chopped**
> 1/4 **cup reduced-fat mayonnaise**
> 2 **tablespoons reduced-fat plain yogurt**
> 1/4 **teaspoon salt**
> 1/4 **teaspoon pepper**
> 4 **lettuce leaves**
> 8 **slices pumpernickel bread**

In a small bowl, combine the turkey, celery, apricots, cashews and onion. Combine the mayonnaise, yogurt, salt and pepper; add to turkey mixture and stir to coat.

Place a lettuce leaf on half of the bread slices; top each with 1/2 cup turkey salad and remaining bread. **Yield:** 4 servings.

Nutrition Facts: 1 sandwich equals 298 calories, 9 g fat (2 g saturated fat), 51 mg cholesterol, 664 mg sodium, 32 g carbohydrate, 4 g fiber, 22 g protein. **Diabetic Exchanges:** 2 starch, 2 very lean meat, 1-1/2 fat.

Make-Ahead Mashed Potatoes

PREP: 40 min. + chilling **BAKE:** 50 min.

This lightened-up holiday staple is such a time-saver on your special days—no more frantically whipping the potatoes while hungry family members and guests hang around the kitchen!
—Marty Rummel, Trout Lake, Washington

> 5 **pounds potatoes, peeled and cut into wedges**
> 1 **package (8 ounces) reduced-fat cream cheese, cubed**
> 2 **egg whites, beaten**
> 1 **cup (8 ounces) reduced-fat sour cream**
> 2 **teaspoons onion powder**
> 1 **teaspoon salt**
> 1/2 **teaspoon pepper**
> 1 **tablespoon butter, melted**

Place potatoes in a large saucepan and cover with water. Bring to a boil. Reduce heat; cover and cook for 15-20 minutes or until tender. Drain.

In a large bowl, mash potatoes with cream cheese. Combine the egg whites, sour cream, onion powder, salt and pepper; stir into potatoes until blended. Transfer to a greased 3-qt. baking dish. Drizzle with butter. Cover and refrigerate overnight.

Remove from the refrigerator 30 minutes before baking. Cover and bake at 350° for 50 minutes. Uncover; bake 5-10 minutes longer or until a thermometer reads 160°. **Yield:** 12 servings (3/4 cup each).

Nutrition Facts: 3/4 cup equals 220 calories, 7 g fat (4 g saturated fat), 22 mg cholesterol, 316 mg sodium, 32 g carbohydrate, 3 g fiber, 7 g protein. **Diabetic Exchanges:** 2 starch, 1 fat.

Moroccan Salmon

PREP: 15 min. **BAKE:** 25 min.

If you're trying to add more fish to your diet, consider this tasty, simple main dish from our Test Kitchen. The baked salmon fillets are topped with sauteed onions, tomatoes, golden raisins and a cinnamon-spice mixture, transforming an ordinary weeknight meal into a dinnertime adventure.

> 2 **cups sliced onions, separated into rings**
> 1 **tablespoon canola oil**
> 2 **cups sliced plum tomatoes**
> 1/4 **cup golden raisins**
> 4 **garlic cloves, minced**
> 1/2 **teaspoon salt**
> 1/2 **teaspoon ground cumin**
> 1/2 **teaspoon ground turmeric**
> 1/8 **teaspoon ground cinnamon**
> 4 **salmon fillets (4 ounces *each*)**
> **Hot cooked couscous, optional**

In a large nonstick skillet, saute onions in oil for 5 minutes or until tender. Add the tomatoes, raisins, garlic and seasonings; cook and stir for 5 minutes.

Place salmon in a 13-in. x 9-in. baking dish coated with cooking spray. Top with onion mixture. Cover and bake at 375° for 25-30 minutes or until fish flakes easily with a fork. Serve with couscous if desired. **Yield:** 4 servings.

Nutrition Facts: 1 serving (calculated without couscous) equals 311 calories, 16 g fat (3 g saturated fat), 67 mg cholesterol, 374 mg sodium, 17 g carbohydrate, 3 g fiber, 24 g protein.

Seafood Salad Pitas

(Pictured below and on page 264)

PREP/TOTAL TIME: 20 min.

You can make this lovely, interesting sandwich as a refreshing light lunch…or pair it with a hearty soup for a change-of-pace supper.   *—Linda Evancoe-Coble, Leola, Pennsylvania*

      2 cups chopped imitation crabmeat (about
          10 ounces)
   1/2 pound cooked medium shrimp, peeled,
          deveined and chopped (about 1 cup)
      2 celery ribs, chopped
   1/2 cup thinly sliced green onions
   3/4 cup fat-free mayonnaise
   3/4 teaspoon seafood seasoning
   1/4 teaspoon salt
   1/8 teaspoon pepper
      4 whole wheat pita breads (6 inches), halved

In a large bowl, combine the crab, shrimp, celery and onions. Stir in the mayonnaise, seafood seasoning, salt and pepper. Cover and refrigerate for at least 2 hours. Spoon into pita halves. **Yield:** 8 servings.

Nutrition Facts: 1 filled pita half equals 162 calories, 2 g fat (trace saturated fat), 27 mg cholesterol, 755 mg sodium, 28 g carbohydrate, 3 g fiber, 10 g protein.
Diabetic Exchanges: 2 starch, 1 very lean meat.

Curried Turkey Vegetable Soup

(Pictured above)

PREP: 15 min. **COOK:** 20 min.

Chock-full of veggies, this aromatic soup has the perfect hint of curry. It's a delicious way to use up leftover holiday turkey.
      —Virginia C. Anthony, Jacksonville, Florida

      2 medium onions, chopped
      2 tablespoons canola oil
      2 to 3 tablespoons all-purpose flour
      1 teaspoon curry powder
      3 cups reduced-sodium chicken broth
      1 cup diced red potatoes
      1 celery rib, sliced
   1/2 cup thinly sliced fresh carrots
      2 tablespoons minced fresh parsley
1-1/2 teaspoons minced fresh sage
      2 cups cubed cooked turkey breast
1-1/2 cups fat-free half-and-half
      1 package (9 ounces) fresh baby spinach,
          coarsely chopped
   1/4 teaspoon salt
   1/4 teaspoon pepper

In a Dutch oven, saute onions in oil until tender. Stir in flour and curry until blended. Gradually stir in broth. Add the potatoes, celery, carrots, parsley and sage. Bring to a boil. Reduce heat; cover and simmer for 10-12 minutes or until vegetables are tender.

Stir in the turkey, half-and-half, spinach, salt and pepper. Cook and stir until spinach is wilted and soup is heated through. **Yield:** 6 servings (2 quarts).

Nutrition Facts: 1-1/3 cups equals 219 calories, 6 g fat (1 g saturated fat), 40 mg cholesterol, 534 mg sodium, 20 g carbohydrate, 3 g fiber, 20 g protein. **Diabetic Exchanges:** 2 very lean meat, 1 starch, 1 vegetable, 1 fat.

Holiday Brussels Sprouts

(Pictured above at right)

PREP/TOTAL TIME: 25 min.

Peas and sprouts mixed with crunchy celery and flavorful bacon make this an appealing side dish. I often add it to my holiday menus. —Jodie Beckman, Council Bluffs, Iowa

> **1** package (16 ounces) frozen brussels sprouts
> **1** package (10 ounces) frozen peas
> **2** medium celery ribs, chopped
> **2** tablespoons butter
> **2** bacon strips, cooked and crumbled
> **2** tablespoons minced chives

Cook brussels sprouts and peas according to package directions.

Meanwhile, in a small skillet, saute celery in butter until crisp-tender. Transfer to a large bowl; add bacon and chives. Drain brussels sprouts and peas; add to celery mixture and stir until blended. **Yield:** 6 servings.

Nutrition Facts: 2/3 cup equals 115 calories, 5 g fat (3 g saturated fat), 12 mg cholesterol, 147 mg sodium, 13 g carbohydrate, 5 g fiber, 6 g protein. **Diabetic Exchanges:** 2 vegetable, 1 fat.

Pork Tenderloin With Fig-Orange Glaze

(Pictured above at left)

PREP: 40 min. + chilling **COOK:** 30 min.

Here's an entree that's low in fat and calories—but doesn't make you feel deprived! The sauce is bursting with fig flavor, seasonings and citrus flair. —Kathy Pettit, Los Angeles, California

> **1-1/2** teaspoons garlic powder
> **3/4** teaspoon pepper
> **1/2** teaspoon salt
> **1/2** teaspoon fennel seed, crushed
> **1/2** teaspoon rubbed sage
> **1/2** teaspoon dried thyme
> **1/8** teaspoon cayenne pepper
> **2** pork tenderloins (3/4 pound *each*)

GLAZE:
> **2/3** cup reduced-sodium chicken broth
> **2** tablespoons brown sugar
> **1** tablespoon molasses
> **1/2** teaspoon balsamic vinegar
> **1/4** teaspoon ground cumin

1/8 teaspoon kosher salt

Dash white pepper

Dash ground cinnamon

1/2 cup chopped orange segments

10 dried figs

1/4 cup water

1 tablespoon olive oil

In a small bowl, combine the first seven ingredients; rub over pork. Cover and refrigerate for at least 2 hours.

For glaze, in a large saucepan, combine the broth, brown sugar, molasses, vinegar and seasonings. Stir in orange and figs. Cook and stir over medium heat until mixture comes to a boil. Reduce heat; simmer, uncovered, for 15-18 minutes or until figs are tender. Stir in water; cool slightly. Transfer to a blender; cover and process until smooth.

In a large nonstick skillet, brown pork in oil on all sides. Spread with half of fig-orange glaze. Place pork on a rack in a shallow roasting pan lined with foil.

Bake at 350° for 25-30 minutes or until a meat thermometer reads 160°, basting occasionally with remaining glaze. Let stand for 10 minutes before slicing. **Yield:** 6 servings.

Nutrition Facts: 3 ounces cooked pork equals 233 calories, 6 g fat (2 g saturated fat), 63 mg cholesterol, 377 mg sodium, 19 g carbohydrate, 2 g fiber, 24 g protein. **Diabetic Exchanges:** 3 lean meat, 1 starch, 1/2 fat.

Mediterranean Bulgur Salad

PREP: 15 min. **COOK:** 20 min.

With this recipe from our Test Kitchen staff, you don't have to choose between healthy eating and taste. Bulgur, beans, cherry tomatoes, toasted pine nuts and olive oil all team up in this vegetarian main-dish salad with delicious results.

3 cups vegetable broth

1-1/2 cups uncooked bulgur

6 tablespoons olive oil

2 tablespoons lemon juice

2 tablespoons minced fresh parsley

1/2 teaspoon salt

1/4 teaspoon pepper

1 can (15 ounces) garbanzo beans *or* chickpeas, rinsed and drained

2 cups halved cherry tomatoes

1 cup chopped cucumber

8 green onions, sliced

1 package (4 ounces) crumbled feta cheese

1/2 cup pine nuts, toasted

In a large saucepan, bring broth and bulgur to a boil over high heat. Reduce heat; cover and simmer for 20 minutes or until tender and broth is almost absorbed. Remove from the heat; let stand at room temperature, uncovered, until broth is absorbed.

In a jar with a tight-fitting lid, combine the oil, lemon juice, parsley, salt and pepper; shake well. In a large serving bowl, combine the bulgur, beans, tomatoes, cucumber and onions. Drizzle with dressing; toss to coat. Sprinkle with the feta cheese and pine nuts. **Yield:** 9 servings

Editor's Note: Look for bulgur in the cereal, rice or organic food aisle of your grocery store.

Nutrition Facts: 1 cup equals 298 calories, 17 g fat (3 g saturated fat), 7 mg cholesterol, 657 mg sodium, 31 g carbohydrate, 8 g fiber, 10 g protein.

Salsa Bean Dip

(Pictured below)

PREP/TOTAL TIME: 10 min.

Served with low-fat chips or fresh veggies, this easy dip is perfect for your health-conscious family members and guests. Pineapple salsa adds sweetness to the smooth blend. For a different twist, substitute peach salsa. —Beverly Smith, Ferndale, Washington

1/2 cup pineapple salsa

1 tablespoon lemon juice

1 can (15 ounces) garbanzo beans *or* chickpeas, rinsed and drained

1/4 cup minced fresh parsley

1/4 teaspoon pepper

Tortilla chips

In a food processor or blender, combine the salsa, lemon juice, beans, parsley and pepper; cover and process until smooth. Transfer to a serving dish. Serve with tortilla chips. Refrigerate leftovers. **Yield:** 1-1/2 cups.

Nutrition Facts: 2 tablespoons dip (calculated without chips) equals 39 calories, 1 g fat (trace saturated fat), 0 cholesterol, 77 mg sodium, 7 g carbohydrate, 2 g fiber, 1 g protein. **Diabetic Exchange:** 1/2 starch.

Lentil Soup

(Pictured below and on page 264)

PREP: 30 min. **COOK:** 40 min.

Legume lovers can easily fill up on this substantial soup without expanding their waistlines. Lentils lend both taste and texture to this stockpot. —*Dorothy Webb, Estacada, Oregon*

- **2 cups sliced fresh carrots**
- **2 celery ribs, chopped**
- **1 large onion, chopped**
- **1 garlic clove, minced**
- **2 tablespoons butter**
- **7 cups reduced-sodium chicken broth *or* vegetable broth**
- **1-1/2 cups dried lentils, rinsed**
- **3 tablespoons medium pearl barley**
- **1-1/2 cups chopped fresh tomatoes**
- **2 tablespoons lemon juice**
- **4-1/2 teaspoons molasses**
- **1 tablespoon red wine vinegar**
- **1/2 teaspoon pepper**
- **Dash *each* dried thyme, basil and oregano**

In a Dutch oven, saute the carrots, celery, onion and garlic in butter until crisp-tender. Add the broth, lentils and barley; bring to a boil. Reduce heat; cover and simmer for 25-30 minutes or until lentils and barley are almost tender.

Stir in the remaining ingredients. Bring to a boil. Reduce the heat; cover and simmer for 15 minutes or until the lentils and barley are tender. **Yield:** 8 servings (2 quarts).

Nutrition Facts: 1 cup equals 219 calories, 3 g fat (2 g saturated fat), 8 mg cholesterol, 601 mg sodium, 35 g carbohydrate, 14 g fiber, 14 g protein. **Diabetic Exchanges:** 2 starch, 1 lean meat, 1 vegetable, 1/2 fat.

Calico Pepper Frittata

(Pictured above and on page 264)

PREP: 20 min. **COOK:** 10 min.

This garden–fresh frittata has all–day appeal. I've served it for breakfast, brunch, lunch and dinner with Italian bread. Because it's made in a skillet, there's no need to heat the oven. —*Loretta Kelcinski, Kunkletown, Pennsylvania*

- **1 medium green pepper, chopped**
- **1 medium sweet red pepper, chopped**
- **1 jalapeno pepper, seeded and chopped**
- **1 medium onion, chopped**
- **1 garlic clove, minced**
- **1 tablespoon olive oil**
- **5 eggs**
- **1-1/4 cups egg substitute**
- **1 tablespoon grated Romano cheese**
- **1/2 teaspoon salt**
- **1/8 teaspoon pepper**

In a large nonstick skillet, saute peppers, onion and garlic in oil until crisp-tender. In a large bowl, whisk eggs and egg substitute. Pour into the skillet. Sprinkle with cheese, salt and pepper.

As the eggs set, lift edges, letting uncooked portion flow underneath. Cook until eggs are completely set, about 8-10 minutes. Cut into wedges. **Yield:** 4 servings.

Editor's Note: When cutting or seeding hot peppers, use rubber or plastic gloves to protect your hands. Avoid touching your face.

Nutrition Facts: 1 wedge equals 201 calories, 10 g fat (3 g saturated fat), 268 mg cholesterol, 559 mg sodium, 10 g carbohydrate, 2 g fiber, 17 g protein. **Diabetic Exchanges:** 2 lean meat, 2 vegetable, 1 fat.

4 hours or until set. **Yield:** 6 servings.

Nutrition Facts: 1 serving equals 95 calories, trace fat (trace saturated fat), 0 cholesterol, 83 mg sodium, 13 g carbohydrate, 2 g fiber, 2 g protein. **Diabetic Exchange:** 1 fruit.

Avocado-Orange Spinach Toss

(*Pictured below*)

PREP/TOTAL TIME: 20 min.

Baby spinach, avocado and a burst of citrus combine in this springtime salad. If you like, substitute fresh orange slices for the mandarin oranges. —*Margaret O'Bryon, Bel Air, Maryland*

    1/4 cup orange juice
  4-1/2 teaspoons lemon juice
      1 tablespoon sugar
      1 tablespoon white wine vinegar
      1 tablespoon canola oil
    1/4 teaspoon grated orange peel
Dash salt
      6 cups fresh baby spinach
      1 can (11 ounces) mandarin oranges, drained
      1 small cucumber, thinly sliced
    1/2 medium ripe avocado, peeled and sliced

For dressing, in a small bowl, combine the first seven ingredients.

Place the spinach in a large salad bowl; top with oranges, cucumber and avocado. Drizzle with dressing and gently toss to coat. **Yield:** 8 servings.

Nutrition Facts: 1-1/4 cups equals 71 calories, 4 g fat (trace saturated fat), 0 cholesterol, 38 mg sodium, 9 g carbohydrate, 1 g fiber, 1 g protein. **Diabetic Exchanges:** 1 fat, 1/2 fruit.

Sangria Gelatin Dessert

(*Pictured above*)

PREP: 15 min. + chilling

Our Test Kitchen home economists came up with this festive finale. White wine gives the gelatin a refreshing twist, but feel free to substitute white grape juice instead.

      1 package (.3 ounce) sugar-free lemon gelatin
      1 package (.3 ounce) sugar-free raspberry gelatin
  1-1/2 cups boiling water
      1 cup cold water
      1 cup white wine
      1 can (11 ounces) mandarin oranges, drained
      1 cup fresh raspberries
      1 cup green grapes, halved

In a large bowl, dissolve gelatins in boiling water. Let stand for 10 minutes. Stir in cold water and the wine; refrigerate for 45 minutes or until partially set.

Fold in the oranges, raspberries and grapes. Transfer to six large wine glasses, 1 cup in each. Refrigerate for

AVOCADO ADVANCE. To quickly ripen an avocado for use in a recipe, place it in a paper bag with an apple. Poke the bag with a toothpick in several spots and leave it at room temperature. The avocado should be ripe in 1 to 3 days.

Black Bean Asparagus Salad

(Pictured below)

PREP: 10 min. **COOK:** 5 min.

For a change from ordinary steamed asparagus, try this different salad idea. The black beans, red pepper, cilantro and cumin give it a Southwestern twist—always popular at potlucks and parties. I also serve this medley with chicken or cheese enchiladas.
—Laurie Jackson, Falcon, Colorado

   1 **pound fresh asparagus, trimmed and cut into 1-inch pieces**
   1 **can (15 ounces) black beans, rinsed and drained**
   1 **medium sweet red pepper, cut into 1/2-inch pieces**
   1 **tablespoon finely chopped onion**
   3 **tablespoons olive oil**
   2 **tablespoons cider vinegar**
   1 **tablespoon minced fresh cilantro**
   1 **garlic clove, minced**
   1/2 **teaspoon salt**
   1/2 **teaspoon ground cumin**
Dash pepper

Place 1/2 in. of water in a large saucepan; add the asparagus. Bring to a boil. Reduce the heat; cover and simmer for 4-5 minutes or until crisp-tender. Drain.

In a bowl, combine the asparagus, beans, red pepper and onion. In a small bowl, whisk the oil, cider vinegar, cilantro, garlic, salt, cumin and pepper. Pour over the vegetables and toss to coat. Cover and refrigerate for at least 2 hours before serving. **Yield:** 8 servings.

Nutrition Facts: 1/2 cup equals 100 calories, 5 g fat (1 g saturated fat), 0 cholesterol, 252 mg sodium, 10 g carbohydrate, 3 g fiber, 3 g protein. **Diabetic Exchanges:** 2 vegetable, 1 fat.

Avocado Tomato Salad

(Pictured above)

PREP/TOTAL TIME: 15 min.

This simple salad is terrific with any kind of Mexican food and makes a super appetizer when spooned on a toasted baguette. The recipe combines fresh tomatoes with avocados, a source of healthy fat.
—Ginger Burow, Fredericksburg, Texas

   4 **cups chopped tomatoes**
   1/2 **cup chopped green pepper**
   1/4 **cup chopped onion**
   1/2 **teaspoon salt**
   1/8 **teaspoon pepper**
   2 **medium ripe avocados, peeled and cubed**
   1 **tablespoon lime juice**

In a bowl, combine the tomatoes, green pepper, onion, salt and pepper. Place the avocados in another bowl; sprinkle with lime juice and toss gently to coat. Fold into the tomato mixture. Serve immediately. **Yield:** 6-8 servings.

Nutrition Facts: 3/4 cup equals 134 calories, 10 g fat (2 g saturated fat), 0 cholesterol, 215 mg sodium, 11 g carbohydrate, 5 g fiber, 2 g protein.

Flaxseed Bread

PREP: 40 min. **BAKE:** 35 min.

Every slice of this hearty, whole grain bread is so satisfying. It's among my all-time favorites! The flaxseed gives the loaf a nutty texture.
—Jennifer Niemi, Kingston, Nova Scotia

1-1/2 **cups whole wheat flour**
1-1/2 **to 2 cups all-purpose flour**
   1 **package (1/4 ounce) active dry yeast**
   1 **teaspoon salt**

1-1/2 cups fat-free milk
1/4 cup packed brown sugar
2 tablespoons honey
2 tablespoons plus 1-1/2 teaspoons butter, divided
1/2 cup ground flaxseed
1/2 cup flaxseed

In a large mixing bowl, combine whole wheat flour, 1 cup all-purpose flour, yeast and salt. In a large saucepan, heat the milk, brown sugar, honey and 2 tablespoons butter to 120°-130°. Add to dry ingredients; beat until smooth. Stir in ground flaxseed and flaxseed until smooth. Stir in enough remaining all-purpose flour to form a firm dough.

Turn onto a lightly floured surface; knead until smooth and elastic, about 6-8 minutes. Place in a large bowl coated with cooking spray, turning once to coat top. Cover and let rise in a warm place until doubled, about 1 hour.

Punch dough down. Turn onto a lightly floured surface. Shape into a loaf; place in a 9-in. x 5-in. x 3-in. loaf pan coated with cooking spray. Cover and let rise until doubled, about 30 minutes.

Bake at 375° for 35-40 minutes or until golden brown. Remove from pan to a wire rack. Melt remaining butter; brush over bread. Cool. **Yield:** 1 loaf (16 slices).

Nutrition Facts: 1 slice equals 169 calories, 5 g fat (2 g saturated fat), 5 mg cholesterol, 183 mg sodium, 27 g carbohydrate, 4 g fiber, 6 g protein. **Diabetic Exchanges:** 2 starch, 1 fat.

Colorful Vegetable Medley

PREP: 10 min. **COOK:** 5 min.

Here's a tasty way to get your daily veggies and a quick side dish for any meal. Our Test Kitchen sprinkled this crisp–tender mixture with fresh parsley, lemon juice and coriander.

2 medium yellow summer squash, sliced
4 teaspoons olive oil
1-1/2 cups fresh sugar snap peas
1-1/2 cups halved cherry tomatoes
3 tablespoons minced fresh parsley
2 tablespoons lemon juice
1/2 teaspoon ground coriander
1/4 teaspoon salt
1/8 teaspoon pepper

In a large nonstick skillet, saute squash in oil for 3 minutes. Add peas and tomatoes; saute 2-3 minutes longer or until crisp-tender. Sprinkle with parsley, lemon juice, coriander, salt and pepper; toss to coat. **Yield:** 4 servings.

Nutrition Facts: 1 cup equals 101 calories, 5 g fat (1 g saturated fat), 0 cholesterol, 159 mg sodium, 12 g carbohydrate, 4 g fiber, 4 g protein. **Diabetic Exchanges:** 2 vegetable, 1 fat.

Baked Veggie Chips

(Pictured below)

PREP: 15 min. **BAKE:** 20 min.

Slices of colorful roasted root vegetables make a fun, festive snack or side. These perfectly seasoned chips are so good, they don't even need dip! —Christine Schenher, Ypsilanti, Michigan

1/2 pound fresh beets (about 2 medium)
1 medium potato
1 medium sweet potato
1 medium parsnip
2 tablespoons canola oil
2 tablespoons grated Parmesan cheese
1/2 teaspoon salt
1/2 teaspoon garlic powder
1/2 teaspoon dried oregano
Dash pepper

Peel vegetables and cut into 1/8-in. slices. Place in a large bowl. Drizzle with oil. Combine the remaining ingredients; sprinkle over vegetables and toss to coat.

Arrange in a single layer in two ungreased 15-in. x 10-in. x 1-in. baking pans. Bake at 375° for 15-20 minutes or until golden brown, turning once. **Yield:** 3-1/2 cups.

Nutrition Facts: 1/2 cup equals 108 calories, 5 g fat (1 g saturated fat), 1 mg cholesterol, 220 mg sodium, 15 g carbohydrate, 2 g fiber, 2 g protein. **Diabetic Exchanges:** 1 starch, 1 fat.

Wild Rice Salad

(Pictured above and on page 264)

PREP: 1-1/4 hours + chilling

Here's a flavorful dish ideal for holidays or anytime. It tastes great chilled but is just as good at room temperature or warmed up in the microwave. —Robin Thompson, Roseville, California

>   3 cups water
>   1 cup uncooked wild rice
>   2 chicken bouillon cubes
> 4-1/2 teaspoons butter
>   1 cup cut fresh green beans
>   1 cup cubed cooked chicken breast
>   1 medium tomato, chopped
>   1 bunch green onions, sliced
>   1/4 cup rice vinegar
>   1 tablespoon sesame oil
>   1 garlic clove, minced
>   1/2 teaspoon dried tarragon
>   1/4 teaspoon pepper

In a large saucepan, bring the water, rice, bouillon and butter to a boil. Reduce heat; cover and simmer for 45-60 minutes or until rice is tender. Drain if necessary; transfer to a large bowl and cool completely.

Place green beans in a steamer basket; place in a small saucepan over 1 in. of water. Bring to a boil; cover and steam for 8-10 minutes or until crisp-tender.

Add the chicken, tomato, onions and green beans to the rice; stir until blended. Combine the remaining ingredients; drizzle over mixture and toss to coat. Refrigerate until chilled. **Yield:** 4 servings.

Nutrition Facts: 1-1/2 cups equals 330 calories, 10 g

fat (4 g saturated fat), 39 mg cholesterol, 618 mg sodium, 43 g carbohydrate, 4 g fiber, 18 g protein. **Diabetic Exchanges:** 2 starch, 2 fat, 1 very lean meat, 1 vegetable.

Scotch Broth

PREP: 2 hrs. 15 min. **BAKE:** 1 hr. 15 min.

Pair your favorite bread with this luscious concoction of lamb, vegetables and barley, and you'll have all a hungry body needs. I skim the fat to suit our lighter way of eating.
—Kelsey Hamilton, Highland Park, New Jersey

>   1 lamb shank (about 1 pound)
>   2 teaspoons canola oil
>   4 cups water
>   2 cans (14-1/2 ounces *each*) reduced-sodium
>   beef broth
>   2 whole cloves
>   1 medium onion, halved
>   1 medium carrot, halved
>   1 celery rib, halved
>   1 bay leaf
>   1/4 cup minced fresh parsley
>   1/4 teaspoon dried rosemary, crushed
>   1/4 teaspoon dried thyme
>   1/4 teaspoon whole peppercorns
> **SOUP:**
>   1/3 cup medium pearl barley
> 1-1/2 cups julienned peeled turnips (1-inch pieces)
>   1 cup coarsely chopped carrots
>   1 medium leek (white portion only), thinly
>   sliced
>   1/4 teaspoon salt
>   1/4 teaspoon pepper

In a Dutch oven, brown lamb in oil on all sides; drain. Stir in water and beef broth. Insert cloves into onion. Add the onion, carrot, celery and seasonings to the pan. Bring to a boil. (Skim off foam if necessary.) Reduce heat; cover and simmer for 2 hours or until the meat is very tender.

Remove lamb shank from broth. When cool enough to handle, remove meat from bone and cut into small pieces. Strain broth, discarding vegetables and seasonings. Cover and refrigerate broth and lamb meat in separate containers overnight.

Skim and discard fat from broth. In a large saucepan, bring broth to a boil. Stir in barley. Reduce heat; cover and simmer for 40 minutes.

Stir in the turnips, carrots, leek, salt and pepper. Return to a boil. Reduce heat; cover and simmer for 15 minutes or until vegetables are tender. Add lamb meat; heat through. **Yield:** 4 servings.

Nutrition Facts: 1-1/2 cups equals 224 calories, 8 g fat (2 g saturated fat), 44 mg cholesterol, 601 mg sodium, 23 g carbohydrate, 5 g fiber, 15 g protein. **Diabetic Exchanges:** 2 lean meat, 1 starch, 1 vegetable, 1/2 fat.

Blueberry Orange Smoothies

(Pictured above)

PREP/TOTAL TIME: 10 min.

I start my mornings with this refreshing, low-fat smoothie. To complete the meal, just add a whole-grain muffin, bagel or slice of toast. —Nella Parker, Hersey, Michigan

- 2 medium navel oranges
- 1 cup fat-free plain yogurt
- 1/4 cup fat-free milk
- 2/3 cup fresh *or* frozen blueberries
- 4 teaspoons sugar
- 1 to 1-1/3 cups ice cubes

Peel and remove the white pith from oranges; separate into sections. Place in a blender; add the yogurt, milk, blueberries and sugar. Cover and process until smooth. Add ice; cover and process until smooth. Pour into chilled glasses; serve immediately. **Yield:** 4 servings.

Nutrition Facts: 1 cup equals 92 calories, trace fat (trace saturated fat), 2 mg cholesterol, 43 mg sodium, 21 g carbohydrate, 2 g fiber, 4 g protein. **Diabetic Exchange:** 1-1/2 fruit.

SIMPLE SECTIONING. To section oranges, cut a thin slice off the bottom and top of the fruit. Rest the fruit, cut sides down, on a cutting board. With a sharp paring knife, remove the peel and white pith. Hold the fruit over a bowl and slice between the membrane of a section and the fruit until the knife reaches the center. Turn the knife and follow the membrane so the fruit is released. Repeat until all sections are removed.

Salmon with Fettuccine Alfredo

(Pictured below)

PREP: 10 min. **BAKE:** 20 min.

Using a few salmon fillets, my imagination and my taste buds, I came up with this twist on an Italian classic. It's a healthy indulgence and makes an impressive entree for company.
—Pat Patty, Spring, Texas

- 4 salmon fillets (4 ounces *each*)
- 1/4 teaspoon coarsely ground pepper, **divided**
- 4 ounces uncooked fettuccine
- 2 garlic cloves, minced
- 1 tablespoon reduced-fat margarine
- 1 tablespoon all-purpose flour
- 1/8 teaspoon salt
- 1 cup fat-free milk
- 4 tablespoons grated Parmesan cheese, **divided**

Place salmon, skin side down, on a broiler rack coated with cooking spray. Sprinkle with 1/8 teaspoon pepper. Broil 4-6 in. from the heat for 10-12 minutes or until fish flakes easily with a fork.

Meanwhile, cook fettuccine according to package directions. In a small saucepan, cook garlic in margarine until tender. Stir in the flour, salt and remaining pepper. Gradually stir in milk. Bring to a boil; cook and stir for 2 minutes or until thickened. Remove from the heat. Stir in 3 tablespoons Parmesan cheese.

Drain fettuccine; toss with cheese sauce. Serve with salmon. Sprinkle with remaining Parmesan cheese. **Yield:** 4 servings.

Editor's Note: This recipe was tested with Parkay Light stick margarine.

Nutrition Facts: 1 fillet with 1/2 cup fettuccine equals 372 calories, 16 g fat (4 g saturated fat), 72 mg cholesterol, 294 mg sodium, 25 g carbohydrate, 1 g fiber, 31 g protein.

Wrap it the Light Way

ROLLING OUT a wholesome, satisfying meal doesn't get much easier than fixing a chock-full wrap. Whether you're looking for a cool lunch or hot dinner, you'll find four family-pleasing choices here.

Have a taste for something Southwestern? Try mouth-watering Calypso Burritos—no one will miss the meat. Or skip the usual tortilla and wrap things up with a crunchy lettuce leaf.

Mexican Lettuce Wraps

(Pictured below)

PREP/TOTAL TIME: 20 min.

This recipe is so versatile—the filling can make a great sandwich, dip or salad. I like to make it ahead and keep it in the fridge for a picnic. —*June Barrus, Springville, Utah*

- 3　**cups cubed cooked chicken breast**
- 1　**can (15 ounces) black beans, rinsed and drained**
- 1　**medium tomato, seeded and finely chopped**
- 1　**can (4 ounces) chopped green chilies**
- 1/2　**cup salsa**
- 1/4　**cup finely chopped onion**
- 1/4　**cup finely chopped sweet red pepper**
- 1　**tablespoon lime juice**
- 1/2　**teaspoon ground cumin**
- 1/2　**teaspoon seasoned salt**
- 1/4　**teaspoon garlic powder**
- 1　**medium ripe avocado, peeled and finely chopped**
- 12　**Bibb *or* Boston lettuce leaves**
- 1/2　**cup reduced-fat sour cream**

In a large bowl, combine the first 11 ingredients. Refrigerate until serving.

Just before serving, stir in avocado. Place 1/2 cup chicken mixture on each lettuce leaf; top each with 2 teaspoons sour cream. Fold lettuce over filling. **Yield:** 6 servings.

Nutrition Facts: 2 wraps equals 259 calories, 8 g fat (2 g saturated fat), 61 mg cholesterol, 478 mg sodium, 19 g carbohydrate, 6 g fiber, 26 g protein. **Diabetic Exchanges:** 3 very lean meat, 1 starch, 1 vegetable, 1 fat.

Shrimp 'n' Mushroom Lettuce Wraps

PREP: 40 min.　**COOK:** 10 min.

Here's a nutritious but special option for a luncheon. To add some hands–on fun, serve the filling on a platter with the lettuce leaves on the side, and let your guests wrap their own. —*Mary Beth Vultee, Ocean Beach, North Carolina*

- 1/4　**cup reduced-fat creamy peanut butter**
- 1　**tablespoon water**
- 1　**tablespoon lime juice**
- 1　**tablespoon cider vinegar**
- 1　**tablespoon reduced-sodium soy sauce**
- 3/4　**teaspoon minced fresh gingerroot**
- 1　**tablespoon chopped jalapeno pepper**
- 1　**garlic clove, peeled**
- 3/4　**teaspoon sesame oil**
- 3/4　**teaspoon honey**
- 1　**pound uncooked medium shrimp, peeled, deveined and coarsely chopped**
- 1/4　**teaspoon salt**
- 1/4　**teaspoon pepper**
- 2　**teaspoons canola oil, *divided***
- 1　**package (6 ounces) portobello mushrooms, coarsely chopped**
- 1/2　**cup chopped red onion**
- 1　**cup canned bean sprouts**
- 1/4　**cup minced fresh cilantro**
- 2　**tablespoons minced fresh basil**
- 4　**green onions, sliced**
- 2　**tablespoons chopped salted peanuts**
- 8　**Bibb *or* Boston lettuce leaves**

For sauce, in a blender, combine the first 10 ingredients; cover and process until smooth. Set aside.

Sprinkle shrimp with salt and pepper. In a large nonstick skillet, saute shrimp in 1 teaspoon canola oil for 4-6 minutes or until shrimp turn pink; remove and keep warm.

In the same skillet, saute the mushrooms and red onion in remaining oil for 5-8 minutes or until tender.

In a large skillet over medium heat, cook and stir the zucchini, carrots and onion in oil for 3-5 minutes or until tender. Stir in the beans, corn, salsa, taco seasoning and cumin. Cook and stir for 5-7 minutes or until vegetables are tender.

Remove from the heat. Stir in cheese and cilantro. Spoon about 2/3 cupful of filling off center on each tortilla. Fold sides and ends over filling and roll up. **Yield:** 8 servings.

Nutrition Facts: 1 burrito equals 349 calories, 7 g fat (2 g saturated fat), 8 mg cholesterol, 744 mg sodium, 55 g carbohydrate, 8 g fiber, 16 g protein.

Pastrami Deli Wraps

(Pictured below)

PREP/TOTAL TIME: 20 min.

I sometimes add horseradish when I make this hearty wrap for my husband. It packs well, too, so it's a terrific choice when you need to brown-bag it. —Nila Grahl, Gurnee, Illinois

- 1/4 **cup reduced-fat spreadable cream cheese**
- 1/4 **cup coarsely chopped roasted sweet red pepper**
- 4 **spinach tortillas (8 inches)**
- 4 **lettuce leaves**
- 4 **slices deli pastrami**
- 4 **slices reduced-fat provolone cheese**
- 1/4 **cup thinly sliced red onion**
- 1 **small sweet red pepper, julienned**
- 1/2 **cup chopped cucumber**

Place cream cheese and roasted pepper in a small food processor. Cover and process until blended. Spread over tortillas. Layer with remaining ingredients; roll up. Secure with toothpicks. **Yield:** 4 servings.

Nutrition Facts: 1 wrap equals 271 calories, 10 g fat (4 g saturated fat), 29 mg cholesterol, 697 mg sodium, 29 g carbohydrate, 1 g fiber, 15 g protein. **Diabetic Exchanges:** 2 lean meat, 1-1/2 starch, 1 vegetable, 1 fat.

Return the shrimp to the pan. Add the bean sprouts, cilantro and basil; cook and stir for 1 minute or until heated through.

Remove from the heat; stir in green onions and peanuts. Divide among lettuce leaves; drizzle each with 1 tablespoon sauce. Fold the lettuce over filling. **Yield:** 4 servings.

Editor's Note: When cutting or seeding hot peppers, use rubber or plastic gloves to protect your hands. Avoid touching your face.

Nutrition Facts: 2 wraps with 2 tablespoons sauce equals 268 calories, 12 g fat (2 g saturated fat), 168 mg cholesterol, 619 mg sodium, 15 g carbohydrate, 4 g fiber, 26 g protein. **Diabetic Exchanges:** 3 very lean meat, 2 fat, 1 vegetable, 1/2 starch.

Calypso Burritos

(Pictured above)

PREP: 20 min. **COOK:** 10 min.

This recipe is so big on flavor, no one notices the burritos are meatless. Any leftovers are perfect for topping a taco salad the next day. —Darlene Deeg, Vernon, British Columbia

- 2 **small zucchini, shredded**
- 2 **medium carrots, shredded**
- 1 **medium onion, finely chopped**
- 1 **tablespoon canola oil**
- 1 **can (16 ounces) kidney beans, rinsed and drained**
- 1 **can (15 ounces) black beans, rinsed and drained**
- 1-1/2 **cups frozen corn, thawed**
- 3/4 **cup salsa**
- 2 **tablespoons reduced-sodium taco seasoning**
- 2 **teaspoons ground cumin**
- 1 **cup (4 ounces) shredded part-skim mozzarella cheese**
- 1/4 **cup minced fresh cilantro**
- 8 **flour tortillas (8 inches), warmed**

Basil Polenta with Beans 'n' Peppers

(Pictured above)

PREP: 35 min. **COOK:** 10 min.

Basil livens up the polenta and black beans in this Italian-style meatless supper. Add a tossed green salad and fruit to complete the light meal. —Kimberly Hammond, Kingwood, Texas

- **3 cups water**
- **1 teaspoon salt,** *divided*
- **1 cup yellow cornmeal**
- **1/2 cup chopped fresh basil**
- **1 medium green pepper, cut into strips**
- **1 medium sweet red pepper, cut into strips**
- **1 medium onion, thinly sliced**
- **3 garlic cloves, minced**
- **1 tablespoon olive oil**
- **1 can (15 ounces) black beans, rinsed and drained**
- **1/4 teaspoon pepper**

In a large saucepan, bring the water to a boil; add 1/2 teaspoon salt. Gradually add cornmeal, stirring constantly. Reduce heat to low. Stir in basil. Cook and stir for 10 minutes or until thick and creamy. Transfer to an 8-in. square dish coated with cooking spray. Cool to room temperature, about 30 minutes.

In a large skillet, saute the peppers, onion and garlic in oil until tender. Stir in the beans, pepper and the remaining salt; keep warm.

Cut polenta into four squares; place on an ungreased baking sheet. Broil 4 in. from the heat for 5 minutes. Turn and broil 5-6 minutes longer or until heated through. Top with vegetable mixture. **Yield:** 4 servings.

Nutrition Facts: 1 polenta square with 1 cup vegetables equals 276 calories, 4 g fat (1 g saturated fat), 0 cholesterol, 795 mg sodium, 50 g carbohydrate, 9 g fiber, 9 g protein.

Roasted Red Pepper Soup

PREP: 10 min. **COOK:** 25 min.

Colorful and smooth, this lovely soup from our Test Kitchen is full of flavor and just as comforting as traditional tomato soup. Using roasted red peppers from a jar makes the recipe quick and easy to fix, and they are just as healthy as fresh peppers.

- **1 large sweet onion, chopped**
- **2 garlic cloves, minced**
- **2 teaspoons butter**
- **2 jars (15-1/2 ounces *each*) roasted sweet red peppers, drained**
- **2 cups vegetable broth**
- **1/2 teaspoon dried basil**
- **1/4 teaspoon salt**
- **1 cup half-and-half cream**

In a large saucepan, saute onion and garlic in butter for 2-3 minutes or until tender. Add the red peppers, broth, basil and salt. Bring to a boil. Reduce heat; cover and simmer for 20 minutes. Cool slightly.

In a blender, cover and process soup in batches until smooth. Remove 1 cup to a small bowl; stir in cream. Return remaining puree to pan. Stir in the cream mixture; heat through (do not boil). **Yield:** 6 servings.

Nutrition Facts: 1 cup equals 135 calories, 6 g fat (3 g saturated fat), 23 mg cholesterol, 753 mg sodium, 21 g carbohydrate, 1 g fiber, 2 g protein.

Fresh Asparagus with Pecans

(Pictured below and on page 264)

PREP: 15 min. + marinating

This is one of my family's special-occasion dishes. We all love the refreshing taste of asparagus, and crunchy chopped pecans are the perfect complement. —Jennifer Clark, Blacksburg, Virginia

- **1 pound fresh asparagus, trimmed**
- **1/4 cup cider vinegar**
- **1/4 cup reduced-sodium soy sauce**
- **2 tablespoons sugar**
- **2 tablespoons olive oil**
- **3 tablespoons chopped pecans, toasted**

In a large skillet, bring 3 cups water to a boil. Add the asparagus; cover and boil for 3 minutes. Drain and immediately place the asparagus in ice water. Drain and pat dry.

In a large resealable plastic bag, combine the vinegar, soy sauce, sugar and oil. Add the asparagus; seal bag and turn to coat. Refrigerate for up to 3 hours. Drain and discard marinade. Sprinkle asparagus with pecans. **Yield:** 4 servings.

Nutrition Facts: 1 serving equals 77 calories, 6 g fat (1 g saturated fat), 0 cholesterol, 164 mg sodium, 5 g carbohydrate, 1 g fiber, 2 g protein. **Diabetic Exchanges:** 1 vegetable, 1 fat.

Baked Flounder with Tartar Sauce

PREP: 20 min. **BAKE:** 10 min.

When I wanted a new twist on flounder, I came up with this oven-baked, lightly breaded fillet paired with a homemade tarragon tartar sauce. Other varieties of fish, such as lake perch, tilapia, sole and orange roughy, work just as well in this recipe.
—*Phyllis Schmalz-Eismann, Kansas City, Kansas*

- **1/3 cup dry bread crumbs**
- **1/4 teaspoon salt**
- **1/4 teaspoon pepper**
- **4 flounder *or* sole fillets (5 ounces *each*)**
- **1 tablespoon olive oil**

TARRAGON TARTAR SAUCE:
- **1/4 cup fat-free plain yogurt**
- **1/4 cup reduced-fat mayonnaise**
- **1-1/2 teaspoons capers, drained**
- **1 garlic clove, minced**
- **1/2 teaspoon sugar**
- **1/2 teaspoon lemon juice**
- **1/2 teaspoon dill pickle relish**
- **1/2 teaspoon Dijon mustard**
- **1/4 teaspoon dried tarragon**

In a small skillet, toast the bread crumbs, salt and pepper over medium heat until lightly browned, stir occasionally. Remove from the heat.

Brush both sides of flounder fillets with oil; coat with the toasted bread crumbs. Place in a 15-in. x 10-in. x 1-in. baking pan coated with cooking spray. Bake at 450° for 6-8 minutes or until fish flakes easily with a fork.

Meanwhile, in a small bowl, combine the sauce ingredients. Serve with fish. **Yield:** 4 servings.

Nutrition Facts: 1 fillet with 2 tablespoons sauce equals 241 calories, 10 g fat (2 g saturated fat), 72 mg cholesterol, 510 mg sodium, 10 g carbohydrate, trace fiber, 26 g protein. **Diabetic Exchanges:** 4 very lean meat, 1-1/2 fat, 1/2 starch.

Spinach-Stuffed Portobellos

(Pictured below)

PREP: 20 min. **BAKE:** 10 min.

With the meaty texture of portobello mushrooms, this marvelous main dish may remind you of a steak dinner! It features a cheesy spinach filling and gets a nice kick from the red pepper flakes.
—*Diane Lombardo, New Castle, Pennsylvania*

- **4 large portobello mushrooms**
- **2 tablespoons olive oil**
- **1 can (14-1/2 ounces) diced tomatoes, drained**
- **1 package (10 ounces) frozen chopped spinach, thawed and squeezed dry**
- **3 tablespoons chopped green onions**
- **2 tablespoons grated Romano cheese**
- **1/4 teaspoon crushed red pepper flakes**
- **1/8 teaspoon salt**
- **1/2 cup shredded part-skim mozzarella cheese**

Remove and discard stems and gills from mushrooms. In a large skillet over medium heat, cook mushrooms in oil for 10-15 minutes or just until tender, turning once.

In a small bowl, combine the tomatoes, spinach, onions, Romano cheese, pepper flakes and salt. Spoon into mushroom caps. Sprinkle with mozzarella cheese.

Place on a baking sheet lined with heavy-duty foil. Bake at 375° for 10-15 minutes or until heated through and cheese is melted. **Yield:** 4 servings.

Nutrition Facts: 1 stuffed mushroom equals 177 calories, 11 g fat (3 g saturated fat), 12 mg cholesterol, 381 mg sodium, 13 g carbohydrate, 5 g fiber, 10 g protein.

Fettuccine with Mushrooms And Tomatoes

(Pictured below)

PREP: 15 min. **COOK:** 15 min.

To perk up an ordinary plate of fettuccine, I add a creamy sauce with mushrooms and tomatoes. I can toss this dish together in 30 minutes, yet it's nice enough to present as a vegetarian entree for guests. —Phyllis Eismann Schmalz, Kansas City, Kansas

- 1 package (12 ounces) fettuccine
- 1 pound fresh mushrooms, halved
- 1 large onion, chopped
- 1 large green pepper, chopped
- 4 garlic cloves, minced
- 1 teaspoon olive oil
- 3 tablespoons all-purpose flour
- 3 cups 1% milk
- 1 teaspoon salt
- 1/4 teaspoon pepper
- 1/2 cup sun-dried tomatoes (not packed in oil), thinly sliced
- 1 cup (4 ounces) shredded reduced-fat Swiss cheese
- 1/4 cup grated Parmesan cheese

Cook fettuccine according to package directions. Meanwhile, in a large nonstick skillet, saute the mushrooms, onion, green pepper and garlic in oil for 4-6 minutes or until vegetables are tender.

In a small bowl, combine the flour, milk, salt and pepper until smooth; gradually stir into mushroom mixture. Add tomatoes. Bring to a boil; cook and stir for 2 minutes or until thickened. Stir in cheeses. Drain fettuccine; toss with sauce. **Yield:** 6 servings.

Nutrition Facts: 1-1/3 cups equals 387 calories, 8 g fat (4 g saturated fat), 17 mg cholesterol, 662 mg sodium, 60 g carbohydrate, 5 g fiber, 23 g protein.

Pronto Vegetarian Peppers

(Pictured above)

PREP/TOTAL TIME: 25 min.

During summer, I serve these with salad and a roll. At the end of the season, I freeze the peppers for winter when produce costs are higher. —Renee Hollobaugh, Altoona, Pennsylvania

- 2 large sweet red peppers, halved lengthwise
- 1 cup canned stewed tomatoes
- 1/3 cup instant brown rice
- 2 tablespoons hot water
- 3/4 cup canned kidney beans, rinsed and drained
- 1/2 cup frozen corn, thawed
- 2 green onions, thinly sliced
- 1/8 teaspoon crushed red pepper flakes
- 1/2 cup shredded part-skim mozzarella cheese
- 1 tablespoon grated Parmesan cheese

Place peppers in an ungreased shallow microwave-safe dish. Cover and microwave on high for 3-4 minutes or until tender.

In a small microwave-safe bowl, combine the tomatoes, rice and water. Cover and microwave on high for 5-6 minutes or until rice is tender. Stir in the beans, corn, onions and pepper flakes; spoon into peppers.

Sprinkle with cheeses. Microwave, uncovered, for 3-4 minutes or until heated through. **Yield:** 2 servings.

Editor's Note: This recipe was tested in a 1,100-watt microwave.

Nutrition Facts: 2 stuffed pepper halves equals 341 calories, 7 g fat (3 g saturated fat), 19 mg cholesterol, 556 mg sodium, 56 g carbohydrate, 11 g fiber, 19 g protein.

Savory Orange Salmon

(Pictured below)

PREP: 5 min. **BAKE:** 20 min.

A simple-as-can-be citrus sauce with garlic and fennel adds zip to these succulent salmon fillets, making them a mouth-watering dinner choice anytime. Try rounding out the meal with a side of healthy steamed broccoli or stunning, yellow saffron rice.
> —Roseanne Turner, Denver, Indiana

- **2 garlic cloves, minced**
- **1 teaspoon fennel seed**
- **1 teaspoon olive oil**
- **4 salmon fillets (1 inch thick and 4 ounces** *each***)**
- **1/2 teaspoon salt**
- **1 cup orange juice**

In a large nonstick skillet coated with cooking spray, cook the garlic and fennel seed in oil for 2 minutes. Sprinkle the salmon fillets with salt; add to the skillet. Top with the orange juice. Bring to a boil. Reduce the heat; cover and simmer for 8-12 minutes or until the fish flakes easily with a fork.

Remove salmon and keep warm. Simmer sauce, uncovered, for 6-9 minutes or until slightly thickened. Spoon over fillets. **Yield:** 4 servings.

Nutrition Facts: 1 fillet with 4 teaspoons sauce equals 249 calories, 14 g fat (3 g saturated fat), 67 mg cholesterol, 363 mg sodium, 7 g carbohydrate, trace fiber, 23 g protein.

Sugar Snap Pea Stir-Fry

(Pictured above)

PREP: 10 min. **COOK:** 10 min.

Our Test Kitchen blended ginger, balsamic vinegar, soy sauce and sesame oil in this Asian-inspired recipe for fresh sugar snap peas. The quick-to-cook side dish will complement just about any spring entree, from ham and lamb to chicken and fish.

- **1 pound fresh sugar snap peas**
- **2 teaspoons canola oil**
- **1 garlic clove, minced**
- **2 teaspoons minced fresh gingerroot**
- **1-1/2 teaspoons balsamic vinegar**
- **1-1/2 teaspoons reduced-sodium soy sauce**
- **1 teaspoon sesame oil**
- **Dash cayenne pepper**
- **1 tablespoon minced fresh basil** *or* **1 teaspoon dried basil**
- **2 teaspoons sesame seeds, toasted**

In a large nonstick skillet or wok, saute peas in canola oil until crisp-tender. Add garlic, ginger, vinegar, soy sauce, sesame oil and cayenne; saute 1 minute longer. Add basil; toss to combine. Sprinkle with the sesame seeds. **Yield:** 6 servings.

Nutrition Facts: 1/2 cup equals 60 calories, 3 g fat (trace saturated fat), 0 cholesterol, 59 mg sodium, 6 g carbohydrate, 2 g fiber, 3 g protein. **Diabetic Exchanges:** 1 vegetable, 1/2 fat.

Zippy Tomato-Topped Snapper

(Pictured below)

PREP: 15 min. **BAKE:** 25 min.

Seafood fans are sure to be lured by this entree sized for two. Serve the fish fillets with a tossed green salad and baked potato.
—*Mary Anne Zimmerman, Silver Springs, Florida*

- 3/4   teaspoon lemon-pepper seasoning
- 1/8   teaspoon salt
-   1   red snapper fillet (3/4 pound), cut in half
- 1/2   cup canned diced tomatoes and green chilies
-   2   tablespoons chopped onion
-   2   tablespoons chopped celery
-   1   tablespoon minced fresh parsley
- 1/8   teaspoon celery seed

Combine the lemon-pepper and salt; sprinkle over both sides of red snapper. Place in an 11-in. x 7-in. baking dish coated with cooking spray.

In a small bowl, combine the tomatoes, onion, celery, parsley and celery seed; spoon over snapper. Cover and bake at 350° for 25-30 minutes or until fish flakes easily with a fork. **Yield:** 2 servings.

Nutrition Facts: 1 serving equals 179 calories, 2 g fat (trace saturated fat), 60 mg cholesterol, 643 mg sodium, 4 g carbohydrate, 1 g fiber, 34 g protein. **Diabetic Exchanges:** 4-1/2 lean meat, 1 vegetable.

Makeover Fancy Bean Casserole

(Pictured above)

PREP: 15 min. **BAKE:** 35 min.

My daughter gave me this terrific recipe, and I've since shared it with many of my friends. It's a wonderful light alternative to the traditional green bean casserole popular at holiday feasts.
—*Venola Sharpe, Campbellsville, Kentucky*

-     3   cups frozen French-style green beans, thawed
-     1   can (10-3/4 ounces) reduced-fat reduced-sodium condensed cream of chicken soup, undiluted
- 1-1/2   cups frozen corn, thawed
-     1   can (8 ounces) sliced water chestnuts, drained
-     1   medium onion, chopped
-   1/2   cup reduced-fat sour cream
-   1/4   cup cubed reduced-fat process cheese (Velveeta)
-     5   teaspoons reduced-fat butter
-   1/3   cup crushed butter-flavored crackers
-     2   tablespoons slivered almonds

In a large bowl, combine the first seven ingredients. Transfer to an 11-in. x 7-in. baking dish coated with cooking spray. In a small skillet, melt butter. Add the butter-flavored cracker crumbs and slivered almonds; cook and stir until lightly browned. Sprinkle over the top of casserole.

Bake, uncovered, at 350° for 35-40 minutes or until heated through and topping is golden brown. **Yield:** 6 servings.

Editor's Note: This recipe was tested with Land O'Lakes light stick butter.

Nutrition Facts: 2/3 cup equals 213 calories, 8 g fat (3 g saturated fat), 17 mg cholesterol, 355 mg sodium, 32 g carbohydrate, 5 g fiber, 7 g protein. **Diabetic Exchanges:** 2 vegetable, 1-1/2 starch, 1 fat.

Artichokes with Lemon-Mint Dressing

PREP: 10 min. **COOK:** 20 min.

Our Test Kitchen cooks liked the fresh-tasting dressing in this recipe so much, they suggest making a double batch to use as a regular salad dressing! If you prefer, thin it with a little milk.

        4 medium artichokes
        1 package (12.3 ounces) firm silken tofu
        4 teaspoons minced fresh mint *or* 1-1/4
          teaspoons dried mint
        4 teaspoons lemon juice
        1 tablespoon olive oil
    2-1/2 teaspoons honey mustard
        1 teaspoon grated lemon peel
      3/4 teaspoon salt
      1/4 teaspoon curry powder
      1/4 teaspoon pepper

Place the artichokes upside down in a steamer basket; place in a saucepan over 1 in. of boiling water. Cover and steam for 20-25 minutes or until tender.

Meanwhile, for dressing, combine the remaining ingredients in a blender or food processor; cover and process until smooth. Serve with the artichokes. **Yield:** 4 servings (1 cup dressing).

Nutrition Facts: 1 artichoke with 1/4 cup dressing equals 154 calories, 6 g fat (1 g saturated fat), trace cholesterol, 615 mg sodium, 18 g carbohydrate, 7 g fiber, 10 g protein. **Diabetic Exchanges:** 1 vegetable, 1 reduced-fat milk, 1 fat.

Tomato Soup with Cheese Tortellini

PREP: 20 min. **COOK:** 40 min.

Tortellini gives this summery tomato soup stick-to-your-ribs goodness. Light and quick to fix, the recipe has become a staple in my kitchen. —*Susan Peck, Republic, Missouri*

        1 large onion, chopped
        1 tablespoon butter
        2 pounds plum tomatoes, seeded and quartered
        3 cups reduced-sodium chicken broth *or*
          vegetable broth
        1 can (8 ounces) tomato sauce
        1 tablespoon minced fresh basil
      1/4 teaspoon salt
    Dash pepper
        1 cup dried cheese tortellini
      1/3 cup shredded Parmesan cheese

In a large saucepan, saute onion in butter until tender. Add the tomatoes, broth, tomato sauce, basil, salt and pepper. Bring to a boil. Reduce heat; cover and simmer for 30 minutes. Cool slightly.

Cook tortellini according to package directions; drain well and set aside. In a blender, cover and process soup in batches until smooth. Return to the saucepan; add tortellini and heat through. Garnish with Parmesan cheese. **Yield:** 8 servings (2 quarts).

Nutrition Facts: 1-1/3 cups equals 114 calories, 4 g fat (2 g saturated fat), 14 mg cholesterol, 609 mg sodium, 15 g carbohydrate, 2 g fiber, 6 g protein. **Diabetic Exchanges:** 2 vegetable, 1/2 starch, 1/2 fat.

Peppered Sole

(Pictured below)

PREP/TOTAL TIME: 25 min.

Here's a dressed-up and delicious treatment for sole. It's the only way my daughter will eat fish...and it's good for her, too!
—*Jeannette Baye, Agassiz, British Columbia*

        2 cups sliced fresh mushrooms
        2 tablespoons butter
        2 garlic cloves, minced
        4 sole fillets (4 ounces *each*)
      1/4 teaspoon lemon-pepper seasoning
      1/4 teaspoon paprika
      1/8 teaspoon cayenne pepper
        1 medium tomato, chopped
        2 green onions, thinly sliced

In a large skillet, saute mushrooms in butter until tender. Add garlic; saute 1 minute longer. Place fillets over mushrooms. Sprinkle with lemon-pepper, paprika and cayenne.

Cover and cook over medium heat for 5-10 minutes or until fish flakes easily with a fork. Sprinkle with tomato and onions. **Yield:** 4 servings.

Nutrition Facts: 1 serving equals 174 calories, 7 g fat (4 g saturated fat), 69 mg cholesterol, 166 mg sodium, 4 g carbohydrate, 1 g fiber, 23 g protein. **Diabetic Exchanges:** 3 very lean meat, 1-1/2 fat.

Meals on a Budget

Clever cooks know you don't need to spend a fortune to serve your family delicious fare. Most of these enticing dishes cost less than $2 per serving!

DOLLAR-SAVVY DINING. Clockwise from top left: Pork in Orange Sauce (p. 286), Grilled Tilapia with Pineapple Salsa (p. 293), Lemon Basil Chicken (p. 288) and Blue Cheese Flank Steak (p. 293).

Marinated Chuck Steak

(Pictured above)

PREP: 10 min. + marinating **GRILL:** 20 min. + standing

Turn inexpensive beef into a real treat with this easy marinade, which tenderizes and boosts the flavor. The cost per serving is about $1.33. —Karen Haen, Sturgeon Bay, Wisconsin

- 1/2 **cup red wine vinegar**
- 1/2 **cup soy sauce**
- 2 **tablespoons lemon juice**
- 1 **tablespoon brown sugar**
- 1 **tablespoon Worcestershire sauce**
- 2 **garlic cloves, minced**
- 1/4 **teaspoon onion powder**
- 2 **pounds boneless chuck steak**

In a large resealable plastic bag, combine the first seven ingredients. Add the beef; seal bag and turn to coat. Refrigerate for 8 hours or overnight.

Drain and discard marinade. Grill steak, covered, over medium heat for 8-10 minutes on each side or until meat reaches desired doneness (for medium-rare, a meat thermometer should read 145°; medium, 160°; well-done, 170°). Let stand for 10 minutes before slicing. **Yield:** 6 servings.

Romano Basil Turkey Breast

PREP: 15 min. **GRILL:** 1 hour + standing

Guests will be impressed when you slice this golden, grilled turkey breast, and you'll love the fact that the entree costs only about $1.83 per person. —Darlene Markham, Rochester, New York

- 4 **ounces Romano cheese, cubed**
- 1/2 **cup fresh basil leaves, torn**
- 4 **lemon slices**
- 4 **garlic cloves, minced**
- 1 **bone-in turkey breast (4 to 5 pounds)**
- 2 **tablespoons olive oil**
- 1/2 **teaspoon salt**
- 1/4 **teaspoon pepper**

Combine cheese, basil, lemon slices and garlic. With fingers, carefully loosen skin from the turkey breast; place mixture under the skin. Secure skin to underside of breast with toothpicks. Rub skin with oil and sprinkle with salt and pepper.

Prepare grill for indirect heat, using a drip pan. Place the turkey over drip pan. Grill, covered, over indirect medium heat for 1 to 1-1/2 hours or until a meat thermometer reads 170° and juices run clear. Cover and let stand for 10 minutes before slicing. **Yield:** 8 servings.

Pork in Orange Sauce

(Pictured below and on page 284)

PREP/TOTAL TIME: 30 min.

There's no need to go out for Chinese when you have this Asian-inspired stir-fry recipe. It pairs nicely with a cucumber salad in vinaigrette dressing. —Marlene Kroll, Chicago, Illinois

- 1 **cup uncooked long grain rice**
- 2 **teaspoons cornstarch**
- 1 **teaspoon sugar**
- 1 **teaspoon ground ginger**
- 1 **teaspoon grated orange peel**
- 1 **cup orange juice**
- 1 **teaspoon soy sauce**
- 2 **celery ribs, chopped**
- 2 **medium carrots, thinly sliced**
- 1/4 **cup lightly salted cashews**
- 1 **tablespoon canola oil**
- 2 **cups cubed cooked pork**
- 1/2 **cup chow mein noodles**
- 1 **green onion, julienned**

Cook rice according to package directions. Meanwhile, in a small bowl, combine the cornstarch, sugar, ginger and orange peel. Stir in orange juice and soy sauce until smooth; set aside.

In a large skillet or wok, stir fry the celery, carrots and cashews in oil until vegetables are crisp-tender. Stir cornstarch mixture and add to the pan. Bring to a boil; cook and stir for 1 minute or until thickened. Add pork; heat through. Serve with rice; top with noodles and onion. **Yield:** 4 servings.

Cornmeal Oven-Fried Chicken

PREP: 20 min. **BAKE:** 40 min.

This home-style fried chicken perks up the dinner table for only $1.69 a serving. Its cornmeal/bread-crumb coating is a nice change of pace. —*Deborah Williams, Wildwood, Missouri*

☑ This recipe includes Nutrition Facts and Diabetic Exchanges.

- 1/2 **cup dry bread crumbs**
- 1/2 **cup cornmeal**
- 1/3 **cup grated Parmesan cheese**
- 1/4 **cup minced fresh parsley** *or* **4 teaspoons dried parsley flakes**
- 3/4 **teaspoon garlic powder**
- 1/2 **teaspoon salt**
- 1/2 **teaspoon pepper**
- 1/2 **teaspoon onion powder**
- 1/2 **teaspoon dried thyme**
- 1/2 **cup buttermilk**
- 1 **broiler/fryer chicken (3 to 4 pounds), cut up and skin removed**
- 1 **tablespoon butter, melted**

In a large resealable plastic bag, combine the first nine ingredients. Place the buttermilk in a shallow bowl. Dip chicken in buttermilk, then add to bag, a few pieces at a time, and shake to coat.

Place in a 13-in. x 9-in. baking pan coated with cooking spray. Bake at 375° for 10 minutes; drizzle with butter. Bake 30-40 minutes longer or until juices run clear. **Yield:** 6 servings.

Nutrition Facts: 1 serving equals 244 calories, 9 g fat (3 g saturated fat), 82 mg cholesterol, 303 mg sodium, 11 g carbohydrate, 1 g fiber, 27 g protein. **Diabetic Exchanges:** 3 lean meat, 1 starch, 1/2 fat.

Spaghetti Supper

(Pictured above right)

PREP: 30 min. **COOK:** 2 hours

I used to love coming home to find my mom making these tender meatballs for dinner. They were one of my favorite meals—and still are! —*Debbie Heggie, Laramie, Wyoming*

- 2 **cans (14-1/2 ounces** *each***) diced tomatoes, undrained**

- 1-1/2 **teaspoons salt**
- 1 **teaspoon sugar**
- 1 **teaspoon dried basil**
- 1 **garlic clove, minced**
- 1/4 **teaspoon pepper**

ITALIAN MEATBALLS:
- 3 **cups soft bread crumbs**
- 1/2 **cup water**
- 2 **eggs, beaten**
- 1/2 **cup grated Parmesan cheese**
- 2 **tablespoons minced fresh parsley**
- 1 **garlic clove, minced**
- 1 **teaspoon salt**
- 1/4 **teaspoon pepper**
- 1 **pound ground beef**
- 1 **pound ground pork**

Hot cooked spaghetti

In a Dutch oven, combine the tomatoes, salt, sugar, basil, garlic and pepper. Bring to a boil. Reduce heat; cover and simmer for 1-1/2 hours, stirring occasionally.

For meatballs: Place bread crumbs and water in a large bowl; let stand for 5 minutes. Stir in the eggs, Parmesan cheese, parsley, garlic, salt and pepper. Crumble beef and pork over mixture and mix well. Shape into 1-in. balls. Place on racks in baking pans. Bake at 400° for 15-20 minutes or until no longer pink.

Stir meatballs into sauce; heat through. Serve with spaghetti. **Yield:** 10 servings (about 5 dozen meatballs).

Editor's Note: To quickly prepare this meal, substitute 2 pounds frozen cooked meatballs (about 60) for the homemade meatballs. You may also prepare just the meatballs, then bake and freeze them for future use.

Lemon Basil Chicken

(Pictured at right and on page 285)

PREP: 15 min. **BAKE:** 1-1/4 hours + standing

For Sunday dinner, a holiday feast or anytime, this tender and fragrant chicken is special. Plus, you fork over just $2.22 per person! —Marguerite Marshall, Carencro, Louisiana

  1 **medium lemon**
  2 **garlic cloves,** *divided*
1/4 **cup minced fresh basil,** *divided*
  1 **broiler/fryer chicken (3 to 4 pounds)**
  2 **tablespoons butter, melted**
1/2 **teaspoon salt**
1/4 **teaspoon pepper**

Finely grate peel from lemon to measure 2 teaspoons. Cut lemon in half; squeeze juice from one half. Set aside. Slice one garlic clove; place sliced garlic, 2 tablespoons basil and remaining lemon half in the chicken cavity.

Place chicken, breast side up, in a shallow roasting pan; rub with reserved lemon juice. Mince remaining garlic; combine with butter and reserved lemon peel. Brush mixture over chicken. Sprinkle with salt, pepper and remaining basil.

Bake, uncovered, at 375° for 1-1/4 to 1-1/2 hours or until a meat thermometer reads 180°. Let stand for 15 minutes before carving. **Yield:** 6 servings.

German Pork Roast

(Pictured below)

PREP: 20 min. **BAKE:** 1-3/4 hours + standing

With potatoes, onions and tomato wedges, this tender roast is my husband's favorite meal. He even asks for it on his birthday. —Camie Hewitt, Redmond, Oregon

  3 **tablespoons olive oil**
  4 **garlic cloves, minced**
  1 **teaspoon lemon juice**
  1 **teaspoon stone-ground mustard**

  1 **teaspoon salt**
1/2 **teaspoon** *each* **dried oregano, thyme and rosemary, crushed**
1/4 **teaspoon pepper**
  1 **boneless whole pork loin roast (3 to 4 pounds)**
  4 **medium potatoes, peeled and cut into wedges**
  3 **medium onions, cut into wedges**
  1 **medium yellow tomato, cut into wedges**

In a small bowl, combine the oil, garlic, lemon juice, mustard and seasonings. Rub over roast. Place on a rack in a shallow roasting pan.

Bake, uncovered, at 350° for 20 minutes. Add the potatoes, onions and tomato to the pan; bake 40-70 minutes longer or until a meat thermometer reads 160° and vegetables are tender. Let stand for 10 minutes before slicing. **Yield:** 8 servings.

Teriyaki Grilled Chicken

PREP: 10 min. + marinating **GRILL:** 40 min.

Here's a super recipe you can use with any chicken pieces you like. Marinate the chicken overnight for an extra flavor boost. —Jennifer Nichols, Tucson, Arizona

1/3 **cup soy sauce**
1/4 **cup canola oil**
  2 **green onions, thinly sliced**
  2 **tablespoons plus 1-1/2 teaspoons honey**
  2 **tablespoons sherry** *or* **chicken broth**
  2 **garlic cloves, minced**
  1 **teaspoon minced fresh gingerroot**
  6 **bone-in chicken breast halves (8 ounces** *each***)**

In a large resealable plastic bag, combine the first seven ingredients; add the chicken. Seal bag and turn to coat; refrigerate for at least 5 hours.

Drain and discard marinade. Prepare grill for indirect heat, using a drip pan. Place chicken skin side down on grill rack. Grill, covered, over indirect medium heat for 40-50 minutes or until a meat thermometer reads 170°. **Yield:** 6 servings.

Gnocchi Alfredo

(Pictured below)

PREP/TOTAL TIME: 20 min.

Frozen gnocchi gives you a head start on this creamy Italian dish. Even using that convenience, the cost is reasonable—just $1.64 per serving. —Jessica Silva, East Berlin, Connecticut

- **2 pounds frozen potato gnocchi**
- **3 tablespoons butter, *divided***
- **1 tablespoon plus 1-1/2 teaspoons all-purpose flour**
- **1-1/2 cups milk**
- **1/2 cup grated Parmesan cheese**
- **Dash ground nutmeg**
- **1/2 pound sliced baby portobello mushrooms**
- **Minced fresh parsley, optional**

Cook the gnocchi according to package directions. Meanwhile, in a saucepan, melt 1 tablespoon butter. Stir in flour until smooth; gradually add milk. Bring to a boil; cook and stir for 1-2 minutes or until thickened. Remove from the heat; stir in cheese and nutmeg until blended. Keep warm.

Drain gnocchi. In a large heavy skillet, cook remaining butter over medium heat until golden brown (do not burn). Add mushrooms and gnocchi. Cook and stir 4-5 minutes or until gnocchi are lightly browned and mushrooms are tender. Serve with sauce. Sprinkle with parsley if desired. **Yield:** 5 servings.

Grilled Country-Style Ribs

(Pictured above)

PREP: 15 min. + marinating **COOK:** 30 min.

These marinated ribs are precooked in the microwave and then finished on the grill. They turn out wonderfully tender with a great smoky taste. —Sue Benning, Menasha, Wisconsin

- **1 cup water, *divided***
- **1/2 cup soy sauce**
- **2 tablespoons lemon juice**
- **2 tablespoons canola oil**
- **1 tablespoon brown sugar**
- **1 teaspoon garlic powder**
- **1 teaspoon pepper**
- **6 bone-in country-style pork ribs (1-1/2 inches thick and 14 ounces *each*)**

In a small bowl, combine 1/2 cup water, soy sauce, lemon juice, oil, brown sugar, garlic powder and pepper. Cover and refrigerate 1/2 cup mixture for basting. Pour remaining mixture into a large resealable plastic bag; add the ribs. Seal bag and turn to coat. Refrigerate for 8 hours or overnight.

Drain ribs and discard marinade; place ribs and remaining water in a 3-qt. microwave-safe dish. Cover and microwave on high for 20-25 minutes or until meat is tender.

Coat grill rack with cooking spray before starting the grill. Drain ribs. Grill ribs, covered, over medium heat for 8-10 minutes or until browned, turning occasionally and basting with reserved marinade. **Yield:** 6 servings.

Chunky Chipotle Pork Chili

(Pictured above)

PREP: 15 min. **COOK:** 20 min.

Perfect for using leftover pork roast, this tasty and easy recipe can be made ahead and reheated. We think it's even better the second day. —*Peter Halferty, Corpus Christi, Texas*

- 1 medium green pepper, chopped
- 1 small onion, chopped
- 1 chipotle pepper in adobo sauce, finely chopped
- 1 tablespoon canola oil
- 3 garlic cloves, minced
- 1 can (16 ounces) red beans, rinsed and drained
- 1 cup beef broth
- 1/2 cup salsa
- 2 teaspoons ground cumin
- 2 teaspoons chili powder
- 2 cups cubed cooked pork
- 1/4 cup sour cream

In a large saucepan, saute the green pepper, onion and chipotle pepper in oil until tender. Add garlic; saute 1 minute longer.

Add the beans, broth, salsa, cumin and chili powder. Bring to a boil. Reduce heat; simmer, uncovered, for 10 minutes or until thickened. Add pork; heat through. Serve with sour cream. **Yield:** 4 servings.

Chicken Potpie

PREP: 70 min. + cooling **BAKE:** 25 min.

This comforting potpie gives you a lot for a little—just $1.83 per serving. It's a meal-in-one with tender chicken and plenty of veggies. —*Valerie Belley, St. Louis, Missouri*

- 1 broiler/fryer chicken (3 to 4 pounds), cut up
- 4 cups water
- 3 medium carrots, halved widthwise
- 2 medium onions, quartered
- 4 teaspoons chicken bouillon granules
- 1 bay leaf
- 1/2 pound whole fresh mushrooms
- 2 celery ribs, cut into 1-in. pieces
- 3 tablespoons butter
- 5 tablespoons all-purpose flour
- 1/2 cup milk
- 1 cup frozen peas
- 1 teaspoon dried basil
- 1 teaspoon salt
- 1/4 teaspoon pepper

BISCUITS:
- 1-1/2 cups all-purpose flour
- 2 teaspoons baking powder
- 2 teaspoons sugar
- 1/4 teaspoon salt
- 5 tablespoons shortening
- 1/2 cup milk

Place chicken, water, carrots, onions, bouillon and bay leaf in a Dutch oven; bring to a boil. Reduce heat; cover and simmer for 25 minutes. Add mushrooms and celery; simmer 15 minutes longer or until chicken is tender.

Remove chicken; allow to cool. Strain broth, reserving vegetables; skim fat. Set aside 2 cups broth (save remaining broth for another use). Discard bay leaf. Remove meat from bones; discard bones. Chop vegetables and cut chicken into bite-size pieces.

In a large saucepan, melt butter. Stir in flour until smooth; gradually add milk and reserved broth. Bring to a boil; cook and stir for 2 minutes or until thickened. Stir in the chicken, cooked vegetables, peas and seasonings. Pour into a greased 2-qt. baking dish; set aside.

For biscuits, in a large bowl, combine the flour, baking powder, sugar and salt. Cut in shortening until mixture resembles coarse crumbs. Stir in milk just until moistened. Turn onto a lightly floured surface; knead 8-10 times. Pat or roll out to 1/2-in. thickness; cut with a floured 2-1/2-in. biscuit cutter.

Place biscuits on top of chicken mixture. Bake, uncovered, at 400° for 25 minutes or until golden brown. **Yield:** 7 servings.

Buttermilk Pot Roast

PREP: 20 min. **BAKE:** 2-1/4 hours

This melt-in-your-mouth beef boasts a wonderfully flavorful gravy. I've been making it for years and have served it to guests countless times. —*Anne Powers, Munford, Alabama*

- 2 tablespoons Dijon mustard
- 1 boneless beef chuck roast (about 3-1/2 pounds)
- 4-1/2 teaspoons onion soup mix
- 1/4 teaspoon pepper
- 8 medium potatoes, peeled and halved

8 medium carrots, halved
8 small onions, cut into wedges
1 cup buttermilk

Spread mustard over roast; place in a Dutch oven. Sprinkle with soup mix and pepper. Arrange vegetables around roast; pour buttermilk over the top.

Cover and bake at 350° for 2-1/4 to 2-3/4 hours or until meat and vegetables are tender. Transfer meat and vegetables to a platter and keep warm.

Skim fat from drippings; bring to a boil. Cook until liquid is reduced to 1 cup; serve with beef and vegetables. **Yield:** 8 servings.

Lemon Chicken Tortellini

(Pictured below)

PREP: 15 min. **COOK:** 25 min.

I like to keep leftover chicken on hand in the freezer to make this saucy main dish...and it never tastes like we're eating leftovers.
—*Lorraine Caland, Thunder Bay, Ontario*

1 package (19 ounces) frozen cheese tortellini
1 pound boneless skinless chicken breasts, cut into 1-in. pieces
2 tablespoons butter
1/2 small sweet red pepper, julienned
2 garlic cloves, minced
3 cups reduced-sodium chicken broth, *divided*
1/3 cup all-purpose flour
1/2 teaspoon salt
1/4 teaspoon pepper
2 teaspoons grated lemon peel
1/2 teaspoon hot pepper sauce, optional
1 package (6 ounces) fresh baby spinach
6 tablespoons shredded Parmesan cheese

Cook tortellini according to package directions. Meanwhile, in a large skillet, saute chicken in butter until no longer pink. Remove and keep warm. In same pan, cook red pepper until crisp-tender. Add garlic; cook

1 minute longer. Add 2 cups broth; bring to a boil.

Combine flour, salt, pepper and remaining broth until smooth; gradually stir into the pan. Bring to a boil; cook and stir 2 minutes or until thickened. Stir in chicken, lemon peel and pepper sauce if desired. Add spinach; cook just until wilted. Drain pasta; toss with sauce. Sprinkle with cheese. **Yield:** 6 servings.

Deluxe Corn Muffins

(Pictured above)

PREP: 15 min. **BAKE:** 20 min.

In my family, these tender, 25¢-per-serving corn muffins are the cream of the crop! The easy, homemade honey butter adds a pleasant hint of sweetness.   —*Angela Lively, Baxter, Tennessee*

1 cup all-purpose flour
1 cup yellow cornmeal
1/4 cup sugar
2-1/2 teaspoons baking powder
3/4 teaspoon salt
1/2 teaspoon baking soda
1 egg
1 egg yolk
1-1/4 cups buttermilk
1/3 cup canola oil
3/4 cup whole kernel corn
HONEY BUTTER:
1/2 cup butter, softened
2 to 3 tablespoons honey

In a large bowl, combine first six ingredients. In another bowl, whisk the egg, egg yolk, buttermilk and oil. Stir into dry ingredients just until moistened. Fold in corn.

Fill greased muffin cups three-fourths full. Bake at 400° for 18-23 minutes or until a toothpick comes out clean. Cool for 5 minutes before removing from pan to a wire rack.

In a small bowl, beat butter and honey until blended. Serve with muffins. **Yield:** 1 dozen (1/2 cup butter).

Italian Supper Sandwich

(Pictured above)

PREP: 40 min. **BAKE:** 20 min.

This baked sandwich is so good—and the bonus is you can make the meatballs and sauce ahead. Try it for a Super Bowl party or other get-together. —Patricia Cornell, Burlington, Kentucky

>   4 cups tomato juice
>   1/2 cup water
>   1/3 cup tomato paste
>   1 tablespoon dried minced onion
> 1-1/2 teaspoons dried basil
>   1/2 teaspoon sugar
>   1/2 teaspoon garlic powder
>   1/4 teaspoon dried oregano
>   1/8 teaspoon paprika
> 1/16 teaspoon cayenne pepper
>   1 loaf (1 pound) Italian bread
>   2 tablespoons butter, softened
>   1 pound frozen cooked meatballs (about 30)
>   1/4 cup shredded Parmesan cheese

In a Dutch oven, combine the first 10 ingredients. Bring to a boil. Reduce heat; simmer, uncovered, for 30-40 minutes, stirring occasionally, or until slightly thickened.

Cut top third off of bread but not all the way through; hollow out top and bottom, leaving a 1-in. shell. Spread with butter.

Add meatballs to sauce; heat through. With a slotted spoon, transfer meatballs into the loaf. Sprinkle with cheese; replace bread top. Wrap loaf in foil. Bake at 425° for 20 minutes or until heated through. Let stand for 5 minutes before slicing. Warm remaining sauce; serve with sandwiches. **Yield:** 6 servings.

Editor's Note: You may use homemade meatballs or a frozen convenience product when preparing this recipe.

Cranberry-Cherry Lattice Pie

PREP: 30 min. **BAKE:** 25 min. + cooling

My mom used to bake this pie for the holidays when I was a girl. But at just 91¢ per slice, you can afford to enjoy it all year long. —J. Tomasi, Toledo, Ohio

>   1 can (21 ounces) cherry pie filling
>   1 can (16 ounces) whole-berry cranberry sauce
> 1/4 cup sugar
>   3 tablespoons quick-cooking tapioca
>   1 teaspoon lemon juice
> 1/4 teaspoon ground cinnamon
>   1 package (15 ounces) refrigerated pie pastry
>   2 tablespoons butter

In a large bowl, combine the pie filling, cranberry sauce, sugar, tapioca, lemon juice and cinnamon. Let stand for 15 minutes.

Line a 9-in. pie plate with bottom pastry; add filling. Dot with butter. Roll out remaining pastry; make a lattice crust. Trim, seal and flute edges.

Bake at 400° for 35-40 minutes or until the crust is golden brown and the filling is bubbly. Cool on a wire rack. **Yield:** 6-8 servings.

Ham & Sweet Potato Kabobs

PREP: 25 min. + marinating **GRILL:** 15 min.

With chunks of pineapple, sweet potato, squash and apple, these ham kabobs are colorful and delicious—perfect served with a green salad. It's a thrifty meal that looks and tastes anything but! —Sandra Hill, Wilson, New York

>   1 large sweet potato, peeled and cubed
>   1 can (20 ounces) unsweetened pineapple chunks
> 1/4 cup butter, melted
>   4 teaspoons brown sugar
>   1 pound fully cooked boneless ham, cut into 1-in. cubes
>   2 yellow summer squash, cut into 3/4-in. slices
>   2 large apples, cubed

Place the sweet potato in a small saucepan; cover with water. Bring to a boil. Reduce the heat; cover and cook for 10-15 minutes or until almost tender. Drain and set aside.

Drain pineapple, reserving juice; set pineapple aside. In a small bowl, combine the butter, brown sugar and reserved juice. Place the ham, squash, apples, sweet potato and pineapple in a large resealable plastic bag; add the juice mixture. Seal bag and turn to coat; refrigerate for 1 hour.

Drain and discard the marinade. On eight metal or soaked wooden skewers, alternately thread the ham, sweet potato, squash, apples and pineapple. Grill, covered, over medium heat for 15-20 minutes or until apples are tender, turning occasionally. **Yield:** 8 kabobs.

Grilled Tilapia With Pineapple Salsa

(Pictured above and on page 285)

PREP/TOTAL TIME: 25 min.

When it comes to summery meals, this seafood entree is hard to beat. It's been a favorite of mine for years and costs just $1.81 per serving. —*Beth Fleming, Downers Grove, Illinois*

☑ This recipe includes Nutrition Facts and Diabetic Exchanges.

>   2 cups cubed fresh pineapple
>   2 green onions, chopped
> 1/4 cup finely chopped green pepper
> 1/4 cup minced fresh cilantro
>   4 teaspoons plus 2 tablespoons lime juice, *divided*
> 1/8 teaspoon plus 1/4 teaspoon salt, *divided*
> Dash cayenne pepper
>   1 tablespoon canola oil
>   8 tilapia fillets (4 ounces *each*)
> 1/8 teaspoon pepper

In a small bowl, combine the pineapple, onions, green pepper, cilantro, 4 teaspoons lime juice, 1/8 teaspoon salt and cayenne. Chill until serving.

Combine oil and remaining lime juice; brush over fillets. Sprinkle with pepper and remaining salt.

Coat grill rack with cooking spray before starting the grill. Grill fish, covered, over medium heat for 3-4 minutes on each side or until fish flakes easily with a fork. Serve with salsa. **Yield:** 8 servings (2 cups salsa).

Nutrition Facts: 1 fillet with 1/4 cup salsa equals 131 calories, 3 g fat (1 g saturated fat), 55 mg cholesterol, 152 mg sodium, 6 g carbohydrate, 1 g fiber, 21 g protein. **Diabetic Exchanges:** 3 very lean meat, 1/2 fruit.

Blue Cheese Flank Steak

(Pictured below and on page 284)

PREP: 10 min. + marinating **COOK:** 10 min.

We lived with my parents for a few months while having a house built, and I took the opportunity to look through Mom's recipe files. One of the many treasures I found was this tasty steak. —*Laurie Nudo, The Woodlands, Texas*

☑ This recipe includes Nutrition Facts and Diabetic Exchanges.

>   1 medium onion, sliced
>   1 garlic clove, peeled and sliced
> 1/3 cup water
> 1/3 cup white wine vinegar
>   2 tablespoons reduced-sodium soy sauce
> 1/2 teaspoon coarsely ground pepper
>   1 beef flank steak (1 lb.)
> 1/2 cup crumbled blue cheese

In a large resealable plastic bag, combine the first six ingredients. Add the steak; seal bag and turn to coat. Refrigerate overnight, turning occasionally.

Drain and discard marinade. Coat grill rack with cooking spray before starting the grill. Grill, covered, over medium-hot heat for 5-7 minutes on each side or until meat reaches desired doneness (for medium-rare, a meat thermometer should read 145°; medium, 160°; well-done, 170°). Let stand for 5 minutes; thinly slice across the grain. Sprinkle with blue cheese. **Yield:** 4 servings.

Nutrition Facts: 3 ounces cooked beef with 2 tablespoons cheese equals 239 calories, 12 g fat (6 g saturated fat), 65 mg cholesterol, 367 mg sodium, 5 g carbohydrate, 1 g fiber, 26 g protein. **Diabetic Exchanges:** 3 lean meat, 1 fat.

Getting in the Theme of Things

Hosting a themed party is a snap when you rely on the festive fare gathered here. So go ahead—invite guests and have some fun with your food!

ENTERTAINING IDEAS. Clockwise from upper left: It's a Pizza Party! (p. 300), Indulge in a Dessert Buffet (p. 298), You Say Potato Bar! (p. 296) and Dine Out on the Deck (p. 302).

You Say Potato Bar!

GUESTS of Alcy Thorne of Los Molinos, California really dig her recurring potato parties. Alcy sets out potatoes and toppings, letting guests fix their own spuds.

Want to host your own potato bar? Our Test Kitchen staff gathered four delicious recipes for potato toppings and featured them here.

To bake the potatoes, rub them with oil, pierce them all over with a fork and bake them on oven racks about 1/2 inch apart at 350° for about an hour, depending on their size. If you are cooking more than four potatoes, add another 10 minutes of baking. (This method also works for sweet potatoes.)

Potato-Bar Chili

(Pictured above and on page 295)

PREP: 10 min. **COOK:** 30 min.

Everyone from children to adults will like this mild, beefy chili. Ladle a generous helping over a hot baked potato and enjoy!
—Alcy Thorne, Los Molinos, California

1-1/2 **pounds ground beef**
  2 **medium onions, chopped**
  1 **medium green pepper, chopped**
  1 **can (28 ounces) diced tomatoes, undrained**
  1 **can (15-1/2 ounces) chili beans, undrained**
  2 **tablespoons sugar**
  2 **teaspoons chili powder**
1/4 **teaspoon salt**
1/4 **teaspoon pepper**
Baked potatoes

In a Dutch oven, cook the beef, onions and green pepper over medium heat until meat is no longer pink; drain. Add the tomatoes, chili beans, sugar and seasonings. Bring to a boil. Reduce heat; simmer, uncovered, for 20 minutes. Serve over potatoes. **Yield:** 7 cups.

Sassy Blue Cheese Potato Topper

(Pictured at top far right)

PREP/TOTAL TIME: 5 min.

This topper works great on a spud or even as a dip with your favorite corn chips. I think it's best made a day ahead of time.
—Ronald James Bishop, Ridgefield, Washington

  2 **cups mayonnaise**
  1 **jar (5 ounces) blue cheese spread**
1/4 **cup finely chopped onion**
1/4 **cup minced fresh parsley**

2 **garlic cloves, minced**
1/4 **teaspoon Worcestershire sauce**
Baked potatoes

In a small bowl, beat mayonnaise and blue cheese spread until smooth. Stir in the onion, parsley, garlic and Worcestershire sauce. Serve over potatoes. **Yield:** 2-1/2 cups.

Chipotle Cheese Sauce

(Pictured at center right)

PREP/TOTAL TIME: 15 min.

Fans of Mexican flavor are sure to love this! It's a smooth, smoky cheese sauce with a hint of heat from chopped chipotle peppers.
—*Melissa Jelinek, Menomonee Falls, Wisconsin*

1/4 **cup butter, cubed**
2 **tablespoons chopped chipotle peppers in adobo sauce**
1/4 **cup all-purpose flour**
1/8 **teaspoon pepper**
2-1/2 **cups milk**
1-1/2 **cups (6 ounces) shredded Colby-Monterey Jack cheese**
Baked potatoes

In a small saucepan, melt the butter over medium heat. Add the chipotle peppers; cook and stir for 2 minutes. Stir in flour and pepper until blended; gradually add milk. Bring to a boil; cook and stir for 1-2 minutes or until thickened. Stir in cheese until melted. Serve over potatoes. **Yield:** 2-3/4 cups.

Quick Hamburger Gravy

(Pictured at bottom right)

PREP/TOTAL TIME: 20 min.

You'll be surprised at how quickly this mild, creamy gravy comes together. And with ground beef, it turns a plain baked potato into a meal. —*Alcy Thorne, Los Molinos, California*

1-1/2 **pounds ground beef**
2 **medium onions, chopped**
1/2 **cup all-purpose flour**
2 **tablespoons beef bouillon granules**
1/4 **teaspoon salt**
1/4 **teaspoon pepper**
5 **cups milk**
Baked potatoes

In a Dutch oven, cook the ground beef and onions over medium heat until the meat is no longer pink; drain. Stir in the flour, beef bouillon granules, salt and pepper. Gradually add the milk; bring to a boil. Cook and stir for 2 minutes or until thickened. Serve over potatoes. **Yield:** 7 cups.

Indulge in a Dessert Buffet

WHAT a tantalizing idea! Invite family and friends over for an afternoon or evening of sampling special desserts. They'll be in sweet-tooth heaven…and you'll find this event is a treat to host.

Just look here for an assortment of rich temptations your guests are sure to love. Our Test Kitchen staff gathered an assortment of goodies, from playful pops made of cheesecake to light but luscious parfaits and delicate tarts with fabulous fillings. Yum!

Cheesecake Pops

(Pictured above)

PREP: 2 hours + freezing

These cute, lollipop–like bites make any occasion memorable. The topping possibilities are endless, and guests can choose their favorite.   —*Evelyn Moore, Elk Grove, California*

   3 packages (8 ounces *each*) cream cheese, softened
   1 cup sugar
   1 cup sour cream
   1 teaspoon vanilla extract
   3 eggs, beaten
   1 cup graham cracker crumbs
   45 lollipop sticks (4 inches long)
   3 packages (10 to 12 ounces *each*) vanilla *or* white chips
   3 tablespoons shortening
Toppings: grated coconut, grated chocolate, assorted sprinkles and chopped nuts

Line the bottom of a 9-in. springform pan with parchment paper; coat paper and sides of pan with cooking spray. In a large bowl, beat cream cheese and sugar until smooth. Beat in the sour cream and vanilla until blended. Add eggs; beat on low speed just until combined. Pour into prepared pan.

Place the pan on a baking sheet. Bake at 350° for 45-50 minutes or until center is almost set. Cool on a wire rack for 10 minutes. Carefully run a knife around edge of pan to loosen; cool 1 hour longer. Cover and freeze overnight.

Remove from the freezer and let stand for 30 minutes. Place the cracker crumbs in a shallow bowl. Working quickly, scoop out 1-in. balls of cheesecake; roll each in cracker crumbs and insert a lollipop stick. Place on waxed paper-lined baking sheets. Freeze for 1 hour or until firm.

In a microwave, melt vanilla chips and shortening at 70% power; stir until smooth. Place toppings in shallow bowls. Dip the cheesecake pops in vanilla chip mixture; allow excess to drip off. Roll in the toppings. Place on waxed paper; let stand until set. Store pops in the refrigerator. **Yield:** 45 cheesecake pops.

Strawberry Mousse Parfaits

PREP: 30 min. + chilling

Sweetened strawberries are layered with a luxurious mousse to create these lovely parfaits. They absolutely melt in your mouth!
—Mary Lou Timpson, Colorado City, Arizona

- 2 packages (10 ounces *each*) frozen sweetened sliced strawberries, thawed, undrained
- 1 tablespoon plus 2 teaspoons cornstarch
- 1 can (14 ounces) sweetened condensed milk
- 2 tablespoons orange juice
- 1/8 teaspoon red food coloring, optional
- 2 cups heavy whipping cream, whipped

Place the strawberries in a food processor; cover and process until pureed. In a small saucepan, combine cornstarch and strawberries until blended. Bring to a boil; cook and stir for 2 minutes or until thickened. Transfer to a large bowl; refrigerate until chilled.

Set aside 1/2 cup berry mixture. Add condensed milk, orange juice and food coloring if desired to remaining mixture; stir until blended. Fold in whipped cream.

Spoon 1/4 cup cream mixture into each of 12 parfait dishes or cocktail glasses. Layer each with 4 teaspoons of reserved berry mixture and 1/4 cup cream mixture. Refrigerate until serving. **Yield:** 12 servings.

Lemon Curd Tartlets

(Pictured below and on page 295)

PREP: 35 min. + chilling

This recipe has been in my collection for over 30 years and never fails to impress. I can always rely on these tartlets to delight even the fussiest person. —Jessica Feist, Pewaukee, Wisconsin

- 3 eggs
- 1 cup sugar
- 1/2 cup lemon juice
- 1 teaspoon grated lemon peel
- 1/4 cup butter, cubed
- 1 package (1.9 ounces) frozen miniature phyllo tart shells, thawed

Fresh raspberries, mint leaves *and/or* sweetened whipped cream, optional

In a small heavy saucepan over medium heat, whisk the eggs, sugar, juice and peel until blended. Add butter; cook, whisking constantly, until mixture is thickened and coats the back of a metal spoon. Transfer to a small bowl; cool for 10 minutes. Cover; refrigerate until chilled.

Just before serving, spoon lemon curd into tart shells. Garnish with raspberries, mint and/or whipped cream if desired. Refrigerate leftovers. **Yield:** 15 tartlets.

Chocolate Ganache Tarts

(Pictured above)

PREP: 30 min. + chilling **BAKE:** 20 min. + cooling

A delectable chocolate filling makes these miniature baked tarts irresistible. You won't have to wait long before hearing "Mmm!"
—Lorraine Caland, Thunder Bay, Ontario

- 1/2 cup butter, softened
- 1 package (3 ounces) cream cheese, softened
- 1 cup all-purpose flour
- 1/2 cup semisweet chocolate chips
- 1/2 cup milk chocolate chips
- 2/3 cup heavy whipping cream

Whipped cream, fresh raspberries and confectioners' sugar, optional

In a small bowl, beat the butter and cream cheese until blended; beat in the flour. Drop the dough by scant tablespoonfuls into greased miniature muffin cups; press onto bottoms and up the sides.

Bake at 325° for 20-25 minutes or until golden brown. Cool for 5 minutes before removing from pans to wire racks to cool completely.

In a small saucepan, melt chocolate chips with cream over low heat; stir until blended. Transfer to a small bowl; cover and refrigerate until firm.

Beat chocolate mixture until soft peaks form. Pipe or spoon into shells. Garnish with whipped cream, berries and sugar if desired. **Yield:** 2 dozen.

It's a Pizza Party!

MAMMA MIA! Who doesn't love biting into a big slice of piping-hot, cheesy pizza? And you can turn your kitchen into the best pizza parlor in town thanks to the crowd-pleasing recipes here.

With all your favorite toppings and a few new twists, these pies are sure to have you saying, "That's amoré!"

Smoked Gouda Spinach Pizza

(Pictured above)

PREP/TOTAL TIME: 30 min.

My daughter created this out-of-the-ordinary sausage pizza as an appetizer. It's cheesy and has a wonderfully smoky flavor.
—*Marie Hattrup, The Dalles, Oregon*

   1 **tube (13.8 ounces) refrigerated pizza crust**
1/2 **pound sliced fresh mushrooms**
   1 **small red onion, chopped**
   2 **tablespoons butter**
   2 **garlic cloves, minced**
   1 **cup Alfredo sauce**
1/2 **teaspoon dried thyme**
   1 **package (6 ounces) fresh baby spinach**
1/2 **pound Italian chicken sausage links, cooked and sliced**
   2 **cups (8 ounces) shredded smoked Gouda cheese**

Unroll dough into a greased 15-in. x 10-in. x 1-in. baking pan; flatten dough and build up edges slightly. Bake at 425° for 10-12 minutes or until lightly browned.

Meanwhile, in a large skillet, saute mushrooms and onion in butter until tender. Add garlic; cook 1 minute longer. Stir in Alfredo sauce and thyme. Spread over crust. Top with spinach, sausage and cheese. Bake for 10-15 minutes or until crust and cheese are lightly browned. **Yield:** 10 pieces.

Garden Pizza Supreme

PREP: 20 min. **BAKE:** 20 min.

This meatless pie is so delicious, colorful and nutritious. Feel free to toss on any vegetables you like from your garden—I do!
—*Pamela Shank, Parkersburg, West Virgina*

☑ This recipe includes Nutrition Facts and Diabetic Exchanges.

   1 **loaf (1 pound) frozen bread dough, thawed**
   6 **slices part-skim mozzarella cheese**
   1 **can (8 ounces) pizza sauce**
   2 **cups (8 ounces) shredded part-skim mozzarella cheese, *divided***
1/2 **cup *each* finely chopped fresh cauliflowerets, mushrooms and broccoli florets**
1/4 **cup *each* finely chopped red onion, green pepper and sweet red pepper**
1/2 **cup pickled pepper rings**

Roll the dough into a 15-in. circle. Transfer to a greased 14-in. pizza pan, building up edges slightly. Place cheese slices on dough. Spread sauce over cheese. Sprinkle with 1 cup shredded cheese, cauliflower, mushrooms, broccoli, onion, peppers and pepper rings.

Bake at 425° for 15 minutes. Sprinkle with remaining cheese. Bake 5-10 minutes longer or until the cheese is melted and crust is golden brown. **Yield:** 8 slices.

Nutrition Facts: 1 slice equals 316 calories, 11 g fat (6 g saturated fat), 28 mg cholesterol, 644 mg sodium, 33 g carbohydrate, 3 g fiber, 19 g protein. **Diabetic Exchanges:** 2 starch, 2 lean meat, 1 vegetable, 1 fat.

Pizza Shop Pizzas

PREP: 40 min. + rising **BAKE:** 15 min.

Without a doubt, this is the best homemade pizza I've ever tried. Even the sauce is made from scratch…yet the recipe is simple to prepare. —Melody Mellinger, Myerstown, Pennsylvania

- 2 packages (1/4 ounce *each*) active dry yeast
- 2-2/3 cups warm water (110° to 115°)
- 4 tablespoons olive oil, *divided*
- 2 tablespoons sugar
- 2 teaspoons salt
- 1/2 teaspoon dried oregano
- 1/4 teaspoon garlic salt
- 6-1/2 to 7 cups all-purpose flour
- 1 tablespoon cornmeal

SAUCE:
- 1 can (14-1/2 ounces) diced tomatoes
- 1 can (6 ounces) tomato paste
- 1 tablespoon olive oil
- 1 teaspoon sugar
- 1 teaspoon salt
- 1/2 teaspoon *each* dried basil, oregano, marjoram and thyme
- 1/4 teaspoon garlic powder
- 1/4 teaspoon pepper

TOPPINGS:
- 4 cups (16 ounces) shredded pizza cheese blend
- 1 package (6 ounces) sliced turkey pepperoni
- 2 cans (2-1/4 ounces *each*) sliced ripe olives, drained
- 1 cup pickled pepper rings
- 1 small onion, halved and sliced
- 1 can (4 ounces) mushroom stems and pieces, drained

In a large bowl, dissolve yeast in 2/3 cup warm water. Add 3 tablespoons oil, sugar, salt, oregano, garlic salt, remaining water and 5 cups flour. Beat until smooth. Stir in enough remaining flour to form a soft dough.

Turn onto a floured surface; knead until smooth and elastic, about 6-8 minutes. Place in a greased bowl, turning once to grease the top. Cover and let rise in a warm place until doubled, about 1 hour.

Punch dough down; divide into two portions. Roll each into a 15-in. circle. Brush two 14-in. pizza pans with remaining oil; sprinkle with cornmeal. Transfer dough to prepared pans; build up edges slightly. Bake at 425° for 5 minutes.

In a small bowl, combine sauce ingredients. Spread over the crusts. Sprinkle with toppings. Bake for 15-20 minutes or until crusts and cheese are lightly browned. **Yield:** 2 pizzas (8 slices each).

Hot Wing Pizza

(Pictured below and on page 294)

PREP/TOTAL TIME: 30 min.

My husband loves this pie, especially when he has a craving for hot wings. If you don't have blue cheese dressing, just substitute ranch. —Danielle Weets, Grandview, Washington

- 3 boneless skinless chicken breast halves (5 ounces *each*)
- 1 tablespoon steak seasoning
- 1/2 cup tomato sauce
- 2 tablespoons butter
- 2 tablespoons Louisiana-style hot sauce
- 1 tablespoon hot pepper sauce
- 1 prebaked Italian bread shell crust (14 ounces)
- 1/3 cup blue cheese salad dressing
- 1/2 cup shredded part-skim mozzarella cheese
- 3 green onions, thinly sliced

Sprinkle chicken with steak seasoning on both sides; grill, covered, over medium heat for 4-7 minutes on each side or until juices run clear. Cool slightly; cut into strips.

In a small saucepan, bring the tomato sauce, butter, hot sauce and pepper sauce to a boil. Reduce the heat; simmer, uncovered, for 10-15 minutes or until slightly thickened. Add chicken; heat through.

Place crust on a 12-in. pizza pan; spread with salad dressing. Top with chicken mixture, cheese and onions. Bake at 450° for 8-10 minutes or until cheese is melted. **Yield:** 6 slices.

Editor's Note: This recipe was tested with McCormick's Montreal Steak Seasoning. Look for it in the spice aisle.

Dine Out on the Deck

BREATHE in the fresh air, bask in the sunshine and enjoy dining alfresco with these reader-favorite recipes. They're perfect for casual parties with friends and family out on the patio or deck.

Start with Watermelon Salsa and Festive Shrimp Tarts as appetizers before digging into Italian Garden Salad as a main dish, all washed down with ice-cold Lemony Cooler. One thing's for sure—with this refreshing menu, you'll have your table all decked out!

Watermelon Salsa

(Pictured above and on page 294)

PREP: 25 min. + chilling

Served with tortilla chips, this snappy mix of melon, jalapeno and black beans will be a surefire hit. In fact, you might want to make extra!   —Iola Egle, Bella Vista, Arizona

☑ This recipe includes Nutrition Facts and Diabetic Exchanges.

 2 cups diced seedless watermelon
3/4 cup finely chopped sweet onion
3/4 cup canned black beans, rinsed and drained
 2 jalapeno peppers, seeded and chopped
1/4 cup minced fresh cilantro
 2 teaspoons brown sugar
 1 garlic clove, minced
1/2 teaspoon salt

In a small bowl, combine all ingredients. Cover and refrigerate for at least 1 hour. Drain if necessary before serving. **Yield:** 3-1/2 cups.

 Nutrition Facts: 3/4 cup equals 129 calories, 1 g fat (trace saturated fat), 0 cholesterol, 78 mg sodium, 33 g carbohydrate, 2 g fiber, 1 g protein. **Diabetic Exchanges:** 1 starch, 1 fruit.

Festive Shrimp Tarts

PREP/TOTAL TIME: 30 min.

These easy, colorful bites made with phyllo tart shells are so fun for parties. You can prepare them ahead and pop them into the oven just before serving.   —Sheri Mosely, Clermont, Florida

☑ This recipe includes Nutrition Facts.

 1 egg, lightly beaten
1/2 cup mayonnaise
 1 tablespoon Dijon mustard
 1 pound frozen cooked salad shrimp, thawed and patted dry
 4 green onions, chopped
 1 can (8-3/4 ounces) whole kernel corn, drained and patted dry
1/4 cup chopped celery
1/4 cup chopped sweet red pepper
 2 tablespoons capers, drained and minced

1 tablespoon minced fresh cilantro
2 garlic cloves, minced
1 teaspoon chili powder
1/4 teaspoon pepper
4 packages (2.1 ounces *each*) frozen miniature phyllo tart shells
1/2 small green pepper, cut into small strips

In a small bowl, combine egg, mayonnaise and mustard. Stir in shrimp, onions, corn, celery, red pepper, capers, cilantro, garlic, chili powder and pepper. Spoon about 2 teaspoons filling into each tart shell.

Place on baking sheets; bake at 350° for 7-10 minutes or until the tops begin to brown. Top with green pepper strips. Serve warm. **Yield:** 5 dozen.

Nutrition Facts: 1 tart equals 49 calories, 3 g fat (trace saturated fat), 19 mg cholesterol, 65 mg sodium, 3 g carbohydrate, trace fiber, 2 g protein.

Lemony Cooler

(Pictured below)

PREP: 15 min. + chilling

Everyone thinks I've gone to a lot of trouble when I present this refreshing drink, but it's a breeze to stir together. Add fresh fruit for a garnish. —Bonnie Hawkins, Elkhorn, Wisconsin

3 cups white grape juice
1/2 cup sugar
1/2 cup lemon juice
1 bottle (1 liter) club soda, chilled
Ice cubes
Assorted fresh fruit, optional

In a pitcher, combine grape juice, sugar and lemon juice; stir until sugar is dissolved. Refrigerate until chilled.

Just before serving, stir in club soda. Serve over ice. Garnish with fruit if desired. **Yield:** 8 servings.

Italian Garden Salad

(Pictured above)

PREP: 35 min. + chilling

This is a great way to use the vegetables my husband grows, and it's always well received. Spaghetti and chunks of chicken make the salad filling. —Lori Daniels, Beverly, West Virginia

8 ounces uncooked spaghetti
1 cup cut fresh green beans
DRESSING:
6 tablespoons canola oil
3 tablespoons sugar
2 tablespoons white wine vinegar
1 garlic clove, minced
1 teaspoon salt
1 teaspoon dried parsley flakes
1 teaspoon dried basil
1/2 teaspoon dried oregano
1/4 teaspoon onion powder
SALAD:
2 cups cubed cooked chicken
1 medium green pepper, julienned
4 ounces Colby-Monterey Jack cheese, cubed
1 medium zucchini, sliced
1 small yellow summer squash, sliced
8 cherry tomatoes, halved
1 small red onion, halved and sliced
Shredded Parmesan cheese, optional

Cook spaghetti according to package directions, adding the green beans during the last 4 minutes of cooking.

Meanwhile, in a large bowl, combine the dressing ingredients. Add the chicken, pepper, Colby-Monterey Jack cheese, zucchini, squash, tomatoes and onion.

Drain pasta and beans; rinse in cold water. Add to the other ingredients; toss to coat. Refrigerate until chilled. Sprinkle with Parmesan if desired. **Yield:** 8 servings.

Substitutions & Equivalents

Equivalent Measures

3 teaspoons	= 1 tablespoon		16 tablespoons	= 1 cup
4 tablespoons	= 1/4 cup		2 cups	= 1 pint
5-1/3 tablespoons	= 1/3 cup		4 cups	= 1 quart
8 tablespoons	= 1/2 cup		4 quarts	= 1 gallon

Food Equivalents

Grains

Macaroni	1 cup (3-1/2 ounces) uncooked	=	2-1/2 cups cooked
Noodles, Medium	3 cups (4 ounces) uncooked	=	4 cups cooked
Popcorn	1/3 to 1/2 cup unpopped	=	8 cups popped
Rice, Long Grain	1 cup uncooked	=	3 cups cooked
Rice, Quick-Cooking	1 cup uncooked	=	2 cups cooked
Spaghetti	8 ounces uncooked	=	4 cups cooked

Crumbs

Bread	1 slice	=	3/4 cup soft crumbs, 1/4 cup fine dry crumbs
Graham Crackers	7 squares	=	1/2 cup finely crushed
Buttery Round Crackers	12 crackers	=	1/2 cup finely crushed
Saltine Crackers	14 crackers	=	1/2 cup finely crushed

Fruits

Bananas	1 medium	=	1/3 cup mashed
Lemons	1 medium	=	3 tablespoons juice, 2 teaspoons grated peel
Limes	1 medium	=	2 tablespoons juice, 1-1/2 teaspoons grated peel
Oranges	1 medium	=	1/4 to 1/3 cup juice, 4 teaspoons grated peel

Vegetables

Cabbage	1 head	=	5 cups shredded	Green Pepper	1 large	=	1 cup chopped
Carrots	1 pound	=	3 cups shredded	Mushrooms	1/2 pound	=	3 cups sliced
Celery	1 rib	=	1/2 cup chopped	Onions	1 medium	=	1/2 cup chopped
Corn	1 ear fresh	=	2/3 cup kernels	Potatoes	3 medium	=	2 cups cubed

Nuts

Almonds	1 pound	=	3 cups chopped	Pecan Halves	1 pound	=	4-1/2 cups chopped
Ground Nuts	3-3/4 ounces	=	1 cup	Walnuts	1 pound	=	3-3/4 cups chopped

Easy Substitutions

When you need...		Use...
Baking Powder	1 teaspoon	1/2 teaspoon cream of tartar + 1/4 teaspoon baking soda
Buttermilk	1 cup	1 tablespoon lemon juice *or* vinegar + enough milk to measure 1 cup (let stand 5 minutes before using)
Cornstarch	1 tablespoon	2 tablespoons all-purpose flour
Honey	1 cup	1-1/4 cups sugar + 1/4 cup water
Half-and-Half Cream	1 cup	1 tablespoon melted butter + enough whole milk to measure 1 cup
Onion	1 small, chopped (1/3 cup)	1 teaspoon onion powder *or* 1 tablespoon dried minced onion
Tomato Juice	1 cup	1/2 cup tomato sauce + 1/2 cup water
Tomato Sauce	2 cups	3/4 cup tomato paste + 1 cup water
Unsweetened Chocolate	1 square (1 ounce)	3 tablespoons baking cocoa + 1 tablespoon shortening *or* oil
Whole Milk	1 cup	1/2 cup evaporated milk + 1/2 cup water

Cooking Terms

HERE'S a quick reference for some of the cooking terms used in *Taste of Home* recipes:

Baste—To moisten food with melted butter, pan drippings, marinades or other liquid to add more flavor and juiciness.

Beat—A rapid movement to combine ingredients using a fork, spoon, wire whisk or electric mixer.

Blend—To combine ingredients until *just* mixed.

Boil—To heat liquids until bubbles form that cannot be "stirred down." In the case of water, the temperature will reach 212°.

Bone—To remove all meat from the bone before cooking.

Cream—To beat ingredients together to a smooth consistency, usually in the case of butter and sugar for baking.

Dash—A small amount of seasoning, less than 1/8 teaspoon. If using a shaker, a dash would comprise a quick flip of the container.

Dredge—To coat foods with flour or other dry ingredients. Most often done with pot roasts and stew meat before browning.

Fold—To incorporate several ingredients by careful and gentle turning with a spatula. Used generally with beaten egg whites or whipped cream when mixing into the rest of the ingredients to keep the batter light.

Julienne—To cut foods into long thin strips much like matchsticks. Used most often for salads and stir-fry dishes.

Mince—To cut into very fine pieces. Used often for garlic or fresh herbs.

Parboil—To cook partially, usually used in the case of chicken, sausages and vegetables.

Partially Set—Describes the consistency of gelatin after it has been chilled for a small amount of time. Mixture should resemble the consistency of egg whites.

Puree—To process foods to a smooth mixture. Can be prepared in an electric blender, food processor, food mill or sieve.

Saute—To fry quickly in a small amount of fat, stirring almost constantly. Most often done with onions, mushrooms and other chopped vegetables.

Score—To cut slits partway through the outer surface of foods. Often used with ham or flank steak.

Stir-Fry—To cook meats and/or vegetables with a constant stirring motion in a small amount of oil in a wok or skillet over high heat.

Guide to Cooking with Popular Herbs

HERB	APPETIZERS SALADS	BREADS/EGGS SAUCES/CHEESE	VEGETABLES PASTA	MEAT POULTRY	FISH SHELLFISH
BASIL	Green, Potato & Tomato Salads, Salad Dressings, Stewed Fruit	Breads, Fondue & Egg Dishes, Dips, Marinades, Sauces	Mushrooms, Tomatoes, Squash, Pasta, Bland Vegetables	Broiled, Roast Meat & Poultry Pies, Stews, Stuffing	Baked, Broiled & Poached Fish, Shellfish
BAY LEAF	Seafood Cocktail, Seafood Salad, Tomato Aspic, Stewed Fruit	Egg Dishes, Gravies, Marinades, Sauces	Dried Bean Dishes, Beets, Carrots, Onions, Potatoes, Rice, Squash	Corned Beef, Tongue Meat & Poultry Stews	Poached Fish, Shellfish, Fish Stews
CHIVES	Mixed Vegetable, Green, Potato & Tomato Salads, Salad Dressings	Egg & Cheese Dishes, Cream Cheese, Cottage Cheese, Gravies, Sauces	Hot Vegetables, Potatoes	Broiled Poultry, Poultry & Meat Pies, Stews, Casseroles	Baked Fish, Fish Casseroles, Fish Stews, Shellfish
DILL	Seafood Cocktail, Green, Potato & Tomato Salads, Salad Dressings	Breads, Egg & Cheese Dishes, Cream Cheese, Fish & Meat Sauces	Beans, Beets, Cabbage, Carrots, Cauliflower, Peas, Squash, Tomatoes	Beef, Veal Roasts, Lamb, Steaks, Chops, Stews, Roast & Creamed Poultry	Baked, Broiled, Poached & Stuffed Fish, Shellfish
GARLIC	All Salads, Salad Dressings	Fondue, Poultry Sauces, Fish & Meat Marinades	Beans, Eggplant, Potatoes, Rice, Tomatoes	Roast Meats, Meat & Poultry Pies, Hamburgers, Casseroles, Stews	Broiled Fish, Shellfish, Fish Stews, Casseroles
MARJORAM	Seafood Cocktail, Green, Poultry & Seafood Salads	Breads, Cheese Spreads, Egg & Cheese Dishes, Gravies, Sauces	Carrots, Eggplant, Peas, Onions, Potatoes, Dried Bean Dishes, Spinach	Roast Meats & Poultry, Meat & Poultry Pies, Stews & Casseroles	Baked, Broiled & Stuffed Fish, Shellfish
MUSTARD	Fresh Green Salads, Prepared Meat, Macaroni & Potato Salads, Salad Dressings	Biscuits, Egg & Cheese Dishes, Sauces	Baked Beans, Cabbage, Eggplant, Squash, Dried Beans, Mushrooms, Pasta	Chops, Steaks, Ham, Pork, Poultry, Cold Meats	Shellfish
OREGANO	Green, Poultry & Seafood Salads	Breads, Egg & Cheese Dishes, Meat, Poultry & Vegetable Sauces	Artichokes, Cabbage, Eggplant, Squash, Dried Beans, Mushrooms, Pasta	Broiled, Roast Meats, Meat & Poultry Pies, Stews, Casseroles	Baked, Broiled & Poached Fish, Shellfish
PARSLEY	Green, Potato, Seafood & Vegetable Salads	Biscuits, Breads, Egg & Cheese Dishes, Gravies, Sauces	Asparagus, Beets, Eggplant, Squash, Dried Beans, Mushrooms, Pasta	Meat Loaf, Meat & Poultry Pies, Stews & Casseroles, Stuffing	Fish Stews, Stuffed Fish
ROSEMARY	Fruit Cocktail, Fruit & Green Salads	Biscuits, Egg Dishes, Herb Butter, Cream Cheese, Marinades, Sauces	Beans, Broccoli, Peas, Cauliflower, Mushrooms, Baked Potatoes, Parsnips	Roast Meat, Poultry & Meat Pies, Stews & Casseroles, Stuffing	Stuffed Fish, Shellfish
SAGE		Breads, Fondue, Egg & Cheese Dishes, Spreads, Gravies, Sauces	Beans, Beets, Onions, Peas, Spinach, Squash, Tomatoes	Roast Meat, Poultry, Meat Loaf, Stews, Stuffing	Baked, Poached & Stuffed Fish
TARRAGON	Seafood Cocktail, Avocado Salads, Salad Dressings	Cheese Spreads, Marinades, Sauces, Egg Dishes	Asparagus, Beans, Beets, Carrots, Mushrooms, Peas, Squash, Spinach	Steaks, Poultry, Roast Meats, Casseroles & Stews	Baked, Broiled & Poached Fish, Shellfish
THYME	Seafood Cocktail, Green, Poultry, Seafood & Vegetable Salads	Biscuits, Breads, Egg & Cheese Dishes, Sauces, Spreads	Beets, Carrots, Mushrooms, Onions, Peas, Eggplant, Spinach, Potatoes	Roast Meat, Poultry & Meat Loaf, Meat & Poultry Pies, Stews & Casseroles	Baked, Broiled & Stuffed Fish, Shellfish, Fish Stews

General Recipe Index

*This handy index lists every recipe by food category, major ingredient and/or
cooking method, so you can easily locate recipes to suit your needs.*

✓ Recipe includes Nutrition Facts and Diabetic Exchanges.

✓ Recipe includes Nutrition Facts and Diabetic Exchanges.

✓ Recipe includes Nutrition Facts and Diabetic Exchanges.

✓ *Recipe includes Nutrition Facts and Diabetic Exchanges.*

✓ *Recipe includes Nutrition Facts and Diabetic Exchanges.*

✓ Recipe includes Nutrition Facts and Diabetic Exchanges.

✓ Recipe includes Nutrition Facts and Diabetic Exchanges.

✓ Recipe includes Nutrition Facts and Diabetic Exchanges.

✓ *Recipe includes Nutrition Facts and Diabetic Exchanges.*

✓ *Recipe includes Nutrition Facts and Diabetic Exchanges.*

Alphabetical Recipe Index

This handy index lists every recipe in alphabetical order so you can easily find your favorites.

✓ *Recipe includes Nutrition Facts and Diabetic Exchanges.*

✓ Recipe includes Nutrition Facts and Diabetic Exchanges.

✓ Recipe includes Nutrition Facts and Diabetic Exchanges.

✓ Recipe includes Nutrition Facts and Diabetic Exchanges.